WOMEN'S FRIENDSHIP
IN LITERATURE

Women's Friendship in Literature

JANET TODD

Columbia University Press
New York

Library of Congress Cataloging in Publication Data

Todd, Janet M   1942–
  Women's friendship in literature.

  Bibliography: p.
  Includes index.
  1. English fiction—18th century—History and criticism.   2. French fiction—18th century—History and
criticism.   3. Women in literature.   4. Friendship in
literature.   I. Title.
PR858.W6T6   809.3′3   79-20175
ISBN 0-231-04562-X   (cloth)
ISBN 0-231-04563-8   (paper)

    Columbia University Press
New York   Guildford, Surrey

FOR CLARA

ACKNOWLEDGMENTS

I WOULD LIKE to thank Carol Smith for her suggestions about my work and Otis Fellows for his helpful reading of the section on Diderot. I owe thanks also to Madelyn Gutwirth for letting me see in manuscript portions of her book on Mme de Staël, A. Walton Litz for general encouragement, and Patricia M. Spacks for her kind remarks and stimulating disagreement. Other debts are to the Oxford University women's group, to whom I presented some of the ideas, to Godelieve Mercken-Spaas, who commented on the book at several stages of its writing, to Julian Todd, who helped compile the bibliography, and to Gloria Cohn, who typed much of the manuscript. Finally I am deeply grateful to the Research Council of Rutgers University and the American Council of Learned Societies for their financial support of my work.

CONTENTS

CONTENTS

WOMEN'S FRIENDSHIP IN LITERATURE

I covenant that your acquaintance be general; that you admit no sworn confidante or intimate of your own sex, no she-friend to screen her affairs under your countenance and tempt you to make trial of a mutual secrecy.

Mirabell, hero of *The Way of the World* (1700) by William Congreve

My wife must have no other companion or friend but her husband; I shall never be averse to your seeing company, but intimates I forbid; I shall not choose to have my faults discussed between you and your friend.

Mr Morgan, villain of *Millenium Hall* (1762) by Sarah Scott and Barbara Montagu

INTRODUCTION

IN *A Room of One's Own* Virginia Woolf lamented that literature rarely depicts female friendship:

> I tried to remember any case in the course of my reading where two women are represented as friends. . . . They are confidantes, of course, in Racine and the Greek tragedies. They are now and then mothers and daughters. But almost without exception they are shown in their relation to men. It was strange to think that all the great women of fiction were, until Jane Austen's day, not only seen by the other sex, but seen only in relation to the other sex.

Woolf's impression is a common one, but it is mistaken nonetheless. Eighteenth-century fiction is rich in presentations of female friendship, by both men and women. At the very beginning of the classical English novel, Samuel Richardson created two women whose friendship became the pattern in life and literature, while a host of women writers before and after him wrote of female ties. The fictional friendship grew out of the idea of the confidante— the correspondent in the epistolary novel or the recipient in the memoir, both favored forms in the eighteenth century. But the confidante is something more than a formal necessity and her tie with the heroine is often minutely analyzed. Although seemingly on the periphery of the plot, she may usurp the center when the perspective on action is changed. In this book I am investigating the literary phenomenon of female friendship, its form and ideology. Because friendship is marked socially by the romantic plot and structured historically by the first female tie, I am also touching on the heterosexual and parental relationships.

1

INTRODUCTION

The eighteenth-century novel almost invariably tells of romantic attachment between a man and a woman, an attachment expressed in conflict. The two sides grapple and spar the length of the book and, whether marriage or death closes the contest, they remain strangers to the end, the captains of their sex. Female friendship is the only social relationship we actually enter in the novel and the only one the heroine actively constructs. The family commonly selects the lover (or the man nominates himself), where the woman chooses the friend. Richardson's Clarissa is free to make a friend, but a husband is imposed.

In the romantic relationship, each partner is no doubt concerned with the beloved enemy, but each is also much taken with his or her own image and position. In female friendship, however, there can be cooperation as well as conflict, and the persistent self-concern which the heterosexual tie seems to demand need not be primary. In female friendship the heroine can momentarily forget the feminine image she must create for a man and relax from the strenuous demands of romantic love. Although the action of the novel usually takes place in the heterosexual plot, its, sentiment may be centered in female friendship. Clarissa elopes and dies for Lovelace, but it is her friend Anna Howe who reveals the drama of her mind.

The mothers of fictional heroines are usually bad and living or good and dead. In the commonest eighteenth-century plot of romance and sexual misadventure, the mother is removed so that her daughter may become an orphan, the most promising of heroines. Daniel Defoe's Moll Flanders, P.C. de Marivaux's Marianne, and Mme de Staël's Delphine all lose their mothers early; in other cases the heroine is parted from her parent during the main action. Susan Ferrier's heroine in *Marriage* journies from home toward the romantic center of her novel. The flawed mothers—those of Jane Austen's Fanny Price and Mary Wollstonecraft's heroines—are weak, dominated by men who blame them for their feebleness, their infidelity, or their fading charms. Such mothers repudiate their daughters, while doting on their male children, substitutes for the men who have in some way turned from them. When this happens, the heroine seems available for female friendship and yet the mother will haunt the new alliance. Where the mother-daughter relationship has been loving, close, and reasonably extended, the heroine is prepared for friendship, as Richardson's Clarissa and Jean-Jacques Rousseau's Julie are; where the tie was rudely severed by real repulsion, the daughter will tend to seek a woman over a male lover, not to enjoy friendship but to relive history. The mothers of Denis Diderot's Suzanne in *The Nun* and Wollstonecraft's Mary in *Mary, A Fiction* both repudiate their children, and neither heroine can achieve a satisfactory friendship; each in different ways looks for the mother who failed her, while revenging herself on the other woman for the first female hurt.

Female friendship involving orphans, mature women, and mutilated daughters is a diverse and rich subject, and inevitably it has been difficult to create a useful paradigm. I have organized the novels according to five categories of friendship—sentimental, erotic, manipulative, political, and social—well aware that the works treated in detail fail to fit neatly into any one of them. Richardson's *Clarissa*, for instance, covers them all, Staël's *Delphine* is manipulative as often as political, and even John Cleland's *Fanny Hill* is not unremittingly erotic. In the section called "The Literary Context" I have elaborated on the five categories—which exist only to order, not to cramp—and here I will offer only brief definitions.

Sentimental friendship is a close, effusive tie, revelling in rapture and rhetoric. Unlike the sentimental romance which so often ruins, it aids and saves, providing close emotional support in a patriarchal world. If heterosexual love has proved violent or painful, it may even threaten and replace this love. Outside the text, sentimental friendship becomes a means of befriending the female reader; through her relationship with her friend, the heroine can display her exemplary state, and under her mask of sentiment, stand as a model for other young ladies who may unwisely yearn to stray. Richardson's *Clarissa* includes the surpassing example of the sentimental tie.

3

INTRODUCTION

Erotic friendship requires physical love. Cleland's *Fanny Hill* exemplifies it with Fanny and her sexual mentor Phoebe, although her other female relationships are simply social and supportive. Similarly Diderot's *The Nun* has an erotic tie, while allowing its heroine Suzanne to enter several manipulative unions.

In manipulative friendship, one woman uses another, controls her and joys in the control. Claire in Rousseau's *Julie* is sentimental with Julie, possibly erotically obsessed, but primarily she is manipulative, ordering her friend's words and deeds both openly and furtively. Sade's Juliette in *Juliette* is manipulative simply because she controls Clairwil through murder.

Political friendship requires some action against the social system, its institutions or conventions. The friendships in Wollstonecraft's two novels, *Mary, A Fiction* and *The Wrongs of Woman,* move toward this action; stunted by female upbringing and childhood pain, Mary cannot progress in friendship although she yearns for it, but in *The Wrongs of Woman* Maria counters and escapes the prison-asylum with a female friend. In Staël's *Delphine* the heroine, aided by friends, surreptitiously battles the institutions of marriage and all the social conventions that trap women.

Social friendship is a nurturing tie, not pitting women against society but rather smoothing their passage within it. If their destiny is almost always sexual and heterosexual in the eighteenth-century novel, women's salvation is social, for they may "fall" sexually, but must rise socially. Here the support and acceptance of other women is essential, since through their teaching of female lore, criminal or conventional, women aid and sustain each other. One may hide the unwanted infant of Moll Flanders in Defoe's novel, another flee to bolster a precarious happiness like the heroine of Mme de Riccoboni's *Jenny Salisbury.* In both cases the friend does not tamper with the central romance, but instead promotes it, working to ease the social life of her friend. Clearly, of all the types of alliance, it is the most accommodating to the romantic plot; yet in Austen's fictive world even this shows a threatening aspect. Throughout *Mansfield*

4

INTRODUCTION

Park, the fearful Fanny Price refuses an appeal for social friendship, while in *Emma* the heroine approaches it only through a series of manipulative ties.

I must preface this study with some self-justification—first, of the period I have chosen. I have dealt with fiction of the eighteenth and early nineteenth centuries, but have shortened the impossible adjective in "eighteenth-and-early-nineteenth-century fiction" simply to "eighteenth-century." I chose the period because it encloses some of literature's most splendid creations of friendship and because, as the first era of the modern novel, it witnesses the rooting of fictional conventions. I am not insisting on the eighteenth-century novel as a single artifact. Of course its exponents are as various as novelists of any later century and its beginning and ending years show contrasts as often as continuities. The rake becomes sentimentalized, for example, or the coquette turns feminist. Yet this fiction has a unity of outlook, concerns, and narrative expression that can justify some generalization about it and can, I hope, excuse Defoe's lodging with Fanny Burney, or Henry Fielding with the Marquis de Sade.

Second, I have chosen to treat both English and French novels, believing that in the eighteenth century there was a back-and-forth relationship across the Channel that brought the two countries almost into one literary realm. Books of one nation were immediately translated and published in the other, creating a climate of mutual literary influence. Richardson had, for example, much effect on Mme Riccoboni, who concluded Marivaux's *Marianne* and very freely translated Fielding's *Amelia* into French. A generation of English literary women, including Mary Wollstonecraft, saw themselves in Rousseau's Julie, while Mme de Staël felt the elopement of Richardson's Clarissa as an event in her own childhood.

Third, I have selected novels for primary treatment because of their primary depictions of women: Samuel Richardson's *Clarissa,* John Cleland's *Fanny Hill,* Denis Diderot's *The Nun,* Jean-Jacques Rousseau's *Julie,* the Marquis de Sade's *Juliette,* Mary Wollstonecraft's *Mary, A Fiction* and *The Wrongs of*

INTRODUCTION

Woman, Mme de Staël's *Delphine*, and Jane Austen's *Mansfield Park* and *Emma*. I have lightly probed other novels in the second part of the book. I have not been comprehensive but I have intended to cover the major types of treatment and give a broad view of eighteenth-century literary friendship. The longest discussion is of Richardson's *Clarissa*, probably the century's most influential novel in its establishing of fictional motifs. I have devoted the whole of the first chapter to its shrewd and disquieting treatment of female friendship within a patriarchal context.

Finally, my main justification is about method. Feminist literary criticism in English has been predominantly an interdisciplinary affair, often brilliantly mingling sociology, history, literature, and biography. Certainly there is room for this kind of criticism in my topic, using actual female friendship of the eighteenth century and relating the literary presentation to the historical background. I have not intended to write such all-inclusive criticism, however. Instead I have concentrated on the text alone. My subject in the first part of the book is the *literary* phenomenon of female friendship, its ideology, the conventions that determine it, and the hidden patterns and repetitions that structure it. Yet I have been fascinated by the biographies of the major authors studied, the immediate context of their creations, and, although I have not wanted to emphasize links between life and literature, I have ended this work by speculating on the authors' experiences of female friendship. The speculations are there not as explanation of the novels but as postlude to them.

To look at female friendship in novels whose plots are usually the heterosexual romance is abruptly to change a critical focus. It is to concentrate on a relationship and an ideology often opposing the main romantic ones; to follow it is sometimes to discover a different fictional trajectory, embittering the comic end or mitigating the tragic. And it is to risk overreading. For inevitably it is a heady business to enter a territory which the acute eye of Virginia Woolf failed to scan. I can only plead that I have tried to be tactful.

PART I

Selected Texts

CHAPTER ONE

Sentimental Friendship

Samuel Richardson's *Clarissa* (1747–48)

RICHARDSON ONCE INTENDED *Clarissa* to be named *The Lady's Legacy*. A curiously reductive title it seems at first, but one which by the end declares itself comprehensive, for the grandfather's legacy of his estate to Clarissa binds the novel. By it she receives the house and valuables that should have gone to her father and brother, and so provokes an antipathy and fear not easily allayed. At the opening of the novel Clarissa displays the will for her friend Anna Howe; both dimly see its importance but neither recognizes its transforming power. By the middle of the book a sadder and wiser Clarissa writes of "the envied Estate, which has been the original cause of all my misfortunes" (V 53).[1] As the novel closes, the last spokesman, Belford, envisions the dead Clarissa trying through her own will to repair the injustice of her grandfather's.

Clarissa partially recoils from the legacy, the gift of potential independence. Although she accepts the estate, she is quick to vest its government in her father. This legacy acts as the "original cause" and sin of the novel, functioning within two opposing contexts. One is called by the libertine Lovelace "the old patriarchal system"—the system in which "that half of the populace which is female is controlled by that half which is male" and in

---

1. Quotations are from *Clarissa or, The History of a Young Lady* (Oxford: Shakespeare Head Press, 1930), 8 vols. References to volume and page number in the text are to this edition.

which "male shall dominate female, elder male dominate younger."[2] The two female friends, Clarissa Harlowe and Anna Howe, create the other context in their letters, expressing it in their equality and yearning for autonomy.

The legacy acts differently according to context: in the patriarchal one it causes social disfunction by exaggerating a weakness in the transmission of property; the patriarchy is reconstructed only as the will is revoked. In the context of female friendship the legacy promises self-determination and is embodied in the grandfather's dairy house, which Clarissa fondly contemplates but never reaches. This is the place of the single life for which both she and Anna yearn, a life opposing marriage but including close female friendship. Such a life tempts Clarissa, and the will sweetens and strengthens the temptation.

The two contexts emerge from the early pages. The novel begins with the letters of the two women, whose relationship is always the latent subject of their discourse. Initially the patriarchal context seems distant, for it is created in the prose of Clarissa and Anna Howe. We soon learn, however, that reality is the reverse, since the women themselves exist within the patriarchy and their actions are conditioned by it. The first open topic is the duel of James Harlowe and Robert Lovelace, patriarchy's two main exponents; between them these men will shatter both the relationship and its prose.

The patriarchy is preeminent in power and size, comprehending most of the relationships of the novel. It includes even the mothers who might seem subversive of it and the lovers who might seem hostile: Mrs. Harlowe and Lovelace ultimately function within the scheme of the father and express him.[3] Because of

2. Kate Millett, *Sexual Politics* (New York: Avon Books, 1971), p. 46.
3. Lovelace's rape of Clarissa can be seen as an extreme but logical act of patriarchy. In *Against Our Will,* Susan Brownmiller argues: "A world without rapists would be a world in which women moved freely without fear of men. That some men rape provides a sufficient threat to keep all women in a constant state of intimidation. . . . Rather than society's aberrants or 'spoilers of purity,' men who commit rape have served in effect as front-line masculine shock troops, terrorist guerillas in the longest sustained battle the world has ever known" (New York: Simon and Schuster, 1975), p. 209.

this connection, the house of harlots becomes a parody, not an antithesis, of the house of Harlowes. Mrs. Harlowe, parted from Clarissa, her brightest expression, darkens into Sinclair,[4] while Mr. Harlowe is transformed into the nakedly powerful and violent Lovelace; as the father, ruling his house with iron authority, becomes victim to the son he begot, so Lovelace, controlling and moving the house of harlots, finally falls prey to the harlots he made.

The female context is less realized than the patriarchal, existing fully in no relationship or institution. A sentimental scheme, it mingles ideal and real, exemplary and flawed.[5] Its proponents, Clarissa Harlowe and Anna Howe, try to act benevolently in a malevolent world and to show in themselves those virtues of compassion, generosity, and kindliness which they are so often forced to deny in action. These virtues are socially expressed most fully in their friendship, which yet remains in great part a potential one. Beside the powerfully realized patriarchal context, the female one sometimes seems tenuous and rather wistful.

The two unequal and opposing contexts are articulated in Clarissa. She is at once the humble maiden and dutiful daughter of the patriarchal family and the exemplary and virtuous woman of the female world. In her family she is a kind of Cinderella, rewarded for her obedience by a godmotherly grandfather, but the reward fails to propel her toward Cinderella's obedient place in the world of men. By her womanly excellence she has set up a hierarchy of values at odds with the male familial one, so incurring the vengeful violence that is the patriarchy in action.

Clarissa's uneasiness in her obedient role appears when she

4. The connection is made by R. F. Brissenden, who calls Sinclair "the nightmare version of the mother." He considers that Mrs. Harlowe shows the morality of a whoremonger when she connives at the scheme to sell her daughter. See *Virtue in Distress: Studies in the Novel of Sentiment from Richardson to Sade* (New York: Barnes & Noble, 1974), p. 181.

5. R. F. Brissenden calls Clarissa the feminine embodiment of the sentimental virtues and ideals; "she believes in man's innate benevolence and in the right of the individual to follow the promptings of his own heart," *Virtue in Distress,* p. 161. For a discussion of the word "sentimental" as used here, see chapter 2 of Brissenden's book.

is reluctant to extend to a husband the patriarchal principle she accepts in the father; she will not move from daughter to wife. Before she ever receives the legacy she has refused suitors and pleaded for the single life.[6] Later, although she continues to reverence her father, she is openly hostile to his displacements: her brother, men in general, and, above all, Lovelace. It seems that she is overtly obedient then, while covertly recalcitrant. Both her father and Lovelace detect her treachery and respond severely. "Father-sick" in her lover's eyes and enamored of a rake in her father's, she can convince neither of her dutifulness.[7]

The legacy, which Anna Howe urges Clarissa to grasp as her own, allows the single life of integrity away from marriage and filial obedience. At the same time it binds Clarissa to the scheme which she is already so fearful of betraying, for the will is a recompense for "dutifulness" (II, 25) to the grandfather. If she uses it to oppose and free herself from the family the grandfather headed, she will no longer be the true legatee. Obedience and integrity collide, then, and Clarissa, the obedient and upright, cannot wholly espouse either.

In the novel three groups of people encircle Clarissa. Within her family she is restricted by father and brother, outside by Lovelace. All form the group of men within patriarchy, a powerful group expressed in the customs and conventions of the society it rules. The second group comprises women within patriarchy, women who have assimilated its views and become its implements. Its main exponents are Clarissa's mother and sister in the family, and Sinclair and the whores outside. On the periphery of

6. According to Margaret Anne Doody, the heroine's desire for a single life had become a convention of the novel by Richardson's time, occurring in the fiction of such popular writers as Mary Davys and Eliza Haywood. See *A Natural Passion: A Study of the Novels of Samuel Richardson* (Oxford: Clarendon Press, 1974), p. 134. Its conventionality need in no way detract from its importance in Clarissa's character.

7. She has, however, thoroughly convinced several modern critics. Norman Rabkin argues that she is duty and convention personified: "Clarissa's behavior throughout the novel is directly attributable to her deification of social law, her instinctive feeling that the conventions of her society constitute an absolute moral command." See *"Clarissa: A Study in the Nature of Convention," Journal of English Literary History* 23, no. 3 (September 1956), 206.

12

this group are the women who reject patriarchal beliefs but who are yet bound through poverty and dependence to act by its rules. Mrs. Norton, Clarissa's nurse, is the prime example of such women. The final group—of women outside patriarchy—is expressed only in Anna Howe. The fluency and extent of her writings proclaim the potential of her group, but her solitude betrays its actual power. All three groups are related arcs in the social circle centering on Clarissa; as the novel begins, the legacy ominously transforms the circle into an elliptical enclosure whose center is simultaneously pulled closer to opposing arcs. Clarissa is trapped in a geometry of relationships and she cannot approach or leave one group without provoking the menace of the others.

1

MEN WITHIN PATRIARCHY

When the novel opens, Clarissa Harlowe, once beloved and esteemed by uncles, parents, and friends, is already on the path to rejection and disgrace. Her grandfather's bounty has freed her siblings, James and Arabella, to display their long-suppressed envy at her excellence, and her latest marriage proposal goads them to active cruelty.

Lovelace, her aristocratic and rich suitor, has alienated the sister by moving his attentions from her to Clarissa and the brother by surpassing him on all counts in college. Finally he alienates Clarissa by his moral inadequacy. Forced to duel, Lovelace wounds the body and pride of her brother and antagonizes the rest of the family. All vow there shall now be no match.

To ensure that Lovelace will lay no claim to Clarissa, the family, urged on by James, introduce to her the vastly rich and utterly worthless Solmes, whom Clarissa detests for his mind and person. A variety of torments· follows to force her agreement to the marriage. All the family, including even her passive but well-meaning mother, join to torment her, and so active are they that the dutiful and virtuous Clarissa even contemplates escaping with

Lovelace, the only person willing and able to aid her. She withdraws from the step, but is ultimately tricked by him into taking it. From his own letters we learn that he has prodded the family into severity to accomplish just this end. Clarissa escapes, accompanied by her father's curse that she may be punished "both *here* and *hereafter*" through the man she has chosen above her family.

After her flight, Clarissa keeps a decorous distance from her abductor, who at first imitates her restraint. Soon, however, he lures her into a London brothel, run by the infamous Sinclair and stocked with women he has ruined. Escaping once she suspects the nature of the place, Clarissa is recaptured by Lovelace who at will can create a whole false environment of relations and friends to delude her. After trying several times to seduce her, he rapes her while she is drugged. Her will, as he and she both assert, remains inviolate.

Lovelace's own account of his motives for rape is complex: revenge on the Harlowes who have so arrogantly dismissed him and on Clarissa who has repeatedly announced her moral superiority and opposition. He is immediately provoked, however, by fear of the whores' ridicule and a desire to prove his continuing "manliness."

After the rape, Clarissa is temporarily mad, then permanently ailing. To some extent she retained her self-esteem through her long and detailed correspondence with Anna Howe; but through Lovelace's machinations, this is interrupted. Her family, meanwhile, remains obdurate. When Clarissa escapes for a second time from Lovelace, she enters her final house, where she prepares elaborately for death, ritually transforming herself into a scapegoat for the sins she cannot quite grasp. She reestablishes the contacts that matter to her now, with Mrs. Norton, her nurse, and with her friend Anna Howe. She dies surrounded by kind strangers, a surrogate family, her own still unforgiving. After her death, she is revenged against her will by her cousin Morden, who kills Lovelace in a duel.

As the summary suggests, the Harlowe family acts in a severely patriarchal world of male kinship and money. It is expressed structurally through the laws and customs of patrilineal descent and primogeniture. The grandfather exists within the spatial and temporal web of patriarchy, emblematically atop his sons, Clarissa's father and uncles, whose gold and authority in turn flow to James, the only male child of the next generation. Because the grandfather has been cheered in his gloomy years by the grace, charms, and kindly ways of his granddaughter, an uncommon Harlowe, he disturbs the web of patriarchy, thus undermining the scheme that demands the gradual aggrandizement of the only true family exponent, the eldest son. The sex of the legatee exaggerates the disturbance. As a woman Clarissa is the property, not the proprietor, of her family and an independent fortune merely diminishes her function as property. The youngest female of the group, she is least suited to distinction, for any distinction must be from, not for, the family.

Clarissa's legacy especially irritates her brother, already somewhat antagonistic to her because of his peculiar situation. In patriarchy the eldest son is privileged as successor and legal usurper of his father.[8] In the Harlowe family James is especially so because he is unique, the only male child of his generation. With his uncles' fortunes and—as was intended—his grandfather's, he would surpass his father in wealth and power. So he has an exaggerated position in the family, and Clarissa is forced to note bitterly how much "is allowed to a son." In fact he largely rules his relatives; the father remains the sign of authority, but is denied much of the substance. The family falls into the hands of a man with patriarchal power but no paternal tenderness.

Clarissa has always accepted that her father, an awesome and totemic figure, should be supreme. Like God, he is manifest mainly in speech, which Clarissa reverences whether it is an oath within the house or a curse outside. But she will not transfer her

8. The position of the eldest son in *Clarissa* is treated by Christopher Hill in "Clarissa Harlowe and her Times," *Essays in Criticism* 5 (1955), 315–40, and by Mark Kinkead-Weekes in *Samuel Richardson: Dramatic Novelist* (London: Methuen, 1973), pp. 127–29. The historical background is discussed by H. J. Habbakuk in "English Landownership, 1680–1740," *Economic History Review* (1940), 6–10.

reverence to her brother, in spite of her family's insistence: "If you govern every-body else, you shall not govern me" (II, 209), she roundly declares. Her opposition is eased because she so heartily disapproves the family goal: the ennobling of the brutish James through his accumulation of wealth. A proper patriarchal goal expressing and strengthening family power, it clashes with Clarissa's sense of right order. This sense is upheld in the novel, for at the end we read of the sorry and just fate of the whore Sally Martin, who with the wealth of her physical charms tried to buy her way up the ranks. She presents a closing analogy to James, whose ambitions begin the book.

Clarissa is hostile to her brother and reverential to her father. But the two cannot really be severed. In much the same way she finds herself resisting the father when she opposes men as a group, ignoring the fact that men merely generalize him. Superficially, men in general seem far removed from the father; so Clarissa can be more aggressive toward this manifestation of patriarchy than she ever was toward her loathsome brother.

She conveys her antipathy to men through repeatedly wishing to remain unmarried—not only because she finds suitors unworthy but also because she shudders at the state they imply. Here, as so often, Anna Howe says openly what Clarissa only suggests, but it seems her horror springs from a true understanding of her family and her mother's married life.[9] Like Anna Howe, she senses that the dynamics of marriage allow all men to become Mr. Harlowes and all women passive and subsumed wives.

Clarissa is constantly subjected to the vast overreaching claims of men. She hears much of the "prerogative of Manhood" (I, 89) and she sees it irresponsibly embodied in her brother. As the family crisis mounts, Clarissa's uncle blames her for her disrespect to this brother, "who is a Man." She realizes it full well.

9. Norman Rabkin turns Clarissa's distaste for marriage into a distaste for nature and a refusal to love. I would argue that Clarissa's dislike of the state is amply justified by the expressions of it she has seen.

She comes to see "manliness" not as courage but as brutal force, and at moments of passionate hatred she throws to her antagonists the most abusive epithet she knows: "My soul is above thee, Man!" she cries to Lovelace, but she could be addressing all the Harlowe males as well. The women of the detested Sinclair house, dreadful as they are in her mind, are never accosted with such generic detestation.[10]

Her loathing of the name images her loathing of the thing. Although the women are partly responsible for her rape, it is men she cannot bear near her. Even before the rape, she commands Lovelace "Begone, man!"; after it she fears most that a man will molest her in her misery in prison, in her dying and after her death. No man, she declares, must see her dead. The loathing is intensified by the rape but Clarissa has always had a hearty dislike of the male sex, oddly contrasting with her reverence for her father. When she is still considering her escape from her father's house, she painfully images the life of women with men:

> Could there be any way to escape this Solmes, a breach with Lovelace might make way for the Single Life to take place, which I so much prefer: And then I would defy the Sex. For I see nothing but trouble and vexation that they bring upon ours: And when once entered, one is obliged to go on with them, treading, with tender feet, upon thorns, and sharper thorns, to the end of a painful journey. (II, 314)

A little later she cries in anguish, "Why had I any concerns with this Sex!" (II,324).

With Robert Lovelace, her suitor and rapist, Clarissa joins in open battle and it is with him that she most clearly opposes both father and brother. In his wealth and power, Lovelace stands at the apex of the patriarchal scheme and in Clarissa's relationship

10. Dorothy Van Ghent investigates Clarissa's hatred of men and concludes, "Perhaps no single word with emotional resonance occurs more frequently in this novel than the word 'man,' " *The English Novel, Form and Function* (New York: Rinehart & Company, 1953), p. 51.

with him we are most shockingly exposed to women's power-lessness and degradation. To investigate women's place in the patriarchy is then largely to investigate Lovelace and his striking similarity to the father Clarissa was born to obey.

Mr. Harlowe and Lovelace insist on their distinction from each other. The father abhors and condemns the licence and licentiousness of the young rake, and the rake detests the tyranny and rigidity of the old father. Lovelace even mocks him as "old prerogative," scorning the "old patriarchal system" within which the Harlowes operate. Yet both men create an environment and character for Clarissa, and demand her submission. Since their actions and aims coincide, Lovelace can truly see the "whole stupid family doing my business for me." Ironically the converse is also true.[11]

The father gives his name to Clarissa, making much of the present. When she must be dutiful, she is addressed by her surname. When she should show duty through marriage, however, the name becomes a mark of shame, derisively stamped on her by her sister. After the rape she sinks below the name, unworthy of it or inappropriate for it; so she interrupts her letter to Anna before the signature as if doubtful what it should be. In the purity of death she becomes again a Harlowe and the name is boldly inscribed on the coffin and proclaimed in the will. But Lovelace also lays claim to Clarissa and forces his claim on her consciousness. When she hesitates in her letter after her rape, it is his name she fears she should write. When she dies he insists that she has died a Lovelace and he asserts that his name should have been emblazoned on her coffin: he is her husband and she "Clarissa Lovelace."

Both men control Clarissa's social status and relationships. The father agrees that a servant shall rule his daughter and that her mother shall be separated from her. Lovelace gives titles, names, and functions to the people who surround her at Sinclair's; he orders their attitudes and actions and so ordains her

11. Dorothy Van Ghent calls Lovelace "indirectly a kind of moral employee of the father," ibid., p. 60.

response. Sometimes he even writes the words his characters speak; it is a theatrical image of a reality that surrounded Clarissa even in her father's house, where mother, aunt and uncles mouthed words dictated by the controlling male.

Both father and Lovelace expect absolute obedience from Clarissa in accordance with their kingly power. The father sees himself in royal terms when he fears to damage his image by revoking the sentence on his daughter. Lovelace frequently styles himself king and emperor and he labels Clarissa's resistance to him "treasonable." Both men urge their absolute power so insistently that they almost destroy the identity of their victim. Clarissa is driven into "a perfect phrensy" by the severe measures of father and brother; Lovelace imposes his physical will in the rape, reducing her to the non-identity of madness.

Lovelace again coincides with the Harlowes in the idea of women as property.[12] Clarissa gives some allegiance to this idea when expressed by her family; but, when exaggerated and exposed in Lovelace, she opposes it strenuously. As the father cannot bear Lovelace having his daughter, so Lovelace cannot bear another man close to her. Both the father and Lovelace are even more averse to her on her own, and both fulminate against her repeated desire to remain single.

Because of their makeshift vision of women, both men view the rape as a property crime. "I can marry her when I will," Lovelace asserts, "And if I do, after prevailing (whether by *surprize*, or by *reluctant consent*) whom but myself shall I have injured?" (IV, 217). Even more shockingly he later asks: "whose property, I pray thee, shall I invade?" (IV, 377). By the rape he damages some Harlowe goods but the damage can be rectified by marriage, the legal buying and paying for the goods.

Lovelace and the Harlowes both insist on marriage after

12. Lovelace displays this attitude when he thinks of Anna Howe as well as of Clarissa. As Katharine Rogers has noted, he hesitates in raping Anna only when he thinks of the injury he would do to Hickman, her lover. See "Richardson's Empathy with Women," *The Authority of Experience: Essays in Feminist Criticism* (Amherst: University of Massachusetts Press, 1977), p. 123.

Clarissa's "fall." Her reaction again shows her pivotal place in patriarchal and female schemes. She will accept her father's right to dispose of his own child since he has created her, but she will not accept the analogy, that she is created anew by Lovelace into a woman and must obey his disposition of marriage. She agrees she can be no man's but Lovelace's, but she insists, against Lovelace and ultimately her father, that she has a right to be her own. The extreme possessiveness is finally seen after her death in Lovelace's frenzied cries that he owns the corpse because he raped the woman, and that he may dispose of it according to his will. Clarissa is freed from them all only by her insentience.

Mr. Harlowe and Lovelace converge again in using words to bring about their victim's fate. The father curses his daughter and his curse—largely fulfilled—resounds through the last part of the novel. So too Lovelace binds Clarissa with his words when he coerces her into silently accepting their marriage; the rape fulfills his boast. More tenuously the novel itself ties Clarissa to Lovelace. Excited by his schemes, he imagines himself a popular rapist arrested and displayed to the crowd in the London streets; it is however Clarissa, not he, who fulfills his words when she is arrested for a false debt and turned into a public spectacle.

As we have seen, Lovelace and her father impose a character, a society, a dutiful scheme and fate on Clarissa. They go even further, trying in their different ways to impose an interpretation on her life and death. Both trivialize what she signifies. The father seeks to make her struggle for integrity—so realized in her correspondence with Anna Howe—into the display of petulance and obstinacy of the spoiled child. He refuses to believe in her dying and death because such pretended acts betray the revenge of the child hoping to make her parents sorry for their meanness.[13] Clarissa is aware of the imposition and she tries to refute

13. Morris Golden responds to the father's interpretation when he sees the last quarter of *Clarissa* as a child's revenge fantasy: "Nowhere else in literature . . . has the self-pity of the punished child managed to exact so complete a revenge on the adult punishers," *Richardson's Characters* (Ann Arbor: University of Michigan Press, 1963), pp. 67 and 177.

it at her death by her forgiving and encouraging letters to her family.

In a similar way, Lovelace seeks to reduce Clarissa, not to the petulant child but to the coy, coquettish mistress or the punctilious prude. He does this in two ways. First he imposes on her the reductive words "Charmer" and "Beauty," putting a coquettish interpretation on her acts and responses, and describing her blushes and tears, her restraint and withdrawals in terms of the sexual game.[14] Since Clarissa exists so largely in Lovelace's prose after her escape from her family, his interpretation is an insistent one. Second, he fools Clarissa herself into using ironically inappropriate words, so reducing her to the pathetic.[15] He makes her accept whores as ladies and crooks as gentlemen, and he describes his deceptions in boisterously cruel letters to his friend. Forced to exist in this fully realized and humorously horrible context, Clarissa often verges on the ridiculous in her defensive or well-meaning gentility and punctiliousness. Indeed so overwhelming is Lovelace's prose creation of Clarissa that Richardson was obliged to provide footnotes asserting his rake's villainy, to keep the reader from succumbing to his libertine world-view and judging Clarissa accordingly.

The physical sign of patriarchy's power is blood, and it is in their joy in blood that the Harlowes and Lovelace most strikingly mirror each other. The Harlowe men by *"nature"* share Lovelace's "triumph in subduing" (I, 252). Toward other men their bloodlust is declared in the duel of swords; toward women, it is manifested in rape. Both the duel and the rape are socially sanctioned and in both the aggressor is socially untarnished. After the rape Lovelace is courted in society, even by women; the duellist is

---

14. Morris Golden points to another method of trivializing when he shows how Lovelace views Clarissa's pathos aesthetically rather than morally or emotionally. For him Clarissa becomes lovely in her tears. Ibid., p. 121.

15. In the brothel she pathetically approves a whore's spurious alliance. Ian Watt discusses this scene in *The Rise of the Novel: Studies in Defoe, Richardson, and Fielding* (1957; Penguin Books, 1972), pp. 239–40.

a hero. The bloody cruelty at the heart of the patriarchal social order is forced on Clarissa consciously when she sees "one half of mankind tormenting the other and being tormented themselves in tormenting" (I, 38), and unconsciously when she dreams of the lustful cruelty which propels Lovelace before ever he has revealed his character and designs.

Lovelace exaggerates the male lust for blood and power, viewing the sexes entirely in its terms. Women for him are trained in resistance that men may have the pleasure of combat. The combat over, men become cruel, and joy in tyrannizing over what they love.

From the bleeding of the beloved object Lovelace derives the most exquisite and painful pleasure. Vividly he visualizes his triumph over the conscience as bloody murder. The blood foreshadows Clarissa's virgin blood—which is hidden from the reader in Lovelace's silence over the rape—and ultimately his own blood from the sword he chose.

The rape itself, related only by a semiconscious Clarissa, is expressed for us in a simulacrum, the scene of the nosebleed which Lovelace exposes in all its frenzy and blood:

> snatching up hastily her head from the chair, and as hastily popping it down again in terror, [she] hit her nose, I suppose, against the edge of the chair; and it gushed out with blood running in a stream down her bosom; she herself too much afrighted to heed it!
>
> Never was mortal man in such terror and agitation as I, for I instantly concluded, that she had stabbed herself with some concealed instrument.
>
> I ran to her in a wild agony—For Dorcas was frighted out of all her mock interposition—
>
> What have you done!—O what have you done!—Look up to me, my dearest life!—Sweet injured innocence, look up to me! What have you done! Long will I not survive you! And I was upon the point of drawing my sword to dispatch myself, when I discovered—[What an unmanly blockhead does this charming creature make me at her pleasure!] that all I apprehended was but a bloody nose. . . . (V, 378)

SENTIMENTAL FRIENDSHIP

The situation resembles the rape: Lovelace is nakedly aggressive and supported by the women of the house against Clarissa, almost unconscious of the event and her effect on others. The rape is further indicated when the nosebleed is valorized, then trivialized. As soon as he sees the blood Lovelace reacts in agony, about to turn the sword on himself, truly an "unmanly" act, for it suggests he sees the rape and the wounding in feminine terms as a fatal blow to autonomy. Quickly he changes, however, to resume his manhood, and the bloody wounding becomes insignificant, an action silly women fuss too much about. Clarissa moves from the "injured innocence" to the "charming creature" and all is translated into the boisterously and humorously cruel mode that is peculiarly Lovelace's.[16]

But the incident simulates more than Lovelace can know. The "terror and agitation" he feels resembles his emotions both after the rape and after Clarissa's death. The distinct horror of the later event is suggested here, for his agony is increased in both cases when he perceives that death has become his successful rival.

Only once in the novel does Clarissa herself actively enter the scheme of blood: in the pen-knife scene shortly after her nosebleed. Both Clarissa's triumph and her defeat, this scene demonstrates the same shifting sexual relationships as the nosebleed scene, but in it Clarissa for once consciously uses the bloody power she so insistently relates to the male.

Lovelace has pretended to reproach Dorcas for planning to aid her mistress. Clarissa is not fooled; instead she is provoked into her most violent and powerful attack on Lovelace and the women:

> ye, vile women, who perhaps have been the ruin, body and soul, of hundreds of innocents (you shew me *how*, in full assembly) know, that I am not married—Ruined as I am, by your help, I

16. Lovelace's changes in mode can be related to his dramatic image of himself. Responding aesthetically and dramatically to events, he erroneously believes that he can always choose and impose on others the mode of drama. For a discussion of Lovelace as dramatist, see Margaret Anne Doody's *A Natural Passion*, p. 114.

bless God, I am *not* married, to this miscreant—And I have friends that will demand my honour at your hands!—And to whose authority I will apply; for none has this man over me. Look to it then, what further insults you offer me, or incite him to offer me. I am a person, tho' thus vilely betrayed, of rank and fortune. I never will be his; and, to your utter ruin will find friends to pursue you. . . .

Madam, said I, let me tell you; and was advancing towards her, with a fierce aspect, most cursedly vexed, and ashamed too—

But she turned to me; "Stop where thou art, O vilest and most abandoned of men!—Stop where thou art—Nor, with that determined face, offer to touch me, if thou wouldst not that I should be a corpse at thy feet!"

To my astonishment, she held forth a penknife in her hand, the point to her own bosom, grasping resolutely the whole handle, so that there was no offering to take it from her.

"I offer not mischief to any-body but myself. You, Sir, and ye, women, are safe from every violence of mine. The LAW shall be all my resource. . . ." (VI, 66–67)

Clarissa breaks through the web of deceit in which Lovelace has trapped her to admit her unmarried state, frightening all her spectators with her active integrity and innocence. At the same time she asserts this integrity in spite of the physical "ruin" and rejects the sexual identity Lovelace had for so long been trying to force on her. Like the body he violated, the body he will touch again will be no more than a corpse.

Certainly Clarissa is triumphant—the women are made fearful, Lovelace retreats humiliated—yet she is so by entering a scheme of blood and vengeance which she elsewhere vigorously opposes. To frighten the women she assumes the identity of rank and fortune she has in the male world; she threatens them with the very family power she has repudiated, as well as with the power of the patriarchal law, an agent whose immoral action is declared again and again in the book.[17] In addition she intimi-

17. Lovelace states he is sure to be acquitted of rape because of his rank and person; Clarissa is arrested for a debt she does not owe. The law, it seems, acts with the cruelty and partiality of the patriarchal family, whose instrument it is.

dates with a weapon, the pen-knife as a feminized sword.[18] She will hurt only herself, so the cruelty is turned inwards; yet it is the same cruel power that characterized the men she despises. At the end of the scene she realizes how far she has strayed into an alien world when she thanks God she has been delivered from herself.

When death really comes, Clarissa rejects its bloody aspect. Turning from "the pursuit of blood," she dies a pallid death urging her defenders to forgo their bloody revenge. But she cannot as easily escape the context of blood as she can the direct use of it. She is tied to her family by blood and it is in blood that they must prove their kinship. The peaceful death of Clarissa provokes the violent death of Lovelace through the mediation of the violent family to which she is inextricably bound.

In *Clarissa* the "old patriarchal system" of the Harlowes, exaggerated by Lovelace, seeks to control the heroine. She sees it work first through the nurturing family; only later can she appreciate its expression in property and violence. By that time, however, she is bound to it by the virtue of obedience to parents, the divinely sanctioned ideal of the system. Her bonds constrict when her grandfather's will uncovers patriarchy's awful dependence on money and when Lovelace's cruelty betrays its habitual expression in blood. Before either event, however, she has been exposed to one of its most disturbing results: the repression and perversion of women. Her mother and sister are the first victims of the father and all he stands for. Clarissa is only his latest.

2

WOMEN WITHIN PATRIARCHY
Property and the law are instruments of patriarchy. Marriage is a legal affair of property and the women who have much to do

18. Dorothy Van Ghent comments on the various images of stabbing—as well as the several sharp instruments—used by Clarissa in the course of the novel. She argues for an erotic context since they are commonly employed when Clarissa is seductively dishevelled,

with it are inevitably marked by patriarchy. Subordinated to the men who control them, they can act only by imitating their masters and acquiring the traits of those men to whom they must submit. Outside legal marriage, women may be similarly marked, depending as they usually do on some exploitation of sexuality, rendered degrading through the existence of marriage. The whores and madams mock the matrons but inevitably echo them. All are subordinate to the controlling male and all act by imitating him. Within the family the Harlowe women, Arabella and Mrs. Harlowe, are the book's most telling examples of patriarchal women; outside it they are shadowed and exaggerated by Sinclair and her whores.

Arabella and her mother clearly display their patriarchal scars: Mrs. Harlowe, well-born and virtuous, is reduced to a weak and accommodating servant of the man she married and the son she bore; Arabella, physically ill-favored, is soured into a jealous and rancorous sister. Both women are wealthy but their money is tied to husband and father; neither receives an uncustomary legacy and neither knows the temptation of independence or female integrity.

Mrs. Harlowe shares much with her daughter Clarissa, called by Anna Howe "her Mother's girl." Like Clarissa she is sensible and compassionate and judged "admirably well qualified to lead." But she leads no one, for she has fully accepted the duty of obedience to her husband and she is governed by this choleric and intolerant man in everything. In her mother Clarissa sees her own future and is puzzled. She admires her and accepts that she owes obedience to the husband; at the same time she sees the dutifulness as weakness. Mrs. Harlowe, Clarissa knows, "must submit to be led," but she admits that her mother errs when she is so.

The English Novel, pp. 315–16. The context of violence is however even more pronounced than the erotic context and the images and instruments seem primarily to indicate the entanglement of the passivist Clarissa in a scheme of violence she cannot easily escape.

SENTIMENTAL FRIENDSHIP

According to Clarissa, her mother has "a gentle and sensible mind, which has from the beginning, on all occasions, sacrificed its own inward satisfaction to outward peace" (I, 30). Clarissa early understands that for the woman "inward satisfaction" and "outward peace" are incompatible, but she can still sever her mother's culpable passivity from the virtue of obedience to the man. Naively she believes that the virtuous and good must rule or influence if they will: "would she but exert that authority which the superiority of her fine talents gives her, all these family feuds might be extinguished" (I, 32). Such naiveté is destroyed as Clarissa's own virtuous exertions fail. If she avoids her mother's psychological constraints, she comes later to appreciate and suffer from her social ones. The peace her mother has so long bought at the cost of her integrity appears less despicable in the violent days that follow.

In the beginning, Clarissa blames her mother for her weakness and abdication of responsibility, while accepting her goodness: "Dear, dear excellence! how could she be thus brought over . . ." (I, 41). Later she drives her mother to explain her weakness and justify her ventriloquist speeches. Urging the hateful Solmes on the daughter whose surpassing value she knows, the mother makes a complex plea which aims both to persuade Clarissa into the role of daughter and to justify her own interpretation of the wifely role:

> You know, my dear, what I every day forego, and undergo, for the sake of peace. Your papa is a very good man, and means well; but he will not be controuled; nor yet persuaded. You have sometimes seemed to pity *me*, that I am obliged to give up every point. Poor man! *his* reputation the less for it; *mine* the greater: Yet would I not have this credit, if I could help it, at so dear a rate to *him* and to *myself* . You are a dutiful, a prudent, and a *wise* child, she was pleased to say, in hope, no doubt, to make me so: You would not add, I am sure, to my trouble: You would not wilfully break that peace which costs your Mother so much to preserve. Obedience is better than sacrifice. O my Clary Harlowe, rejoice my heart, by telling me I have apprehended too much!—I see your

27

concern! I see your perplexity! I see your conflict [loosing her arm, and rising, not willing I should see how much she herself was affected]. I will leave you a moment.—Answer me not—[For I was essaying to speak, and had, as soon as she took her dear cheek from mine, dropt down on my knees, my hands clasped, and lifted up in a supplicating manner]. I am not prepared for your irresistible expostulation, she was pleased to say. I will leave you to recollection: And I charge you, on my blessing, that all this my truly maternal tenderness be not thrown away upon you. (I, 103)

It is a revealing speech, created both by the mother who makes it and the daughter who records it and contextualizes it. The mother argues for her own way of total obedience, even though it reduces her husband to a "poor man" and herself to a nullity. She is consoled by her merit, but we do not learn in whose eyes, divine or earthly, this exists.

In the name of this negative merit, she appeals to Clarissa's duty, prudence, and wisdom. It is a chilling list of qualities—as negative in their way as the mother's meritorious meekness—and they contrast with the kindness and justice Anna Howe constantly finds in her friend. These negative virtues Mrs. Harlowe subtly reduces, and duty to parents degenerates in her speech, from honor of them into a slavish surrender to their power. All the while Clarissa is kept to her dutiful image.

Mrs. Harlowe has sacrificed her own less patriarchal virtues of kindness, justice, and sympathy. In her speech, she reveals her sacrifice at the same time as she demands Clarissa's obedience, suggesting that such obedience annihilates these virtues. "Obedience is better than sacrifice," she declares ambiguously, but Clarissa must see by now that the two may be identical, and that obedience is contingent not on justice but on power.

Indeed the mother herself seems aware of what she implies and, alarmed at it, breaks off to appeal by name to her daughter. But the address in part realizes her implication: combining the familiar name of the loved child with the family name causing the love and demanding duty, it hints that Clarissa is loved because she is a daughter who may be sacrificed to the man whose name marks her. The naked power behind the loving relationships of the family is disclosed and further words would make it only more abhorrent. So the mother retreats from the daughter, pausing only to ensure that her "truly maternal tenderness" will be rendered truly patriarchal.

By recording both the speech and her own response to it, Clarissa makes the monologue into a kind of dialogue between herself and her mother, and between speech and action. Clarissa, the narrator, watches her mother watching her and notes that her mother rises to avoid her own emotion, as well as her daughter's. In Clarissa's interpretation, her action belies her sureness about the sacrifice she has made and is demanding of another.

Clarissa too watches herself as she falls into the kneeling position. The action should suggest humility and sacrifice, but here, as she and her mother know, it signifies resistance. Her mother reacts to the significance not the action and withdraws into the veiled threat of denying her blessing and "maternal tenderness" unless Clarissa becomes obedient and acquiesces in the sale of herself. It is the sacrifice in action: the admirable mother reduced to the methods of the father, the "poor man" she fears and half despises. The words "maternal tenderness" are as divorced from their meaning as Clarissa's capitulating action, as the surface of the speech from its depths, and as, finally, the mother from the daughter.

As the conflict within Clarissa develops, Mrs. Harlowe responds more harshly. In the beginning she has mouthed the words of father and son, while softening them often with outbursts of tears and affection for her stronger daughter. Later Clarissa's obstinate integrity seems to question her own sacrificial choice and indeed to nullify it in the domestic war she causes. The warmth and affection become rarer and Mrs. Harlowe grows alienated from the non-Harlowe segment of her character. Anna Howe later sees her as a shadow Harlowe, a woman divorced from her maternal function, and she roundly declares:

I pity no Mother that puts it out of her power to show maternal Love, and Humanity, in order to patch up for herself a precarious and sorry quiet, which every blast of wind shall disturb.

29

SENTIMENTAL FRIENDSHIP

I hate tyrants in every form and shape: But paternal and maternal tyrants are the worst of all. (IV, 74–75)

In *Clarissa* character is often visibly expressed. People apprehend one another through an expression of the eyes or through momentary tableaux. A displaced effect occurs with the motif of the mirror.[19] To Clarissa, the mirror may reveal herself as she is seen, as the seductive and fragile maiden, the "broken lily," or it may expose Lovelace, the humbly grieving, as wrathful and vindictive. In another confrontation between Clarissa and her mother, the daughter glimpses her parent in a mirror and, as in the earlier pleading scene, catches an image belied by word and deed. But she is unsure whether she has discerned her mother's true self distanced in the mirror or whether she is creating with the lineaments of her mother the maternal image she needs. The mirror alienates, and mother and daughter are both hardened through their confusion. The mother is vexed because she has revealed herself or because she suspects Clarissa of imposing a revelation on her; the daughter stiffens because she has either been fooled or betrayed.

The image in the mirror is formed when Clarissa and her mother are alone, crying out their loss of each other as they converse about the trivia of the household:

Mr. Harlowe talks of dining out to-day, I think, at my Brother Antony's.—

Mr. Harlowe!—Not my Father! Have I not then a Father!—thought I?

Sit down when I bid you.

I sat down.

You look very sullen, Clary.

I hope not, Madam.

If children would always be children—parents—And there she stopt.

19. Dorothy Van Ghent has an excellent discussion of the use of mirrors and other special devices for seeing, which she relates to the epistolary form of *Clarissa*. See *The English Novel*, pp. 48–49. Margaret Anne Doody treats the mirror image alone, showing its tendency to reveal truth when the world is false and to represent the false when the world appears as it really is, *A Natural Passion*, p. 207.

She then went to her toilette, and looked in the glass, and gave half a sigh—The other half, as if she would not have sighed could she have helped it, she gently hem'd away.

I don't love to see the girl look so sullen.

Indeed, Madam, I am not sullen.—And I arose, and, turning from her, drew out my handkerchief; for the tears ran down my cheeks.

I thought, by the glass before me, I saw the *Mother* in her softened eye cast towards me: But her words confirmed not the hoped-for tenderness. (I, 130)

To Clarissa Mrs. Harlowe reveals her maternal side in the mirror, where alone she sighs and displays the *"Mother."* When she turns, she is all Harlowe, abrasive and scornful. The "mother" is reduced for her daughter to an image in the mirror—perhaps false, perhaps true, who knows?—while in the room she is absent.

Her disappearance disturbs all family relationships. In her discourse the father loses the paternal in the patriarchal, turning from father into "Mr. Harlowe." But he was always distant and fearsome; we do not see the idyllic family that Clarissa speaks of before Lovelace destroys it, and when we first meet Mr. Harlowe he is already angry and imperious. With the mother it is quite different, for we have had hints of her warmth. Her alienation from Clarissa and from herself, imaged in the hard, distant mirror, becomes even more terrifying.

In Clarissa's story her sister Arabella plays the ugly stepsister, as her mother declines into the cruel stepmother. Less favored in person and parts, Arabella is distinguished from Clarissa so energetically that they seem indeed only tenuously related. Arabella is indolent, envious, spiteful, and unrelenting, and her taunting treatment forms the nadir of her sister's sufferings under her father's roof.

The general cause of Arabella's envy is Clarissa's superlative merit and physical charms; the particular cause is Lovelace's favor. When he rejects Arabella, he is beyond her reach and she can retaliate only by rejecting Clarissa. She does this by vigorously pushing her first toward the hateful Solmes, then out of her father's house, and finally, after the disgrace of the rape, into death or Pennsylvania, both harsh alternatives. So severe is Arabella in her envy and rejection that Clarissa feels almost as much wounded by her sister as by Lovelace. The sororial wound festers because hidden; conceiving her domestic duty so highly Clarissa struggles to love and respect Arabella and she can rarely relieve herself by recriminating. Only later when Arabella remains merciless as Clarissa's sufferings increase is the struggle largely abandoned. Then Clarissa comes to accept her sister as unsisterly and, when her friend Anna is momentarily cruel, she uses Arabella as the very touchstone of cruelty, seeing her style in Anna's rebukes.

Clarissa instinctively perceives Arabella as masculine, for she has long equated evil with masculinity. Arabella is cruel like a man, even bloodthirsty. She displays her passion for Lovelace in lust for his death, as Lovelace shows his love for Clarissa in rape. Clearly the adjective "masculine" is used abusively for Arabella (as later for Sinclair) to imply the harshness and impetuous cruelty Clarissa finds in men but not in herself or, formerly, in her mother:

> what a hard-hearted Sex is the other! Children of the same parents, how came they by their cruelty?—Do they get it by travel? Do they get it by conversation with one another?—Or how do they get it?—Yet my Sister, too, is as hard-hearted as any of them. But this may be no exception neither: For she has been thought to be masculine in her air, and in her spirit. She has then perhaps, a soul of the *other* Sex in a body of *ours.*—And so, for the honour of *her own,* will I judge of every woman for the future, who, imitating the rougher manners of men, acts unbeseeming the gentleness of her own Sex. (III, 216)

Yet, as Clarissa knows, women owe obedience to the male sex: father rules mother, brother rules sister. Being more masculine must imply being more important, more powerful. By attacking Arabella for masculinity, then, she is criticizing cruelty in her sister but also upholding in a way the patriarchal scheme at its base. Arabella is condemned not only for being cruel, but also for trespassing on male ground. Lovelace may boast of his femininity; a woman is always shamed by her masculine side.

Clarissa thinks highly of the sisterly function; a sister should be a friend by blood, a person who shares, comforts, and supports. It is the only relationship that is potentially equal within the rigidly hierarchical family; when this is marred by conflict, the family becomes indeed a place of warfare.

In the Harlowe household, the relationship is early spoiled by Arabella's envy. When Lovelace abandons his mistaken suit of her, she abandons entirely her sisterly pretensions. To the physical, mental, and spiritual inequality between her and her sister, she joins a social one. Henceforth she and Clarissa will be simply rivals—a possibility always contained in patriarchal sisterhood, where women must compete through waiting for men. The energies of Arabella have no outlet but in taunting her more successful and more favored sister.

The cruelty of Arabella is realized on page after page of Clarissa's miserable letters from her home. A typical example comes from the early part of volume I:

> My Sister came to me soon after—Sister Clary, you are going on in a fine way, I understand. But as there are people who are supposed to harden you against your duty, I am to tell you, that it will be taken well if you avoid visits or visitings for a week or two till further order.
>
> Can this be from those who have authority—
>
> Ask them; ask them, child, with a twirl of her finger.—I have delivered my message. Your Father will be obeyed. He is willing to hope you to be all obedience, and would prevent all *incitements* to refractoriness.
>
> I know my duty, said I; and hope I shall not find impossible conditions annexed to it.
>
> A pert young creature, vain and conceited, she called me. I was the only judge, in my own wise opinion, of what was right and fit. She, for her part, had long seen into my specious ways: And now I should shew everybody what I was at bottom.

Dear Bella, said I! hands and eyes lifted up—why all this? dear Bella, why—

None of your dear, dear Bella's to me.—I tell you, I see thro' your *witchcrafts* [that was her strange word]. And away she flung; adding, as she went, And so will everybody else very quickly, I dare say.

Bless me, said I to myself, what a Sister have I!—How have I deserved this?

Then I again regretted my Grandfather's too distinguishing goodness to me. (I, 50–51)

Clarissa degenerates from "Sister Clary" through "child" to "a pert young creature" and the equality necessary for sisterly friendship is destroyed. The relationship functions within a context of domination, where family controls society—Clarissa is refused exit—and father controls children. Arabella dominates Clarissa through their father's business; his message gives her the superiority she had long coveted.

As Clarissa perceives the horror that may result from being obedient to family law and accepting family hierarchy, she concludes that duty may be limited. Since Arabella may dominate her sisterly rival only as long as the father's justifying power is supreme, she is especially provoked by Clarissa's limiting conclusions.

She is further provoked when her sister attempts to reduce her to equality through kindness. Calling her "dear Bella," Clarissa shows herself sympathetic and amiable beyond family necessity, and again the family pattern of dominance and submission is questioned. Arabella is the more incensed as these qualities remind her of how Clarissa successfully appealed to the grandfather, and so placed herself clearly over her elder sister in power. The memory allows her to accuse Clarissa of playing a crafty hand in the power game; through her accusation Arabella reelevates herself and again rejects equality.

This analysis of Arabella's speech is partially confirmed when Clarissa juxtaposes her sister's anger with her own lament for her grandfather's favor. By so doing she hints at the provocation—conscious or unconscious—of her own behavior. It is as though she wishes somehow to express her anger at female perversion in the family and chooses to do it through arousing her sister (rather than her mother) to the kind of spitefulness she can openly combat. Later when she writes to her sister begging her to appeal for her, she alludes to the period of Lovelace's fake courtship of Arabella and to his obvious attractiveness, although she is aware that her sister continues to love the man. Following this with the address "my sister, my Friend, my Companion, my Adviser," (I, 205) she seems to be demanding rejection. When it comes, she responds almost with relief: in her mind there arose "a rancour" that was new to her.

After Clarissa leaves her father's house, she has little further to do with the alienated mother and the persecuting sister. But she does not escape them, for both are displaced negatively within the brothel. Sinclair carries out the mother's cruel aim of shattering her daughter's autonomy; while the whores, her "daughters," find in Clarissa their most tempting rival.

Ian Watt has noted Clarissa's progress from the house of Harlowes to the house of harlots.[20] The linguistic connection ensures that we see how similar are the establishments and their organizers. The terrifying Sinclair may seem far from the weak and submissive Mrs. Harlowe, but their functions collide; both women minister to men and preside over houses whose genteel veneer barely hides the brutality beneath.

Sinclair shares with Mrs. Harlowe a mothering function and her whores become her daughters whom she, like Mrs. Harlowe, wishes to sell. Like other mothers, Sinclair aims to increase her family; since her daughters are born through rape and seduction, she is eager to promote these activities. She and her whores conspire "to break the resisting spirit" (IV, 372) of young women, especially of such superlative ones as Clarissa. As Lovelace says, "the highest joy every infernal Nymph of this worse than infernal

20. *The Rise of the Novel*, p. 269. Watt comments on how close Richardson himself comes to making the verbal association.

35

habitation *could* have known, would have been to reduce this proud Beauty to her own level" (V, 17–18).

Following Mrs. Harlowe again, Sinclair tries to impose behavior and attitudes on her "daughters." Both, however, go too far too quickly with Clarissa, thus shocking where they would convince. The sudden horrific epiphany of Sinclair before the rape is prefigured in the sudden strangeness and cruelty of the gentle mother. Clarissa is driven in both cases to wonder and shudder. She is transformed neither into the wholly subservient Harlowe daughter nor into the abandoned harlot.

The whores follow Arabella in judging Clarissa solely as a rival. Sally Martin and Polly Horton share Arabella's passion for Lovelace and her hatred for the female autonomy and integrity they have forfeited. When the whores revile and taunt Clarissa, they reenact the cruel scenes with Arabella in the family house. Through the reenactment we come to appreciate that what Clarissa kindly terms Arabella's "severity of . . . virtue" (VIII, 29) is identical in the patriarchal scheme with the severity of vice. Patriarchal virtue is simply being within a father's house, vice without it.

The rape—the ultimate human horror for Clarissa—is strangely associated with Sinclair and the whores, who implicate the Harlowe women they displace. Clarissa's short, drugged description centers on Sinclair: "some visionary remembrances I have of female figures, flitting, as I may say, before my sight; the wretched woman's particularly" (VI, 191).[21] As we see the whores cajoling and coercing their victim into the evil house, we remember Arabella and her maid, who tug and pull Clarissa toward the sinister "Moated-house," where the marriage-rape of

21. Responding to Clarissa's "appalling conviction that Sinclair was somehow at the heart of the matter," Judith Wilt has argued that Sinclair is both instigator of and actor in the rape. As further evidence she cites Lovelace's reiterated complaint that it is the whores who drive him on and his admission that he has within him something of the woman: "He Could Go No Further: A Modest Proposal about Lovelace and Clarissa," *PMLA* (January 1977), 19–32. It is a provocative idea, wittily presented, but it founders, I believe, on the nature of the evidence. As I argue below, Sinclair is almost entirely created by Clarissa and Lovelace and in their prose she is devil and beast as well as rapist.

Solmes should be perpetrated; as we hear of Sinclair flitting before Clarissa's sight while Lovelace rapes her, we may recall the mother flitting through the Harlowe household as the men press her daughter inexorably toward the hated husband.

The rape is powerful partly because it does implicate so many. It compels Clarissa to see the controlling and evil influence of a scheme to which she has assented, however unwillingly. Through her mother and sister she appreciated how patriarchal power could act through women; Sinclair and the whores confirm the lesson. The rape mortally wounds because the rapist is in a way father, lover, sister, and mother.[22]

When Clarissa is imprisoned for debt through the trickery of the whores, she most perceives their envious hatred and she again learns a painful lesson. Enduring their taunts and scoffs, she is inevitably reminded of her siblings: "O my Sister!—O my Brother!—Tender mercies were your cruelties to this!" The attacks in fact follow closely Arabella's. Sally mocks Clarissa for not being married, for motives and actions below her—"a young creature who would have bilked her lodgings"—and for her pious protestations and attitudes—"Your religion, I think, should teach you, that starving yourself is Self-murder" (VI, 276). It is Clarissa's very autonomy, integrity and virtue that have provoked Sally and Arabella. To destroy these qualities has been their primary aim.

In prison Clarissa is again the victim of whores, sister, and mother, all of whom have envied and distrusted her monied independence. Mrs. Harlowe, once rich, lost her will and fortune in Mr. Harlowe, while Arabella exists only to transfer property from father to husband. The whores must prey daily on men to survive. But imprisonment for poverty teaches the rich Clarissa that money—however coveted—cannot give independence, for power derives not from money alone but from the meshing of money, cruelty, and the law. Helpless, kind, and rich, she cannot

22. Later, when the whores reduce Clarissa to a victim of the law she had once so proudly invoked, she is further shocked to understand how comprehensive is the evil scheme she is simultaneously entering and fighting.

use her wealth to bribe her way to freedom: she could not buy her mother and sister with the legacy when she offered it in place of herself, and later she failed to purchase even the meanest whore. In contrast Lovelace supports the brothel with his money, legal immunity, and brutal habits; legally, financially, and physically powerful, he can buy almost anyone.

The Harlowe and Sinclair women tell this truth to Clarissa, apprising her of the tainted complexity of power. The legacy in Harlowe Place seemed an exit intermittently repudiated; later the exit appears blocked unless she would enter through it a whole scheme of cruelty and coercion. Between them, then, the two sets of patriarchal women reinterpret the legacy and render it a dubious route to female autonomy.

When Clarissa apprehends Sinclair and the whores as supremely evil, she hints at another resemblance between the Harlowe women and their displacements. Like the mother and Arabella, Sinclair and her "daughters" live through the expression of others. Their motives are imputed, not stated, and we hear more of their effect than of their actions. The mother and sister, however, did write occasionally, although they mostly used the father's or brother's words. Sinclair and the whores are even more hidden, existing entirely in other people's prose.

All the writers conspire to impose a diabolic, masculinized character on Sinclair, and the language in which she exists is always extreme. Lovelace, for example, sees her as the power of darkness who must betray him. He blames her for urging the rape and for ensuring Clarissa's death by her brutal treatment. Before the rape he speaks of his own divided psyche in terms of a fight between himself and the women, forgetful that he has made them whores and that he alone brought Clarissa to the house:

> How do these creatures endeavour to stimulate me! A fallen woman is a worse devil than even a profligate man. The former is incapable of remorse: That am not I—Nor ever shall they prevail upon me, though aided by all the powers of darkness, to treat this admirable creature with indignity. (III, 338–39)

But he betrays himself in his concluding clause:

> So far, I mean, as indignity can be separated from the trials which
> will prove her to be either woman or angel.

Clearly the infernal women allow Lovelace the exquisite pleasure
of brutality with high motives and they allow him also the comfort that, because society refuses their remorse, the women must
exceed himself in dreadfulness. Sinclair the silent can become his
scapegoat as well as society's.

When Lovelace is at his most powerful and most lustful, he
again has a vision of Sinclair, this time as bestial rather than infernal:

> The old dragon straddled up to her, with her arms kemboed
> again—Her eye-brows erect, like bristles upon a hog's back, and,
> scouling over her shortened nose, more than half-hid her ferret
> eyes. Her mouth was distorted. She pouted out her blubber-lips, as
> if to bellow up wind and sputter into her horse-nostrils . . . . (V,
> 313)

Certainly it is a revolting sight but one which tells us more of the
seer than the seen. Surely here is an image of Lovelace's bestial
passion rather than of any woman, even one with infernal intentions. To avoid the negative reductiveness into which such visions
of women lead him, Lovelace must, perversely, reduce Clarissa to
an angel. He must rape her to prove women may be innocent.[23]

After Lovelace has indeed treated his "admirable creature
with indignity" and rendered her truly an "angel" in death, he is
still found blaming Sinclair, whom Belford amply terms the
"mother" of his mind. Yet Lovelace will not accept such kinship
and urges diabolic possession, reducing the women again to elements in his fantasy. He fulminates against the dark power in
which he sees himself enmeshed:

23. In Lovelace's exaggerated views of the women, we can see his thwarted idealism,
an idealism connected with the patriarchal desire to have women supremely pure and supremely subservient. Women are either angels like Clarissa or devils like the whores, and
he betrays his polarized view when he angrily terms the whores infernal nymphs.

Had I carried her [I must still recriminate] to any other place than to that accursed woman's—For the potion was her invention and mixture; and all the persisted-in violence was at her instigation, and at that of her wretched daughters. (VIII, 269)

But he deflates such fantasy and shows how it reverses reality when he qualifies the "daughters" with the clause *"who have now amply revenged upon me their own ruin, which they lay at my door."* If the daughters are thus unwillingly justified, his "mother" and theirs deserves some less imaginary and egocentric analysis.

To Lovelace the whores, like Sinclair, are mostly devils and creatures of darkness in description. In action, however, they become pathetic and fallen women. Of Sally he writes heartlessly:

Because this little devil made her first sacrifice at my altar, she thinks she may take any liberty with me: And what makes her outrageous at times, is, that I have, for a long time, *studiously* as she says, slighted her too readily offered favours: But is it not very impudent in her to think, that I will be any man's *successor?* (IV, 283)

The devil is diminutive and further reduced to the abandoned and slighted woman.

At the end of the novel the whores emerge a little more clearly from the murk of other people's emotions when Belford narrates their histories. They still do not speak for themselves of course, but at least we hear a version of their biographies. Sinclair is never so revealed and even her real name remains hidden.

Both Sally and Polly are children of defective parents who raise them without siblings. Sally's parents ape quality, Polly's mother acts the child. Neither girl receives moral or intellectual instruction and neither can develop integrity; both are taught to see themselves—their beauty or accomplishments—solely in relationship to men and the marriage only men may confer.

Within their families, Sally and Polly are far freer than the Harlowe daughters and both fall easily to the marauding libertine. As Belford says of Sally:

A bad education was the preparative, it must be confessed: And for this Sally Martin had reason to thank her Parents: As they had reason to thank themselves, for what followed: But, had she not met with a Lovelace, she had avoided a Sinclair; and might have gone on at the common rate of wives so educated; and been the Mother of children turned out to take their chance in the world, as she was; so many lumps of soft wax, fit to take any impression that the first accident gave them; neither happy, nor making happy; every-thing but useful; and well off, if not extremely miserable. (VIII, 293)

Without Lovelace they would have had a dreary but not disastrous fate—similar to that of Arabella, brought up in the conventional family shadowed by the properly dominant and restricting male. They differ in fate primarily because they are more attractive than Arabella, for all are affected by Lovelace and none is especially repulsed by his shaky morals. Indeed before Lovelace abandoned his suit, Arabella had resolved to treat him more freely.

In upbringing Clarissa is distinguished from her peers only in the instruction of her nurse, Mrs. Norton, and in the companionship of Anna Howe. Both help her to develop morally and intellectually. The education she receives is not vocational, for it aims at the autonomous woman of integrity. The patriarchal education variously exposed in Arabella, Sally, and Polly, fits a woman to be a mistress or a wife and pits her against all other women with whom she must compete for these roles.

Clarissa oscillates between the patriarchal view of infernal women and a female view of corrupted beings, implements of patriarchy. Sometimes she shares Lovelace's diabolic vision and looks to him for protection. At other times she sees Sinclair expressing Lovelace's physical power and cruelty, which he himself takes pains to hide. Sinclair becomes not the powerful mother of Lovelace but his obedient daughter, keeping his house and arranging everything by his commands, as Clarissa had done for her own father.

When she considers the whores alone, Clarissa is torn between horror at their effect on her and pity for their situation: *"Women to desert the cause of a poor creature of their own Sex in such a Situation, what must they be!*—Then, such poor guilty sort of figures did they make in the morning after he was gone out" (V, 57). Dimly Clarissa sees that she and the whores are victims, and she is disturbed that they cannot all make common cause. The contiguity of clauses suggests why, for the whores are bound fast in a system of power that has destroyed any opportunity of free female bonding; they are together solely because of their master. Their horrific powerful nature clearly depends on Lovelace too; when he is "gone out," they do not become virtuous autonomous women but merely "poor guilty" things. Like Arabella, the little importance they have is contingent on the male.

While Clarissa occasionally accepts the whores as active and primary agents of evil, Anna Howe firmly holds to her view of dependent women. She agrees that in Lovelace's prose Sinclair and the other women have been created "still wickeder" than himself, but she manages to slash through the construct to discover that "these women were once innocent. It was *man* that made them otherwise. The first bad man, perhaps, threw them upon worse men: Those upon still worse, till they commenced devils incarnate" (VIII, 194). Anna gives the supernatural a natural birth and allows patriarchy and hell as alternative breeding grounds for she-devils.

Through hating Sinclair and the whores, who exaggerate tendencies glimpsed in mother and sister, Clarissa comes to accept that she is separated from the women of her family. Toward the end of her life she finds a new sister in Mrs. Smith and a new mother in the "widow-lodger Lovick." But the strangeness persists in these and all other pseudo-family relationships Clarissa enters into in her last refuge. Kind and caring as Mrs. Lovick and her companions are, they can say throughout: "We are all strangers about her in a manner" (VII, 448).

The mothers and sisters, however, cannot so easily escape

Clarissa. Arabella is finally trapped in the fate she intended for her sister, tied to a man who combines the avarice of Solmes with the profligacy of Lovelace. Through Clarissa the whores lose Lovelace, their master, and they die after following her progress through violence and law.

The mothers are even more closely attached to Clarissa. Mrs. Harlowe dies shortly after her daughter, thinking of her in her last hours, while Sinclair laments her in an agonizing and tumultuous death, the opposite of Clarissa's.[24] Each in a way dies of Clarissa and with her. The weak-willed Mrs. Harlowe has no justification as a mother without Clarissa, and she becomes but a shadow of her husband, while the powerful Sinclair, who failed to make Clarissa her own, is repulsed in her function and power. The patriarchal scheme of violence and property Sinclair has entered is questioned and for the "masculine" woman there is no return to the feminine. The conflict involving Clarissa, which the mothers struggled not to enter, has killed them.

Clarissa must relate to both Harlowe and Sinclair families and be imprisoned in their houses. Her tie with her old nurse Norton is far more voluntary. Mrs. Norton has reared and educated her; according to Anna Howe, it was to Norton's "care, wisdom, and example" that she was "beholden for the groundwork of her taste and acquirements." Clearly Norton has set Clarissa on the road to female excellence; she cannot however ensure her charge's female autonomy, for she has no money and no position. While this poverty of state frees her from the cruder constraints of patriarchy, it also renders her impotent within its scheme. She may head Clarissa toward the female context, but not truly enter it herself.

On her last birthday, the dying Clarissa wrote to her nurse and educator, Mrs. Norton:

> You, who love me so dearly: Who have been the watchful sustainer of my helpless infancy: You, by whose precepts I have been

24. Significantly Sinclair's death is due to a fall when drunk; Clarissa's death is also due to a "fall" when drugged.

so much benefited!—In your dear bosom could I repose all my griefs; And by your piety, and experience in the ways of Heaven, should I be strengthened in what I am still to go through.

But, as it must not be, I will acquiesce. (VI, 420)

What must not be is a closeness between Clarissa and Mrs. Norton which surpasses that between Mrs. Harlowe and her child. Clarissa, the loving and dutiful daughter, must keep her regard fixed primarily on the mother who is bound to her by the father's name. To put Mrs. Norton before her parent is to lessen the importance and power of the family, an unacceptable action in patriarchy. Psychologically, too, such ranking and separation of mother and surrogate is unacceptable, since it parts Mrs. Harlowe from her best expression. When Norton is close to Clarissa and the Harlowe house, mother and daughter are most thoroughly alienated, and it is only when Mrs. Harlowe takes up her old correspondence with her daughter's nurse that she can show again her motherly side.

Clarissa herself tries not to separate her mother and Norton, often fighting her inclination to accept her nurse as her true parent, the mother of her mind. Throughout the novel she admits great affection for Norton, however, and, as her mother's harsh weakness is exaggerated, she is tempted to look primarily to her nurse, the woman from whom she has derived her strength and virtue. In her sufferings she comes even closer to Norton; both women have withstood the scorn and arrogance of the rich and mean, and both have been so schooled in torment that they look only to an afterlife for respite. Thus it becomes increasingly hard for Clarissa to hold out against the unfamilial temptation and, in the depths of her misery after Lovelace has raped her and her family repulsed her, she cries out to Norton:

Surely you are mine own Mother; and, by some unaccountable mistake, I must have been laid to a family, that having newly found out, or at least suspected, the imposture, cast me from their hearts, with the indignation that such a discovery will warrant.

O that I had indeed been your own child, born to partake of

your humble fortunes, an heiress only to that content in which you are so happy! Then should I have had a *truly* gentle spirit to have guided my ductile heart, which force and ungenerous usage sit so ill upon; and nothing of what has happened would have been. (VI, 139)

Clarissa's fears and longing emerge from what is unstated as well as stated. Her fantasy that she is really Mrs. Norton's child relieves her family of a guilt that is here her burden as well as theirs, for even in fantasy she, like her family, accepts that only consanguinity (or marriage) justifies love. The unloving family is exonerated and she need not love them.

In place of her own family, she would put the humble and poor Mrs. Norton and the present horror would be obliterated. As Norton's child she would be free of the context of property and power, and Lovelace would have nothing to revenge or subdue. The *"truly* gentle" Norton would be parent and womanly ideal for her, and she would have escaped the conflict between patriarchal values and female autonomy in which she is enmeshed. Certainly "nothing of what has happened would have been."

But, as Clarissa knows, it is all a treasonable fantasy and she must not indulge it. Quickly she checks herself. Later, as she approaches death, she keeps Norton away, fearful that she might indeed take the mother's place. In her posthumous letter, she thanks her nurse for her care and instruction, but makes no mention of her filial love. She is in death the daughter of her mother. But it is the mother herself who at the end rivets the bond between Clarissa and her nurse—a bond which Clarissa had so often feared and appreciated. In her grief Mrs. Harlowe wails to Mrs. Norton: "You was the dear creature's more *natural* Mother!" (VIII, 92).

Norton cannot truly function within the female scheme during Clarissa's persecutions; old and penniless, she is dependent on the Harlowes and forced to act in their context or not at all. Yet she provides a bridge for Clarissa between patriarchal and female schemes; she establishes Clarissa's integrity and yearning

45

for autonomy and, in the loving relationship she forms with the child, foreshadows the loving, admiring, and more equal friend who will nurture and support the woman.

3

WOMEN OUTSIDE PATRIARCHY

Against the patriarchal scheme, against the array of father,· brother, uncles, and lover, of patriarchal women, of the law, property, and power, Anna Howe thrusts her friendship with Clarissa.[25] It is an action which provokes the immediate charge of masculinization. But Anna is not masculinized into dominating or competing like Arabella and Sinclair, and the relationship she fosters is free from patriarchal attributes. She does not seek to possess her friend, although she is closer than any blood relative and more ardent than any predatory lover. Because of the freedom she allows, she is most tempting to Clarissa, who yet remains uneasy at the desire she so conspicuously exhibits.[26] Anna severs love from domination and undermines the patriarchal economy of desire. Her action attracts and repulses Clarissa, daughter of the Harlowes, as well as "paragon of [her] sex."

"I set not up for a perfect character," (II, 138) Anna declares and her lack of ambition frees her from much of Clarissa's conflict.[27] She is further freed by her situation: more than the

25. When David Daiches reduces the novel to relationships, he lists those "between master and servant, between parents and children, between debtor and creditor, between suitor and sought," and he finds them all "in some sense, symbolic of the relationship between man and God," "Samuel Richardson," *Literary Essays* (London: Oliver and Boyd, 1956), p. 33. He omits the relationship between friend and friend, which is distinguished from the others in not symbolizing the unequal relationship between man and God.

26. Dorothy Van Ghent relates the emotionalism of Clarissa's friendship with Anna Howe to the particular character of male-female relationships, *The English Novel*, p. 320.

27. Some critics regard Anna Howe as the norm. "Her spirit, even good sense, and moral solidity comprise a convincing norm in the novel," writes Norman Rabkin in "*Clarissa:* A Study in the Nature of Convention," p. 216, while Elizabeth Bergen Brophy calls her "the voice of normality," *Samuel Richardson: The Triumph of Craft* (Knoxville:

other women of the novel she can aspire to female autonomy and repudiate the role of dutiful daughter because this role is imposed only by a mother. Anna has no father and no brother, wealth sufficient to be freed of financial constraints and insufficient to invite marauding males. From her feminine haven, she regards the towering patriarchy of the Harlowes and can be sceptical of its power and careless of its virtues. Her understanding of its limits is clearer than Clarissa's, but the novel proves she is only hazily aware of its strength. Her view is painfully clarified by the end.

The perfect Clarissa, ideal woman and ideal daughter, is largely created by Anna. In her prose, the excellence of Clarissa initially shines forth. The first letter of the novel breathes Clarissa's surpassing grace and talent and at the end, as Belford and Anna jostle each other for space to construct their paragon, it is again Anna who urges her excellence: "She was the nearest perfection of any creature I ever knew" (VIII, 246). Between the sentimental extremes of course Clarissa tells her own story, describing excellence in action, but it is Anna as correspondent and inquirer who prompts the description and encourages it. As the women's correspondence becomes attenuated, Clarissa's story grows less clear, falling into allegory and incoherence. She needs the image of herself in Anna's writing to continue her own recreation. Divorced from this image, the conflict overwhelms, for it is in this correspondence alone that her female autonomy is respected. Separated from Anna's prose and her own self-creating response, the woman is raped into a daughter and wife.

The friendship of Clarissa and Anna differs from patriarchal relationships in being uncommercial, peaceful, and equal. Neither woman buys, sells, or steals the other. Neither shrinks from cri-

University of Tennessee Press, 1974), p. 94. Mark Kinkead-Weekes argues that she serves to express a more normal reaction than Clarissa and so acts as a safety valve for our own less than ideal feelings, *Samuel Richardson: Dramatic Novelist*, p. 158. In *Samuel Richardson and the Eighteenth-Century Puritan Character* (Hamden: Archon, 1972), Cynthia Griffin Wolff sets Anna up as Clarissa's conscience; their correspondence serves as Clarissa's diary. These views are certainly justified by the text, but they tend to ignore Anna's peculiar social situation, her perverse treatment of Hickman, and her final position as unwilling wife.

ticizing or from being criticized when necessary; neither "gives a byas against justice." The equality essential for such generosity and criticism cannot be attained in relationships between men and women. It is absent too from the wider society where justice from the law becomes impossible.

Equal, improving, and generous as the friendship is, it is most strikingly marked as fervent. Anna's declarations of love for Clarissa are the only ones given and accepted in the novel, and they contrast with the contempt and coldness both women throw to their male lovers. Anna woos Clarissa in her prose, caressing her friend by enumerating her qualities: "I could write a quire . . . upon a subject so copious and so beloved as is your praise" (II, 182). As Clarissa is tormented, Anna urges her suit, establishing herself against the power of all the Harlowes and Lovelaces of the world. No man is good enough for her Clarissa, for none can love as fiercely as Anna. "You know how much I love," she reiterates, "If it be possible, *more* than I love *myself* I love you." Her love has no temporal bounds: "I must, I will love you; and love you for ever" (III, 295) and no spatial ones: "what is the whole world to me, weighted against such a friend as you are?" (IV, 84). It is given biblical sanction by its echoes of *Ruth* when Anna asserts, "I would accompany you whithersoever you went" and by its allusion to the story of David and Jonathan when Clarissa acknowledges that her friend's love for her *"has passed* the love of women."

With the reference to David and Jonathan, erotic hints inevitably intrude. Anna's love for Clarissa is fervent and physical. She falls easily into physical metaphors for their interaction; criticism becomes a kind of erotic wounding that goes "deeper than the skin" and the chastisement feels—as well as is—good.[28] Anna longs to be with Clarissa to take the place not only of cruel father and mother but of lover as well. When she sees her friend dead in her father's house, Anna wails:

28. Morris Golden has noted how Anna deliberately provokes Clarissa's rebukes, "wishing to be hurt by her, and at the same time masochistically taking the serious hurt as evidence that her correspondent loves her," *Richardson's Characters*, p. 51.

. . . why . . . was she sent *hither?* Why not to *me?* —She has no
Father, no Mother, no Relations, no, not one!—They had all renounced her. I was her sympathizing friend—And had not I the
best right to my dear creature's remains —And must Names, without Nature, be preferred to such a Love as mine?

Again she kissed her lips, each cheek, her forehead;—and
sighed as if her heart would break— (VIII, 87)

These are the questions and actions of the lover and are painfully
reminiscent of the anguished outburst of Lovelace. Clarissa's
spirit was much to Anna, but her body, it seems, was also precious.

Anna insists that the friendship is unique—fervent, erotic,
generous, judicious, and critical. Within the patriarchal scheme
there cannot be its equal and there are few people daring enough
to reject this scheme to enter into a relationship so potentially
subversive, questioning as it does the values, polarities, and inclu-
siveness of patriarchy. Lovelace has his friend Belford but he reiterates his domination over him: he dramatizes this in writing
when he largely ignores Belford's actual letters, instead dictating
words and coercing his friend into attitudes of his own choosing.
Arabella finds a friend only in her subordinate maid, while
women who form an admiring backdrop to Anna and Clarissa
are not shown capable of such deep affection.[29] In the brothel
the women come together only for self interest and part for the
same reason. In the world of the novel, then, Anna can truly say
"I love you, as never woman loved another" (I, 27), a sentiment
echoed throughout the book and repeated with only a change of
tense in her final testament: "I loved the dear creature, as never
woman loved another" (VIII, 88).

So intense is Anna's love that she feels enveloped in her
beloved. "You are me," she constantly avers. When Clarissa is
praised, Anna is proud: "The praise was yours . . . and I enjoyed it" (I, 63); when Clarissa's honor is threatened, Anna's is

29. We do not hear much of the earlier friends of Clarissa and Anna, but we do see
them forming a network against the male world. Anna Howe learns of the obscene nature
of Clarissa's London lodgings through a relay of female informants.

implicated: "is not your Honour my Honour?" (V, 47); when Clarissa is humiliated, the humiliation is Anna's as well. This identity is cruelly parodied in Lovelace's fantasy that he is fooling the women, degrading them, and raping them in tandem.

The repetition of oneness, like the repetition of uniqueness, is fulfilled in Anna's parting words: "We had but one heart, but one soul, between us: And now my better half is torn from me,— *what shall I do?*" The selves of the women were interconnected and their autonomy was strangely symbiotic. When Anna says that Clarissa drags her whithersoever she goes, even into death, she is right. The dead Clarissa is manifested in the married Anna.

The friendship of Anna and Clarissa is expressed in writing. In the beginning both women accept their correspondence as one of the joys of their life; as Clarissa's miseries increase, both consider it their only joy. They write for themselves, and their letters are secret to an extent, as all personal correspondence must be. But, unlike Lovelace and Belford, Clarissa and Anna do not write in a secret code. The letters when taken may be read and, as Clarissa approaches death, her letters—those she is writing and those she has written—begin to fulfill their public potential and to move toward a wider readership than Anna.[30] After her death, Clarissa's letters alone can vindicate her; if it is her virtue that justifies her in heaven, it is her prose that does so on earth.[31]

Because the female correspondence is in a code available to everyone, it can be subverted. In the beginning of the novel Lovelace has already shown his subversive power when he forces Clarissa to repeat the words he writes. We do not see his letters directly, but they are paraphrased, quoted, and interpreted by Clarissa for her friend. So they insinuate themselves into her epistolary world, assuming its attributes. It is hard to discern the

---

30. David Daiches relates the public nature of the letter to the public nature of the moral dramas, "Samuel Richardson," p. 28.

31. In *Seduction and Betrayal* (New York: Vintage Books, 1975), Elizabeth Hardwick makes a related point when she discusses the significance of the epistolary form in *Clarissa*. Of the heroine she writes: "Words are her protection," pp. 207–8.

villain or remember him when he expresses himself within the ingenuous correspondence of the two loving friends.

Of course such subtle penetration does not satisfy Lovelace;
he must enter dramatically. His desire to rupture the correspondence of the two friends parallels his physical desire; when
he reads the letters, he is horrified at the hatred they express for
him and longs to rape Anna as well as Clarissa. Lovelace succeeds
in breaking the unity of the friends and, when he forges Anna's
letter, he enters with his words into their hearts and minds.
Clarissa and Anna are sundered and each is lowered in the eyes
of the other. Anna's proud boast, that "No *man* shall write for
me," is nullified. Female autonomy is destroyed by male pen or
penis.

In their letters, Clarissa and Anna are closer than Lovelace
and Belford but have far from identical voices. Sometimes Anna
states the antipatriarchal viewpoint and Clarissa, fearing it, re-
futes, parries, or qualifies; at other times she clothes the subversive sentiments of Anna in the conventional prose of patriarchy.[32]
The topics they cover range far, from literature and religion to
daily chores. Most keenly they investigate subjects directly relating to themselves, their identities as women—daughters, wives,
and people of honor.

Clarissa and Anna are both conscious of being women
(which makes doubly offensive Lovelace's use of this term for the
sexually awakened). But Anna is most clearly proud of the label
and sad at the limitations it imposes. She sees that women have
been made defective by pernicious education, designed to subordinate them to men, and that later, when they enter the social
game of courtship, they do so as standing targets. Clarissa notes
that the situation dissipates heterosexual love in women who
have such small power of choice. Men, made insolent and arrogant by privilege, become as little human as the women they

---

32. Morris Golden generalizes the point: "Anna serves to say the things about the
characters which Clarissa, limited by her more refined nature and upbringing, cannot,"
Richardson's Characters, p. 50. For example, Clarissa echoes in dutiful language Anna's
contempt for the Harlowe uncles.

oppress. In Anna's writing they sink to "Monkeys" and "Baboons," stupid, other, and frightening in their mischief.

Because she so deeply distrusts men, Anna tries to persuade Clarissa to put herself as far as possible from their power. She constantly urges her friend to take up her legacy and admit that she prefers spinsterhood to all other states. But Clarissa, trapped in the patriarchal scheme far more tightly than Anna, fears using patriarchal law and property against the very embodiment of patriarchy, her father. When Anna insists "Justice is due to ourselves, as well as to every-body else" (II, 9), Clarissa doubts the sentiment. Nothing in the patriarchal scheme suggests that she is owed either legal or social justice.

Anna is so insistent on the single life for herself and Clarissa because she sees all dealings between the sexes as warfare: "It vexes me to the very bottom of my pride, that any wretch of that Sex should be able to triumph over a Clarissa" (III, 98), she laments. The sexes are hostile and Clarissa's position at the apex of both schemes for women makes her supremely significant and vulnerable. For patriarchy the most dutiful daughter must be violated to become a dutiful woman and wife, while for the female scheme Clarissa, the virtuous and single, must remain physically, morally, and spiritually autonomous if her sex is to be other than contingent.

Because she perceives the hostility, Anna constantly urges Clarissa to throw out the conventions of patriarchy while fighting its exponent. "Punctilio," the rules by which Clarissa ordered her social conduct when in her family, "is out of doors the moment you are out of your Father's house," Anna declares. Later she advises Clarissa to forget the decorum designed by men for women in a domestic setting, and accept the power game on which she is embarked with Lovelace. But Clarissa has no practice in such games and she is hampered because she has too well internalized the rules of the dutiful daughter. She cannot reject these rules without alienating herself.[33]

While Anna forthrightly denounces marriage, Clarissa

33. But even Anna fails to see how intense is the power game and how deep is male hostility. Her spirited advice constantly falls short of the situation.

echoes more mildly many of her views. Both see it as a state of bondage, when the woman sacrifices her name, her fortune, and in a way her identity:

> To give up her very Name, as a mark of becoming his absolute and dependent property; To be obliged to prefer this strange man to Father, Mother, — to every-body: —And his humours to all her own. (I, 223)

Both Anna and Clarissa reject the argument that women must marry because they need to be protected by a man: Clarissa asserts that their upbringing causes the need, while Anna acidly points out that "this brave man will free us from all insults but . . . His own" (II, 150). Again both women reject the prescribed triumph of marriage over friendship. Anna resolves to live single as long as Clarissa's friendship remains an option; thinking obediently of marriage Clarissa yet concludes that one of its greatest evils is its power to destroy "the strictest friendship . . . all at [the husband's] pleasure."

Because they care about female autonomy, Clarissa and Anna agonize over female honor. It is a difficult concept that links patriarchal and female schemes. In the former it appears little more than virginity; in the latter it is sometimes coupled with dignity, so composing in part the autonomous woman. According to Anna, Clarissa is fearless in "points where her Honour, and the true dignity of her Sex are concerned" (II, 22).

The concept is tested after Clarissa is raped. In the madness that follows she accepts that she is "no longer what I was in any one thing" (V, 327). Yet she interrupts herself with the question and answer "In any one thing did I say? Yes, but I am; for I am still, and I ever will be, *Your true*—." She gives herself no name for she is no longer Clarissa Harlowe, but she exists still in her truth to Anna. Later she is less sure of this and, dying, she reiterates: "I am not what I was, when we were *inseparable* Lovers" (VI, 348). Anna and Clarissa had loved the honor of each other and, when it is destroyed in the patriarchal scheme, their friendship is shaken.

The exit from this dilemma is created by Clarissa when she

distinguishes her soul from her honor and hints that women have erred in confusing the two. Lovelace has taken her honor indeed, but since her will was uninvolved he has left her soul. This becomes the important element for the two women who see their mistake in trying to reinterpret so patriarchal a concept. Now Anna talks of Clarissa in terms not of honor but of soul: "I love not my Soul better than I do Miss Clarissa Harlowe" (VII, 34). The progression is, however, otherworldly, for, as honor is found too earthly, so the soul is proved eternal. It is not in friendship. that Clarissa will realize her soul but in death.

The letters of Clarissa and Anna form a dialogue on many subjects—social organization, marriage, female honor. The relationship between the two voices is shifting, sometimes close, sometimes distant. The viewpoint and tone coincide only to break apart a page later. One letter comments on the written and unwritten text of a previous letter; the next is rigorous in ignoring implications. Anna intermittently appreciates the awfulness of her friend's predicament and occasionally shares her intimate and painful knowledge of patriarchal power. Clarissa realizes, alternately accepting and rejecting, the flaming love of Anna.

Caught in patriarchy's conflict with the feminine scheme, Clarissa cannot wholeheartedly return Anna's love, seeing it detracting from the primary love of family. Anna must be more obedient, more subservient even, to her mother, Clarissa constantly urges; she must be a dutiful daughter and marry if her mother's choice is not totally repugnant to her. Both Clarissa and Anna desire the single life, but Clarissa partly ascribes her own desire to the clear unworthiness of her suitors and she believes Anna has no such excuse.

Yet she is tempted by Anna's love and she regrets that her friend is not within the family where alone the unmarried woman may wholeheartedly love. She wishes Anna had married her odious brother James and so become a sister, for the tie would have justified their affection. Later she wants Anna married to Hickman so that Anna may receive her. Clarissa can accept the love of an unrelated woman only when the woman's first affection is to a husband.

But Anna becomes neither Clarissa's sister-in-law nor her married friend; instead she asserts her identity as lover. Clarissa is uneasy, even frightened by her "flaming Love" (III, 381), often questioning its propriety. She is fearful when Anna threatens to come to her, stay with her, and accompany her as her shadow wherever she goes, and once she finds Anna *"guilty* of . . . an act of Love."

When Anna goes vigorously but ill-advisedly to war with the Harlowes on her friend's behalf, Clarissa rebukes her:

> Forgive me, my dear, but I must tell you that that high-soul'd and noble friendship, which you have ever avowed with so obliging and so uncommon a warmth, altho' it has been always the subject of my grateful admiration, has been often the ground of my apprehension, because of its unbridled fervor. (IV, 90)

There is a coldness here that speaks not only of Clarissa's distress at Anna's awkward aid but of her uneasy fear of "unbridled" friendship. She attacks Anna because her feelings are unique and warm, characteristics on which she knows her friend has prided herself. As at the beginning of the novel when she blamed her for criticizing the Harlowes, Clarissa is here both admiring and disapproving; the gentle opening suggests both attitudes, for Anna is dear to Clarissa, who indeed requires to be forgiven for such an attack—and yet Clarissa "must" tell and attack. The fervor of her friend is seductive and must be repulsed. The coldness Clarissa conveys is, then, a compound of uneasiness and half-hearted rejection.

Anna is well aware that she makes Clarissa uneasy; she tries, she writes, to rein in her passion. Often, however, it surges out in elaborate eulogies of Clarissa's virtues. In the midst of one, Anna interrupts herself in a way that foreshadows Clarissa's rebuke:

> Forgive me, my beloved friend. My admiration of you (encreased, as it is, by every letter you write) will not always be held down in silence; altho', in order to avoid offending you, I generally en-

deavour to keep it from flowing to my pen, when I write to you.
. . . (II, 69)

Anna's "admiration"—so distinct from Clarissa's "grateful admiration"—is expressed even as she denies that it has yet found expression.

Anna's love is constant and vigorous until, through Lovelace's tricks, she is persuaded to accept a false image of Clarissa; influenced by it, she doubts her friend's purity of will. Once these doubts are removed, she becomes doubly rapturous, spurred on not only because she reveres and admires her friend, but because she feels guilty toward her. Even now she tries to "hold down" her praise, the written form of her passion, allowing it to flow over only when Clarissa cannot receive it. To Lovelace's cousin she writes:

> You know not how I love her!—My own Soul is not dearer to me, than my Clarissa Harlowe!—Nay, she *is* my Soul—For I now have none—Only a miserable one, however—For she was the joy, the stay, the prop of my life. Never woman loved woman as we love one another. It is impossible to tell you half her excellencies. It was my glory and my pride, that I was capable of so fervent a Love of so pure and matchless a creature. (VI, 260)

To a third person Anna can write freely of Clarissa, implicating her in her own rapture. She repeats her constant theme, that Clarissa and she are one person and that the friendship is uniquely loving, while she makes her sentiments Clarissa's as well. "We" love fervently, she can assert, for there is none to be disquieted by her audacious boast.

Anna rivals Lovelace for Clarissa. Insistently she urges her suit above the man's, pressing her friend to go with her and take her money. On one occasion she hides fifty guineas in the leaves of a book celebrating friendship.[34] Through this money she seems eager to lure Clarissa into the female scheme, as earlier she had

---

34. The book is John Norris's *Miscellanies,* a collection of poems praising friendship and depicting the union of virtuous souls in heaven. It is described in Margaret Anne Doody's *A Natural Passion,* p. 156.

wished to keep her out of the patriarchal one through the legacy. But Clarissa catches what Anna is about and in spite of her need returns the guineas. She will have no subordinate part in the system of money power whether it approaches in male or female guise.

Anna bitterly complains that Clarissa constantly repulses her aid; once she even tries to shame her into accepting it by appealing to the contest with Lovelace:

> I beg, my dearest Clarissa, that you will not put your Anna Howe upon a foot with Lovelace, in refusing to accept of my offer. If you do not oblige me, I shall be apt to think, that you rather incline to be obliged to *him,* than to favour *me,* And if I find this, I shall not know how to reconcile it with your delicacy in other respects. (III,44)

Addressing Clarissa as her dearest and calling herself Clarissa's own, Anna pleads her legitimacy beyond the usurping Lovelace. Her lightly threatening tone foreshadows her truly threatening one when she declares she will break forever if she finds Clarissa has indeed chosen Lovelace and accepted his favor.

After the rape, Anna impetuously rejects Clarissa who, she feels, has repudiated female autonomy and virtue and taken an unworthy lover over her friend. The slight is personal to Anna as well as general to the sex. When she learns her error, she laments that she has added to her friend's sorrow, and she is deeply ashamed that her jealous love has cast out her reverence. For a moment Anna has approached Lovelace in attitude. Thereafter she redoubles her expressions of admiring and tender affection.

The rape is a turning point in friendship for Clarissa as well. She has suffered the worst from men and their patriarchal scheme, and has withstood it only through rejecting the life which seems indelibly patriarchal. With her rejection, the conflict is immediately stilled. Anna is less threatening to the family, now beyond their daughter's reach, and Clarissa can accept less uneasily the "flaming Love." To Anna's mother she avows: "My Miss Howe's friendship was all the comfort I had or expected to have in this world" (VI, 120), and she images more perfectly than ever before the friendship that has always been the pride of Anna's life: "Miss Howe and Clarissa Harlowe . . . who were the happiest creatures on earth in each other's friendship" (VI, 32).

Such acceptance of the friendship culminates when Clarissa places Anna above her family:

> How much more binding and tender are the Ties of pure Friendship and the Union of Like minds, than the Ties of Nature! Well might the Sweet-Singer of Israel, when he was carrying to the utmost extent the praises of the friendship between him and his beloved friend, say, that the Love of Jonathan to him was wonderful; that it surpassed the *Love of Women!* What an exalted idea does it give of the Soul of Jonathan, sweetly attempered for the sacred band, if we may suppose it but equal to that of my Anna Howe for her fallen Clarissa! (VI, 405)

Clarissa accepts Anna's love, here revising the biblical scheme by surpassing the love of men. Yet she can do so because she is dying and because she is abasing herself below the exemplary daughter and woman she had desired to be. She is the "fallen Clarissa" and her family can never again accept her love. Rejected, Clarissa in turn rejects the ties of kinship and the patriarchal scheme of father and lover they imply for women. In the shadow of death the female autonomy Anna has represented becomes for a fleeting moment possible for her.

As she comes nearer to death, however, Clarissa gains in self-esteem through her own singleness of purpose. She becomes less self-abasing if more self-critical, and the conflict continues. Her letters to Anna again censure her for putting another woman before both parent and lover. When Mrs. Lovick urges her to live for such a friend as Anna, Clarissa by now understands that to live is to live for more than her friend and to be forever in conflict; only when alienated from a part of herself can she feel singly. As she lies dying, she calls Anna's friendship "the dearest consideration to me now" and wishes that she were near; yet she knows she has refused her friend's coming. She lists Anna's meanings to her *"Sweet and ever-amiable Friend—Companion—*

Sister—Lover" (VII, 461), allowing her to engross all physical, spiritual, and moral relationships, while simultaneously giving away Anna's portrait to Hickman in marriage.

Throughout the novel Lovelace strenuously opposes the friendship of Clarissa and Anna both overtly and covertly. First, he tries to tamper with its written expression, so destroying the impetus behind it. He partially succeeds in his attempt, for Clarissa is sundered from her friend, who is driven to reject her. The correspondence and the friendship are reestablished only when Clarissa eludes Lovelace. More subtly Lovelace subverts the correspondence by making it an agent in his own villainies. The insolent letters of Anna goad him to revenge on Clarissa. When he wavers in his cruel purpose, he rereads the letters, converting Clarissa's chief comfort into an oblique instrument of torment.

Second, Lovelace menaces the friends when he aims to abuse them both so violently that they will be incapable of friendship. Clarissa he has in his power and he subjects her to a whole gamut of physical and mental tortures. Anna he torments in fantasy; he yearns to capture "the vixen girl" and he conjures up around her elaborate scenarios of abduction and rape. He will lure her to London, reduce her to a whore, anything in short that will destroy her self-respect and render her unworthy and unfit for friendship.

Third, he makes new images of the women so that the friendship will disintegrate of itself. On Anna he foists a degenerate image of her friend, the Widow Bevis ("bloated, and flesh-coloured"), so different from the tall and dignified presence of the living Clarissa and the pallid figure of the dying one. By this shocking appearance, Anna is jolted into apostasy.

Lovelace cannot easily foist a corrupt image of Anna onto Clarissa, although he can use Anna's words to authenticate his own lies. Clarissa can believe that her uncle has relented toward her as Lovelace falsely affirms, because she knows Anna has approached her family on her behalf. For others, however, Lovelace can employ his image-making art more directly, and through these strangers endanger the friendship from without. For the women in Clarissa's first refuge he makes a malicious Anna, "an arrogant creature, a revengeful, artful, enterprizing, and one who, had she been a Man, would have sworn and cursed, and committed Rapes, and played the devil" (V, 145). The women are convinced and aid him in his campaign against the friends.

To these women (and to us, the readers, who ultimately must create the friendship in our minds), he insinuates that Anna is motivated in her violence less by love for Clarissa than by love for himself. The insinuation is made more plausible for the reader when Anna admits that Lovelace might well have suited her more than Hickman and when Lovelace alludes to her early passion for a rake—a passion conquered only through the support and guidance of Clarissa. Anna, Lovelace hints, may be opposed to him because she wishes to punish a friend who destroyed her happiness in the past and is again destroying it. Insidiously the novel lends some support to his hints, for Anna almost invariably increases her friend's misery by her actions. When she rails against the Harlowes, they become harsher to Clarissa and retreat from any possible tenderness; when she contrives escapes for her and denounces Lovelace, she incites him to greater violence.

Lovelace's impudent idea that Anna favors him is further strengthened when he sees her as someone who would be a rake if born a man. Frequently he connects his own inventive spirit and violent contrivances with Anna's and he subjects her to the kind of admiration he usually reserves only for himself: "This girl's a devilish Rake in her heart. Had she been a man, and one of us, she'd have outdone us all in Enterprize and Spirit" (IV,189). Besides being a crushing indictment of patriarchy's education of its sons, the passage reduces Anna to a libertine manqué and throws doubt on the scheme of female autonomy she so vociferously asserts.[35]

35. Clarissa and Morden also relate Anna to Lovelace through her spiritedness. Morden notes that because of this quality Anna would have made a good man. It seems that the men coopt spiritedness for the male scheme, a view internalized by Clarissa when she finds it inappropriate in Anna.

SENTIMENTAL FRIENDSHIP

Fourth and finally, Lovelace attacks the idea of female friendship directly, undermining its basis and mocking its expression. Such attacks cannot influence the image Anna and Clarissa form in their letters, but, like the hints of Anna's rakish inclinations, it may affect our re-creation.

Lovelace disdains "these high flights among the Sex":

these vehement friendships are nothing but chaff and stubble, liable to be blown away by the very wind that raises them. Apes, mere apes of *us!* they think the word *friendship* has a pretty sound with it; and it is much talked of; a fashionable word: And so, truly, a single woman, who thinks she has a Soul, and knows that she wants something, would be thought to have found a fellow-soul for it in her own Sex. But I repeat, that the word is a *mere* word, the thing a *mere* name with them; a cork-bottomed shuttle-cock, which they are fond of striking to and fro, to make one another glow in the frosty weather of a Single State; but which, when a *man* comes in between the pretended *inseparables,* is given up, like their Music, and other maidenly amusements; which, nevertheless, may be necessary to keep the pretty rogues out of active mischief. They then, in short, having caught the *fish,* lay aside the *net.*

Thou hast a mind, perhaps, to make an exception for these two Ladies. With all my heart. My Clarissa has, if *woman* has, a soul capable of friendship. Her flame is bright and steady. But Miss Howe's, were it not kept up by her Mother's opposition, is too vehement to endure. . . .

. . . as to these two Ladies, I will grant thee; that the active spirit of the one, and the meek disposition of the other, may make their friendship more durable than it would otherwise be; for this is certain, that in every friendship, whether male or female, there must be a man and a woman spirit (that is to say, one of them, a *forbearing* one) to make it permanent.

But this I pronounce, as a truth, which all experience confirms; that friendship between women never holds to the sacrifice of capital gratifications, or to the endangering of life, limb, or estate, as it often does in our nobler Sex. (V, 274–75)

The passage demands to be fully quoted, for it is as clever and comprehensive an attack as Lovelace ever makes on the rela-

61

tionship which so disturbs him. We can resist it only by remembering its context. To a man he frequently despises and always ignores, Lovelace denounces female friendship, exalting the nobler male variety. He is writing shortly before he rapes Clarissa.

Lovelace makes a multiple assault on female friendship. He starts by judging it a poor copy of the male, thereby reducing women to "apes" as Anna has reduced men to "monkeys" and "baboons"; but where Anna stresses men's alien animality in the comparison, Lovelace is galled mainly by women's imitation: parody detracts from the noble male.

Accepting the expressions of friendship in Clarissa and Anna, Lovelace attacks again by separating these expressions from a deeper reality, severing sign from signified. Friendship for women is only a word or a name; there is nothing beyond. By attacking generally, Lovelace ensures particular criticism of Clarissa and Anna, whose whole friendship is for us a sign, the written expression of a reality we must take on trust.

In addition, Lovelace tries to coerce female friendship into the patriarchal context it has evaded. Subordinate women must, he declares, desire and submit to dominant men and, because men alone can confer status and power, they must be the sole and constant concerns of women. Elsewhere he vacillates between anger and disbelief at Clarissa's desire to remain single; here he reduces all women's desire for autonomy to a ploy to attract a man, a segment of the elaborate game of attack and defense which he believes female education fits all women to play. Female friendship becomes coquettish, affected, and man-centered.

Lastly, Lovelace combats the friendship by suggesting the libidinous nature of women which must rivet them to men. Female friendship may substitute for a while, but the amorous language of substitution is a "maidenly" amusement which must be rejected when real male love intrudes and defines the woman. The friendship of Clarissa and Anna has survived beyond most because of Anna's male "spirit." Through this, Lovelace believes she may be stimulated like the amorous male. She loves because she is opposed.

Lovelace partially succeeds in his campaign against the friendship of Anna and Clarissa. He is supported by the patriarchy he epitomizes and he manages—by fooling and using women and by subverting the image of the friends and of female friendship—to gain what Clarissa's family had proposed by simple proscription. But his success seems neither longlasting nor complete. The friends return to each other and reestablish their relationship, for the written expression, not the reality, has been subverted and the images created are proved false. Although doubts may remain, we as readers must be ashamed of them and to a large extent we end convinced by Anna's record of intimacy.[36]

Yet all is not as it was. If Lovelace fails directly to sever the friendship, he does prepare the way for a new destroyer, death. His irruption into Clarissa's life ensures that she will jettison the life he has tainted and abandon the conflict in which friendship has its being. By causing her death, he returns her to her father and severs her friendship forever.

Clarissa's death occurs away from both the father who disowns her and the lover she disowns; her last thoughts for the absent are for women, Anna Howe and Mrs. Norton, who represent the female life she could not and dared not attain. Yet her progress to death is clearly conventional in direction. She falls from patriarchal grace and moves from her father's house to her Father's house, to expiate in death her sin in life. Mr. Harlowe and God are united in her metaphoric letter to Lovelace, written just before she dies: "I am setting out with all diligence for my Father's House. . . . I am . . . taken up with my preparation for this joyful and long-wished for journey" (VII, 187–88).

Obviously death comes to Clarissa in sexual and familial,

36. On several occasions in the novel Richardson manipulates our response to make us regret former doubts and beliefs. An example occurs when we learn we have, with Lovelace's aid, been fooled into believing Captain Tomlinson trustworthy and Clarissa too wary.

not friendly, terms. She wishes, she declares, "to be wedded to my shroud" and later she believes, in Lovelace's words, that she is "breeding death." The coffin is her father's house and she dies as she reenters it in the pure state only death can now impose.

Clarissa once said of her father: "I would rejoice to owe my death to him, as I did my life." Extreme obedience certainly, it would remove a burden of guilt which she had always been quick to assume.[37] She will die for as well as by the father, and she is relieved that he does not by his presence or last-minute forgiveness disturb the simplicity of her dissolution.

On her coffin Clarissa has the Harlowe name inscribed, so completing a pattern of names latent in the book. Often the Harlowes and Lovelace have insisted she assume their names; at other times the Harlowes have been shamed by the kinship their name asserts. Clarissa herself has been unsure of what she deserved to be called, wavering after the rape between father and lover. After her death Anna cries out against the tyranny of names, proclaiming the love of a female friend whose function gives her no title in patriarchy and no claim to her beloved. But Clarissa does not at the end approach Anna in namelessness; instead she dies into the Harlowes, whose name will mark her forever.

"A will of my own has been long denied me," Clarissa laments. She has been prevented from acting by her family and indeed from speaking, for they had feared her persuasive power. Even in death she is constrained, and her last will is marked by the fear of disobedience, strong throughout her life. But the will expresses too the hopelessness that eases her dying. The conflict of patriarchal and female has, it seems, proved too strong for her and to avoid further bloody action she must conform to the patriarchal order as best she can. So she revokes the grandfather's will that had allowed her nonconformity and leaves her property

37. When her father's anger was excessive Clarissa refused to blame him, as Anna urged, instead expressing her resentment in illness and fainting. When he remained obdurate, she accused herself of pride in her own goodness. Her resentment against Lovelace is turned into the threat of violence to herself.

to its proper owner, her father. She reestablishes the convention of patriarchy and gives to the man the power she had wrongly received.

Money, the male instrument, cannot bring peace or legitimate power to a woman. Anna will carry out the feminine function of distributing alms to Clarissa's poor and marry the man her mother chose, but she will not receive the legacy of independence.

Clarissa functions where she conforms to convention and wills only what the patriarchy wills—the father promptly assumes the estate, the friend marries and takes a husband's name. Where she tries to thwart its action, she fails completely. Conscious of the bloodiness of the Harlowes, she enjoins her cousin Morden, the present instrument of the family, to eschew the blood feud. But such passivism is against the nature of a Harlowe. The woman does not control the man, the faultless the faulty. As Clarissa the innocent knows, the patriarchy is guilty and her will could control for good only someone outside it. Morden accepts his place within and kills Lovelace in spite of Clarissa. "What a torment is it to have a will without a power" (IV, 80), her mother had lamented, and the words could have been her daughter's. Anna remains neither her executor nor her gentler avenger.

As an agent of female autonomy then, female friendship clearly fails, and Clarissa has escaped, not resolved, the conflict in which it engages. So much of her experience has confirmed what she both feared and desired to believe—that the "Ties of pure Friendship" are more binding and tender than the patriarchal ties of the family and its surrogates—yet she is not made courageous by the knowledge but rather despairing for herself and fearful for others. She will not be the prophet of a new order. So her will, her written testament toward patriarchy turns herself and her friend from friendship. She dies a daughter and Anna lives a wife.

The female sex is "inferior in nothing to the other, but in want of opportunities," Anna declares; yet she ends defined by a husband, aiming to live the exemplary life within patriarchy Clarissa had once planned to lead—organizing charities and distributing the Harlowe superfluities. She largely obeys Clarissa's will, then, and becomes her surrogate, but her life without Clarissa is no longer self-expressed. Anna cannot tell her story or create her own character—as Clarissa could not when Lovelace broke the correspondence. At the end of the novel she enters Hickman's house and Belford's prose and is lost to us.

The subtlety and ambivalence of Richardson's depiction of female friendship is well caught in the obituary on friendship written by Morden, the best of the Harlowes—who yet, as Anna knows, remains unworthy of his dead cousin:

> *Friendship* . . . is too fervent a flame for female minds to manage: A light, that but in few of their hands burns steady, and often hurries the Sex into flight and absurdity. Like other extremes it is hardly ever durable. Marriage, which is the highest state of friendship, generally absorbs the most vehement friendships of female to female; and that whether the wedlock be happy, or not.
>
> What female mind is capable of two fervent friendships at the same time?
>
> This I mention as a *general observation:* But the friendship that subsisted between these two Ladies affords a remarkable exception to it: Which I account for from those qualities and attainments in *both,* which, were they more common, would furnish more exceptions still in favour of the Sex.
>
> Both had *enlarged,* and even a liberal education: Both had minds thirsting after virtuous knowledge: Great readers both: Great writers—. . . Both generous. High in fortune; therefore above that dependence each on the other, that frequently destroys the familiarity which is the cement of friendship. Both excelling in *different ways,* in which neither sought to envy the other. Both blessed with clear and distinguishing faculties; with solid sense; and from their first intimacy . . . each seeing something in the other to *fear,* as well as to *love;* yet making it an indispensable condition of their friendship, each to tell the other of her failings

and to be thankful for the freedom taken. One by nature *gentle;* the other *made so,* by her *love* and *admiration* of her exalted friend—Impossible that there could be a friendship better calculated for duration.

I must, however, take the liberty to blame Miss Howe for her behaviour to Mr. Hickman. And I infer from it, that even women of sense are not to be trusted with power. (VIII, 185–86)

The passage is rich in echoes. Morden reiterates Anna's boast that the friendship is unique, and Lovelace's declaration that women are usually incapable of true friendship. He also echoes Clarissa. After she had been lured to a brothel with promise of marriage, she writes to her loving friend that marriage is the highest state of friendship. The ironic context of the original modifies Morden's repetition and hints at the irony of the whole disquisition on female friendship and marriage.

As the echoes suggest, Morden's speech is a hybrid, an effort to do justice to the female scheme from inside a firmly patriarchal context. He apparently accepts the uniqueness that is Anna's pride but uses it against her sex—"female minds" and female fervor are denigrated not exalted by the women's admirable example.

On the qualities the two friends shared, Morden is eloquent. They were both educated, intellectually eager, sensible, generous, and independent. In short they were equal friends, and their love precluded jealousy and condescension. Yet he declares friendship most supremely expressed in marriage, a condition so unequal that in it the man legitimately absorbs the woman. Anna exemplifies the state by ironically reversing its pattern of inequality, dominance, and subordination through abusing her power over the man in courtship.

Morden's censure of Anna influences in retrospect the whole eulogy of friendship. He blames her for her fickle behavior to Hickman, seen as inconsistent with her generally noble character. But Anna's inconstancy to the man is the obverse of her constancy to the woman and her distaste for Hickman is contingent on her desire for Clarissa.[38] Morden errs in perceiving that Clarissa and Anna subvert the general rule that women (or men indeed) cannot simultaneously sustain two fervent relationships. Unequal marriage and equal friendship remain contradictory and opposing.

In describing the friendship, Morden equivocates, praising and undermining with the same phrases. His equivocation is clearest in his use of tense. He judges Clarissa and Anna so admirable and so compatible that their relationship need never die. Through largely avoiding main verbs, his prose gives it an illusion of timelessness, and, following a string of unlimited phrases, Morden can exclaim at the friendship's endurance. We are then jolted to remember that it is in fact already dead and that Morden is describing the past. The present is reserved for his arrogant inference about women of sense and for marriage, the actual relationship to which women must and should submit.

The past tense, in which Morden at the end of the novel envelops Clarissa and Anna, connects the friendship with the grandfather's legacy, the past when the novel opened. Both legacy and friendship have exacerbated Clarissa's conflict between two variously accepted goods, patriarchal obedience and female autonomy, and both have partially propelled her out of the subordinate condition necessary for obedience into an acceptance of autonomy. But the partial nature of the movement vitiates it. The two schemes are opposed and no one can straddle them. Clarissa's ambivalence toward patriarchy results in its reaffirmation. The legacy is restored to the father, and Clarissa, who embodies its female potential, is dead. Morden follows his eulogy of his cousin by revoking her will: arming himself instead with the will of the Harlowes, he sets forth sword in hand to kill the man Clarissa had implored him to spare. The lady's legacy becomes the memory of a friendship that could have endured forever and a man dying a bloody death.

---

38. Katharine Rogers sees behind Anna's ill treatment of Hickman the conscious desire that he will release her. She believes Anna motivated by a generalized hostility toward men springing from their exploitation of women, "Richardson's Empathy with Women," p. 134.

CHAPTER TWO

Erotic Friendship

John Cleland's *Fanny Hill* (1748–1749)

1

AN ORPHANED GIRL, not yet fifteen, is lured to London where she is easily duped by a procuress. In time she accepts prostitution, a profession in which, in this male fantasy, she delights and prospers. Her career is episodic; now a kept mistress and now a professional whore, she moves through men, varying the social and sexual positions. Finally at nineteen, wealthy and independent, she bestows herself on her "true love," the man who has taken her virginity; with him she settles down to a respectable life of marriage.

So runs the story of *Memoirs of a Woman of Pleasure,* better known as *Fanny Hill,* whose antithesis is the cautionary tale of a whore's decline and death—William Hogarth's *The Harlot's Progress,* for example. In this the deflowered woman is pursued to her bitter end; in *Fanny Hill,* the whore's career is rewarded by society's highest prize: marriage with money. The trajectory of vice establishes the mode: Hogarth's plot and message are stern and unrelenting, those of Cleland ironic and urbane. They share, however, an exemplary intent. Hogarth suggests an ideal of respectable marriage, from which his whore is forever barred; Cleland shows a similar ideal, only attainable for a poor woman through a carefully planned and orderly life of vice. The distinction is caused and exemplified by female friendship. Hogarth's Moll Hackabout has no friend and no guide, while Cleland's Fanny Hill is escorted by female mentors through every stage of her ascending career.

The immediate effect of *Fanny Hill* is confusing. Although married virtue is exemplary, so is vice; Fanny prospers through vice and writes a paean to marriage. Heterosexual married love is the apex, not only the antithesis, of sexual variations which include a lesbian one; virtue is celebrated not after Fanny and her readers have rejected vice but after they have glutted themselves on it. Sexuality in all its guises fills the novel and it is always out of wedlock; yet Cleland could write of his book as he later wrote of Henry Fielding's *Amelia:* "The chief and capital purport of this work is to inculcate the superiority of virtuous conjugal love to all other joys."[1]

To reconcile the novel's messages—the exemplary one of virtuous marriage and the exemplary one of vicious sexual freedom—we must look at the text—especially the relationships through which it fulfills its plot. *Fanny Hill* is a transvestite work, written by a man as if it were female memoirs. Fanny, the older narrator, tells the story of her younger days and it is in the main her language we hear. She writes her memoirs in the form of two long letters to a female correspondent; so she adds to the dual consciousness of the memoir form (the younger actor and older narrator) the interaction of writer and recipient peculiar to the letter. The younger Fanny enters into relationships within these memoir-letters and her partners are clothed with the narrator's commentary, reflecting her older consciousness and her epistolary aim; Fanny and her friends must be deciphered through the older narrator.

The older Fanny has, she declares, arrived at a stage "when all the tyranny of the passions is fully over and my veins roll no longer but a cold tranquil stream. . . ." (p. 50).[2] In keeping with

1. *The Monthly Review* (December 1751), 512.
2. The page numbers refer to the Putnam paperback edition of *Fanny Hill*, edited in 1963 by Peter Quennell. The controversy concerning the text and the first edition is sum-

her staid time of life, she is given to moralizing, especially at the end when she dispenses her "tail-piece of morality." Perhaps, then, the narrator can be judged the moral interpreter of the young girl's vicious ways, now safely past and repented. But the punning language betrays such judgment. It is no pious matron who refers to her message of decency as a "tail-piece" and makes her phrase a single thread in a tissue of puns that have covered and conditioned every description and comment in the novel.[3]

The relationship of narrator and character is not then primarily a parental, hierarchic one; rather the two women represent temporal steps in a single consciousness. The young Fanny is the older narrator in the making; her ingenuous and free qualities are not rejected for the narrator's sophistication and experience but contributory to them. Her curiosity, the agent of her transformation, is fulfilled rather than simply abandoned: it gives way to a knowledge that precludes further curiosity. The older narrator differs from the young girl in being more knowledgeable, judgmental, and conventional, but she has learned to be so as a younger woman and on herself she rarely passes judgment. Instead of morally placing her younger self, she luxuriates in the pleasure of reexperiencing her; since this narcissistic pleasure is not questioned, the appearance, attitudes and acts of the young woman avoid judgment as well.

The young Fanny uses her sexuality wisely and gives the older narrator the benefit of her experience. Both reader and character learn that the young girl's exploitation of her physical charms in the past establishes the narrator's achieved maturity and happiness in the present. The achievement is mediated by her

---

marized in Appendix A of William H. Epstein's *John Cleland: Images of a Life* (New York: Columbia University Press, 1974). For the reader of *Fanny Hill* the most important disagreement concerns the inclusion or exclusion of the homosexual encounter which Fanny spies toward the end of the book. The Quennell edition excludes it as a later interpolation.

3. B. Slepian and L. J. Morrissey draw attention to many comic metaphors, synonyms, and puns in their review article "What is Fanny Hill?" in *Essays in Criticism* 14 (January 1964), 65.

perception that for women sexuality is fate, that it is political and may be manipulated.

The young Fanny's experiences teach that women's world is reductive, that for them virtue is reduced from right conduct to chastity. She learns that men have defined the ideal of chastity for women and made it incompatible with success in their own terms—riches, power, position—within their world. Such success can be achieved only through marriage, but for a woman without riches and position, marriage to obtain them is impossible. This female dilemma governs the plot of *Fanny Hill* and wittily marks its language.

Sexually, Fanny must function within two systems, the male and the female, although the female one is—far more than Clarissa's sentimental female scheme—contingent on the male and has little potential for autonomy. The first, the male, requires women to be virginal before marriage and faithful afterwards, to espouse the ideal of virtue as chastity or virginity, and to respect social classes and conventions. The second, the female, teaches women to mock virginity, even parody it, to despise and manipulate class and convention, and sell and flaunt their sexuality. It teaches too that they must pay lip-service to the male system and, when they achieve success in marriage, accept this system and seem to promote it. By the end of her tale, the narrator has taught that women must *achieve* position and happiness through female understanding—an understanding handed on in female relationships—but *maintain* these by both accepting the male view and partly rejecting female relationships. In other words, Fanny must both climb and spurn a ladder of women to achieve success in a male world.

2

The first, overarching female relationship in the novel is between Fanny and the woman who receives her letters. It is a prototypical one, both the model and reversal of the female relationships into which the young Fanny enters. In it one woman educates another in female knowledge by explicit discourse and example; when the education is complete, the educating woman leaves or is dismissed. The relationship reverses the pattern of the narrative, for it makes Fanny the mentor, not the pupil.

The friendship of Fanny and her correspondent is one of "unreserved intimacies," in which the written word is forced to do duty for the sexual act. Fanny's account of her sexual exploits in London springs from the friend's curiosity, in much the same way as the exploits themselves spring from Fanny's youthful curiosity about London and sexual matters. In the memoirs she yields sexually to satiate her curiosity; by writing she yields to her friend's curiosity and satiates it. Her narrative of her sexual life, sent to her friend, forms an erotic encounter through which the friend comes to "know" Fanny as Fanny herself came to know her numerous sexual partners. In the second letter she complains that she must comply "with a curiosity that is to be satisfied so extremely at any expense"; in her narrative she has frequently and extremely expended herself to satisfy her clients.

Through her confessional memoirs, then, Fanny is initiating her friend into female sexual knowledge, leading her into the kind of female association from which she has herself profited and from which she has graduated. Such an association is formed to preserve its members in a hostile male society and to transmit the purely female knowledge of female activity necessary for success. Fanny and her friend form the first educational female association of the novel.

Since the association is based on the letter, it is prominent primarily when the letter form intrudes, at the opening and closing of the two long sections of the novel. The break between the first and second letters establishes the novel's structure, which images Fanny's success and determines the stages of her relationship with her correspondent. The first letter recounts the fall from innocence and rusticity to sophisticated experience—in the context, however, of the accepted happy outcome: "I emerg'd, at length," says Fanny on the first page of her history, "to the enjoyment of every blessing in the power of love, health, and fortune to bestow; whilst yet in the flower of youth" (p. 3). The correspondent must be aware of this outcome and is reminded of it by the break, which occurs at the lowest point in Fanny's career. The second letter begins with Fanny as a professional whore and ends with her a respectable married woman. It is recuperative and upward moving according to conventional morality; yet the correspondent cannot be unaware that the whole of Fanny's life has led ineluctably toward the blessed state of marriage and fortune.

The opening of the second letter exemplifies the decorum of modesty which Fanny, now moving toward success, and the older narrator, now consolidating it, must espouse. She had hoped, she declares to her friend, that "instead of pressing me to a continuation, you would have acquitted me of the task of pursuing a confession, in the course of which my self-esteem has so many wounds to sustain" (p. 105). There is nothing to suggest that during her adventures Fanny, a poverty-stricken orphan at the beginning, loses much self-esteem, and the employment of "wounds," undercuts the modest female disclaimer. When Fanny witnesses a sexual encounter in her first brothel, she sees the newly used female sexual organ as a "recently opened wound" and when she loses her virginity to her lover, she speaks again of a fresh bleeding wound. The word exists in a sexual context and it retains its connotations when Fanny uses it for her confession, the written equivalent of her sexual life. Through it she ensures that her friend will both regard her adventures in the conventional, male-imposed way and understand in a female way the need for them.

At the end of the novel, Fanny is established in life, married, wealthy, and chaste, given to praising virtue and railing against vice. Yet it was of course vice, reduced for women to sexuality without marriage, that made her prosper; it is knowledge of this that she gained from female friends and which she is now dispensing to her female correspondent through her confession. These contradictions inform the virtuous protest with which she closes her letter:

in the bosom of virtue, I gather'd the only uncorrupt sweets: where, looking back on the course of vice I had run, and comparing its infamous blandishments with the infinitely superior joys of innocence, I could not help pitying, even in point of taste, those who, immers'd in gross sensuality, are insensible to the so delicate charms of VIRTUE. . . . (p. 213)

. . . mark, how spurious, how low of taste, how comparatively inferior its joys are to those which Virtue gives sanction to, and whose sentiments are not above making even a sauce for the senses, but a sauce of the highest relish; whilst Vices are harpies that infect and foul the feast. (p. 214)

Vice, once necessary knowledge for survival and success, becomes inferior in joy to virtue and then infectious and foul, a progress that indicates how adroitly Fanny is manipulating her terms. In case her friend does not yet see how necessary to the maintenance of fortune and happiness such a disparaging attitude is, Fanny sharply warns her:

You laugh, perhaps, at this tail-piece of morality . . . you think it, no doubt, out of place, out of character; possibly too you may look on it as the paltry finesse of one who seeks to mask a devotee to Vice under a rag of a veil, impudently smuggled from the shrine of Virtue. . . . But . . . give me leave to represent to you, that such a supposition is even more injurious to Virtue than to me. (pp. 213–14)

The puns and allusions to Fanny's old trade throughout this discourse teach as much as the expressed sentiments. The hidden nature of female knowledge is urged while the same words force the friend to accept and parrot conventional morality. But Fanny's sharpness has a further function: it distances the friend. Female intimacies are necessary for women who are learning success, but for women who have learned all and achieved success, they are detrimental. The intimate friend must dwindle into an acquaintance who may visit occasionally.

3

My maiden name was *Frances Hill.* I was born at a small village near *Liverpool,* in *Lancashire,* of parents extremely poor, and, I piously believe, extremely honest.

My father, who had received a maim on his limbs that disabled him from following the more laborious branches of country-drudgery, got, by making of nets, a scanty subsistence, which was not much enlarg'd by my mother's keeping a little day-school for the girls in her neighborhood. They had had several children; but none lived to any age except myself, who had received from nature a constitution perfectly healthy.

My education, till past fourteen, was no better than very vulgar; reading, or rather spelling, an illegible scrawl, and a little ordinary plain work composed the whole system of it; and then all my foundation in virtue was no other than a total ignorance of vice, and the shy timidity general in our sex, and the tender stage of life when objects alarm or frighten more by their novelty than anything else. But then, this is a fear too often cured at the expence of innocence, when Miss, by degrees, begins no longer to look on a man as a creature of prey that will eat her. (p. 4)

So begins Fanny's account of her life. But these opening paragraphs convey the narrator as well as the teen-age girl, and the interaction of the two consciousnesses—the older woman's and the young Fanny's—is as much the subject of the discourse as the history itself. Through the consciousness of both we see Fanny's mother who forms, historically, the first of Fanny's female relationships.

Fanny, whose "maiden" name is ironically retained throughout her escapades, is the daughter of parents marked by the conventional attributes of poverty and honesty. The younger Fanny is properly impressed by the combination, but the older narrator—by adding "I piously believe"—suggests both the simplicity of her younger self and the ironic knowledge of the older woman who has learned that poverty may not imply honesty but that honesty certainly implies poverty. The irony of the narrator distances but does not destroy the naive picture of the maiden Fanny.

The father is a maker of nets, a worthy occupation for the parent of so alluring and ensnaring a daughter. The maim on his limbs further connects father and child through the sexual connotation of wounding.[4] Like her father, Fanny, as a woman, is maimed or wounded—socially in her own view and sexually in a male-oriented one—and she too has nothing to do but make nets for men, an occupation with which she far exceeds her father's "scanty subsistence." The mother is a teacher and her poverty instructs her daughter in the worth of the kind of education she peddles. Clearly, book-learning is not the way for women to flourish, a fact reinforced by the contiguous deaths of her children. Only Fanny, the uneducated, escapes into life and success. Her "perfectly healthy" constitution distinguishes her from her parents and dead siblings and it is essential for her rise. Yet, the mother is not entirely without influence on the daughter, for she leaves her two inestimable qualities or skills: innocence, and the ability to write—even if illegibly.

Innocence is a key term in the novel, where it gradually acquires connotations quite different from its original ones. Like her virginity, from which she soon learns to sever it, Fanny uses innocence adroitly to attract and control her male clients. In the early pages she sees innocence as virtue and untried virginity. Later she comes to see it as sexual ignorance which need not imply physical virginity. Toward the end of her career she accepts its importance quite as much as her mother, but defines it very differently. She sees it now as a female weapon forged through male cruelty and she refers to "that innocence which the men so ardently require in us, for no other end than to feast themselves with the pleasure of destroying it, and which they are so grievously, with all their skill, subject to mistakes in." The hostility rebounds on men, and innocence when most abused is most ferocious.

Fanny first claims she learned reading from her mother, but she corrects herself, aware perhaps that she has used this skill only rarely. She reads the address of the employment agency and

4. The maim suggests the foot injury of Oedipus, which Freudian analysis—through linking the phallus and the foot—has associated with castration.

is thus set on the road to vice, but no other changes are precipitated in this way. The letters of her lover Charles, like the pledge of their love, "miscarried" and the affronted client Mr. H... refuses to write to her. So she is correct when in her narrative she substitutes spelling or writing for reading as the legacy of her mother. Through writing Fanny develops prodigiously until she can construct the whole elaborate edifice of her memoirs themselves; through them she becomes a link in the chain of female knowledge.

A more shadowy maternal legacy is the image of marriage that descends to Fanny. The mother is "tender" and "fond" toward her husband—she dies when he dies—and she provides a worthy instance of marital devotion (as of marital subservience even in death) that helps her errant daughter see the positive aspect of the married state. Unlike fallen women from harsher backgrounds—Jemima in Mary Wollstonecraft's *The Wrongs of Woman*, for example—Fanny can marry and love, for she has learned from her mother that marriage may be based on love; at the same time of course her poor mother teaches her that it should also be based on money.

In these introductory paragraphs, while the narrator ironically foreshadows Fanny's progress throughout the novel, she provides the conventional attitude toward it—an attitude her correspondent must both accept and understand how to suspend. The narrator implies that, since her education was so deficient and her foundation for virtue so shaky, it is no wonder that Fanny went astray. Such an interpretation displays an ill-prepared and uneducated girl searching for the real meaning of virtue in a world of corrupt and ignorant females. The flippant generalization about women being ignorant rather than innocent is the first of several belittlings of women which punctuate the novel whenever Fanny is about to take a momentous, wicked, and well-advised step. Here Fanny falls because she is ill-prepared and weak like all women; but the narrator well knows too that she must fall to rise and that, had her mother been more strenuous in her educating, Fanny would never have "emerg'd . . . to the enjoyment of every blessing."

4

After her parents die together, Fanny becomes an orphan—the correct state for a poor woman who would advance in fictional society; death or distance must remove the incriminating family. After her loss Fanny enters into a series of relationships with older women who figure in her life as governesses or mentors. Through these she matures, gradually learning to appreciate the hidden springs of society and to manipulate its conventions. By so doing, she obtains the spoils otherwise denied to women.

In depicting the female relationships, the book again displays the double consciousness at work within it. The older narrator, who has learned the male-imposed vision, sees such friendships as evil; so she usually begins her account by describing the friends as false, cunning, corrupting, or polluting. Yet the young Fanny is trusting and, in a way, right in her trust, for these friends give her the knowledge she must have to prosper. And of course the author's plot bears her out, for, however the older narrator may fulminate against them, it is these women who direct her toward her conventionally happy and safe conclusion.

The first of the false/true friends is Esther Davis, a young woman on a visit from London to Fanny's village. She arouses Fanny's curiosity about the great city and impresses her with her tawdry clothes. Throughout the novel, Fanny is much taken with dress and her attitudes chart the course of her maturation. When she is callow and inexperienced, "innocent" in the novel's early terminology, she finds Esther's finery irresistible. Later, when she is a "fallen" woman, she comes to admire modest, tasteful attire by instinct. By the time she ends her career in wealth, she has adopted a style of "plainness and simplicity . . . with studied art."

When the two young women arrive in London, Esther suddenly becomes strange and cool. Perhaps her finery has suggested her trade and she does not care to be encumbered with the budding Fanny. Before she leaves, however, she puts into Fanny's hand the address of an employment agency. It is there that Fanny meets the procuress Mrs. Brown, subsequently her mentor; in a way then Esther Davis has handed Fanny over to the next stage of her education. Her own part was to invite her to London and awaken her curiosity. Such curiosity is by no means socially proper; yet it is essential if Fanny is to progress and "make her fortune." Having got her to school, Esther Davis disappears.

When Fanny meets Mrs. Brown, she believes she has found a respectable friend. Wiser later, she observes that Mrs. Brown is less grand than ridiculous in her velvet mantle in the middle of summer; she sinks in Fanny's view from a "lady" to a "beldam." Yet the young girl's first impression is not altogether false; like Esther Davis, Mrs. Brown is a necessary agent in her life and a true friend in her very real distress. In Cleland's euphoric scheme, the prostitution she orders is the route to happiness.

The brothel to which Mrs. Brown takes Fanny is the main school for women who would learn the female knowledge of manipulation through sexual submission—manipulation hidden from us in the severer accounts of Sinclair's brutal establishment. Mrs. Brown's brothel functions in the secular fictive world rather like the convent in the religious—at one point in *Fanny Hill* the madam is called "the venerable mother Abbess." Both brothel and convent are set apart for the transmission of special knowledge and both are exclusively female. But both are fantasies doubly ordered and structured by men: in the novels' society, men have created them, and their fictional creation is also a male affair. The brothel differs from the convent, however, since it caters directly to men in the world. Because more openly dependent, it is less likely to become a parody of male institutions than the convent, which has a fascinated, fearful attitude to the world it has rejected; the brothel teaches women how to use and manipulate men's weaknesses and quirks, not fearfully to imitate them.

The older narrator is of course dismayed to see her younger self decoyed into the brothel and trapped there. Yet she fails to obscure her own earlier delight; she was, she says, "pleased with my cage, and blind to the wires." Indeed there is something attractive about the society of the brothel if one can overlook its glaring defects. Mrs. Brown wants to be "more than twenty mothers to Fanny" and, unlike the hierarchic society it preys on, the brothel is democratic.

Both of these advantages need qualification, however. First, while Mrs. Brown and later Mrs. Cole express maternal feelings for Fanny, both nurture her the better to sell her. For Fanny, the mother-daughter relationship is rendered economic, most nurturing when most clearly commercial. Her natural mother neither tended her nor appreciated her marketability. Second, the brothel does not cause equality among its women; rather, it admits it, for all women are in a way equal—all gain status and prestige through their male sexual partners. Fanny comes to this knowledge only slowly, for at first she is surprised at women's democratic ways: when Mrs. Brown invites her to sit down with her at their first meal, she demurs, feeling it "could not be right, or in the order of things."

Initially Fanny believes the house a respectable one and the whores cousins of the mistress. Yet even then she conveys her eagerness for brothel life: she is excited at the prospect of exchanging her "country cloathes for London finery" and ready to have done with her rustic innocence. Soon she is introduced to the main agent in its destruction, Phoebe, named her "tutoress elect." With Phoebe, Fanny enters the closest relationship with a woman in the novel and experiences erotic female friendship for the first and only time.

5

Phoebe initiates Fanny into sexuality and autoeroticism. It is an easy task, for Fanny, innocent only because ignorant, is immediately responsive. And she learns that her identity is her sexuality. As Phoebe exclaims in the midst of love-making, "What a happy man will he be that first makes a woman of you"; it is the reductive use of "woman" employed by Lovelace in *Clarissa,* but here it suggests a social truth not lost on the educable Fanny.

The first lesbian act is condemned by the respectable narrator as lewd and licentious, but the excitement of it comes through the prose as Phoebe's hands roam "like a lambent fire." Because Fanny perceives Phoebe herself as ugly—possibly all of thirty-five, with loose breasts and large cavity—the encounter is more narcissistic than lesbian. Through Phoebe, Fanny comes to value herself as a sexual object, a necessary step in self-awareness and self-esteem in a world where she must trade in herself. She perceives that her own breasts are firm, her skin smooth, and her pubic hair soft and silky. Phoebe is her mirror and she learns to gaze fondly into it. As she explores herself, her gaze and consciousness move from sexual part to sexual part until she reaches "the quick itself." From then she watches, as if a separate entity, her own physical reactions. She sees herself inflamed "beyond the power of modesty to oppose," excited by "lascivious touches," her limbs extended and her breath heaving. Finally "I saw myself stretch'd nak'd"; a few minutes earlier, she had been too modest to undress to her shift before Phoebe. Her consciousness of her mind and body expands as her sexual awareness spreads to each erotic part. At the end she is both thoroughly aroused and thoroughly shameless. Her mental virginity has been conquered.

After Phoebe has initiated her sexually, Fanny first describes herself in detail. The description is of course in the older narrator's prose, a prose which shows how fully she had been socialized into attitudes proper for success. The younger Fanny has delighted in her physical charms for their own sake, but the narrator presents them primarily as objects designed for men and valorized by them. Fanny is beautiful, as Phoebe had taught her to realize, but the narrator accepts this beauty only when ratified by men:

> I was tall, yet not too tall for my age . . . my shape perfectly straight, thin waisted, and light and free, without owing any thing to stays; my hair was a glossy auburn, and as soft as silk, flowing down my neck in natural buckles, and did not a little set off the whiteness of a smooth skin . . . my eyes were as black as can be imagin'd, and rather languishing than sparkling, except on certain occasions, when I have been told they struck fire fast enough . . .

82

In short, all the points of beauty that are most universally in
request, I had, or at least my vanity forbade me to appeal from
the decision of our sovereign judges the men, who all, that I ever
knew at least, gave it thus highly in my favour. (pp. 18–19)

Phoebe herself realizes that only men can give value and purpose
to Fanny's beauty and at one point she sighs "Oh! that I were a
man for your sake!" Only then would her admiration be potent
and significant.

In the novel, Fanny moves through three stages of the narcissism which is a large component of female knowledge. This
narcissism is of the type Freud classified as autoerotic, in which a
part of the body contemplates and takes joy in another part. First
she views herself through a female and defines her charms
through contrast—she is attractive and desirable, as Phoebe is
not. Then she comes to look through men's eyes and define herself with their criteria. She is beautiful because they judge her so
and have her "in request." Finally as the older narrator she contemplates herself and lovingly depicts and transfixes her younger
image in her prose.

The progression suggests that narcissism is the only erotic
state that is allowed to exist primarily for women. Its existence
allows the young Fanny to concentrate on the commercial aspect of her sexual relationships since they do not comprise her
whole sexual feelings. In addition it enables the older woman to
have some erotic pleasure without jeopardizing her respectability.
Yet the state is not entirely free of commerce. Through the distancing of her body which autoerotic narcissism implies, Fanny
can the more easily see it as a commodity distinct from her essential self. So she can assess it with a critical eye and sell it well.

The older narrator is harsh on Phoebe and the sexual knowledge she gives by word, look, and touch. Yet in her harshness she
suggests Phoebe's function: "The first sparks of kindling nature,
the first ideas of pollution, were caught by me that night; and
. . . the acquaintance and communication with the bad of our
own sex, is often as fatal to innocence as all the seductions of the

other" (p. 16). Such innocence was slightingly mentioned in the opening pages where it was resolved solely into "a total ignorance of vice." Phoebe has taught a proper appreciation of self as object and commodity and such knowledge far surpasses in value the ignorant innocence women are expected to prize.

Phoebe herself emerges only partially from the narrative. She initiates young women into the brothel, teaching them desire and desirability without harming their marketability. Fanny comments on her activity and her partiality for women:

> Not that she hated men, or did not even prefer them to her own sex; but when she met with such occasions as this was, a satiety of enjoyments in the common road, perhaps too, a secret bias, inclined her to make the most of pleasure, wherever she could find it. (pp. 15–16)

Lesbianism in Phoebe is presented as a variation of heterosexuality; perhaps Phoebe prefers men, but perhaps she is merely unperturbed by the gender of her lover. Certainly she is aroused by Fanny for she gives her kisses "as fierce and fervent as ever I received from the other sex," but she provokes no responding passion in Fanny, who, through Phoebe, learns to love not another woman but herself. Phoebe stimulates Fanny solely to prepare her for men. The autoeroticism she teaches is part of the preparation Fanny must undergo if she is to be successful in her manipulation of men; she must comprehend her value and love herself first. It is no part of the education for success that she should love Phoebe.

If Phoebe had kindled a mutual passion, she would have precluded Fanny's success, for women have no power, riches, or status to convey and society in this novel recognizes only heterosexual unions. A homosexual one is not socially functional and can have no end beyond itself. Indeed its freedom from economics and status may make it socially subversive, for the partners may question the whole system of political and economic sexuality which Fanny is learning; such questioning can only be harmful where the goal is conventional social success.

The subversive possibility of homosexuality, male or female, may lie behind the outraged reaction to male homosexuality Cleland gives to Fanny at the end of her social education.

Before Phoebe has finished her course in sexual politics, Mrs. Brown sells Fanny's virginity to an ogrish gentleman named Mr. Crofts, before whom she is displayed as in a market. Certainly Mrs. Brown acts reprehensibly but no more than Fanny does herself later—although with more tact and taste—when she is self-employed. The encounter is a disaster and Fanny is saved from complete violation by a nosebleed, "which did not a little tragedize the scene." As in Clarissa, one bleeding does for another and serves to impress both the man and the watching woman, who terminates the assault. Fanny has learned to use a female weapon, which she will employ to great effect in a male world that makes a peculiar fetish of virgin blood.

The disaster with Mr. Crofts indicates that Fanny is in need of further education from Phoebe, although it underscores her progress as well. She repulses her assaulter, she realizes, not out of "virtue" but out of a particular aversion. She cannot reproach Mrs. Brown and Phoebe for their cruelty to an innocent girl, for she has already lost that character. Technically Fanny retains her virginity on which so much store is set by male society. But, as the novel shows, this is no great commodity in the female world, and indeed Fanny soon yearns to be rid of it altogether. Later she parts with it easily to the man she chooses, finding no change in herself when it goes; later still, she fakes a new maidenhead and sells it well. Innocence or mental virginity does, however, have significance for her and it is the loss of this that she perceives when she analyzes her rejection of Mr. Crofts.

Like Clarissa before her, Fanny responds to a significant change by falling sick. After the débacle with Mr. Crofts, she grows feverish, as she will again when she learns that Charles her lover has been spirited away. Like so many other heroines, Fanny in fact sickens or goes numb on crucial occasions throughout the novel. When she first arrived in London and feared its evil she fell into a deadened state; when Mr. Crofts tried to violate her, she was paralyzed as she felt his predatory male sexuality. Later she is stunned when Mr. H... urges his suit. At each change in position or status, then, she loses consciousness, either through feverish delirium or through a mental numbness that removes her from reality. She is absolved from responsibility and can retain her "innocence" in spite of all appearances: the actions occur to her when she is unconscious, not herself, and so her essential self remains untouched.

When the fever abates, a new Fanny emerges, ready and eager to be educated by Phoebe into the role of whore. As the narrator remarks, she was "indebted to the girls of the house" for the corruption of her innocence. By this time, however, the perennial quality of Fanny's innocence is becoming obvious, while the corruption resolves itself into "the first tinctures of pleasure," an altogether less threatening concept.[5] Phoebe gives her pupil a well-balanced course. Like the friend for whom the memoirs are written, Fanny is already curious and she welcomes Phoebe's explanation of "all the mysteries of Venus." After explaining, Phoebe demonstrates, first with a comic scene of the fat Mrs. Brown, which destroys forever any remaining lesbian tendencies in Fanny, and second with a romantic scene, aimed at allaying her fears of male penetration and arousing her enthusiasm for the male organ. Through these scenes, Fanny and the reading friend are turned into voyeurs. So Fanny's education is a complex system of which discourse and voyeurism are two components; the third is of course her own experimentation and proof.

6

In his account of early fiction, John J. Richetti has noted the eighteenth-century use of the convention that "once a woman has been ruined, her appetite for vice (which may have been virtually nonexistent before the act) is automatic and insatiable." He gives

5. Other high-sounding concepts are also ambiguous. When Fanny says she "made a vice of necessity," she breaks a collocation and suggests the closeness of virtue and vice in her scheme.

a wonderful example from Captain Smith's *The School of Venus* (1715–16) of Madam Charlton who was rigidly virtuous until seduced by trickery:

> . . . but when once she came to relish those forbidden Pleasures and grow wanton in the Enjoyment of them, she grew as intemperate as Messalina: having the Impudence of a Bawd, and the Lasciviousness of a common courtezan.[6]

Fanny follows this model, even though her initial sexual encounter is lesbian; once aroused she becomes insatiable. She throws herself into the arms of the first man she meets—fortunately her future true love, Charles—and, escaping from the brothel with him, urges him to become "the murderer" of her virginity.

Phoebe has taught Fanny about the sexual organs and given her, through her person and propositions, correct regard for the penis, the organ which dominates the sexual economy of the novel. Michael Shinagel has counted at least fifty euphemisms for it, some of the more picturesque being "red-headed champion," "column of the whitest ivory," "furious battering ram," and "master member of the revels." The euphemisms for the female sex organ are far less numerous but they remain colorful; they include "nethermouth," "dark and delicious deep," "pouting-lipt mouth," and "embowered bottom-cavity."[7] Clearly the reality of the two sex organs accounts in part for the rigid and aggressive male metaphors and vacant, cavernous female ones, but the contrast is so insistently expressed that we may suspect that a male view is intruding. The suspicion is confirmed by Fanny's two first sexual encounters.

When she described her experience with Phoebe, she concentrated on her own appearance, which she could see and which autoerotically aroused her. When she depicts her sexual encounter with a man, even when she is describing their battle

---

6. *Popular Fiction Before Richardson: Narrative Patterns 1700–1739* (Oxford: Clarendon Press, 1969), p. 41.

7. "Memoirs of a Woman of Pleasure: Pornography and the Mid-Eighteenth-Century English Novel," *Studies in Change and Revolution: Aspects of English Intellectual History 1640–1800*, ed. Paul J. Korshin (Menston: Scolar Press, 1972).

array rather than the battle itself (military metaphors abound in the novel), she concentrates on her own dark, deep, devouring aspect. In the heterosexual account with Charles and her later clients, she gives, it seems, a penis view of women.

During their time together, Charles urges Fanny toward convention, refines her dress, and makes her aware of the joys of a stable heterosexual union. But he does not marry her, for she remains unworthy, and he does not provide for her. When he is carried off to the South Seas, the idyl is over and Fanny is left without married respectability or fortune. At this juncture her avaricious landlady, Mrs. Jones, steps in to direct her away from a relationship which can whet her appetite for success, happiness, and respectability, but not fulfill it. Through Mrs. Jones, Fanny is set on the path of vice, pleasure, and prosperity.

After Charles leaves, Fanny falls ill, and, as in her first illness, she is nursed back to health by a woman who aims to exploit her endowments. In both cases she is tied to a woman through gratitude or fear. Phoebe and Mrs. Jones can thus coerce her into acts and attitudes she originally found repugnant but which conform to their financial interests and further her own. When Fanny recovers from her second illness, Mrs. Jones gives her the bill and hints at the debtors' prison.

The narrator presents Mrs. Jones as thoroughly nasty; so far, however, all women characters have been presented so and the hostile attitude seems partly the young Fanny's, but mostly the older narrator's achieved one. Mrs. Jones is selling her tenant to the highest bidder, but this, as Fanny learns later, is what all women must do. Mrs. Jones is wrong not so much in what she does as in the duplicitous way she does it, for she never consults Fanny about her schemes. Yet perhaps she is well-advised to be secret, for Fanny is not yet ready to choose correctly for success. With Charles, she declares, she "could have made a pleasure of the greatest toil, and worked my fingers to the bone, with joy." As Phoebe and Mrs. Jones could have told her, such was not the route to marriage and prosperity. By arranging her seduction by the wealthy and aristocratic Mr. H... Mrs. Jones provides Fanny with the only means to such ends. The plot, then, divulges what the narrator must have learned but never admits.

Mr. H... takes Fanny when she is numb and deadened with grief. Yet through an act in which she has been in "a trance of lifeless insensibility," responsive as "a death-cold corpse," she is transformed from the lover of Charles into the mistress of Mr. H.... She is depreciated in the transformation, for, where the sexual experience with Phoebe had led to greater self-esteem, the sexual act here decreases it. She "suffered, tamely, whatever the gentleman pleased." The use of the word "gentleman" at this point indicates a social difference that puts Fanny clearly in the lower class. Immediately too Mr. H... is her "master" and his penis a "truncheon"; Fanny is bound to the man and kept in place by his weapon. This time she blames herself and by implication all women. She was, she says, "betrayed by a mind weakened by a long severe affliction."

As at the outset of her London adventure, Fanny now disparages women, accepting the male evaluation of them: "Violent passions seldom last long," she considers, "and those of women least of any" (p. 71). She can say this even though in Mr. H... she is directly confronted with a far more transient male passion. When finally she responds to Mr. H... , her idea of women sinks still lower; she yields to her own lustiness "as mere woman."

Once again Fanny sees the end of her "innocence" in her liaison with Mr. H.... At their initial encounter she lay "passive and innocent"; the first adjective assumes the second. When she becomes responsive, however, she feels it is her "first launch into vice." Each time she makes a sexual move, she must invoke the powerful emotive words "innocence," "vice," and "virtue"; but progressively these become less and less effective and appropriate. Fanny trots them out as the correct response to events which, as an older narrator, she must, but barely can, see in this conventional and polarized way.

In her liaisons, Fanny traverses the three main classes of

89

eighteenth-century England, parodying in a way the ideal of each. In the brothel, with her tawdry finery and rustic naiveté, she was in the lowest rank, fair game for an aging rapist, and she exemplifed the fate of a girl who is poor but honest in a dishonest world that prizes wealth above all else. With Charles, Fanny moved in dress and sophistication into the middle class and for a time passed as a married woman, a state to which however she could not and did not then aspire. With Mr. H..., she enters the aristocratic world as a kept mistress and she imitates the life and airs of the fine lady. By this time, Fanny is well aware that women are of little importance, whatever their station. Having tasted upper-class female life, she pronounces it silly, flat, insipid, and worthless, and she indignantly snorts that ladies "ought to treat the men as their tyrants, indeed! were they to condemn them to it." Later she learns the intellectual pleasures of the humbly born but immensely rich "rational pleasurist" and with his fortune settles comfortably into the middle class whose representative, Charles, she marries.

Fanny is impressed by Mr. H...'s aristocratic birth and riches, but from Phoebe and Mrs. Brown she has learned democratic tendencies, which she expresses when she prefers Will the servant as a lover over his master Mr. H.... She seduces Will because she has seen Mr. H... seducing her maid. When she is discovered, Mr. H... haughtily alludes to the double standard for men and women, disdaining however to explain it to one so much his inferior. She is inferior of course in both class and sex.

But Fanny is immune to artistocratic scorn, for by now she knows her worth is classless; her active seduction of Will seems to have strengthened her self-esteem and when Mr. H... casts her off, she finds she has often longed for liberty. Remembering what she has learned from Mrs. Brown, Phoebe, and Mrs. Jones, she is confident of herself and her value in a world she now knows to be debased: "the stock of youth and beauty I was going into trade with could hardly fail of procuring me a maintenance" (p. 102).

After the sojourn with Mr. H... , Fanny is thrown back into the female world of entrepreneurs. At this point the narrator surrounds her with a bevy of envious women who insult her and mock her fall. Earlier in her memoirs, when she had described her own youthful beauty, she had mentioned the crowd of jealous and rancorous females who would not allow her just praise. Yet in both cases, the malicious women are not particularized and it seems that again the narrator (and with her the author) is going beyond the novel's experience to an accepted stereotype: that women must envy other women's beauty.

Overwhelmingly in the novel, the women the young Fanny meets are beneficial to her, helpful and admiring of her looks. The most outstanding of these is Mrs. Cole, who becomes Fanny's trustiest instructor. Mrs. Cole does Fanny nothing but good in the scheme of the novel; yet even for this relationship, the narrator must in part make the ritual obeisance to conventional morality: "I could not have put myself into worse, or into better hands."

"A gentlewoman born and bred," Mrs. Cole keeps a small elegant establishment for select clients, some of whom see themselves as "the restorers of the golden age and its simplicity of pleasures, before their innocence became so unjustly branded with the names of guilt and shame." The "innocence" Mrs. Cole provides is then an innocence of free sexual experience; it appeals to Fanny, who, nonetheless, learns that she must continue to pay lip-service to the rustic innocence as ignorance which she has repeatedly lost. In Mrs. Cole's house, the whores sit modestly sewing throughout the day and are transformed into women of pleasure only at night.

Mrs. Cole is a woman of refinement and sophistication and she ratifies these qualities in Fanny, who has acquired them through intensive education. Mrs. Cole enjoys debauchery if polished and depravity if elegant. Financially sensible but never mercenary, kindly to her "daughters" but not overpowering, she works the system but does not unnecessarily exploit it and she herself is not exploited. Like the other women—Mrs. Brown, Phoebe, and Mrs. Jones—she helps Fanny to succeed in a world she well understands; unlike her predecessors, she helps intentionally and directly. She presents the ideal female friend and mentor in the novel.

Fanny enters Mrs. Cole's establishment and begins a new phase of her career; she is transformed from "a private devotee to pleasure into a public one." She intends now to put her "person out to use, either for interest or pleasure, or both" (p. 106). Her life is compartmentalized: the older Mrs. Cole is mother and mentor; the other whores, her contemporaries, are her friends and sisters; the male clients are her lovers. It is the fragmentation necessary for success. Before Fanny was ready to understand this, the older Phoebe, who passed herself off for young, had tried to combine all these roles and satisfy her friend mentally, emotionally, and physically.

Fanny and Mrs. Cole are closely related. The older woman is attracted to the younger because she sees a resemblance in her to "an only daughter whom she had lost." The narrator distrusts this reason but her distrust and the several hints she throws out about Mrs. Cole's unworthiness are not borne out by the story; the young Fanny seems correct in her view of her new friend as a mother, the sort of mother she needs since she has travelled so far from the poor Lancashire one who noticed neither her ignorance nor her budding beauty. Fanny and Mrs. Cole soon become tied by "one of those unaccountable invincible sympathies that, nevertheless, form the strongest links, especially of female friendship" (p. 106). She gains "entire possession" of Fanny, who comes "to regard, love, and obey her implicitly."

Like her male lovers, Fanny's female mentors span the classes, but, because their status is contingent on their sexual clients, their birth and type are more difficult to gauge and Fanny sets out by being completely wrong in her judgments. She is fooled by Mrs. Brown's velvet mantle and magnificent back parlour into thinking her the height of respectability; only later does she see that all was "set out to the most shew" and that Mrs. Brown and Phoebe keep only an indifferent brothel. Mrs. Jones too initially seems better than the mean-minded former mistress she turns out to be.

With Mrs. Cole, however, Fanny begins to judge rightly. Mrs. Cole is a real gentlewoman, "reduced" to earning an immoral living, and she differs from the other bawds by being less mercenary and more epicurean—she pursues her trade "partly through necessity" and partly "for the sake of the trade itself." Unlike the coarse Mrs. Brown, she does not take part in unseemly manner in the erotic events she stages; instead she watches her protégé, Fanny, the image of her daughter, and participates through her. She lives vicariously through the younger woman in the same way as the older narrator whom she resembles. Throughout the novel the female mentors move successively closer to the image of the narrator; Mrs. Cole takes this progression to its conclusion.

Since Mrs. Cole exists at the apex of the female educational scheme it is appropriate that her establishment should be a melange of all the classes and an education for each. In it there is both order and equality, while the "refinements of taste and delicacy" mingle "with the most gross and determinate gratifications of sensuality." The women of the house are at once whores, modest bourgeois women, and fine ladies. As whores, they depend on the men for whom the establishment is maintained, but the men do not allow them to recognize their lowly and dependent position and insist on treating them as ladies. Among themselves the women formed a little domestic "family of love, in which the members found so sensibly their account, in a rare alliance of pleasure with interest, and of a necessary outward decency with unbounded secret liberty" (p. 107). For Fanny, it combines the havens of the aristocratic Mr. H... and the middle-class Charles, but it is based on firmer financial foundations than either. Among the women there is both solidarity and equality and no one feels jealous; the beautiful Fanny brings a good "stock" to the house and the business of all is improved. The commercial relationship once again nurtures.

To initiate Fanny into their sisterhood, the women tell stories of their defloration. The confessions knit them together and, for the reader, generalize Fanny's own history, since, more clearly even than she, these women emphasize the female sexual reality. Each woman loses her virginity in a world that sets absolute store by it and each would have been battered and torn to pieces but for Mrs. Cole. Ruin, which, in the male system, means the loss of virginity in women, is now seen actually to mean the poverty and sickness often attendant on it. At Mrs. Cole's, women are not ruined in this sense but saved from ruin. As for virginity, Mrs. Cole shows its worth by reducing it to its bloody sign and then reproducing it in a tumbler in every bedpost. The blood need only be spilt out for the most hardened whore to be named a virgin.

With Mrs. Cole, Fanny explores a wide sexual scene and she is taught to tolerate almost all quirks and oddities. She takes part in elegant after-dinner orgies and sumptuous bathing bacchanals; she alternates a hair and glove fetishist with a flagellant and satisfies the effete and concupiscent Mr. Norbert as well. Through her clients she comes to understand with Mrs. Cole that "pleasure, of one sort or another," is "the universal port of destination, and every wind that blew thither a good one, provided it blew nobody any harm" (p. 166). But it must be pleasure without risk. When Fanny, left unsatisfied by Mr. Norbert, resorts to a common sailor, she is mildly reproved by Mrs. Cole for "being so open-legg'd and free." Pleasure does not include the pox.

Through her sexual adventures, Fanny learns tolerance but is confirmed in her perception that the highest good in society is married love with a fortune, for it combines sexuality with financial security. Most of the characters she meets are married off with competences before being dismissed: Mr. H... , his servant Will, and two of her friends from Mrs. Cole's. Fanny too can now aim at this blissful sexual and financial state since she has assimilated women's knowledge of the world, while understanding that she must hide it behind a conventional façade of language and gesture.

8

Fanny's experience—which prepares her for marriage—shows that marriage and sexual freedom are compatible and that a woman can accept and participate in both. Ultimately the ironic female knowledge of the world exists within a context of the conventional male order and the sexually liberated world is contained within a world of marriage. A woman's success requires her to understand and act in both worlds. Female knowledge may be potentially subversive, the book suggests, but in Fanny's case it is used to gain conventional success. Phoebe might have won her to lesbian sexual and social attitudes, but instead she simply prepared her for heterosexual prosperity. The truth of this is emphasized by Fanny's extreme attitude toward *male* homosexuality, the only sexual practice which is allowed to represent a truly different sexual realm in the novel and the only one which absolutely horrifies her.

Fanny started her sexual career as a voyeur; toward the end she returns to the role. At an inn, she lodges next to two young men whom she suspects because they eagerly enter their room and lock their door behind them. Through a hole pricked in the partition (Cleland delights in the geography of voyeurism), she watches what she calls the "criminal scene" and, bursting with rage and indignation, she rushes to raise the house. So zealous is she to bring the miscreants to justice that she trips and knocks herself senseless, so allowing them to escape. Again she is lifeless at the crucial moment.

Later Mrs. Cole gives two convincing if punning explanations for Fanny's distaste which do not altogether account for her exaggerated horror: she explains that, since sexuality is women's power, its use by men alone harms women, diminishes this power, and lessens trade, and she adds further that homosexuals mock and parody the faults and failings of women:

though she might be suspected of partiality, from its being the common cause of woman-kind, out of whose *mouths* this practice tended to take something more than bread, yet she protested against any mixture of passion, with a declaration extorted from her by pure regard to truth; which was that whatever effect this infamous passion had in other ages and other countries, it seem'd a peculiar blessing on our air and climate, that there was a plague-spot visibly imprinted on all that are tainted with it, in this nation at least; for that among numbers of that stamp whom she had known, or at least were universally under the scandalous suspicion of it, she would not name an exception hardly of one of them, whose character was not in all other respects, the most worthless and despicable that could be, stript of all the manly virtues of their own sex, and fill'd up with only the worst vices and follies of ours; that, *in fine*, they were scarce less execrable than ridiculous in their monstrous inconsistence, of loathing and condemning women, and all at the same time apeing all their manners, airs, lips, skuttle, and in general, all their little modes of affectation, which become them at least better than they do these unsex'd male-misses. (pp. 182–83)

It is a harsh and complex explanation which yet hints at a deeper, more fearful reason. For women who are successful in society, like Fanny and Mrs. Cole, sexuality has become an economic commodity, which they buy and sell, trade for money and marriage. A sexual relationship which is neither an economic one nor, like that of Phoebe and Fanny, a preparation for the market throws in question the whole elaborate scheme which successful women have erected and accepted. In a way it sheds doubt on the value of the success to be achieved and the means of achieving it, and it stresses that women—in spite of all their contingent cleverness—are ultimately subordinate and reduced. It is the kind of revelation that undermines success and shatters female self-esteem.

This explanation is boosted by the details of Fanny's horror. More than the other women at Mrs. Cole's she is appalled at the idea of sodomy, which homosexuality here implies. It first intrigues her when she hears the adventures of Emily, one of her fellow-whores. Emily had gone to a ball disguised as a shepherd and had been taken at costume-value. When the man discovers his mistake, he gallantly decides to make the best of the situation, but, in Emily's words, he sets himself on her in a "mis-direction" so that she fears "losing a maidenhead she had not dreamt of." When she complains and resists, the man is "brought . . . to himself" again and is persuaded into "the right road." As Emily—not usually a timid woman—recounts her story, Fanny notes the "remains of the fear and confusion" in her face. Whether or not projected onto Emily, certainly such fear and confusion mark Fanny herself. She calls the homosexual practice "universally odious" and also "absurd," for she cannot see how one could "force such immense disproportions."

The sodomy scene at the inn disabuses her and she perceives that nature can arrange the apparently impossible, a lesson she had learned for heterosexuality from the romantic scene staged by Phoebe. From the homosexual incident, however, she discovers also that sexuality need not center on women or on the vagina, by which she has come to set such store. Indeed there seems a whole sexual system where women no longer function as objects of desire—a system they cannot enter or subvert. By running to tell the people at the inn what she has seen, Fanny tries to contain it, but she is summarily silenced by her fall and rendered powerless.[8]

The crucial nature of the homosexual episode is suggested by the structure of repetition in the book. Fanny began at Mrs. Brown's with a combination of homosexuality and voyeurism; here almost at the end of her sexual education she experiences a similar combination and she rejects both components. Her voyeurism is cut short by her fall into senselessness and blindness, which terminate her curiosity—the agent of her education

---

8. The controversy about the homosexual description reinforces this point. If Cleland did not write it, the encounter becomes the only sexual one not described in detail in the novel, suggesting that Fanny, when she relives her life story, is still silenced by it. If, however, the description was written by Cleland and excised under pressure from the government in later editions, again it seems that Fanny is silenced; this time it would be through the mediation of the censoring establishment rather than her male creator.

in both cases—while homosexuality is rendered horrifying and alien to her. Fanny has seen all she has to see and her eyes must now be shut; at the same time she has rejected any scheme that might question the value of herself as a sexual object and of the success she will achieve. Certainly she is ready for marriage. First, however, she must have a fortune.

At Mrs. Cole's Fanny has flourished and, by the time the household is dissolved, she has followed the counsels of her "faithful preceptress" so well that she has "a reserve of eight hundred pounds . . . exclusive of cloaths, some jewels, some plate." She is ready to enter the respectable middle class and, in preparation, she adopts a life-style "strictly within the rules of decency and discretion: a disposition in which you cannot escape observing a true pupil of Mrs. Cole" (p. 198). In this role she soon meets with an elderly "rationalist pleasurist" who completes her conventional education by teaching her to appreciate mental as well as physical pleasure; more importantly, he leaves her his fortune. At nineteen Fanny emerges from her life of vice into affluence and independence. It wants only Charles to complete the picture of felicity. And, on cue, he arrives.

Fanny of course is overjoyed and she offers him her fortune which he at first refuses. Soon, however, he is prevailed on to receive it only if she will be his wife, an invitation which she gratefully accepts, mindful of his generosity in marrying one so lowly as herself. By marrying Charles—who has returned from his travels more or less destitute—Fanny continues the work of the grandmother who had earlier supported him in style from her annuity. In the novel as a whole we see much of women's work, but only a few of the men—Charles when away and Fanny's father—are actually described as working and these are strikingly unsuccessful. It is fitting that Fanny's efforts and money should support the gentleman.

To Charles' male superiority and responsibility, Fanny then adds her fortune and the couple go off to a life of wedded bliss, founded on her sexual prowess and female knowledge but cemented by the conventional morality of the male world. At the end Fanny, who has arranged and paid for everything, bows before "that peculiar scepter-member which commands us all." Her education—and her reading friend's—is complete.

Fanny Hill is the story of a woman adapting to a male system of belief; she learns the conventional code of behavior governing sexual and social relationships, while at the same time assimilating and acting by a quite different, potentially subversive code. In the novel, however, the subversion is contained and the conventional code ultimately dominates, because it determines the language and because it is the male-imposed one in a fictive world which defers to the male principle. This domination is ironically but conclusively illustrated in the culminating marriage, in Fanny's later life, and in the education of her son.

According to the female system, one of the silliest and most destructive male conventions is that a woman must be a virgin until she gives the gift of her maidenhead to the man she marries. In Fanny's life, there are many slips between the gift and the marriage, but she does marry the man who deflowered her. The convention may be mocked in the novel but it is also reestablished. The same effect occurs with the concluding statement of morality: it is partly parody because of its lubricious context, but it accords with the convention that requires a woman to hold and express a rigid moral philosophy.

The male system dominates too because the older Fanny not only chooses it to maintain her status and fortune but *must* choose it because of her age. Writing her memoirs probably in her late thirties——the surmised age of the weatherbeaten Phoebe—Fanny can no longer play the double system. Only in memory can she relive those scenes in which she was the center and chief attraction, and only through her pen can she narcissistically contemplate what once was mirrored in the eyes of of all her beholders. Autoeroticism was Fanny's first sexual impulse and, as she lays down her pen, it is her last. The conventionality she enters is imposed as well as chosen. All she can do is tell.

At the end of the novel the young Fanny disappears and the older narrator and her husband Charles remain. Charles, we learn, educates his son by leading him through "the most noted bawdy-houses in town; where he took care he should be familiarized with all those scenes of debauchery, so fit to nauseate a good taste." The narrator admits the danger of the experience but only, she declares, for a fool, and "are fools worth so much attention?" We are jolted here into understanding that, like the son of Charles and Fanny, we too have been taken on a tour of the bawdy-houses. Also like the son, we are fools if we have not understood that the message, although potentially dangerous, never becomes so. It remains urbane, worldly, and ultimately conventional.

Through this incident we are also jolted into realizing that our tour has been with Fanny alone, and that we are completely ignorant of the lore passed on by father to son, by man to man. At the very end of the novel, with Charles and his son, we glimpse an alien system not designed for women at all, one from which they are in fact excluded. And it is Charles who implies the writer. Revealing his fantasy of the female system, not his knowledge of his own, the male author disturbs the reader with his silence. The female relationships startle and intrigue but even the sexual-experimental friendship with Phoebe and the sexual-didactic one with Mrs. Cole are refused such disturbing power.

Denis Diderot's *The Nun*
(started in 1760, published 1796)

Diderot thought long and deeply about women. He considered their psychological nature and their sexual needs; above all he reflected on their difference from men. In an essay entitled "On Women," he tried to pinpoint some of the distinctions, but his analysis is overwhelmed by its subject: women emerge from most of it not fragmented into analytical categories and qualities but distanced by their otherness.

Like so many men before him, Diderot gives passion to women, along with obsession, cruelty, hysteria, and pain, all

100

qualities and sensations which men themselves usually fear. In his prose women are reduced to the irrational shadow of reasonable men, and the old dichotomy inevitably intrudes: "If we have more reason than women, they have much more instinct than us."

All this is conventional and dreary enough. But Diderot does not stop with his statement of otherness; he reacts to it and in his reaction comes close to understanding if not the psychological reality of women, at least their social one, enveloped as they are in the very attitude he has himself exemplified. Movingly he writes of the physical misery of female life, the menstruation, pregnancy, and daily restrictions. He mentions the sadness of old age for women whose physical charms were their very reason for being. Above all, he understands well the nature of the sexual trap, into which women both must and must not venture. Bitterly and accurately he translates the man's whispered "I love you" into a woman's terms:

> If you are willing to sacrifice your innocence and way of life to me, to lose the respect you have for yourself and obtain from others, to move in society with downcast eyes, at least until you have acquired shamelessness through promiscuous ways, to renounce all claim to honesty, to kill your parents with grief and give me a moment of pleasure, I will be very obliged to you.[9]

Diderot's disconcertingly ambivalent essay points to the ambivalence of his great novel of female love, *The Nun*. In it he treats women in their passionate and obsessional aspects, showing not only that monastic life is unnatural for all people but that under it women in particular lose their tenuous hold on reason. Yet, as in his essay "On Women," a sympathy underlies the thesis and obscures it. Diderot both recoils from the obsession, madness, and hysteria he portrays in the convent and hints at their social cause even outside convent life. On a still deeper level, however, the recoil and the hint are symptomatic of a fear

9. "Sur les femmes," *Oeuvres de Diderot,* ed. André Billy (Paris: Bibliothèque de la Pléiade 1962), p. 957.

101

of women's otherness. Diderot's very understanding of the nature of the sexual trap and the misery of women's progression from pregnancy in youth to neglect in age must have suggested to him that women might not always wish to embrace such a life. If they were relieved of their association with irrationality and obsession, they might well refuse to do so. To see the fear of women's refusal of men underlying the social awareness of women's sorry state in a man's world, itself buried beneath the Enlightenment thesis about the evil of seclusion, we must interrogate the novel directly, especially its strange narrator Suzanne Simonin and the erotic relationships into which she almost enters.

1

Diderot's *The Nun* is the first novel in English or French to treat lesbianism seriously, explicitly, and decently. It is a disquieting work, whose shifting points of view unsettle rather than confuse. It states a clear thesis, that the institution of monasticism is corrupting and that people, especially women, secluded from general society become warped and monstrous. The women in the book are pitiful because they have been wrongfully imprisoned either with or without their consent. They are even more pitiful, the novel seems to assert, because in many cases they have embraced their imprisonment and accepted that an exclusive female society can satisfy all their needs. In this acceptance they have gone against nature and their fate must be madness, sickness and death. Case histories of the insane, diseased, and dying punctuate the book and underline the thesis by making it seem generally and necessarily true.

The Nun takes the form of an appeal of an escaped nun, Suzanne Simonin, who is imploring a kindhearted Christian nobleman, M. de. Croismare, to interest himself in her predicament. The appeal is expressed through the history of Suzanne's trials and sorrows, designed to move the reader to pity and then action. To gain such pity, Suzanne must recapture the moments themselves, not record them through the lens of hindsight; although the work is in the form of the memoir, like *Fanny Hill*, it recounts events rather as a journal or as daily letters. Suzanne, almost unaging in the novel, moves through the scenes in the same state of mind in which she once experienced them. The narrative is reenactment, and no experience is allowed to cloud the innocent vision of the nun who begins her narration at sixteen and ends it at about twenty-seven, but who remains until almost the end the virginal adolescent in body and soul.[10]

The story of *The Nun* can be briefly told, but the telling of it belies its effect. Because of her illegitimacy, Suzanne Simonin is devoted by her mother to a religious life for which she feels no vocation and which she regards with distaste. She tries hard by direct refusal, insubordination, and appeal to escape such a life, but fails at all attempts. The bulk of the novel traces her experiences at the three convents in which she is confined: at Sainte-Marie, where she is placed as a child; at Longchamps, where she wilts under the conflicting influence first of the spiritiaul Madame de Moni and then of the sadistic Sainte-Christine; and last at Arpajon, where she arouses the longing of the Superior. Just before the madness and death of this Superior, the novel subsides into fragments, ostensibly because Suzanne has lost confidence in herself and her absolute innocence. She escapes from the convent aided by a priest, who, almost automatically, assaults her once outside the convent walls.[11] Abandoned in an alien world and marked by the convent she has so much abhorred, she makes her appeal to the Marquis, recreating herself in a persuasive new image for the reading eyes of her judge.

10. The problem of Suzanne's age is discussed by Roger Lewinter in the introduction to *La Religieuse, Oeuvres complètes* (Paris: Club français du livre, 1969–70), 505–6. As he points out, Diderot's sister Angèlique, whom Diderot's daughter regarded as the model of Suzanne, died insane in a convent at about this age.

11. There is debate about the identity between the priest who suggests Suzanne's escape and her assaulter. The text is unhelpful: "the new confessor is being persecuted by his own superiors, and he persuades me to escape from the convent," writes Suzanne, and a few lines later she describes herself "on the way to Paris with a young Benedictine" who violently assaults her. Earlier she has described Dom Morel as a passionate young Benedictine, still under forty, which suggests that he and the assaulter are one, but, if this is the case, it is odd that she does not name him. For this study I have assumed the two men are the same.

Told thus, the novel appears picaresque, with a unity given only by the constant figure of the wide-eyed and receptive heroine. We would expect her to move through the scenes gaining experience and bitter knowledge, but above all presenting vividly the weird and squalid situations she falls into and the equally weird people who make and control them. This is partly the case. The interest in the novel is immediately and strikingly external. It is the Superiors rather than Suzanne who live in her pages. But Suzanne herself does not develop; rather she gradually reveals herself, and she does so not through self-analysis but through her seemingly clear and naive presentation of other women. Slowly, indistinctly at first, these become less external agents than aspects of Suzanne and her primary relationship with her mother. Such a complex and dark image cannot drive the Marquis to intervene. The abrupt translation of the strange nun into the fair victim of a rapist is a brilliant device of fiction and fact. At a stroke, the rescue is made unambivalent and necessary.

To approach Suzanne in and through the text is no easy matter, for the web of the narrative traps and obscures. But it is a necessary effort, for she forms the center of the book and the web is spun from her entrails. First, however, we must come to terms with her apparent naiveté as character and narrator.

Suzanne stresses her naiveté throughout the novel.[12] She understands nothing until she hears it in words, although her own relation of events clearly illuminates the significance of gesture, glance, and sigh. The profession of naiveté and youthful candor is of course most useful to a first-person narrator, for it allows her to ascribe to herself unselfconsciously and artlessly the most flattering virtues. Suzanne is quick to relate compliments and to emphasize ingenuously her distinction from her sisters and the other nuns she encounters. Her naiveté is most striking when she describes the powerful emotion she inspires in others. It is Su-

---

12. The problems of Suzanne as narrator are discussed by Georges May in *Diderot et "La Religieuse"* (New Haven: Yale University Press, 1954) and by Robert J. Ellrich in "The Rhetoric of *La Religieuse* and Eighteenth-Century Forensic Rhetoric," *Diderot Studies III*, ed. Otis Fellows and Gita May (Geneva: Librairie E. Droz, 1961).

zanne's purpose to be ignorant of its meaning and, in the beginning of the story, she presents emotion externally, as if it existed naturally and independently of her, although she contrives that her influence will clearly appear. When she is dragged to make her vows in Sainte-Marie, she does not *know* the reaction of the congregation she has hand-picked to be moved by her display, but she hears and records the sobs; in Longchamps she only guesses at the feeling she has been at pains to evoke: "apparently I was a very touching sight to my companion" (p. 71).[13]

Suzanne asserts she has no tendency to hypocrisy; yet frequently her action suggests this quality. When the first Superior comes in with a letter she clearly wishes to discuss, Suzanne will not play the game and pretends to be ignorant of it. She gives damning evidence about the character of Simonin, her legal father, and then declares we must close our eyes to it; she wishes to reveal the evil without implicating herself in the revelation.

The episode of Simonin points to another problem of Suzanne's naïveté. Throughout the novel there is striking interplay of speech, writing, silence, and gesture. Abrupt silence and gesture are most revealing of character, for through them the women censor themselves and hint at their most painful impressions or inadvertently disclose what their speech intends to hide. Suzanne records the moments in herself and others, just as she relates the laconic and highly charged dialogues which she joins with her friends. But she records too the power of the written word over all the women of the convent. Each nun is bound by her signature of admission and renunciation, and each is thereby related helplessly to a legal and political world dominated only by men. Over and over again the force of the written word is stressed. Suzanne's agreement to enter a convent, written to her mother, binds her, while her spoken doubts are unimportant; her written appeal against her vows throws the convent into turmoil as her spoken lamentations never do.

It is strange and disquieting then to realize that Suzanne,

13. The page numbers refer to the Penguin edition of *The Nun*, translated by Leonard Tancock, 1974.

who describes herself gesturing and speaking among women, is all the while writing—recording speech, gesture, and silence on paper, making a written display for the Marquis who can be forced to act only through the power of writing. Again, then, we are faced with a problem of apparent naiveté and actual artfulness—a disparity between Suzanne's ingenuous speech and gesture and the conscious, manipulative recording of them in writing. Inevitably her naiveté emerges as a rhetorical device, designed to persuade the Marquis of her innocence and virtue, while allowing him to perceive the ghastliness of all who persecute her. She can disclaim her part in revealing Simonin's faults, but she has recorded them for all to see.

Suzanne supports her naiveté within the story with a literary naiveté, equally disturbing and suspect. She opens her narrative by giving her character as writer, a character which of course must influence her presentation within the story: "I shall describe part of my misfortunes without talent or artifice, with the ingenuousness of a girl of my age and with my natural candour" (p. 21). When reading the novel for the first time, it is impossible to know that Suzanne is twenty-seven or twenty-eight when she writes her history, but it is possible to note the contrast between this disclaimer and the concern a few sentences earlier to flatter the Marquis into a receptive mood and to understand his character so that the narrative may be adjusted to it.

Even more striking—although we must wait the length of the novel to see it—is the final postscript, written by Suzanne after she has reread her narrative:

> P.S. I am overwhelmed with fatigue, surrounded by terrors, and peace has deserted me. These memoirs, which I wrote hurriedly, I have just re-read at leisure, and I have noticed that without the slightest intention I had shown myself in every line, certainly as unhappy as I was, but much more attractive than I am. Could it be that we think men are less affected by a picture of our troubles than by a portrait of our charms? And do we count on its being easier to seduce them than to touch their hearts? I have too little experience of them, and I have not studied them sufficiently to know. And yet supposing the Marquis, who is reputed to be the

106

most delicate of men, were to persuade himself that I am addressing myself not to his charity but to his lust, what would he think
of me? This thought worries me. In reality he would be quite mistaken if he ascribed to me in particular an instinct common to all
my sex. I am a woman, and perhaps a bit coquettish, who can
tell? But it is a result of our nature, and not of artifice on my part.
(pp. 188–9) [14]

The admission of disingenuousness undercuts the display of innocence—a large part of Suzanne's established character—while
it seeks to reestablish it after the violent scenes at the close of the
book. Another aim is to obscure again the association of Suzanne
with the powerful medium of writing, an inappropriate association for one who represents herself so insistently as helpless victim. She wrote, she declares, "hurriedly," almost instinctively,
that is, without the premeditation which is the hallmark of writing. As with her revelation and simultaneous rejection of Simonin's wrongdoing, Suzanne here intends to keep the spontaneous and ingenuous image of speaker while preserving this image
in the permanent medium of writing.

With some suspicion, then, we must look again at Suzanne
and her story and, as we probe the text, turn a probing eye on its
narrator. Like the characters themselves, we must try to pry into
Suzanne's devastating innocence and implacable naiveté.

2

Suzanne's mother displays herself only occasionally and always
in displaced or unequal ways: she is found towering above the
small child or rather the grown woman made childlike in her
obeisance; she is seen briefly and enigmatically through the eyes
of the men who enter her life, and finally she appears displaced
by the impersonal letter, which indicates the end of spontaneous
communion between mother and child. [15]

14. The p.s. was added to the novel over twenty years after the original composition.
15. Suzanne's relationship with her mother is brilliantly investigated by Lewinter. I
disagree in part with his attempt to impose the Freudian Oedipal model on Suzanne, but I
am indebted to his analysis of the novel for many of the points elaborated in this section.

EROTIC FRIENDSHIP

Within her family, Suzanne is a Cinderella figure, flanked by
two ugly sisters. Like most writing heroines, she is a product of
defective parents: her father is aloof and austere, her mother un-
sympathetic, even hostile. At first Suzanne is at a loss to explain
why her family neither loves nor nurtures her, but, as she
watches her less favored sisters reach marriageable age, to be
dispatched with handsome dowries to suitable husbands, and
learns that she is to be devoted to a religious life of seclusion, she
becomes, she says, suspicious of her birth. Constrained to live out
her novitiate of two years in the convent of Sainte Marie, she
plans a dramatic escape in the first of the tableaux she images for
herself at crucial moments in her life. Before relatives, friends,
and priests, assembled to hear her vows and witness her marriage
to Christ, she answers "No" to the ritual questions of vocation
and intent. Her speech of justification is cut short by one of the
nuns who mass anonymously and ominously round her throughout the novel—rather like the envious and rancorous women the
narrator of *Fanny Hill* had seen circling her younger self. She is
taken home by her mother in disgrace.

Suzanne's journey to her childhood home provides the setting for one of the few meetings of mother and child. To appreciate its bizarre and symbolic quality, we must look ahead at Mme
Simonin's explanation of her rejection of her daughter. Suzanne
is illegitimate and has become for her mother the embodiment of
her sin against her husband and her religion. But she is more.
Mme Simonin was abandoned by her lover, whose image has obsessed her through all the years of Suzanne's growing up; the
daughter also becomes then the embodiment of her obsession
with the faithless lover, and Suzanne's personal charms—incessantly mentioned in the novel—emphasize her association both
with the charms of the lover and with Mme Simonin's sexuality.

> I took the seat in front and the carriage set off. We sat opposite
> each other for some time without a word, my eyes were lowered
> and I dared not look at her. I don't know what went on in my in-
> nermost soul, but suddenly I flung myself at her feet and laid my
> head on her knees, saying nothing, but sobbing and gasping for

breath. She pushed me away roughly. I did not get up, my nose began to bleed, I nevertheless seized one of her hands and made it wet with mingled tears and blood as I kissed it, saying: 'You are still my mother and I am still your child.' She pushed me even more roughly, snatched her hand away from mine and said: 'Get up, you miserable girl, get up.' I obeyed, sat back on the seat and drew my hood over my face. She had put such firm authority into her tone of voice that I felt I ought to spare her the very sight of me. My tears and the blood from my nose mingled together and ran down my arms, and I had it all over me before I noticed. I gathered from the few words she said that her dress and underclothes had been stained and that it annoyed her. (p. 34)

The blood mingling with the tears is a powerful image, physical and spiritual, erotic and religious.[16] The two women, both fearful of the female sexuality that inevitably and firmly binds them, are baptised in the mixture, which—in the female context—relates to the blood and pain of defloration, menstruation, and childbirth. Suzanne's gasping for breath thickens the erotic atmosphere and foreshadows the panting breath in the sexual encounter of herself and the Superior of Arpajon. In *Clarissa* the nose bleed was a simulacrum for the rape and it momentarily frightened the whore, present to witness another deflowering. In *Fanny Hill* the intended rape ended in a "nose gushing out blood"; the blood was related to the virgin blood the rapist wanted, but it was displayed as well to impress and move another woman to pity.

As the blood and tears are eroticized by present and future contexts, they are spiritualized by the past. It is Christ whom Suzanne with her resounding "No" has refused to marry and serve. Although always pious, she has not accepted the sacrifice of herself to the sacrifice of Christ, imaged in the blood and tears of the crucifixion. Instead she here inserts herself in place of the

16. Stressing the importance of body-language in the novel, Herbert Josephs sees this blood as both pure and impure: "Suzanne is an innocent victim sacrificed to rage and whose own rage can only be implicit in the novel's varied gestures." See "Diderot's *La Religieuse:* Libertinism and the Dark Cave of the Soul," *Modern Language Notes* 91 (1976), 753.

Christ who demands sacrifice of both her and her mother for the sin against Simonin, the father.

Mme Simonin, however, cannot accept Suzanne as female sexual principle and she spurns the morality it implies. She is aghast at the dirtiness of the female blood. Thrusting Suzanne away, therefore, she rejects her as female sexuality; speedily she returns to her husband's house, where at once she shuts her daughter up in her room to avoid again the contamination of her blood.

What then can we make of Suzanne, the sacrificed daughter who bows before her mother and the principle of female sexuality, while at the same time forcing on this mother a baptism of female blood and tears? Is she sacrificed, or would-be sacrificer? All that can be said is that, in the impulsive gesture, she desires to come close to the mother who has always distanced her. Suzanne displays her blood through desire of the mother and fear of sacrifice to male morality and male religion. She fails to gain her object and still her fears. It is one of her only failures in relationship; later she will again make a Christlike physical display of her wounds and a verbal one of her sorrows, and her effect will be intensely appreciated.

The importance of the scene with her mother is immense. It sets the pattern—reversed and convoluted as it becomes—of future relationships. Like these, it is ended or valorized through the mediation or expression of a man. Back in her father's house, Suzanne is told by her mother's confessor that she is indeed illegitimate. The crucial knowledge is not given directly from woman to woman so that it may be set in a female context; it must pass through a man. Later at Longchamps Suzanne's conscious knowledge of the sadism of the Superior, and at Arpajon the awareness of the sexuality of the Superior, both come through men who fit the female facts into a male world of reference and analysis.

After the confession has been divulged to Suzanne, another interview between mother and daughter follows. In it Mme Simonin spells out her feeling of misery and disgrace at her sexual fall and her loathing for Suzanne, who represents her pain. But her most intense feeling arises from quite a different source. Suzanne, it seems, represents not only the disgrace of sexuality but the fascination of it. Mme Simonin expresses her revulsion at the sight of her daughter and we expect that the "hateful betrayal" she laments will be her own of her husband; in fact it is the betrayal by the lover:

> "you are a constant reminder of such hateful betrayal and ingratitude on the part of another man that I cannot bear the thought; the vision of this man always rises up between you and me, he spurns me, and the loathing I have for him recoils on you." (p. 40)

It is a strange avowal to a daughter she has wronged.

Although Mme Simonin asserts the surface reason for Suzanne's sacrifice—"God preserved both you and me so that the mother might atone for her sin through her child"—she implies the deeper one, that the daughter must be entombed for life because she possesses the charm, the sexual power, and the destructiveness of the lover. By so entombing her, Mme Simonin ensures that such power will be hidden. Perhaps too the passion she clearly expresses for the lover in her outpouring of loathing has been channelled to the daughter: the lover has escaped her, but the daughter, shut in a convent for life, can never escape her or entertain a rival.

During the interview, Mme Simonin exclaims to her daughter: "You possess nothing and never will." Clearly this is far from the truth. Devoid of material goods, Suzanne possesses musical and verbal skills as well as physical charms beyond the other women of the novel. For Mme Simonin similar charms characterize her faithless lover rather than her lawful husband. In an agony of passion, she merges daughter and lover; in so doing she mentally reverses the tableau of the carriage ride. Imagining herself falling before the child of her lover, as Suzanne had fallen before her and as she had fallen before the lover who spurned her, she cries, "My child, if it were only necessary to throw

111

myself at your feet to make you. . . ." She interrupts herself, for the reversal has forced her to acknowledge lover and daughter as one, and she hurls at Suzanne the reproach she must so often have thrown at the lover: "But you have no feelings, you have your father's hardness of heart." The juxtaposition of Suzanne with her father impresses because a moment earlier Mme Simonin has referred to her husband as Suzanne's father. By mentioning the natural father, she is in a way beginning to accept her daughter: she provides for her a character, admittedly still not her own, but at least distinct from the sacrificial one she has imposed throughout childhood. The triangle of mother, Suzanne, and Simonin has been replaced by the truer and more natural one of lover, mother, and child.

Here then is a moment of partial understanding: Mme Simonin views her daughter more frankly than before and admits haltingly her own femaleness and sexuality. Suzanne has come nearer than ever to the mother she has so long desired. For the female union of mother and daughter, it is a crucial time.

> At that moment Monsieur Simonin came in. He loved his wife, he saw the state she was in, he was a violent man. He stopped dead, gave me a terrible look and said:
> "Leave this room!"

The possibilities are blighted by the irruption of Simonin. Suzanne can only approach her mother in his absence, for his presence scotches all female association.

For Suzanne, both interviews have ended violently. To the second there is no successor and she is kept away from her mother from that time on, communicating with her only by letter. Her female relationship has then been spoiled and the effect is immediate; she cannot relate to other people in her life, once familiar but now strangely alien. Simonin, the austere ruler of her childhood, becomes a disturbing figure: "Since I had known that he was not my father his presence had filled me with terror." From the strangeness of mother and father, Suzanne flees to the convent.

EROTIC FRIENDSHIP

When Suzanne enters the convent of Longchamps, she seems the same naive but determined woman as before. She does not analyze her mother's rejection or think about the warped adulthood she has just achieved. It is only as the relationship of mother and child is obsessively reiterated that we are allowed a glimpse of the truth: that she is seeking in the women she entangles aspects of the mother who has repulsed her. Perhaps she is seeking through many the primal union she had desired with only one, but her effect on the women suggests quite otherwise: that she is ranging the female world to madden and destroy through her erotic power the mother whose sexuality she has both suffered and expressed.

3

The first of Suzanne's surrogate mothers is Mme de Moni, described in the narrative as humane and spiritual, affectionate and dignified: "She was a sensible woman who understood the human heart, she was indulgent, though nobody needed to exercise it less, for we were all her children" (p. 46). The gifts of divine eloquence and mystical communion are also hers and, under this powerful personality, Suzanne sleepwalks through the vows that bind her to female society and imprison her for life.

The relationship between Suzanne and Mme de Moni is the most positively presented in the book. Suzanne responds to her Superior's remarkable qualities with rapture and reverence. But the description of the relationship is curiously prefaced. Almost forgotten as the recipient of the appeal, M de Croismare is suddenly invoked by Suzanne at this point: she begs him, if he intends rescuing her, to hide her musical talents because, as she says, they will betray her and conflict with the obscure life she intends to lead. The interpolated appeal follows hard on Suzanne's impressive display of musical emotion before her Superior—she has sung Rameau impressively and movingly—and the detailed description of it. Through contiguity of narrative elements, then, rather than through analysis, Suzanne's motives for display are questioned and her spiritual version of the union of herself and Mme de Moni thrown lightly in doubt.

Like all the women of the novel, Mme de Moni exists only through Suzanne, who describes the relationship in terms that fix both women in a web of flattery: "I don't know whether I ought to tell you," begins Suzanne, "that she had a great affection for me and that I was by no means the least of her favourites. I know that this is very great self-praise. . . . If there were anything I could find fault with in Madame de Moni it would be that she let her taste for virtue, piety, candour, meekness, talent and integrity be seen too obviously" (p. 46). It is indeed an impressive set of virtues that Suzanne takes from her Superior into herself, and to accept them the reader needs all the proof Suzanne provides of her naiveté.

Such virtue and charm are of course not lost on the sensitive Mme de Moni and she is affected as deeply and decisively by Suzanne as Mme Simonin was before her. With her talents, beauty and invulnerable naiveté, Suzanne seduces her Superior from her pious communion with God, forcing her to recognize but never express the erotic desire so long subsumed in the mystical experience. "It seems that when you come to me," Mme de Moni laments to Suzanne, "God withdraws and my spirit falls silent, and in vain I try to work myself up, I hunt for ideas and seek to lift up my heart. I find I am just an ordinary woman and an insignificant one, and I am afraid to say anything" (p. 48).

From Mme de Moni, Suzanne succeeds in driving out the male God she has failed to dislodge from the mind of her mother. No longer supported by a powerful divinity, Mme de Moni dwindles into a woman and is silenced. To the Superior's anguished analysis, Suzanne counters: "Suppose it were God making you silent!" Suzanne refers to a divine sign of her own lack of vocation but, since she makes God responsible for what Mme de Moni has just assigned to her, she seems also to be making herself interchangeable with the God to whom she has been sacrificed.

EROTIC FRIENDSHIP

The struggle between God and Suzanne for Mme de Moni intensifies as the Superior tries to reestablish her character through praying and through coercing Suzanne into her own pious context. But again the silence of Suzanne triumphs. This time the reproach is subtly erotic and maternal: "Ah my dear child," sighs Mme de Moni, "what a cruel effect you have had upon me!"

The night before Suzanne is to make her vows, Mme de Moni pleads with God, for she seems to accept Suzanne's radical disjunction from him. In the morning, emerging from her struggle, she has again shrunk into the ordinary woman; sitting on Suzanne's bed with an expression of "bewilderment and grief" on her face, she questions her protégée and the dialogue is as highly charged and revealing as a catechism:

Had I slept well?
"Deeply . . ."
"Didn't you think of anything during the night?"
"No."
"No dreams?"
"No." (pp. 49–50)

Through her questioning of sleep and dreams, Mme de Moni is prying into the fascination of Suzanne, her apparent innocence and naiveté. Suzanne has slept dreamlessly and deeply while the Superior has prayed in agony. The erotic feelings that Suzanne denies for her conscious and unconscious self have been awakened in Mme de Moni, who is unprepared for them since they have entered in so innocent a form. Agitated and aroused, she leaves Suzanne to avoid seeing the ritual dressing of the nun; she turns both from the sacrifice and from the display of physical charms.

In the relationship with Mme de Moni, Suzanne comes closest in her narrative to admitting mutual seduction. She does it, however, in a curiously displaced way. Of Mme de Moni, she writes:

her object was not seduction, but that is what she achieved, for when you left her your heart was on fire, joy and ecstasy shone in your face, and your tears were so sweet! . . . Some of them [the nuns] have told me that they felt a longing for consolation spring up within them like the desire for a great pleasure, and I think I might have reached that state myself had I grown more accustomed to the experience. (pp. 47–48)

Suzanne admits the sweet pain and fascination of the contact, while indicating her own refusal of it. At the same time she suggests her influence over the Superior, for her description is of a woman distributing the favors of her personality among many. It is the establishment of the exclusive relationship with Suzanne later that unbalances this personality and reduces it to its components.

Shortly after she has encountered Suzanne, Mme de Moni dies—at the same time as Mme Simonin, whom she has replaced. On her deathbed she recovers her old character and welds again the aspects of her personality.[17] She becomes eloquent and her eloquence is once more given to all. Fittingly she dies among her many followers and she abandons the grief and tears displayed only in her relationship with Suzanne. A measure of her regained composure is that she leaves her meditations to Suzanne; she will live for her in the displaced medium of writing, not in the close spontaneous one of speech and gesture through which she has all too clearly revealed herself. Indeed we can say she has lost nothing from the relationship with Suzanne—except perhaps her life.

4

With Mme de Moni's death, the convent comes under the rule of a far less spiritual character, Sister Sainte-Christine. With this change, a strange metamorphosis occurs in Suzanne; in a way possessing Mme de Moni in life, she now clearly possesses her in death: "I looked like our former Superior when she used to console us," she says, although, as usual, she presents her opinions through the mouths of others. "My appearance had filled them

17. Georges May has noted that Mme de Moni on her deathbed resembles the dying Socrates, pp. 229–30.

with the same awe" (p. 71). The spiritual aspect of Mme de Moni, jeopardized in her life, now reappears convoluted in Suzanne and with it, we can suppose, the awesome power she had described to Suzanne: "Among all these creatures you see round me, so docile, so innocent, so gentle, indeed, my child, there is scarcely one, yes, scarcely one, I could not turn into a wild beast."

Suzanne's new power is masochistically displayed in the torment and torture she drives Sainte-Christine to inflict. Supporting Mme de Moni's system, Suzanne opposes the new Superior in her religious beliefs and practices; she intensifies and personalizes the opposition by noting the erotic element in the convent, an element with which she will not be contaminated. She throws out "some indiscreet remarks . . . on the subject of the suspicious intimacy between some of the favourites" and between the Superior and a young priest, and thus goads Sainte-Christine into persecution. As persecutor, the Superior is forced into the role of Simonin; as he tormented Suzanne when he apprehended her relationship with his wife, so Sainte-Christine tortures her when she sees the merged personality of Suzanne and Mme de Moni. Simonin and Sainte-Christine are further linked through the narrative method: the house of Simonin and the convent under Sainte-Christine are much more realized as physical contexts than the convents of Mme de Moni and the Superior of Arpajon. The vagueness of the latter forces the reader to concentrate on the subtle revelation of relationship and psychological state, not on the temporal incidents and development.

The episode with Sainte-Christine is the middle of the novel, and a curious structural progression culminates in it. Suzanne, it seems, frequently exists in triangular relationships, torn and ultimately destroyed by conflict. Within her family she begins conventionally enough as the daughter flanked by mother and father. The triangle then shifts to the mother, daughter, and lover, both women still being controlled by a male figure. The new triangle has been formed through the mediation of another man, the confessor. The triangle of Mme de Moni is more obscure but

117

emerges from her relationship with both Christ and Suzanne. It is broken by death, the action of Christ. With Sainte-Christine, and a loving nun named Ursule, Suzanne is for the first time locked into a triangular situation with two women. Her response seems to be masochistically to invest one of the women with the male power of action and punishment. From the logic of the structure as well as from Suzanne's goadings, Sainte-Christine seems fated to torture and Suzanne to suffer.[18]

The scenes with the sadistic Sainte-Christine are the most Gothic of the novel. They are set on a ghostly stage, with deathly props, lit only by fires and flickering candles. In this macabre atmosphere, Suzanne is subjected to a series of hideous tortures: she is in turn reviled and ignored, kept endlessly awake, starved, and confined in a dark solitary cell. Such treatment punishes her for her closeness to the former Superior, but the bond is rather strenthened than weakened. Worn out by persecution, Suzanne at length falls ill and soon is "at death's door." There she enacts the dying scene of Mme de Moni, surrounded by nuns, dispensing to them comfort and wisdom, as her Superior had done before her. Earlier too she had associated herself with Christ as she had done obliquely with Mme de Moni:

> "Oh God, I pray for pardon for my misdeeds, even as You did for me on the Cross."
> "What pride!" they exclaimed. "She compares herself with Jesus Christ and us with the Jews who crucified Him." (p. 66)

Persecuted and reviled as she is, Suzanne's power increases. Through the love of Mme de Moni and the hate of Sainte-Christine, she has grown to such a stature that she electrifies the other

18. In his essay, "Diderot's *Supplément* as Pendant for *La Religieuse*," Otis Fellows summarizes other triadic divisions in *The Nun*: the memoirs of Suzanne are in three parts, her life with the Simonins, her convent existence, and her experience in Paris; her monastic adventures occur in three convents; three priests intervene on her behalf; and Suzanne points out that three people very close to her die one after the other, her mother, legal father, and Mme de Moni. Finally, Fellows notes that in *The Nun* Diderot often uses the tricolon with its arrangement of words or phrases in groups of three, *Literature and History in the Age of Ideas. Essays on the French Enlightenment Presented to George R. Havens* (Ohio State University Press, 1975), pp. 229–43.

nuns with love, hate, or both intermixed. Sainte-Christine has spread it abroad that Suzanne is possessed, and her devastating effect on one young woman confirms the story and reveals how overpowering—erotically and spiritually—she has become:

> One of the youngest was at the end of the corridor and I was going towards her, there was no way of avoiding me and she was seized with a terrible panic. First she turned her face to the wall and muttered in a shaky voice: "My God, my God, Jesus, Mary!" But still I came on towards her, and when she felt me near she hid her face in her hands for fear of seeing me, leaped in my direction, hurtled right into my arms and yelled: "Help! help! mercy! I am lost! Sister Sainte-Suzanne, have pity on me!" And with those words she fell back senseless on the floor. (p. 85)

Forced to be the Satan of the convent, Suzanne is addressed here in words appropriate for Christ. The nun, terrified by her presence, runs to her, not from her.

Suzanne's personality strikes powerfully and less ambivalently on the gentle, sensitive Sister Ursule. The friendship of the two women has all the devotion of the Moni-Suzanne one, but the effect is no longer mutual. It is Sister Ursule alone who is devastated and who, like Mme de Moni before her and the Superior of Arpajon after her, must die.

Sister Ursule befriends Suzanne during her torture. As Suzanne suffers in body, she endures in mind. Emerging into a painless interval, Suzanne is astounded at the deathly face of her sympathetic friend. "I love you," replies Sister Ursule, "and you ask me that! It was high time your ordeal ended, for it would have killed me" (p. 111).

Even more than Mme de Moni, Sister Ursule exists for Suzanne through speech—the huddled conversation or muffled sound—and through gesture. She too, however, leaves to Suzanne her writing when she dies. She differs from Mme de Moni, however, when she instructs her friend to burn it, an instruction with which Suzanne readily complies, troubled by no twinges of curiosity. She has already thoroughly known Ursule through her pallid face and strained whisper.

Sister Ursule does not, then, communicate with Suzanne through writing, but she is a means for the writing of her friend to reach the male world, for which it is designed and through which it has power. Through her, Suzanne appeals beyond the convent and so saves her own life.

Suffering repeated tortures and protracted starvation, Suzanne at one point approaches death—but she refuses to die. Sister Ursule on the other hand is obsessed by Suzanne's suffering and semi-death, and as Suzanne recovers she declines. The illness it seems was "infectious" and soon Sister Ursule comes to the death Suzanne avoided. Like Mme de Moni, however, she escapes finally from Suzanne's powerful fascination:

> she took my hand and held it tight as though she would not or could not let it go. "And yet it must be," she said as she did let it go. "It is God's will. Good-bye, Sister Suzanne. Give me my crucifix." (p. 116)

Through Suzanne she arrives at death, but, like Mme de Moni, she dies back into Christ. Suzanne is absent when she dies.

The written appeal through Ursule is only partly successful and Suzanne is condemned to spend the remainder of her days cloistered from the world; because of her sufferings she is, however, allowed to move to a third convent, Sainte-Eutrope d'Arpajon. There she encounters the Superior and enters into her final and most explicit female relationship. In it she is forced to confront her own nature at last and to learn what logically as older narrator she knows throughout. In the episode the seductiveness of innocence is invoked most clearly for M de Croismare outside the text, as well as for the Superior within it.

5

Suzanne's detailed introduction of the Superior is arresting. It works primarily through gesture and speech:

> She is short and quite plump, yet quick and lively in her movements, her head is never held straight on her shoulders, there is always something wrong with her clothes, her face is good-look-

ing rather than plain, and her eyes, one of which, the right one is higher and larger than the other, are full of fire and far-away looking. When she walks she swings her arms backwards and forwards. Should she want to speak, she opens her mouth before sorting out her ideas, so she tends to -um and -ah somewhat. Should she be sitting down she wriggles in her chair as though something were bothering her, forgetting all sense of decorum she lifts her wimple so as to scratch, crosses her legs, asks you questions but does not listen when you answer, says something to you, loses the thread and stops short, has forgotten where she is, gets annoyed and calls you a great silly, foolish, stupid if you don't set her on the right track again; she is sometimes familiar to the point of my-dearing you, and sometimes haughty and imperious to the point of disdain; her moments of dignity are short, she is in turn compassionate and hard, her ever-changing expression indicates the disconnectedness of her mind and all the instability of her character. (pp. 121–22)

The combination of such a character in the Superior and such acute criticism in Suzanne again strikes at the narrator's proclaimed naiveté and artlessness. It is not without reason that she is nicknamed Sainte-Suzanne the Reserved by the nuns of Arpajon.

The Superior, it would seem, takes pains to reveal herself. Suzanne relates her liking for scourging and her sudden compassion when it begins, followed by her kissing of the nun, her caresses and flattery of skin, neck, and hair. But her erotic feelings are general; although later we learn that she has had a sexual relationship with a young nun, Sainte-Thérèse, she is not at this stage exclusive in her desires. The convent, all exclaim, is happy under her rule and her concupiscence seems to trouble no one in particular.

The arrival of Suzanne changes everything. As at Longchamps, she is careful to display herself: she pleases with her musical skills and physical charms. Soon the Superior is caught fast in a passionate longing that is both erotic and maternal; Suzanne becomes her "dear little friend" and is addressed caressingly in child language.

As the Superior's longing grows, Suzanne increases her own

arousing behavior. She plays for the Superior and questions her desire innocently and provocatively, while herself remaining untouched: "Oh, Reverend Mother," exclaims Suzanne to the libidinal Superior, "could I be fortunate enough to possess something you would like and which would soften your heart?" The predictable answer is physical, not verbal, and is recorded correctly by the unmoved Suzanne: "She lowered her eyes, blushed and sighed—really just like a lover." It is the very innocence of Suzanne that drives her wild: "What innocence!" she cries, "How she appeals to me!" (pp. 133–38)

The relationship of Suzanne and the Superior, described with all the naiveté and ingenousness the narrator can muster, is both complicated and elucidated by Sainte-Thérèse, the discarded lover, whose terror and longing foreshadow the Superior's. The presence of Sainte-Thérèse works in two directions. In her we see the sexual action Suzanne cannot or will not describe for herself (she goes to the Superior when Suzanne flees her); on the other hand she prevents Suzanne from sexual contact when it seems inevitable. One night the Superior contrives to enter Suzanne's bed to "warm herself":

> She held out her arms, but I had my back to her; she took me gently and pulled me towards her, passed her right arm under my body and the other above and said: "I am frozen, and so cold that I am afraid to touch you for fear of hurting you."
>
> "Dear Mother, you need not be afraid of that."
>
> Immediately she put one hand on my breast and the other round my waist, her feet were under mine, and I pressed them so as to warm them, and she said: "Oh my dear, see how my feet have warmed up at once because there is nothing between them and yours."
>
> "But," I said, "what is there to prevent you from warming yourself everywhere in the same way?"
>
> "Nothing, if you are willing." (pp. 150–51)

Certainly the provocation is extreme and Suzanne is saved from the consequences by the violent knocking of Sainte-Thérèse: "I had turned round, and she had opened her nightdress, and I was

122

on the point of doing the same when suddenly there were two violent blows on the door."

Sainte-Thérèse fills yet another function: she is the third element in the triangular relationship we have come to expect of Suzanne. Certainly this relationship is the most striking so far, for the male element is entirely lacking. As always, conflicts arise in the triangle, but slowly Suzanne wins over both the Superior and Sainte-Thérèse; it is therefore potentially the most positive triad and the most subversive to the heterosexual norm which the novel, through its male spokesmen, insistently supports. The intervention of the two male confessors at the close of the book breaks it and, ultimately, causes the death of all three women.

Suzanne is linked with the Superior through speech, never writing, and, in this relationship, speech reaches its apotheosis in the female confession. Suzanne relates her life history as a confession to the Superior, from whom she obtains absolution and who, as she proceeds, relives her sufferings and in Christic manner takes them upon her. So Suzanne is relieved of the burden of experience and the Superior is seduced by mingled pain and pleasure into worshipping her as the wounded Christ:

> "Fancy crushing those arms with ropes!" And she took my arms and kissed them. "Drowning those eyes in tears!" And she kissed them "Drawing groans and wailing from that mouth!" She kissed that too. "Condemning that charming, serene face to be constantly clouded by sadness!" She kissed it. "Making the roses of those cheeks wither!" She stroked them with her hand and kissed them. "Robbing that head of its beauty! tearing out that hair! loading that brow with sorrow!" She kissed my head, brow, hair. (p. 142)

The Christ image adheres to both women and each is in a way worshiped by the other. Much later this inward, female relationship will be shattered by another, external confession, as the Superior speaks not directly to Suzanne but through the male confessor who breaks the blasphemous unity forever.

The friendship of Suzanne and the Superior is openly erotic for all but Suzanne. Her rhetorical naiveté allows her to delineate the very sounds and gestures of desire without being a party to them and, through humor, to distance the erotic moments from herself and from the reader; the naive presentation prevents our coming close to the Superior and sympathizing with her erotic longings:

I followed her in. In an instant she had opened the keyboard, produced a book, moved up a chair, for she was quick in her movements. I sat down. Thinking I might be chilly she removed a cushion from the chairs, which she put in front of me and bent down, took my feet and placed them on the cushion. Then I played some pieces of Couperin, Rameau and Scarlatti, during which she lifted a corner of my collar and rested her hand on my bare shoulders, with the tips of her fingers touching my breast. She was sighing and seemed oppressed, breathing heavily. The hand on my shoulder pressed hard at first but then ceased pressing at all, as though all strength and life had gone out of her and her head fell onto mine. Truly that hare-brained woman was incredibly sensitive and had the most exquisite taste for music, for I have never known anybody on whom it had such an extraordinary effect. (pp. 134–35)

The erotic power of Rameau as played and sung by Suzanne is one of the delights of the novel.

As the relationship progresses, Suzanne describes even more vividly the sexual ordeal of her friend, while still disclaiming both her own part in arousing desire and her understanding of it:

She fell silent, and so did I. She seemed to be experiencing the most exquisite pleasure. She invited me to kiss her forehead, cheeks, eyes and mouth, and I obeyed. I don't think there was any harm in that, but her pleasure increased, and as I was only too glad to add to her happiness in any innocent way, I kissed her again on forehead, cheeks, eyes and lips. The hand she had rested on my knee wandered all over my clothing from my feet to my girdle, pressing here and there, and she gasped as she urged me in a strange, low voice to redouble my caresses, which I did. Eventually a moment came, whether of pleasure or of pain I cannot say, when she went as pale as death, closed her eyes, and her whole body tautened violently, her lips were first pressed together and moistened with a sort of foam, then they parted and she seemed to expire with a deep sigh. I jumped up, thinking she had fainted, and was about to go and call for help. She half opened her eyes and said in a failing voice: "You innocent girl! it isn't anything. What are you doing? Stop . . ." I looked at her, wild-eyed and uncertain whether I should stay or go. She opened her eyes again; she had lost her power of speech, and made signs that I should come back and sit on her lap again. (pp. 137–38)

This incident is described by Suzanne as typical, one of many, taking place at no special time. But, as it progresses, its typicality—which tends, like Suzanne's naiveté, to distance the reader from its events—evaporates and it becomes particular and precise; this is especially so as Suzanne comes tentatively to act and to respond. Significantly she feels in silence. But she does not describe her own symptoms to the Superior or cry out in pain or pleasure; rather she returns to her own cell and there accepts her responsive state while swiftly explaining it. Her explanation reestablishes her character of innocence and naiveté, while it allows her to be still the reactor not the actor; it is she who has been infected by sexuality, not the Superior.

I had never experienced anything like it. My eyes closed in spite of me and I fell into a little doze, although I never usually sleep in the daytime. When I woke up I questioned myself about what had passed between the Superior and me. . . . The result of my reflections was that it was probably an affliction to which she was subject, then another thought came, that perhaps the malady was catching, and that Sainte-Thérèse had caught it and I should too.

While Suzanne sees herself as infected, the novel suggests differently: the idea of infection links the disease of sexuality with the illness which killed Sister Ursule at Longchamps. This nun too had loved Suzanne and had died of an infection caught from her.

The echoic relation of Sister Ursule and the Superior of Arpajon suggests that the explicitly erotic episodes at the final convent are not completely distinct from the earlier episodes of Suzanne with other female associates. Indeed the situation at Arpajon has been foreshadowed both dramatically and verbally throughout the narrative. Most insistent and curious, however, are the parallels between the spiritual Mme de Moni and the concupiscent Superior of Arpajon, parallels which force both women into a single context and make both in a way aspects of the rejecting mother. These aspects Suzanne with pitiless naiveté and goodwill destroys.

Verbal echoes abound, but most striking are the gestures and attitudes which suddenly recall the other women in Suzanne's life. The most arresting example occurs when the scatterbrained Superior of Arpajon follows the dignified Mme de Moni in contemplating Suzanne in her sleep. Both are moved by the sight, both become uneasy, and both question the erotic power they feel. Like Mme de Moni, the Superior interrogates Suzanne, incredulous of her combination of seductiveness and deep innocence: she feels how regular her pulse is and tries to understand that Suzanne has in fact no disturbing inner life, no dreams and no wakefulness. As at Longchamps, so at Arpajon, she sleeps "soundly." In both convents she sleeps while other women are condemned to watch.

Mme de Moni, Sister Ursule, and the Superior of Arpajon are most clearly linked in the chain of death: Mme de Moni dies after the trauma of meeting Suzanne; Sister Ursule dies of an infectious disease caught from Suzanne; Sainte-Thérèse catches her Superior's illness and dies when Suzanne intensifies it. Of Sainte-Thérèse's death we know little, but the dying Mme de Moni and Sister Ursule seem to escape and die into Christ or at least away from Suzanne. Only the Superior of Arpajon dies of and into Suzanne.

Her death following frenzy and madness is a spectacular one. Suzanne's confessor has taken a serious view of the Superior's lusts and cautioned Suzanne to avoid her. Suzanne obeys and reduces her friend—and the once happy convent she rules—to a disordered mass of emotion. Suzanne's power over a woman, placed in the position of her mother, is now complete:

she has become the exclusive beloved of the Superior and has replaced Christ as the object of devotion. When Suzanne told the story of her life to the Superior, displaying her mental and physical sufferings, the Superior made devotion to each wounded part and worshipped as devoutly as she had ever worshipped the wounded Christ. Now in her agony of madness and death, the Superior can neither return to Christ nor rid herself of Suzanne:

"If only I could lose my memory! . . . If I could go back into the void, or be born again! . . . Don't call the confessor. . . . I would rather you read me the Passion of Our Lord Jesus Christ . . . Read it . . . I am beginning to breathe again . . . One drop of His blood is enough to purify me . . . See, it is gushing forth from His side . . . Hold that sacred wound above my head . . . His blood flows down over me, but will not stay there . . . I am lost! . . . Take that Crucifix away from me . . . No, bring it back."

It was brought back and she held it tight in her arms, kissed it everywhere, then said: "These are her eyes, this is her mouth; when shall I see her again? Sister Agathe, tell her I love her, let her know the state I am in and that I am dying." (p. 182)

Sinking into the abyss of death, the Superior wishes to go back into the nothingness before birth. She wishes to rid herself of the knowledge Suzanne refused to gain. This erotic knowledge is her identity, now vested in Suzanne. To exorcise the younger woman she invokes the Christ she has betrayed, but it is too late. The blood of Christ flows over her, reenacting the scene in the carriage of Suzanne and her mother. Suzanne's blood both stuck and stained and the mother rejected it; Christ's blood will not stick to the Superior and she is forced to reject him. The crucifix turns into the image of Suzanne, for it is she whom the Superior has long worshipped.

6

Dom Morel, Suzanne's final confessor, is a shadowy and potent figure in the novel. Towards the end, it is he who follows a long line of male interveners in stating what appears the reasonable

127

and "correct" interpretation of the Superior's madness and death. To appreciate the "ex cathedra" appearance of his words, he must be seen as the heir of Simonin, the lawyer who pleads Suzanne's case, and the Archdeacon who studies it. Each stage of Suzanne's life is ended through male intervention, and these men form a backdrop of remote power and reason that contrasts with the frenzied hothouse of the convent. Truly, then, we seem to be in the world of Diderot's essay "On Women," where men have the reason, women the instinct and passion. Indeed, when the lawyer pleads the case Suzanne blames him for being too reasonable, too moderate, and too general; when she tells her own story, to the Superior and throughout the novel to M de Croismare, she electrifies and moves. Yet the arguments of the lawyer against forced monasticism are given fully and they stand out from the surrounding drama as thesis and conclusion. When Dom Morel speaks, he is in the tradition of such men.

First of all he dispatches Suzanne's innocence through an overheard confession, as earlier Mme Simonin's confessor had dispatched her ignorance of her birth. In both cases the world changes and the kindly, sensitive Superior suddenly becomes abominable and monstrous. Dom Morel immediately gives a reasonable, social origin for the monstrosity:

> "She was not cut out for her way of life, and this is what happens sooner or later when you go against the universal law of nature: this constraint deflects it into monstrous affections which are all the more violent because they have no firm foundation. She is a sort of maniac." (p. 176)

And so the Superior is mad because she is shut up and monstrous because lesbian. Female eroticism is unnatural and is itself madness. Suzanne loses her innocence, gains male reason, and comes to the proper connections.

Strangely, although so much of the book supports this view, the last actions of Suzanne and Dom Morel radically question it. After she has learned the truth, Suzanne and her narrative appear fragmented, and her power, completely expressed over the Superior, seems to decline. At this moment she identifies herself for the first and only time with a man, as if through power and knowledge she had achieved a male state. Of Dom Morel she says:

> And so it was that our similarity of character, together with that of the events in our lives, made us enjoy each other's company more as we saw more of each other. The story of certain moments in his life was that of mine, the story of his emotions was that of mine, the story of his soul was that of mine. (p. 174)

It is one of Suzanne's few moments of self-analysis and it turns out to be bitterly and ironically true.

In the fragments at the end of the novel, Suzanne is persuaded to escape with Dom Morel. Promptly and automatically he reduces her to a powerless woman by assaulting her. His transformation from soul mate to libertine is as sudden as hers from powerful seducer to hapless maiden. Outside the novel, Suzanne is meant to die from the fall she suffered while escaping. But she has been killed psychologically already. She existed—if vampirically—through her female relationships. Denied them and strangled by the male equation of madness and female eroticism, she must die. If her revenge on her mother is complete, her mother's revenge on her is ironically accomplished. She dies from a "fall," guilty through her conduct with a man. She has expiated her mother's sin by first reversing it and then reenacting it.

The relationship of Dom Morel and Suzanne breaks forever the pattern of female friendship. The triangle of women, culminating in the trio of Suzanne, the Superior, and Sainte-Thérèse, is replaced by that of Suzanne, the Superior, and Dom Morel, where Dom Morel holds and wields the power sexually and psychologically. The male presence is restored to the novel and we can now move to the two triads of the final pages, where the male is both all-powerful and absent. In the one is Suzanne the narrator, remarking on Suzanne the character, displayed for the eyes of the Marquis de Croismare; in the other Suzanne the narrator, Suzanne the character and Diderot, the male author. It is he who has manipulated all and has allowed, for a handful of pages, a woman to write of an erotic and self-sufficient female relationship before she must destroy it through his means.

The conjunction of Suzanne and Dom Morel also fulfills the pattern of speech and writing. The confession—the powerful instrument of female friendship—is made to Dom Morel and the Superior is reduced to the helpless and inarticulate state of Mme Simonin, who also gives knowledge through a man. With the aid of Dom Morel, Suzanne too deteriorates to the condition where she must appeal in writing to a man; her appeal is the written version of what she had spoken seductively to the Superior of Arpajon. She tries to combine writing and speech into a doubly powerful instrument, but ultimately it is speech that is subsumed into writing. In much the same way, Suzanne is subsumed into the male context where she dwindles into a helpless and dependent woman.

On female relationships *The Nun* is ambivalent, and its ambivalence reflects its male author's ambivalence toward women. Male pronouncements against exclusive female society and erotic friendships are prominent, but the last comes from the libertine Dom Morel. The convent is squarely condemned, but the life Diderot depicts outside its walls is no more inviting than that within: Mme Simonin has paid with her life and the life of her daughter for one sexual error, quite acceptable in a man; as soon as she leaves the convent Suzanne is subjected to a vicious assault; her unpleasant sisters lose their coveted property to their husbands and are swiftly weighed down with children. The musical convents of Longchamps and Arpajon before Suzanne's violent irruption into them present very real alternatives, and even the hostile eyes of Suzanne cannot entirely obscure this.

Diderot's novel is disquieting for, like his essay "On Women," it does not allow us to condemn and dismiss, while at the same time it prevents us from accepting. Like the essay, too, the book encases many views and possibilities that are neither complementary nor confused. The erotic women—especially the

130

Superior of Arpajon—are made separate from the narrator by her rhetorical naiveté and her later male knowledge, and they are condemned by the reasonable spokesmen. Yet these women exist fully and disturbingly, and the novel becomes far more than the male voyeur's view of lesbianism. It is this disturbing complexity in the center of the book to which the Victorian Lord Morley was no doubt reacting when he declared in dismay: "It is appalling, it fills you with horror, it haunts you for days and nights, it leaves a kind of stain on the memory." [19]

19. Quoted by Arthur M. Wilson in *Diderot* (New York: Oxford University Press, 1972), pp. 387–88.

CHAPTER THREE

Manipulative Friendship

Jean-Jacques Rousseau's *Julie* (1761)

I imagined love and friendship, the two idols of my heart, in the most ravishing of forms, and took delight in adorning them with all the charms of the sex I had always adored. I imagined two women friends, rather than two of my own sex, since although examples of such friendships are rarer they are also more beautiful. I endowed them with analogous but different characters; with features if not perfect yet to my taste, and radiant with kindliness and sensibility. I made one dark, the other fair; one lively, the other gentle; one sensible, the other weak, but so touching in her weakness that virtue itself seemed to gain by it. I gave one of them a lover to whom the other was a tender friend and even something more; but I allowed of no rivalry. . . . Being captivated by my two charming models, I identified myself as far as I could with the lover and friend.[1]

THE TWO WOMEN in Rousseau's *Julie or the New Eloisa* are Julie and Claire; the man, the lover and friend, is nameless but for a pseudonym and must be called Saint-Preux. We face the inevitable triangle, it seems, for literary female friendship is rarely allowed to exist in a pair.[2] Saint-Preux forms the third potent ele-

1. *The Confessions of Jean-Jacques Rousseau*, trans. J. M. Cohen (Harmondsworth: Penguin Books, 1975), pp. 400–1.
2. François Van Laere has noted Rousseau's fondness for triangles in his fiction. Distinguishing between female-dominated and male-dominated figures (between the initial triangle of Julie, Claire, and Saint-Preux, and the later one of Julie, Wolmar, and Saint-

ment, embodying the author and endowed with his seeing eye. The *Confessions* suggests the reader will view the two female friends through this eye, which will itself demand attention. The mediator between the reader and the two women will be the adoring male Saint-Preux.

Yet when we turn to *Julie* and look at the two "ravishing" heroines, the effect is not quite as anticipated. Love and friendship, the two idols of Rousseau's heart, do indeed comprise the novel, but they are not easily defined or severed, and the relationships that express them are strikingly ambiguous. Saint-Preux and Julie are lovers, but so, incipiently, are Saint-Preux and Claire. Julie and Claire are friends, and perhaps—to steal Rousseau's coy phrase—"something more."

1

LOVE

Julie or the New Eloisa is a long and serpentine novel, whose structural coils shift alarmingly when approached. It is divided into six books, but it falls with seeming clarity into two parts and a coda.[3] In neither part does much happen considering the inordinate length, but the initial drama of passionate love primarily occurs in the first. This story is the traditional one of a daughter, Julie, who falls promptly and irrevocably in love before consulting her father, the baron. She chooses Saint-Preux, the informal tutor of the household, and her love is chaste, passionate, and sentimental. With so unpatrician a choice, a wedge is driven between Julie and her parents, and the parental function devolves on her cousin Claire. When Claire is present, chastity and sentimentality are preserved, but when she is absent, all is sullied by sexuality.

Preux), Rousseau gave the greater power to the male. *Une Lecture du temps dans "La Nouvelle Héloïse"* (Neuchâtel: La Baconnière, 1968), p. 40.

3. The two parts are the time before Saint-Preux's long voyage and the time after he returns; the coda concerning the death of Julie joins both parts by reactivating the passionate Julie of the first.

MANIPULATIVE FRIENDSHIP

With the mania for varied repetition that afflicts the chief characters, Julie follows her seduction with its reversal. Saint-Preux is enticed to spend a night in the sanctuary of the bedroom itself. It is the last titillation the reader is allowed. Julie's father, absent while such havoc was played with his daughter, returns to avenge the disgrace to his blood. He severs Julie from Saint-Preux and confirms the breach by insisting she marry his old friend, the noble M de Wolmar. His insistence becomes compelling when Julie's mother, long ailing, dies at the height of the drama, seemingly a victim to its tension. Grief-stricken and guilt-ridden, Julie is reinstated as daughter and led to the altar of parental duty. Saint-Preux in time embarks on a voyage of four years, one of fiction's longest.[4] The first half of the novel closes on the youth of the lovers.

In such a Cornelian drama, we would expect the lovers to hold center stage. Claire seems essential only as the confidante, wearily named the *"constant* cousin" by Saint-Preux and calling herself the "duenna of eighteen."[5] And, as expected, the action is dominated by Julie. She is the principal object of everyone's view and her every gesture is followed, observed, and meticulously recorded.[6] She is analyzed and evaluated more than described (we remain surprisingly unacquainted with her appearance), but her actions and context are lovingly depicted. Of the four main characters Julie alone is given a full name and family background. We know only the married name of Claire; the mother is

4. It may even have been longer since Rousseau is confused about the period. There are hints that the time should be six years or even eight.

5. Most critics have ignored Claire or treated her only in passing as an unnecessary character (John Charpentier in *Rousseau, the Child of Nature* [New York: The Dial Press, 1931], p. 190) or as a literary relic of Richardson (Daniel Mornet in *Rousseau: l'Homme et l'oeuvre* [Paris: Hatier-Boivin, 1950], pp. 80–81.) The two most sustained attempts to understand her character and function are David Anderson's "Aspects of motif in *La Nouvelle Héloïse*," *Studies on Voltaire and the Eighteenth Century* 94 (1972), 25–72, and Hans Wolpe's "Psychological Ambiguity in *La Nouvelle Héloïse*," *University of Toronto Quarterly* 28, no. 3 (April 1959), 279–90. David Anderson discusses primarily the symbolic importance of Claire, Hans Wolpe the erotic.

6. François Van Laere argues that Julie absorbs the sensibility of others, who all wish to give their souls to her. By the end of the novel she has become a messianic archetype, a redeemer, and the book forms a kind of "Imitation of Julie," resembling that of Christ, *Une Lecture du temps*, p. 76.

dead, and the brother and father hazily rendered. Saint-Preux's name is hidden behind the pseudonym Claire bestows and he is without family. Wolmar conceals his name and country while hinting at the high nobility of his birth. Julie alone is the daughter of palpable parents, existing in a realized location; she marries and lives in her father's house in a community of husband, children, servants and laborers, whom we come to know because of her. Even her effects are more vital than other people's: her letters are saved and read by all, while her clothes are viewed with rapture by friend and lover alike. All the characters center on and live in Julie, and it is as hard for the reader as for them to switch regard to anyone beyond her. Indeed such switching seems a furtive act, the secret spying on the hidden photographer. To spy on Claire is especially treacherous since her eye is one of the most potent and all-encompassing in this novel of voyeurs.[7] But we must be guilty of such furtiveness if we are to look beyond the clarity of Claire, the friend, and discern the ambiguity of the friendship into which she enters.[8]

The passion of Saint-Preux and Julie is romantic, often death directed, often a subtle battle for sexual mastery. By Julie it is sometimes imaged as addictive poison while at other times she sees it as a precipice to which she is unwillingly compelled. The lovers are shamed and degraded in the combat with each other and with their passion. Both Saint-Preux and Julie see love as madness and irrationality: under its influence Saint-Preux declares that his brains are turned and his senses disordered, while Julie views herself as a divided being, whose other half becomes Saint-Preux. He is part of her existence and she owns but a partial mind.[9]

7. The major treatment of voyeurism in *Julie* occurs in Jean Starobinski's *Jean-Jacques Rousseau: La Transparence et l'obstacle* (Paris: Gallimard, 1971) and *L'Oeil vivant* (Paris: Gallimard, 1961).

8. As the remainder of the study will show, I would quarrel with Starobinski's assumption of Claire's transparency (complete openness), *La Transparence et l'obstacle*, p. 105.

9. The fullest discussion of passionate love's association with death and suffering is in Denis de Rougemont's *Love in the Western World*, trans. Montgomery Belgion (New

MANIPULATIVE FRIENDSHIP

In opposition Claire creates herself as the reasonable and protecting friend, a fitting companion to the impetuous heroine of sensibility. Moderate, commonsensical and humorous, she counters the passionate excesses of Saint-Preux and the fulsome responses of the lovers. Saint-Preux points out that she reasons better because she does not love and that indeed she has become "more knowing than her preceptor."[10] With the arrogance of the lover, however, he treats this preeminence ironically: "though we have sometimes smiled at her pretensions, she is really the only one of the three who retains any part of our reading" (I, xii).

To Julie, Claire at first brings wholeness. In her initial letter, Julie begs Claire's return, discerning "You alone can restore me to myself" (I,vi). After her fall, which occurs while Claire is away, Julie names Claire her tender friend, guardian angel and

York: Pantheon, 1956). In "Female Sexuality and Narrative Structure in *La Nouvelle Héloïse* and *Les Liaisons dangereuses*," Nancy K. Miller analyzes the seduction of Julie, noting that, while Saint-Preux has presented himself as the victim of love and of Julie, his passive stance is not without violence. She comments too on the struggle between the lovers, for where Saint-Preux wants sensual recognition, Julie requires platonic love organized according to the pattern of courtly love, *Signs* 1, no. 3 (Spring 1976), 615–19. Christie McDonald Vance sees Saint-Preux's confession of love as "a kind of aggression" and she notes that, until Julie's marriage, confusion in the feelings of the two lovers dominates their relationship, *The Extravagant Shepherd: a study of the pastoral vision in Rousseau's "Nouvelle Héloïse,"* in *Studies in Voltaire and the Eighteenth Century* 105 (1973), pp. 77–79.

10. There is no modern unabridged English version of *Julie.* I have used the French Pleiade text in *Jean-Jacques Rousseau: Oeuvres Complètes* (Paris: Bibliothèque de la Pleiade, 1969); the numbers in my text refer to the volumes and letters of this edition. I have, however, quoted from an English translation of the eighteenth century, *Julia; or, the New Eloisa* (Edinburgh: J. Bell, J. Dickson, and C. Elliot, 1773). The first English version appeared in April 1761; the translator was William Kenrick and his text formed the basis of all eighteenth- and nineteenth-century translations. His work has been criticized by James H. Warner in "Eighteenth Century English Reactions to *La Nouvelle Héloïse*," *PMLA* (September 1937), 803–19, and by Judith H. McDowell, the translator of the modern abridged version of *Julie* (University Park: Pennsylvania State University Press, 1968). They accuse Kenrick of inappropriately using the conventional style of the eighteenth-century English novel of sentiment, a style unsuited to the impassioned tone of the original. However, I do not judge Kenrick's version so harshly; the problems of translation are eternal, and the prose style of the eighteenth-century novel, however misleading, may be less alien to Rousseau than the informal and engaging style of the twentieth century.

only resource, blaming her for her absence: "Cruel Claire! to leave me when I stand most in need of your assistance!" (I, xxviii). In Claire alone the poison of self-contempt from indulged passion has an antidote: she alone brings self-esteem to Julie.

As passion becomes more and more controlling, however, Julie is reduced, parted from her reason and her self-esteem, and, caught between her lover's frenzy and her father's anger, she seems almost to vest her rational qualities in Claire. Now Claire must act for her, not with her, since she cannot bring wholeness; despairingly Julie writes: "I have no resource, my dear friend, but in you. Let me prevail on you then to think, to speak, to act for me. I put myself into your hands: whatever step you think proper to take, I hereby confirm beforehand every thing you do; I commit to your friendship that sad authority over a lover which I have bought so dear" (I, lxiii).[11] Claire inevitably appears the reasonable rival of the passionate Saint-Preux, helping Julie retain her sanity, acting for her when necessary, and guarding her when possible from the consequences of passion.

Yet the impression Claire gives is far more complex than such dualism suggests. When Julie invests in her the "sad authority" over a lover and puts herself into her friend's hands, we suspect that she accepts rather than confers authority. Throughout the novel Claire is relied on, condemned, appreciated, and obeyed by the lovers, but none of their statements does justice to her brooding presence. Claire is a personage beyond her supportive meaning for Julie and indeed beyond her prose re-creation of herself as an affectionate and sensible friend. Despite her name she remains elusive and unclear.

Julie's crises of love occur in Claire's absences; indeed so habitual is this pattern that we can almost see this absence as their essence. The love of Saint-Preux springs up when Claire is away

11. Claire and Julie not only help each other but also play each other's roles, as David Anderson has pointed out. Under emotional stress, Julie affects behavior patterns similar to Claire, "Aspects of motif," pp. 50–51. That these patterns are associated with stress suggests that Claire cannot be so easily identified with reasoned calmness as she appears to wish.

mourning La Chaillot, her governess; it is consummated when Claire leaves again. Her return resolves crises, often cruelly but always decisively. When Saint-Preux is banished the first time, Julie is reduced to a confusion of passion and apprehension; she cannot completely confide in Claire or find comfort in her until— in true heroine fashion—she is plunged into a feverish illness. Then Claire returns as confidante and supporter, summoning Saint-Preux to save her friend. The illness past, the father angered, and the town gossiping about the liaison, Claire again dispatches Saint-Preux. Such episodes make Claire one of the few people in the novel whose actions balance her words.[12] Since actions are the most obscure elements in an epistolary novel, here perhaps is one cause of Claire's elusiveness.

Claire's motives are as elusive as her actions. Although she seems rigorous in countering the excesses of Julie's love, she in fact functions to encourage them. In the grove at Clarens, Julie's father's house, she takes part in an erotic game. She kisses Saint-Preux first, as earnest of the kiss from her more desired cousin. The orgasmic kiss of Julie and Saint-Preux that follows she both witnesses and shares.[13] It becomes the lyrical antecedent of the sexual act Julie blames Claire for not preventing.

At the end of the novel we learn that Claire has come to love Saint-Preux; perhaps she already does so in the grove, enjoying him vicariously through Julie, while simultaneously working to part the lovers she envies. Yet ultimately Claire refuses Saint-Preux, and never for one moment through six volumes lets him

---

12. Patrick Brady has analyzed the plot of *Julie* in terms of the pattern of correspondence. He notes that of the 163 letters of the novel, Saint-Preux writes 65, receives 62; Julie writes 53 and receives 60; while Claire writes only 26 and receives 19. Yet her letters dominate during crises; the seduction and separation are marked by the replacement of the lovers' dialogue by a series of four letters dominated by Claire, "Structural Affiliations of *La Nouvelle Héloïse*," *L'Esprit Créateur* 9, no. 3 (Fall 1969), pp. 208–9.

13. Hans Wolpe discusses this scene with reference to a well-known engraving by Deveria which renders Rousseau's ambiguity: "Julie swoons under the caress of Saint Preux, but quite as close to her as the young man, Claire supports her, watching, eyes wide open in an expressionless face. Julie's dress is light, Claire's dark, and while Julie abandons her lips to Saint Preux, she yields her hand—to Claire," in "Psychological Ambiguity," p. 282.

come before Julie in her regard. If there is erotic feeling here for Saint-Preux, vicariousness seems essential to it; it is Julie in love who ravishes.

The kiss in the wood is not the only erotic encounter to which Claire is privy. At Julie's invitation Saint-Preux enters her bedroom and arouses himself with a passion for her underwear:

> Every part of your scattered dress presents to my glowing imagination the charms it has concealed. . . . Heavens, what a charming shape! how the top of the stomacher is waved in two gentle curves—luxurious sight! the whalebone has yielded to their impression—delicious impression! let me devour it with kisses!—O gods! how shall I be able to bear—Ah! methinks I feel already a tender heart beat softly under my happy hand; Julie, my charming Julie, I see, I feel thee at every pore. We now breathe the same air. (I, liv) [14]

A private ecstasy it appears, and yet Claire has shared it through a letter. Again we are not told who it is that interests her in this scene. Does she enjoy Saint-Preux through watching his fetishism or does she rather respond to the ravishing effect of Julie's sacred garments?

Certainly the love of Julie and Claire is no secret in the novel and its relationship to the passion of Julie and Saint-Preux casts an odd light on Claire's persistent identification with reason. In an early letter Claire writes: "The ardent and tender friendship which hath united us, almost from our cradles, expanded our hearts, and ripened them into sensibility, too soon, perhaps for our repose" (I,vii). Like the lesbian tie of Fanny Hill and Phoebe, the friendship of the two women has prepared the way for heterosexual passion; clearly, however, it has not given way. The friendship remains so close that Saint-Preux is sometimes uneasy about it, writing bitterly of "a friend and cousin, who seems to breathe only for your sake." At other times he is transported by the image of friendship which he sees as a similacrum of his love:

14. Discussing Saint-Preux's apparent fetishism here, Starobinski notes how Julie's clothes receive the effluvia of her presence and become sanctified for Saint-Preux. They act as visible messengers of the ideal Julie, *L'Oeil vivant*, p. 116.

139

it was ecstacy itself, to see two such perfect beauties embrace each other so affectionately; your face reclined upon her breast. . . . I grew jealous of such a friendship, and thought there was something more interesting in it than even in love itself. . . . No, nothing, nothing upon earth is capable of exciting so pleasing a sensation as your mutual caresses; not even the sight of two lovers would have yielded such delight. (I, xxxviii)

Yet his contemplation does not lead him to understand more profoundly the fondness of Julie and Claire; instead he becomes ecstatically aware of Julie alone, while Claire disappears: "O how could I have admired, nay, adored your dear cousin, if the divine Julie herself had not taken up all my thoughts." Such a loving process can help interpret Claire's contemplation of Saint-Preux in Julie's bedroom. In this book all ecstasy and desire lead inexorably to Julie.

On the eve of her marriage to M d'Orbe Claire analyzes herself and concludes that her prime identity is indeed as friend:

as a woman, I am a kind of monster; and by whatsoever strange whim of nature it happens, I feel that my friendship is more powerful than my love. When I tell you that my Julie is dearer to me than yourself, you only laugh at me; and yet nothing can be more certain. Julie is so sensible of this, that she is more jealous for you than you are for yourself. (I,lxiv)

Like Anna Howe, Claire will not marry until all is well with her friend. The marriage she contemplates is reduced to tranquil reasonableness, while the female relationship is exalted into passion.

When the friendship seems actually threatened, it flames out from Claire's pen even more brightly. Saint-Preux's protector Lord Bomston has offered the lovers an asylum in England away from the tyranny of the father. Julie is sorely tempted, but shrinks back when she contemplates the loss of parents and cousin:

even you my dear Claire; you my gentle friend, so well beloved of my heart; you, who from our earliest infancy have hardly ever been absent from me a day; shall I leave you, lose you, never see you more? (II, iv)

Claire replies to such treason by declaring her love and promising (or threatening) to accompany Julie wherever she goes:

Can you think there subsists between us but an ordinary connection? Do not mine eyes communicate their sparkling joy in meeting yours? Do you not perceive in my heart the pleasure of partaking your pains, and lamenting with you? Can I forget, that, in the first transports of a growing passion, my friendship was never disagreeable; and that the complaints of your lover could never have prevailed on you to send me from you, or prevent me from being a witness to your weakness? This, my Julie, was a critical juncture. I am sensible how great a sacrifice you made to modesty, in making me acquainted with an error I happily escaped. Never should I have been your confident had I been but half your friend: no our souls felt themselves too intimately united for any thing ever to part them. . . . You know that an unparalleled affection for you possesses my heart, and almost stifles every other sentiment. From my infancy I have been attached to you by an habitual and irresistible impulse; so that I perfectly love no one else. (II, v)

Earlier when Julie had considered fleeing with Saint-Preux, Claire had replied not entirely with humor: "I would have sought you out to the ends of the earth to kill you" (I, xxx).

Claire expresses love furiously but only when her friendship is threatened. At other times she seems content occasionally to substitute her love for the primary passion of Saint-Preux and to comfort when Saint-Preux is cruel. Yet the glimpses of her furious love hint that such appearance masks a deeper reality. Claire is powerful and manipulative in action and is indeed for the lovers a sort of *dea ex machina* of the plot. It need not be shocking then to realize that in the first part of *Julie* Claire does in fact coopt the love of Julie and Saint-Preux, forcing its events into the history and geography of female friendship.[15]

15. Both Saint-Preux and Claire try to control the time and space of Julie. Constantly they need to know where she is and when she arrives or leaves; at the same time both anticipate her future and remake her past.

MANIPULATIVE FRIENDSHIP

According to Jean Starobinski, to look at something is to aim at protecting it.[16] The eye penetrates the personality of another, establishing a relationship between itself and its object. Claire joins the other compulsive gazers in looking at Julie, but her looking—and the knowing it implies—penetrates more deeply than the look of any other. Julie is often wrong in her regard—for example, she errs about Babi, her maid, whom she trusts to have burnt Saint-Preux's letters, and about her husband's ignorance of her early liaison; Saint-Preux is conspicuously astray when he sees Lord Bomston as his rival. Claire is rarely wrong and her look is ubiquitous. There is hardly a letter that she does not see. Even the drafts of the letters of Saint-Preux to Julie find their way through Lord Bomston to Claire. She looks everywhere, seeking out hidden thoughts in Julie and her lover, foreseeing events and revealing old ones. She anticipates the fall of Julie and so insinuates herself even into this action. In a strange way she insists she caused it. "I alone am responsible," she declares, since seeing or foreseeing is for Claire knowledge and action.

With her powerful and coercive look, Claire influences Julie at every turn. She hides and reveals things as she wills. When she lowers the veil over Julie's sexual fall, for example, it is lowered and nothing further is discovered. She is keeper of the veil, and, as she raises or drops it, so the other characters see.[17] It is a role dramatically fulfilled only in Julie's death.

For Julie, Claire often becomes not only the interpretative eye but even the seeing one, and she views the world far more through Claire than through Saint-Preux, whose vision we expected to dominate the novel. Claire's prose alone allows Julie to see the quarrel of Saint-Preux and Lord Bomston, as well as the latter's rash but generous testament on behalf of his friend. On both occasions Julie must act on Claire's information and with

16. *Jean-Jacques Rousseau.*
17. In *Jean-Jacques Rousseau,* Starobinski fully discusses the significance of the veil in all its manifestations. Frequently it functions as an obstacle to be removed before transparence or clarity can be achieved.

Claire's aid.[18] A more startling example of such vicarious seeing occurs when Julie falls ill shortly before her mother dies. In her fever she sees what she takes to be a vision of Saint-Preux by her bedside. Her sight is clouded and she cannot distinguish between dream and reality. It is Claire who aligns Julie's sight with reality by confirming that Saint-Preux was indeed no ghost; she herself was present and conceived the scene for Julie's benefit.

The element of control and manipulation in Claire's constant looking at and for Julie is unmistakable. It is an element that can be found in many of Claire's dealings with the lovers, especially during Julie's crises. Initially when Julie is caught up in her passion Claire seems diminished—Saint-Preux fills her soul and pushes Claire aside. Yet it is in the passionate crises—often precipitated by her absence or playful tricks—that Claire becomes most indispensable. After Julie's fall and during her illnesses, Claire mediates between the lovers. She speaks and acts for Julie, entering into her life in undoubted possession. She is not displacing Julie to approach Saint-Preux, but rather appropriating Julie by taking over her love. Julie accepts the control: "Let me prevail on you then to think, to speak, to act for me," she begs.

But Julie has declared herself a divided being; it is not enough, then, for Claire to control only her friend. Half of her resides with Saint-Preux. To her fiancé, M d'Orbe, Claire writes, "I am even so strongly interested in every thing which concerns her that her lover and you hold nearly the same place in my heart" (I, lxiv). When she exiles Saint-Preux to save Julie from further tension between father and lover, she celebrates her victory by making Saint-Preux accept his exile. Where she had once been resented as an unwelcome companion of the woman he wished to enjoy alone, she now becomes Saint-Preux's cousin, as charming to him as to Julie, and like Julie he comes to rely on her for his action and thought. "Abandon me not, Claire," he

18. David Anderson notes that Julie's absence from the scene of action at the time of the quarrel of Saint-Preux and Lord Bomston is not explained. He concludes that Rousseau must have intended the quarrel to be settled through a letter from Claire. "Aspects of motif," p. 51.

prays, "assist me to recover my former self, and let your gentle counsel supply the dictates of reason to my afflicted heart" (II, x).

Claire even manages to enter the lovers' correspondence. When Saint-Preux is sent on his European travels, he writes to both cousins together. The replies written by Julie incorporate Claire's sentiments. Julie may mildly grumble at such control when she terms Claire's strictures on Saint-Preux's style "hyper-criticisms," but the joint letter is testament to her general acceptance. When Julie sends her portrait to Saint-Preux, Claire again is present in the gift and in the giving. One portrait goes to Saint-Preux, and one to Claire, and it is Claire who has dictated the images they enshrine. Her mediation here is so extreme that even Saint-Preux mildly rebels, objecting to Claire's taste in covering Julie's head with flowers; in revenge he hires a painter to simplify the image and make it his own.

Claire's control over her beloved Julie through her relationship with Julie's lover is almost complete during Saint-Preux's exile. She may then enter a cool marriage with M d'Orbe, knowing that it will not endanger the primary friendship. Circuitously this marriage precipitates the final crisis for the lovers, a crisis which seems to nullify Saint-Preux forever.

Mindful of Claire's dignity as a wife and the subordinate position it implies, Julie insists on taking back from Claire the love letters of Saint-Preux which she had been guarding. Less watchful than her cousin, she allows these to fall into the hands of her mother, so speeding her toward the death she had long been courting. The guilt kills all Julie's slender hopes of Saint-Preux, for she sees the poison of his love entering her mother, and fatally wounding her.[19] The marriage to the father's friend and substitute, Wolmar, can alone reinstate the daughter. To announce this marriage Claire takes over the correspondence with

19. Noting that the mother dies after discovering Julie's secret correspondence, Nancy Miller concludes, "The pen/dagger/phallus that kills Julie's filial innocence thus indirectly destroys the maternal principle as well." "Female Sexuality and Narrative Structure," p. 625.

Saint-Preux which she had before merely entered. It is Claire who gives Julie the married character for Saint-Preux and asserts that she has become Madame de Wolmar; more triumphantly Claire declares, "Your mistress is no more; but I have regained my friend."

Before the opening of the book there existed a female triad consisting of Claire, Julie, and their governess, La Chaillot. The entry of Saint-Preux, breaking the female community, is simultaneous with La Chaillot's death. But only Julie removes her love to the male preceptor; Claire remains grieving, faithful to the community of women and to Julie as female relative.

In Julie's first letter to Claire we see the conflict that this first difference between the two young women causes. Julie tries to wean Claire from the dead Chaillot, declaring that she has sorrowed long enough. She seeks to end the extreme sorrow in two ways: by degrading La Chaillot in Claire's eyes and by putting herself in the place of reverence. La Chaillot is blamed for eroticizing their childhood, for giving dangerous lessons to young girls, for titillating with cautionary tales of love. So convinced is Julie of her own story that she even comes to see divine intervention in her governess's death: "who knows but heaven may have taken her from us the very moment in which her removal became necessary to our future happiness" (I, vi).[20] It is an odd spurning of the female at the moment when the male preceptor is corrupting her heart with actual letters of love. For Claire it is not a convincing hypothesis.

Julie is far more successful in her bid for substitution. "Will you forget the living because of the dead?" she demands. Claire answers by holding fast to both La Chaillot and Julie, quoting her governess's appreciative words of Julie and the flippant judgment on herself. In her picture we come to see the nature of the

---

20. The utter self-centeredness of the characters in *Julie* is occasionally almost beyond belief. Julie's statement here is equalled only by Saint-Preux's exclamations after the death of Julie's mother: "what is the life of a mother . . . what is the existence of the whole world, to the delightful sensation by which we were united?" (III, iii).

golden age of Claire. La Chaillot, the surrogate mother of both girls, welds them together into a closer kinship than nature has allowed, making one family whose adored center is Julie. It is a family of shifting relationships, for La Chaillot is not only a mother to the motherless Claire, but her sister as well, and the cousins regard each other variously as mother and child. La Chaillot provides the context of closeness for Claire and Julie to act out their drama of familial closeness, and her stories gently eroticize it. In this secure world Claire seems blissfully happy and we can perceive the meaning for her of the irruption of Saint-Preux. La Chaillot is dead and only Julie remains to mitigate Claire's orphan state. Claire must keep Julie as mother, child, and sister if she is not to be unremittingly alone.[21]

Existing separately from the hothouse of the female triad are the parents of Julie. They are a traditional pair, the mother weak and benevolent, the father possessive and tyrannical. Caught like Clarissa between judgment and affection, Julie vacillates between views of her father as the best and the most barbarous of men and between acceptance of her mother as the most loving of women and the most cruel.

Julie's mother, less exclusive than the lover, seems less threatening to Claire than Saint-Preux. When Julie is clearly a daughter, Claire still has the close role of sister, and there is no expulsion and no carping at her constant presence. So Claire fosters Julie's ties with her mother and contemplates with foreboding any relaxing of them. And the baroness too is caught in her perceptive regard: "your mother's suspicions are daily increasing," Claire declares to an unconscious Julie, and she divines the hidden motivation of maternal conformism as well as benevo-

21. In the second part of the novel when Claire has in a way become mother and child to her cousin, Julie rejects La Chaillot more forcefully: "You confide in the opinion of La Chaillot; who, because of your vivacity of disposition, judged you to be little susceptible of heart; but a heart like yours was beyond her talents to penetrate. La Chaillot was incapable of knowing you, nor does any person in the world know you truly but myself" (V, xiii). Claire counters by synthesizing her own and Julie's views: La Chaillot saw and understood that Claire's heart was absorbed in Julie's and that her cousin "alone stood in the place of the whole world."

lence: "if she did not dread the violence of your father's temper, I am certain she would already have opened her mind to him; but she is conscious that the blame would fall chiefly on herself" (I, lvi). Claire understands that the mother clings to the daughter against the father out of weakness. Through such a mother Claire can approach her friend without fearing the strength of the mediator. When Saint-Preux and the mother struggle for Julie, Claire sides easily with the mother.

As the baroness approaches death, Claire increases in power, emboldened by Julie's extreme grief and the mother's pain. At the end Claire controls both mother and daughter, commanding the absence and presence of Saint-Preux and arranging all correspondence. When the mother wishes to write humbly and fondly to Saint-Preux, Claire tears up the letter, preventing direct communication. She will have no mother humble herself before her daughter's seducer, she declares; at the same time she ensures her own position of universal mediator. Like the daughter, the mother must—and does—speak through Claire.

Julie's father is a domestic tyrant of a familiar kind, irritable, and arrogant, proud of his masculinity and his patrician birth. He opposes his daughter's union with Saint-Preux with all the weapons at his command. First he tries to appeal to her well-developed sense of duty. When passion still seems powerful against this stern weapon, he uses violence and emotional coercion. Claire is witness to all his attempts, which are meticulously related to her by her cousin.

The great scene of father and daughter is staged when the baron learns of Saint-Preux's pretensions to Julie. It starts with a confrontation of arrogant husband and meek, apologetic wife: "He began by exclaiming violently . . . against such mothers as indiscreetly invite to their houses young fellows without family or fortune." For some time he rails against the complicity of women but can draw little response from his intimidated wife. Ultimately, however, he provokes her into praise of Julie, whose actual peccadilloes neither one suspects. In the course of this paean the father becomes so disturbed by the idea Saint-Preux embodies that he abruptly loses all restraint, revealing to the frightened women the ultimate source of his power, his physical strength:

> He took notice of my looks, cast down, and affrighted, in consequence of my remorse; and if he did not construe them into those of my guilt, he did into looks of my love; but to shame me the more, he abused the object of it in terms so odious and contemptible, that in spite of all my endeavours, I could not let him proceed without interruption.
>
> I know not, my dear, whence I had so much courage, or how I came so far to trespass the bounds of modesty and duty; but, if I ventured to break for a moment that respectful silence they dictate, I suffered for it, as you will see, very severely. For heaven's sake, my dear father, said I, be pacified: never could your daughter be in danger from a man deserving such abuse. I had scarce spoken, when, as if he had felt himself reproved by what I said, or that his passion wanted only a pretext for extremities, he flew upon your poor friend, and for the first time in my life I received from him a box on the ear: nor was this all, but, giving himself up entirely to his passion, he proceeded to beat me without mercy, notwithstanding my mother threw herself in between us, to screen me from his blows, and received many of those which were intended for me. At length, in running back to avoid them, my foot slipt, and I fell down with my face against the foot of a table.
>
> Here ended the triumph of passion, and begun that of nature. My fall, the sight of my blood, my tears, and those of my mother, greatly affected him. He raised me up with an air of affliction and solicitude; and having placed me in a chair, they both eagerly inquired where I was hurt. I had received only a slight bruise on my forehead, and bled only at the nose. (I, lxiii)

Shame follows rapidly and the father soon becomes remorseful: "Surely, my dear, there is no confusion so affecting as that of a tender father, who thinks himself to blame in his treatment of a child."

There is much of interest in this violent scene. First, of course, we have seen it before. The nosebleed gives it away if nothing else. But this is the first time that we have had a father so directly involved. When Lovelace caused Clarissa's nosebleed and "the fine gentleman" Fanny Hill's, the two men were intent on rape. This would be too strong a word for the action of Julie's father, but certainly some of its elements are present. The scene itself derives in part from sexual jealousy, the fear that the woman whom the father owns has slipped from his possession. The blows rain on both mother and daughter. Later we learn from Claire that the baron is given to sexual straying and that he has responded paradoxically by mistreating his wife; the blows he gives her may form a pattern with his earlier treatment.

After the bloody wounding of Julie, the father is appeased—almost like a satisfied lover or a husband secure in his wife's virginity. He relents not one whit to the rival, Saint-Preux, but he feels his danger less. Julie is reinstated as his property, whether as daughter or lover. Indeed, in reasserting his claim he succeeds more than he knows. The nosebleed is but the foreshadowing of the greater bleeding from miscarriage; through his blows, the father has murdered the child of Julie and Saint-Preux, the pledge of their love and their only route to future union. The child would have been Julie's first born, the dangerous one of unfamilial love; when she bears another son, it will be in the image of the father's closest friend.

After his brutal declaration of paternal power and authority, the baron takes great and uncommon pains to make Julie feel the comforts of being a daughter. Frequently he addresses her as daughter, instead of the habitual Julie, and after supper he even places her on his knee. It is a paternal knee, not a lover's, and the father restrains an impulse to embrace his daughter. Julie gives the impulse and its restraint a gentle interpretation:

> a certain gravity, he was ashamed to depart from, a confusion he durst not overcome, occasioned between a father and his daughter the same charming embarrassment, as love and modesty cause between lovers; in the mean while a most affectionate mother, transported with pleasure, secretly enjoyed the delightful sight. (I, lxiii)

Transports and remorse mingle together and mother and daughter are strangely confounded.

149

This is not, however, the end of the incident. In the other literary nosebleeds, the feminine blood has been displayed for female eyes. *Julie* is no exception. The scene of paternal brutality and passion is hidden from the lover, but minutely depicted for Claire who alone is aware of all its elements. It is Claire for whom, ultimately, the blood flows and it is Claire to whom Julie turns at the end of the letter with the agonized plea that she will take over her mind, voice, and pen, and deal with lover and father alike: "Let me prevail on you then to think, to speak, to act for me." The outcome of the appeal is the dismissal of Saint-Preux and through it the neutralization of the father's passion. In the marriage with Wolmar, which Saint-Preux's absence allows, Julie becomes a wife and, most importantly for Claire, her friend again. In the second half of the novel the father dwindles into a shadow of his former self. His authority and even his physical force are spent.

After she has married Wolmar with much filial duty but without love, the new Julie writes a letter to Saint-Preux which forms the center of the novel. In it she recapitulates the course of their love and her progress from Saint-Preux to Wolmar. It is the letter of a wife, a woman who has gained authority through Claire. After her mother's death, Julie asserts, she felt her "incomparable friend" was never more great or more deserving wholly to engross her heart: "Her virtue, her discretion, her friendship, her tender caresses, seemed to have purified it" (III, xviii). For the marriage with Wolmar she learns from the judicious example of Claire, who has in a way married to provide just such a model for her beloved cousin. In the Orbe marriage Julie sees a couple "with a gentle and refined affection, which nourishes the mind, which prudence authorizes, and which reason directs." At the marriage with Wolmar, Claire is on hand, and she blesses the union with her presence. With Wolmar in charge, Claire can be for Julie both parent and lover.

2

MARRIAGE
The last three volumes of the novel recount the married life of
Julie and Wolmar. We meet them some six years after their wedding, surrounded by their two boys and a host of happy domes-
tics. Together they have established at Clarens a model community, autocratic certainly but benevolent and secure too. It is the
image of Wolmar's mind and marriage.

By this time Claire has lost her husband and, with her little
girl, is free to devote herself entirely to her cousin. Against the
background of Clarens, she allows her own personality and character to open. If Claire dominated with her hidden eye the first
half of the novel, she dominates the second with a more visible
one. Her approaches to Julie become less tortuous and the relationships she aims to establish are more distinct, though still
mediated.

When we first meet her again, Julie, happy in her society of
Clarens, is working to draw into it the two people her marriage
seemed to exclude. Claire is invited to live in the Wolmar household with her daughter, to be a surrogate mother to Julie's children; Saint-Preux, now returned as a reformed lover, is to be included as tutor and surrogate father. To try his worth and his
wife's virtue, Wolmar devises a series of tests in which the erst-
while lovers are forced to reenact the past by visiting the scenes
that enshrine it. Through these incidents, Saint-Preux is brought
to learn that he loves a past Julie and that he esteems and
cherishes the present Mme de Wolmar. Chastened, he accepts
Wolmar as his friend and mentor and prepares to move into
Clarens. But Julie remains uneasy at his reformation and she
urges him to cement his growing friendship with Claire by marriage. For different reasons both demur, although Saint-Preux
hints that he might ultimately comply. Before he can be further
tested, he is compelled to leave for Italy to aid his friend Lord
Bomstom.

151

MANIPULATIVE FRIENDSHIP

In this second part of the novel, Claire seems to have a rival as seer and controller. Wolmar characterizes himself as a living eye, a passionless man who would if possible be all observation. He is rational, judicious, acute, and wonderfully knowing. His environment mirrors him. "The economy he has established in his household, is the image of that order which reigns in his own breast," declares Saint-Preux on experiencing him. Like Claire he seems to know all that passes and he can impose his will on others through his knowledge. It is said too that he once felt something like passion for Julie and he cries for the first and only time as she expresses love for him in death. Yet the reader does not feel his passion or really experience his obvious control over others; indeed, the much-vaunted control seems unsubtle beside Claire's insidious one. Claire, the passionate friend with her reasonable counsel and controlling eye continues to dominate.[22]

In the second part, the relationship of Julie and Claire blossoms, now no longer in the shadow of Saint-Preux. The first letter of Julie establishes the tone:

> My dear and tender friend, we are both sensible how much time, habit, and your kindness have rendered our attachment more strong and indissoluble. As to myself, your absence daily becomes more insupportable, and I can now no longer live for a moment without you. The progress of our friendship is more natural than it appears to be; it is founded not only on a similarity of character, but of condition. As we advance in years, our affections begin to centre on one point. We every day lose something that was dear to us, which we can never replace. Thus we perish by degrees, till at length, being wholly devoted to self-love, we lose life and sensibility, even before our existence ceases. But a susceptible mind arms itself with all its force against this anticipated death: when a chillness begins to seize the extremities, it collects all the genial warmth of nature round its own centre; the more connections it loses, the closer it cleaves to those which remain, and all its former ties are combined to attach it to the last object. (IV, i)

22. Hans Wolpe has noted that Claire sets the pace in the second half of *Julie* and that her character imposes itself far more than Wolmar's. "Psychological Ambiguity," p. 285.

MANIPULATIVE FRIENDSHIP

Julie accepts Claire as the shadow of mother and lover, those two ties she has lost, and anticipates their closeness in death.

Both women wish closeness—even more, it seems, than in their early days—and Wolmar considers that two such intimates should not live asunder. Claire has lost her husband and, although she has felt no passion for him, she grieves at his loss. She grieves perhaps too for her years apart from Julie, for the tears Julie accuses her of shedding privately are swiftly dried when their union is assured. On her part, Julie avidly desires association with Claire, for her cousin enshrines not only the dearness of the present but the sweetness of the past, and she couches her appeal to her friend in terms of the history they both share: "I have not forgotten the time when you would have followed me to England. My incomparable friend! it is now my turn" (IV, i). Julie images their union through family and function; they will become one in both. At the same time her image is melancholy and resigned:

> I am indebted to you for all the blessings I enjoy, I see nothing but what reminds me of your goodness, and without you I am nothing. Come then, my much loved friend, my guardian angel; come and enjoy the work of your own hands, come and gather the fruits of your benevolence. Let us have but one family, as we have but one soul to cherish it; you shall superintend the education of my sons, and I will take care of your daughter; we will share the maternal duties between us, and make our pleasure double. We will raise our minds together to the contemplation of that Being, who purified mine by means of your endeavours; and having nothing more to hope for in this life, we will quietly wait for the next, in the bosom of innocence and friendship. (IV, i)

When Claire answers this letter she laughs at its elegiac tone; her broken sentences—echoing the breathless style of Saint-Preux's passion—mock Julie's calm assumption that in their friendship all passions are spent.

Claire has been happy in marriage; yet after it she reiterates the sentiment expressed on its eve, that Julie is primary. "While he [her husband] was living, he shared my affections with you;

153

when he was gone, I was yours entirely" (IV, ii). Like Anna Howe she shows the reluctance of the female friend to marry, but like Clarissa she realizes that for a woman in society marriage may be the only route to freedom:

> If my determination had depended on myself alone, I should never have married. But our sex cannot purchase liberty but by slavery; and before we can become our own mistresses, we must begin by being servants. Though my father did not confine me, I was not without uneasiness in my family. To free myself from that vexation, therefore, I married M. d'Orbe. He was so worthy a man and loved me with such tenderness, that I most sincerely loved him in my turn. (IV, ii)[23]

She has made a conventionally good wife, it seems, but she has done so by repressing much of herself. She has not laughed enough for seven years, she declares, and her gaiety of spirits has been miserably confined. She has missed passion and its extremes of joy and sorrow. It is after the respectful contemplation of her husband that she rapturously describes the meaning of her friend throughout the years:

> I love you, though you eclipse me! Julie, you were born to rule. Your empire is more despotic than any in the world. It extends even over the will, and I experience it more than any one. How happens it, my dear cousin? We are both in love with virtue; honour is equally dear to us; our talents are the same; I have very near as much spirit as you; and am not less handsome: I am sensible of all this; and yet notwithstanding all, you prescribe to me, you overcome me, you cast me down, your genius crushes mine, and I am nothing before you. (IV, ii)

Claire abases herself even further:

> it is certain that nothing but your gentleness and affability of manners could entitle me to the rank of your friend: by nature, I ought to be your servant. Explain this mystery if you can.

23. It is irrelevant but nonetheless interesting to learn that in his copy Napoleon crossed out the passage concerning women becoming their own mistresses, *Jean-Jacques Rousseau: Oeuvres complètes*, II, 1578.

MANIPULATIVE FRIENDSHIP

It is the reader, not Julie, who is burdened with this mystery and is left wondering which of the two friends is so overpowering. Certainly in the book the world turns on Julie, but the impression remains that Claire turns it. Even this image of Julie, the attracting and irresistibly compelling, is Claire's and the reader is drawn to Julie through the agency of her friend.

The love of Julie and Claire burns on as strongly as ever and, even more clearly than in their girlhood days, it includes the love of Saint-Preux. Claire continues to control the relationship and to direct its course. "I had rather talk of him with you, than think of him by myself" (IV, ii), Julie insists before Saint-Preux returns. And indeed Claire is present in all her thoughts of her former lover. When Saint-Preux arrives in person, he holds the name Claire dictated and he communicates with her, accepting Julie's desire that he treat the two cousins as one. As he does so, his particular passion is partially neutralized and he ceases to threaten either woman. After staying a while with Julie, he leaves for Claire declaring "for as yet I have but half seen Julie, not having seen her cousin; that dear and amiable friend, to whom I am so much indebted, and who will always share my friendship, my services, my gratitude, and all the affections of my soul" (IV, vi). He goes partly to talk of Julie no doubt, for both lovers now seem to speak more openly and sincerely with Claire than with each other.

In the period that follows, Wolmar recapitulates the love affair of Saint-Preux to exorcise it. In each event Claire is a witness or a presence, and Julie has much need of her and her counsel. The first test is the repetition of the passionate kiss in the grove, which Claire presided over and enjoyed. Wolmar insists on a replay of the scene to cure the lovers of their emotion and desanctify the place. Julie begins her account of the bizarre ritual by reiterating her youthful appeals to Claire:

My dear friend, is it not decreed that you are on all occasions to be my safeguard against myself? and that after having delivered

155

me with so much difficulty from the snares which my affections laid for me, you are yet to rescue me from those which reason spreads out? (V, xii).

Claire is the obvious recipient of the account since she alone possesses the past, present, and in a way the future, for Wolmar has communicated to her his schemes for taming Saint-Preux.[24] Her eye encompasses all and her judgment alone is all-enveloping.[25] With such perception she cannot ignore the difference in the reenactment of the kiss. In the first episode, Saint-Preux, Julie, and Claire had formed a loving triangle; when the place of Claire is taken by Wolmar, the kiss loses its power.

The next testing of Saint-Preux also displays the influence of Claire. Over his wife's protests Wolmar insists on leaving the former lovers alone. They go out on the lake and a storm blows them to the spot hallowed by Saint-Preux's vigil for Julie during his exile. It is a place of love and its memories are strong. Under the influence of this place Saint-Preux tries to resurrect the old Julie, effaced by Mme de Wolmar. The attempt fails and both are upset and silenced. Following this episode Julie writes to her husband, but she will not relate the events; rather she advises him to go to Claire, so that she may tell him what has passed in his absence. Claire must be the interpreter of Julie and Saint-Preux for Wolmar.

The last testing of Saint-Preux is independent of Wolmar, for it involves his growing love of Claire.[26] Certainly both Claire and

24. In her account of the event Julie confirms what Claire has suspected, that Wolmar was informed of her past before their marriage. Here, then, is another example of Claire's perceptive power.

25. Occasionally in the second part when she considers Wolmar, Claire seems to doubt her own powers. Once she advises Julie to go to her husband for advice. "Do not depend on yourself, for you do not know how to do yourself justice," she counsels, "nor on me, who even in your indiscretions never considered any thing but your heart, and always adored you; but refer to your husband . . ." (IV, xiii). In the presence of Wolmar, the epitome of reason, Claire sometimes fashions for herself an image of female sensibility.

26. Concerning the love of Claire and Saint-Preux, critics have been divided. Lester Crocker sees Claire motivated by love for Saint-Preux throughout the novel, "Julie ou la nouvelle duplicité," *Annales Jean-Jacques Rousseau* 36 (1963–65), 105–52. Hans Wolpe

Saint-Preux admit to an interest in each other and there is a mutual physical attraction. Yet the signs are clear too that Julie is supreme for both and that, as Claire later puts it, each one loves the other because they both love Julie. It is his affection for Julie that makes Saint-Preux most interesting to Claire and it is Claire's enthusiasm for Julie that attracts Saint-Preux. This is most evident in Claire's journey to Julie's house and in her ecstatic arrival, in marked contrast to the restrained arrival of Saint-Preux. Saint-Preux's account of her deportment on the trip sets the atmosphere:

> She is now more sprightly and agreeable than ever; but unequal, absent, giving little attention to any thing, and seldom replying; talking by fits and starts; in a word, given up entirely to that restlessness which is natural to us, when just on the point of obtaining what we have long and ardently desired. One would have thought, every minute, that she was afraid of being obliged to return. Her journey, tho' so long deferred, was undertaken so precipitately, that it almost turned the heads of both mistress and domestics. A whimsical disorder appeared throughout the whole of her little baggage. If her woman imagined, as she did every now and then, that she had left something behind, Claire as constantly assured her she had put it into the seat of the coach; where, upon further inquiry, it was not to be found. (V, vi)

Certainly Claire is in a tumult of love (strikingly similar to the excited state of the Superior of Arpajon), and it is not Saint-Preux who inspires it, although his presence is a necessary condition and he certainly responds to it. Claire is travelling to live with her cousin in a household where no other adult openly inspires Julie's passion. She is moving to center stage and her agitation is uncontrollable.

sees her dominated by passion for Julie at all times and he judges her love for Saint-Preux as "no more than a thrill," "Psychological Ambiguity," p. 289. To Patrick Brady, Claire's possible relationship with Saint-Preux may mean vicarious self-fulfillment for Julie, "Structural Affiliations," p. 217. Regarding Saint-Preux rather than Claire, David Anderson argues that Claire represents a potential threat to his voluntary celibacy and consequently the destruction of his dream of an ideal, nonerotic life, "Aspects of motif," p. 43.

The arrival is even more revealing; it is expressed in one of those *tableaux vivants* of delicious sensibility which the eighteenth century so enjoyed. It mirrors the tableau of the first part, watched ecstatically by Saint-Preux, who then busied himself in reducing its elements to Julie alone. Here both actors and audience are increased and there is a professional quality to the performance:

> Claire had prepared for her a fine compliment, in her way, a compound of affection and pleasantry; but, on setting her foot over the threshold, compliment and pleasantry were all forgotten; she flew forward to embrace her friend with a transport impossible to be described, crying out, Ah! my dear, dear cousin! Henriette [Claire's daughter], seeing her mother, fled to meet her, and crying out *Mama, Mama*, ran with so much force against her, that the poor child fell backwards on the floor. The effect of the sudden appearance of Claire, the fall of Henriette, the joy, the apprehensions, that seized upon Julie at that instant, made her give a violent shriek, and faint away. Claire was going to lift up the child when she saw her friend turn pale, which made her hesitate whom to assist; till seeing me take up Henriette, she flew to the relief of Julie; but, in endeavouring to recover her, sunk down likewise in the same state. (V, vi)

If the reader inevitably thinks of Jane Austen's advice to the sentimental heroine to run mad if necessary but to eschew fainting, the effect on the fictional spectators is undeniably serious. Saint-Preux demands of Lord Bomston, "Where is the heart of iron whom such a scene of sensibility would not affect?" Certainly such a heart does not reside in the cold Wolmar: "Instead of running to Julie, this fortunate husband threw himself on a settee, to enjoy the delightful scene." For Wolmar and Saint-Preux the scene includes both cousins and neither is effaced. It is in this triumphant context that Claire and Saint-Preux's mutual love ripens. It is predicated on the fulfillment of Claire's love for Julie and on the taming of Saint-Preux.

As at the end of the novel's first section, Claire now controls Saint-Preux. A look from her checks a tender memory of Julie, and she and Julie even ration his drink to prevent any wicked descents into drunken irrationality. To Claire he is all gratitude. He recognizes that she kept him from Julie, so giving him an opportunity to purify his affection and his heart. Both Saint-Preux and Claire understand the nature of their love. Only Julie mistakes it and urges their marriage. But after much persuading and withdrawing, Claire has the final word on it in the last letter of the novel: "a man who was beloved by Julie, and could resolve to marry another woman, would in my opinion, be so base, and unworthy a creature, that I should think it a dishonour to call such a one my friend; and with respect to myself, I protest to you that the man, whoever he be, that shall presume to talk of love hereafter to me, shall never in his life have a second opportunity" (VI, xiii). To this there can be no answer.

In the first section of the novel Julie was defined as daughter and lover; hence her tragedy. Now she defines herself as mother and belatedly as lover. In the first part she sacrificed herself to her duty as daughter; in the coda she will sacrifice herself—more literally so—as mother. Certainly Julie's identity as mother must attract Claire, who seeks to enter the maternal relationship with her. Indeed Julie herself dimly recognizes that Claire must enter it when she laments that Wolmar, the man she loves "above all others in the world," is not, like her, intoxicated with fondness for their children; in his place she wants a "friend, a mother, who can be as extravagantly fond of my children, and her own, as myself."

The main route to Julie as mother is through Henriette, Claire's only daughter. Claire idolizes the girl, stressing her facial likeness to Julie. Indeed she seems to idolize her mainly as a new Julie and as a route to the old one. When Saint-Preux leaves Claire's house for Julie's, he takes with him a "pretty little present," Claire's Henriette. "Where you and my daughter are, what part of me is wanting?" asks Claire. By uniting the two she exaggerates the object of her passion and at the same time vicariously embraces the Julie whom she cannot yet see. "While

159

you are reading this, she is already in your arms," she imagines, "she is happier than her mother" (IV, ix).

Because Henriette resembles Julie, around whom the world turns, this child becomes far more prominent than the two sons of Julie and Wolmar. Her education is of paramount importance because it is the education of another Julie: "I consign all maternal authority over to you," says Claire to Julie, "correct my failings; take that charge upon yourself, of which I acquitted myself so little to your liking . . . to render her dearer to me still, make another Julie of her if possible" (IV, ix). Claire takes pleasure in suggesting that Henriette prefers Julie to her own mother, and she enjoys passing off the child as her cousin's. Because Julie's maternal feelings are called forth by Claire's child—the child Claire created in Julie's image—Claire can in a way become Julie's daughter and Julie her mother. Especially so since there is much of Claire in Henriette: she is, for instance, endowed with her mother's powerful regard. In her one letter to Claire she reveals Julie as we do not see her until Julie's own revelation at the end. Julie has been writing to Claire to persuade her to marry Saint-Preux; Henriette notes and records the tears and agitation attending the writing, so telling her mother (and the reader) far more than Julie's urgings.

Henriette is to marry Julie's son, to whom she is already devoted. But this son is a shadowy presence in the novel, hardly mentioned by Claire in her correspondence. The planned match is therefore manifested for the reader far more in the mothers whose union it is to symbolize. Like Saint-Preux, Henriette is to mediate between Claire and Julie; like Saint-Preux too she has a life of her own and Claire must struggle to control her daughter's actions and meaning.[27]

27. For a discussion of Henriette and Claire, see David Anderson's "Aspects of motif." He argues for a rivalry between Claire and her daughter, while at the same time seeing the union of Henriette with Julie's son as "a kind of projected synthesis of Claire and Julie," p. 57.

DEATH

When Saint-Preux leaves Julie for the last time to travel with Lord Bomston to Italy he has a dream in which he experiences the death of Julie's mother, told to him by Claire. But as he looks he sees Julie take her mother's place on the deathbed. Her face is covered with a veil, which her voice forbids him to touch; he cannot see her further or know her again. So frightened is Saint-Preux by the dream-vision that he exclaims to Lord Bomston that he is forever severed from Julie. His agitation is extreme and his friend returns with him to Clarens to quell it. When he nears the place, Saint-Preux overhears the voices of Julie and Claire—speaking, it is later explained, of Claire's love for Saint-Preux. He hears but he does not see, and he returns to Lord Bomston proud of having escaped the slavery of his eyes. To Claire he declares that the veil is now torn aside, that veil which for so long obscured his reason. "All my unruly passions are extinguished," he exults. With his new passionless acceptance of Julie he can say to Claire, "You are both dearer to me than ever, but my heart knows no difference between you, nor feels the least inclination to separate the inseparables" (V, ix). The mother's death heralded the eclipse of Julie's passion; Julie's dream-death ensures the transcendence of Saint-Preux's. He is content henceforth not to see, where before his eyes had been greedy for Julie. Her death can therefore have no importance for him, for it is the death of the body for which he has ceased to feel a passion.

The dream affects the characters in strikingly different ways: Saint-Preux transcends it to approach Julie in a purer realm without veils, while Lord Bomston thinks it merely a dream. Claire, however, who knows the power of the eye, remains caught in it, hindered by the obscuring cloth. Unlike Saint-Preux she cannot dominate the dream and for her it becomes a prediction. So she reproaches Saint-Preux for refusing to look when he could and for having cast off the dream so cleanly. In revenge she appropriates it to become guardian of the veil.[28] From Saint-Preux she has received a present of an Indian veil of gold, embroidered with pearls. When Julie dies, fulfilling the dream, Claire joins this real present to the imagined veil, so fashioning reality into a symbol.

Julie dies from a mysterious illness following a fall into the water while rescuing her son. Six months of bliss have passed with all the characters circling contentedly within her orbit. After holding together Claire, Saint-Preux, Wolmar, Lord Bomston, and the children, there is for Julie nothing further to wish for. "Come death when thou wilt!" she exclaims, "I no longer dread thy power; the measure of my life is full, and I have nothing new to experience worth enjoyment" (VI, viii). When the child tumbles into the water and she rushes to save him, it is an understandable response, which yet fulfills a hidden longing.[29]

Julie does not die at once, for, like Clarissa, she means to have a public and exemplary death. In the following days she preaches religion to the pastor and love and duty to all who surround her. Yet, curiously, the death is not really dominated by Julie at all, but rather by Claire. In death Julie must play for her friend all her roles and play them only for her.

Of all the lovers of Julie, Claire is the most loudly distressed by her illness. Wolmar even fears for her reason, that reason with which she was once so persistently associated. Now, in the shadow of death, Claire's love erupts clearly and distinctly, analogue of Saint-Preux's early obsessive and death-directed passion. She who had mediated through love and loved through mediation is for the first time face to face with love's immediate form.

Weakened by grief and care so thoroughly that she, not her

28. Starobinski notes the imaginative prefigurations in *Julie* before a description of a real occurrence, *L'Oeil vivant*, p. 124. Through her part in these prefigurations Claire becomes intimately involved with the actual event, whether it is the "fall" of Julie or her death.

29. Ronald Grimsley writes that Julie's death is "an accident and yet also a logical result of the implications of her own life," and that her further life could only have been a "decline," *Jean-Jacques Rousseau: A Study in Self-Awareness* (Cardiff: University of Wales Press, 1961), p. 149.

friend, seems dying, Claire can be persuaded to rest only by sharing Julie's bed. In the morning Wolmar enters the room to find Claire

> sitting on the settee, spiritless and pale, or rather of a livid complexion, her eyes heavy and dead; yet she appeared calm and tranquil, but little, and doing whatever she was told to without answering. As for Julie, she appeared less feeble than overnight: the tone of her voice was strong and her gesture animated; she seemed indeed to have borrowed the vivacity of her cousin. (VI, xi)

It is an ambiguous, passionate, and vampiric scene of love, which Julie later tries to interpret conventionally. Holding Claire's hand she states to the assembled onlookers what her cousin has meant for her.

> I am a woman, and yet have known a true friend. Heaven gave us birth at the same time; it gave us a similarity of inclinations, which has subsisted to this hour: it formed our hearts one for the other; it united us in the cradle; I have been blessed with her friendship during my life, and her kind hand will close my eyes in death. (VI, xi)

But when death comes Claire does much more than close Julie's eyes, and her action is of a piece with the exhausted night of love:

> I was alarmed at a low, indistinct noise that seemed to come from Julie's room [writes Wolmar]. I listened, and thought I could now distinguish the groans of a person in extremity. I ran into the room, threw open the curtain, and there—O Saint-Preux! there I saw them both, those amiable friends, motionless, locked in each other's embrace, the one fainted away and the other expiring. I cried out, and hastened to prevent or receive her last sigh; but it was too late; Julie was no more. (VI, xi)

In a way both women die, for Claire is never again herself, a whole person. The embrace is passionate, welding love and death, fulfilling Julie's predictions of her fatal passion for Saint-Preux.

MANIPULATIVE FRIENDSHIP

After the death, Claire is completely overwhelmed. So attenuated is she that she lives only in Wolmar's prose, and the letter describing Julie's death and her own distraught reaction is one of the few she never sees. Her controlling eye is blinded and her mind and pen made impotent.

> As soon as I was a little recovered from my first surprise, I inquired after Mme d'Orbe; and learned that the servants were obliged to carry her into her own chamber, where at last they were forced to confine her to prevent her returning into that of Julie; which she had several times done, throwing herself on the body, embracing, chafing, and kissing it in a kind of phrenzy, and exclaiming aloud in a thousand passionate expressions of fruitless despair. (VI, xi)[30]

For the first time in the novel, Claire is reduced to insentience. Her extreme grief and frenzy now dominate, and she has moved to center stage and unmediated relationships. The price of centrality and directness is the loss of the furtive seeing eye.

Claire's impotence is displayed in all the roles she once controlled and coveted. First, she destroys her own image as reasoning friend when she goes mad. Wolmar's picture of her state is truly frightening:

> On entering her apartment, I found her absolutely frantic, neither seeing nor minding any thing, knowing nobody, but running about the room, and wringing her hands, sometimes uttering in a hollow voice some extravagant words, and at others sending forth such terrible shrieks as to make one shudder with horror. On the feet of the bed sat her woman, frightened out of her wits, not daring to breathe or stir. (VI, ix)[31]

30. Of this scene Hans Wolpe remarks: "the ambiguity is preserved only by one fact: we are dealing with a *dead* body." He notes too that the convulsions that shake Claire in her madness resemble those which overwhelmed Saint-Preux when Julie was about to yield. "Psychological Ambiguity," p. 288.

31. Roger Kempf has discussed the importance of hands in *Julie*. For example, the characters write, act, express love with hands, and Saint-Preux even catches smallpox from Julie's. See "Sur Le Corps de Julie," *Critique* 22 (October 1966), 800–1. Here Claire's lack of control is indicated in her purposeless, reflexive action.

Claire does not quickly recover, and Wolmar grows exasperated at the irrationality of her grief: "Every thing she says, every thing she does, looks like madness; I am obliged therefore to put up with every thing, and am resolved not to be offended."

Second, Claire loses control of Julie through Saint-Preux. In the last letter Julie writes, she admits that she has always loved Saint-Preux and she anticipates their pure union in another state. The image that her lover has guarded of the past Julie has never disappeared, and through death alone its promise may be fulfilled. In this final confession Julie escapes the controlling look of Claire, who does not see the letter or enter the relationship it describes. She has no part in this heavenly union and she will not form the mystical community of Clarens by marrying Saint-Preux and perpetuating the memory of Julie. At the moment of her consummated passion she loses the lovers and the triangle is broken.[32] Claire is excluded.

Finally, she loses control in the maternal sphere, into which she has thrust herself directly. The dying Julie has told her children to look on Claire as their mother, to replace their dead one. Yet, when Claire faces the child whom Julie rescued, she can only repulse him as she repulses Saint-Preux. Julie has died a mother but not for Claire.[33]

To heal Claire's mind, Wolmar, master of the bizarre cure, dresses up Henriette to impersonate Julie at the table from which Claire has fled because of Julie's brooding absence:

> Henriette, proud to represent her little mamma, played her part extremely well; so well indeed, that I observed the servants in waiting shed tears. She nevertheless always gave the name of mamma to her mother, and addressed her with proper respect. At length, encouraged by success and my approbation, she ventured to put her hand to the soupspoon, and cried, *Claire, my dear, do you chuse any of this!* The gesture, tone, and manner, in which

32. Starobinski reads the ending as a turning back to love—with God as the third element in the triangle of Julie and Saint-Preux. *Jean-Jacques Rousseau,* p. 141.

33. Julie's death echoes her mother's; both women die to save their children—whether from moral disgrace or death.

she spoke this, were so exactly like those of Julie, that it made her mother tremble. (VIII, xi)

When the child speaks with Julie's voice, the identification Claire has earlier urged and controlled is too much for her sanity: her madness leaps forth, as it had against Julie's son.

Paradoxically, Claire is the last person to see Julie. Because of the grotesque antics of the servants who believe Julie still lives, the body is kept unburied until it begins to decay. To hide the bloated face, Claire covers it with the veil that Saint-Preux had given her. As she does so, she curses the hand that will dare lift it, so surrounding Julie with a controlling magic, her last act of power in the novel. Julie will be buried veiled. But in covering Julie's face, Claire has of course hidden her from her own view, at a time when no further mediation is possible. Unlike Saint-Preux, she cannot transcend this veil and she cannot escape Julie's fatal fascination. Having lost sight of Julie directly and indirectly, she falls into her power and is dragged downward into her death.[34]

The novel ends with Julie's complete mastery over the cousin who has controlled her for so long: "I feel myself drawn as it were involuntarily to her tomb," writes Claire to a silent Saint-Preux. "I shudder as I approach." She hastens to Julie whose voice calls her from death, "Claire! where art thou? O my Claire! what detains thee from thy friend?—Alas! her grave has yet but half her ashes—" (VI, xiii).

Claire's progress through Julie's novel is finally an ironic one. In the first part of the book she approaches her beloved Julie cleverly and furtively, through a double mediation: she encourages Saint-Preux so she may express her own love and op-

---

34. Anne Srabian de Fabry interprets Claire's death in a different manner; she sees it as symbolizing the triumph of friendship or virtuous passion over love or vicious passion, "Quelques Observations sur le dénouement de la Nouvelle Héloïse," The French Review 46 (October 1972), 7.

poses him when he seems to rival her; at the same time, she moves toward Julie through her mother, manipulating her into a weapon against the dangerous lover. In the second part of the novel Claire's passion for Julie is still mediated, sometimes through Saint-Preux and sometimes through her daughter Henriette. But, in the cool marriage with Wolmar, it is more direct than during the Saint-Preux liaison, more clearly controlling and less furtively manipulative. Now Claire openly orders all her mediators while fearing no rival. But her progress cannot be halted and inevitably she continues to move toward Julie, entering at last a direct, unmediated relationship where she may become lover and parent or child, instead of approaching through them. It is a disastrous move, for Claire's control is most effective when most mediated; her love turns against itself and Claire the controller becomes the controlled. If Claire has ordered Julie's life, Julie orders Claire's death and the relationship is at last reversed.

Claire's manipulation of Julie is of a special kind in fiction. In most eighteenth-century novels of manipulative friendship (*The Life of Marianne* by Marivaux, examined in chapter six, and *The Nun* in some of its ties) the friend manipulates the other woman to benefit herself or to fulfill some neurotic childhood need. In *Julie,* however, Claire acts for love though coercing others to act for her and manipulates her beloved Julie into actions that will support the love. The manipulation and mediation are essential to the living passion, for they not only hide an emotion that is unacceptable when open and direct but also obscure its dangerous, deathly aspect. For Claire can never in life come close enough to Julie, and manipulation and mediation appear at last necessary barriers, not approaches to love. At the end of the novel when her love is unmediated and unmanipulative and when the reason she appeared to embody is entirely conquered, she loses herself in irrational, spontaneous, and immediate passion; and she is pulled toward the death which love has for her always contained.

MANIPULATIVE FRIENDSHIP

The Marquis de Sade's *Juliette* (1797)

The Marquis de Sade, that freest of spirits to have lived so far, had ideas of his own on the subject of woman: he wanted her to be as free as man. Out of these ideas—they will come through some day—grew a dual novel, *Justine* and *Juliette*. It was not by accident the Marquis chose heroines and not heroes. Justine is a woman as she has been hitherto, enslaved, miserable and less than human; her opposite, Juliette represents the woman whose advent he anticipated, a figure for whom minds have as yet no conception, who is arising out of mankind, who shall have wings, and who shall renew the world.[35]

Through a thousand and more pages Juliette (the exemplary woman of the Surrealist, Guillaume Apollinaire) is educated in the wiles and ways of an evil world. She has much to learn, or rather unlearn, since the Sadian world is one of reversals and contradictions.[36] In it the traditional rules of society are confounded and social functions denied. The incest taboo, at the root of social organization, is revoked: father must lie with daughter (or more insistently with son); daughter must abuse parent.[37] Procreation—because familial—is eschewed, and sodomy and homosexuality exalted. In a context of social negation Juliette must learn that human beings are alone, unrelated to any others. With self-confidence they can become gods, sublimely self-possessed and

35. Quoted in Austryn Wainwright's introduction to his translation of *Juliette* (New York: Grove Press, 1968). References to *Juliette* in the text are to this edition. Maurice Tourné follows Apollinaire when he sees Sade denouncing the enslavement of women in his division of them into two antithetical types, Penelope and Circe, the enslaved object woman and the energetic libertine. According to Tourné, the latter is Sade's future woman, feminine in beauty and grace but masculine in intelligence and energy, "Pénélope et Circé, ou les mythes de la femme dans l'oeuvre de Sade," *Europe* (October 1972), 71–88.

36. A full discussion of Sade's nihilism can be found in Lester Crocker's *Nature and Culture* (Baltimore: Johns Hopkins Press, 1963), pp. 399–429.

37. Claude Lévi-Strauss has shown that the incest taboo is the basis of human society since it necessitates an exchange of women and a forging of alliances beyond the blood group. See *The Elementary Structures of Kinship* (Boston: Beacon Press, 1969), p. 481.

self-obsessed. But the self they tend is reduced to its erotic component; being is sexualized.[38]

In the Sadian world, two main classes confront each other: libertines (or tyrants) and victims.[39] The libertines are evil, the victims virtuous or weak. The libertines prey on their victims and their less vicious fellows, deriving pleasure from cruelty. Their obsessive algolagnia is fed by a complex philosophy that finds joy in sensation from whatever source and demands attention solely for the self. If one enjoys another's pain, this pain is justified, for the self feels only what is its own.

The libertine philosophy which Juliette must digest is articulated throughout Sade's works; it is repeated almost as insistently as the orgies of cruelty and sex expressing it. In *Juliette* it triumphs in speech and action. Evil is invariably crowned with success, and misfortune descends on all who falter in its service; in a trice the virtuous shudder can translate tyrant into victim. The system is ratified divinely—or rather naturally, since Nature is here the awful abstraction. *Juliette* ends with the death of Justine, the personification of perfect and perverse virtue; she dies slashed from mouth to vagina by lightning.

The death of Justine, virtuous victim and sister of the vicious Juliette, suggests a familiar distinction between tyrant and slave. In the eighteenth-century novel it is women, like Clarissa, who are raped and degraded by the hero, or, if they escape this fate like Julie and Suzanne, are murdered by their authors. In the lusty and violent world of Sade we might expect the butchering of females to be a common pastime of the puissant male, and we could hardly gasp at women's universal enrollment in the ranks of victims and slaves. Yet, according to Apollinaire, the Marquis has penned a revolutionary work contradicting all social forms

38. Simone de Beauvoir notes Sade's sexualization of existence in *The Marquis de Sade: Must We Burn Sade?* (London: John Calder, 1962), p. 18.

39. Roland Barthes distinguishes five classes of Sadian characters. On the top are the great libertines like Clairwil and Noirceuil; on the bottom are the wives. He notes that across classes there is no communication. *Sade, Fourier, Loyola* (Paris: Editions du Seuil, 1971), pp. 30–31.

and formulae. If he can annihilate the duty of parent and child and dissolve the ties of society, can he not also trample on the ultimate social absolute, that men should control women? Is it possible that Juliette is indeed the revolutionary being of the surrealists and that the vicious circle has opened momentarily to liberate society's primary slaves?

Sadian characters do not think; they act and harangue. So Juliette may be approached only through relationships. She tells her own educational story and her telling of it proves its object has been partially fulfilled, for a mark of a grand libertine is the ability to speak lengthily and lubriciously.[40] Her success derives from a graded schooling in which, like Fanny Hill's, women figure prominently. Her relationships with these women, like other "friendships" in the novel, are an anomaly in the Sadian scheme where the ultimate criminal is solitary and autonomous; yet they are justified repeatedly by the characters who seem as perplexed by them as the reader.[41] The arch-libertine Saint-Fond legitimizes friendship by basing it firmly on self-interest, "the only rule I know for judging oneself and others intelligently," but he ends his days the victim of the "friend" he here addresses. Female relationships must be plagued by equal ambiguities in a novel where philosophy and action meet and part with startling rapidity. Since the woman falls easily into the slavish stance before men, however, female friendships may mediate rather than mitigate the essential libertine autonomy.

Among the myriad fragmentary and momentary relationships into which Juliette enters with women, three stand out:

40. Barthes has fully discussed the function of speech in Sade's works. He considers that the master or tyrant is one who speaks. *Sade, Fourier, Loyola*, p. 36. Georges Batailles has, however, stressed the oddity of violent people speaking at such length, concluding that the language of Sade is that of the victim, *L'Erotisme* (Paris: Editions de Minuit, 1957), p. 211.

41. Jean Biou has noted that paradoxically the libertines enjoy being together and that they achieve an almost Rousseauvian transparency, "Deux oeuvres complémentaires *Les Liaisons dangereuses* et *Juliette*," *Colloque d'Aix-en-Provence sur le Marquis de Sade, 19 et 20 fevrier 1968* (Paris: Armand Colin, 1968), p. 109. For a further discussion of the Sadian emphasis on isolation and negation of the other, see Georges Batailles's *La Littérature et le mal* (Paris: Gallimard, 1957), p. 128, and *L'Érotisme*, p. 186.

the one with Delbène when she is still a child at the convent; with
Clairwil, the powerful libertine whose cruelty impresses even
Saint-Fond; and with Durand, the older sorcerer and poison
monger. All of these relationships educate Juliette and they en-
close and structure both her life and her novel. The book opens
with the display of Delbène, climaxes in the friendship of Clairwil, and closes on the sombre affection of Durand. If Juliette is
indeed the new woman, then these relationships should progress
so that the child might mature into the autonomous woman, ultimately requiring an equal female companion only for pleasure.
Through these women Juliette should learn to throw off all social
inhibitions, to seduce her father, kill her child, and pollute the
world in all possible postures. She need not murder her friend so
long as she derives pleasure from her; when she does not, however, she must be ruthless. Above all she must be free of female
control, neither manipulated nor dominated by a woman. No
libertine man in *Juliette* would be otherwise.

1

The seduction of Juliette by Delbène, Superior of the traditionally
lubricious convent, is quick and decisive, shaming the subtle
overtures of Diderot's libidinous nun. The reader is left to eye
warily the remaining bulk of this enormous novel, which must
sustain so vicious an overture.

Juliette's development with Delbène is impeccable in the Sadian scheme. At the age of nine she was already a sexual entity,
fulfilling her own needs by herself; soon self-interest required
another, and she was ready for Delbène. Certainly no sentimental
affection is lost between adept and acolyte: Juliette notes that
"among recluse women the thirst for the voluptuous is the sole
motive for close friendship" (p. 4). To this Delbène adds a similarly selfish cause: "For a libertine intelligence, there is no more
piercing pleasure than that of making proselytes" (p. 52).

Having picked her new pupil, Delbène does not waste time
on preliminaries. Invited to a luncheon, Juliette enters the orga-

171

nized debauchery to which she and the reader will henceforth be constantly subjected. Directed by the professional Delbène she speedily learns the mechanics of sex, the imperative of wilder and wilder contortions. She apprehends the heady alliance of pain and pleasure, lust and torture. Above all she learns what an earlier pupil terms "being"; at the outset of Juliette's journey in lubricity, this graduate of the convent exclaims to her mentor:

'tis you I am indebted to for an understanding of myself and the meaning of my existence. You have trained my mind, you have rescued it from the darkness wherein childhood prejudices enshrouded it. Thanks alone to you I have achieved being in the world. (p. 8)

Being is sexual and for Juliette it is first defined through another woman.

It matters that her initial mentor is a lesbian. Delbène speaks of her "uncommon liking" for women and her relative lack of desire for men—although like all Sadian libertines she will use whatever flesh is at hand. For Sade the lesbian is primarily a rebellious figure, outside the social heterosexual model and barred from procreation. Through characters and authorial footnotes he praises this woman, finding her superior in grace and intelligence to the contemptible wifely female. That Juliette is initiated first by such a woman augurs well for her future progress in libertinism, but it means little for her development in female friendship. Lesbianism in Sade is not a sure route to female solidarity.

Delbène teaches Juliette an odd combination of act and analysis, the mark of all the grand libertines. Philosophy is here as insistent as lust, and even amidst true believers the Sadian hero must preach—repeatedly, for repetition of act and description alone delivers pleasure. A truly consummated act is one that has been constantly committed, described, and analyzed. The prompter of action is the imagination, which coerces to ever more varied repetition; every body must be enjoyed to the limit, and perfectly mutilated before death meanly intervenes.[42] Since

42. Barthes discusses the importance of the imagination in the Sadian vocabulary; he suggests that it is the Sadian term for language itself. *Sade, Fourier, Loyola,* p. 36.

every thought or fantasy becomes compelling, the richest criminal is richest in imagination. Philosophy requires imaginative cunning, which in turn compels action. All elements must coalesce for the true libertine life.

The main components of Delbène's philosophy are common to all the libertines. She raves at length against "the fantastical God" of Christianity and against the stupid morality of virtue, which misguided humans have erected on the fantasy. She teaches Juliette the "naturalness" of evil and the rightness of cruelty that brings pleasure. Sensation of the self arises as the new divinity, which all that is not the self must serve:

> If Nature has constituted my intimate structure in such a way that it is only from the infelicity of my fellows that voluptuous sensation can flower in me, then 'tis so because Nature would have me participate in the destruction she desires. (p. 99)

No libertine dissents from this creed and Juliette adopts it forthwith.

Although Delbène's pedagogy resembles that of the male debauchees, she delves further than they into the female predicament. Lengthily she analyzes the folly of virginity and chastity in a woman: "how can folly," she demands of a receptive Juliette, "be carried to the point where one believes a female creature is worth more or less for having one part of her body a little more or a little less enlarged?" She teaches that modesty is but a stimulant to lust, and motherhood and family ridiculous snares for the foolish girl. Yet, while the libertine herself should avoid all ties, eschewing the social compact of parent, child, or spouse, she should strenuously deny freedom to others; "Always find some means for obtaining entire control over others, over, that is, their lives" (p. 81), she counsels Juliette. It is essential advice for a woman, little emphasized by the male instructors.

But Delbène teaches Juliette a subtler lesson as well. Although lesbian, she relishes above all the joys of sodomy, and she brandishes a dildo on each sexual occasion. Juliette is satisfied by women, but she is manipulated in her desire by Delbène's example. Soon she contracts the Sadian preference for sodomy over other sexual methods and she longs to rape a virgin, the honored male act from which women seem debarred. She communicates her fantastical longing to Delbène, who knows that no urge must go unattended. In an orgy of cruelty and lust, Juliette deflowers the child she chooses; earlier she herself was similarly served by Delbène.

The episode is bizarre beyond the simulation of male activity. When Juliette was first let free to choose a victim, she picked Justine her sister, a woman most like herself. Considering this action, one suspects she primarily desires to assault her own body as a man. The woman, it seems, is still defined by rape.

The final lesson Delbène gives to Juliette launches her on the road to bigger and better viciousness. Mouthpiece of all contradictions, like the true Sadian libertine she is, Delbène follows her discourse on female friendship and complicity with a statement of faith in isolation.[43] "I haven't the slightest germ of belief in that *bond of fraternity*" (p. 100), she exclaims to her friend. It is all too true. When Juliette finds her parents dead and her fortunes ruined, there is no reentry into the convent. Refusing even to open the gates to her, Delbène shows her how prosperity loathes misery. Juliette is cast into the world, her two virginities lost and her mind contaminated with a libertine philosophy she is burning to practice.

2

Juliette sets out to conquer Paris and her weapons are not negligible. She has youth, beauty, a lusty and vicious character, and a deep commitment to herself. Inevitably she succeeds, but she does so in the conventional female way—through whoring. Unlike her predecessor Fanny Hill, however, she sees her prostitution not as means alone but as both means and end, for she

---

43. Roger G. Lacombe has drawn attention to the disparity between speech and attitude in the Sadian character, especially in the character of Olympia, who boasts that death for her will be a voluptuous treat but who cringes before the reality, *Sade et ses masques* (Paris: Payot, 1974), p. 195.

glories in the name of whore. Unlike Fanny again, she retains her libidinous interest in women.

At this crucial stage of her life Juliette's main teacher is the archlibertine, Noirceuil, an older man who takes a fancy to her body, but admires too her "subtler mind." When she answers his boast, that he has killed her parents, with the words "Monster . . . thou art an abomination, I love thee" (p. 149), she is speedily taken into favor and installed in his house as mistress, to pander to his mental and physical whims and to torture his meek wife. Certainly she has come far from destitution, but for all her mastery she is mistress not master in the household.

Noirceuil confirms the insidious lesson of Delbène. While Juliette often insists she prefers women as sexual partners—or rather accomplices—she reverences above all the sexuality of the phallus. She capitulates in both act and analysis. After one of Noirceuil's lengthy harangues, she exults: "I see no more, I comprehend no more save through your eyes, with your mind," and she wishes, she declares, to be led by this man in everything. Such abasement must gratify Noirceuil and he is quick to exploit it. Juliette may commit all manner of crimes and outrages, glutting herself on indiscriminate sex and murder, but in the end she must hold one god and one value only. "This tool," says Noirceuil, pointing to his penis, "is my god, let it be one unto thee, Juliette: extol it, worship it, this despotic engine, show it every reverence, it is a thing proud of its glory, insatiate, a tyrant . . ." (p. 185).

Noirceuil cannot keep to himself such a prize as Juliette. Soon she is coveted by Saint-Fond, his friend, the minister and virtual ruler of France. Easily she is given to him, for, in spite of her "subtler mind," she is but a woman-object and can be bartered. She concurs wholeheartedly in her sale: "I am yours," she asserts, "a woman, I know my place and that dependence is my lot" (p. 207). Noirceuil qualifies such abjectness, distinguishing the libertine "cerebral" woman from the wifely female, the truly despicable object of male lust. Yet both he and Saint-Fond know the rights of the puissant male: "I would have you a woman and a slave unto me and my friends, a despot unto everyone else" (p.

207). Juliette changes masters, then, and varies her scenario of ferocity, but she continues subject to the penis.

Saint-Fond uses Juliette as procuress and poisoner, traditional female roles. At gargantuan banquets she is instructed to serve food and victims, and both living and dead flesh must be superb. Interestingly she must prove her worthiness for so honored a place in the minister's entourage by poisoning a woman, but her continuance in favor depends on her unfailing respect for the male and adoration of the phallus.

License is Juliette's and she acts to the depths of her lewd desires. But she cannot be called free. Her duties as hostess of Saint-Fond's iniquitous parties are onerous, and his hideous sexual practices are not always to the taste even of so sexually robust and unsqueamish a woman. In spite of her slavish avowals of devotion, Juliette appears to feel a lack, as she never did with Delbène. Her subservience and unease converge when she asks Noirceuil to find her a female friend.

The story of Juliette and Clairwil fills the center of the novel, binding its halves together as an earlier Julie and Claire had straddled and knit their volumes. Their association is long, vocal, and active. Clairwil is the heir of Delbène but not her double. Like her predecessor she teaches, but she goes beyond the pedagogical; on education and sex is built an edifice of friendship that here transcends both motives.

Clairwil enters clearly as mentor. Juliette has asked Noirceuil for a friend and contemporary model, a woman a bit older than herself: ". . . I'd want her to love me," she stipulates, "to have tastes like mine, passions like mine . . . I'd want her to have a certain ascendancy over me, but that without seeking to dominate me" (p. 262). She is not quite asking for the seemingly equal friendship of Noirceuil and Saint-Fond, but she clearly wants something beyond the heterosexual slavery she knows. Clairwil does not disappoint; when Juliette becomes acquainted with her, she exclaims, "I wish if I possibly can to become iden-

176

tical to you; henceforth Juliette shall know no happiness until she has taken on all your vices" (pp. 288–89).

Clairwil seems formed to liberate Juliette as a woman. Inspiring awe rather than love, she is tall in person, fiery, majestic, and sensual; unlike the cowardly Saint-Fond and other male libertines, she is without fear. Knowledgeable even in chemistry and physics, she savors philosophy with the best. Above all she abounds in imagination, that essential quality for survival in the Sadian world, and she can promote and perfect an orgy with the richest embellishments. No possibility for cruelty ever seems to escape her fertile mind.

Like Delbène Clairwil is primarily lesbian, although her sexual preference is more fully expressed in crime than in lust. "I adore women . . . I'm depraved," she exults, and in true libertine fashion she bases her desire on her own self-enjoyment:

I find nothing more unjust than a law that prescribes a mingling of the sexes in order to procure oneself a pure pleasure; and what sex is more apt than ours in doing unto each other that which we do singly to delight ourselves? Must we not, of necessity, be more successful in pleasing each other than that being, our complete opposite, who can offer us none but the joys at the farthest remove from those our sort of existence requires . . . ? (p. 276)

The corollary of this preference is in Clairwil an utter detestation of men, which she tries throughout their association to inflict on Juliette. "Never for one instant forget that he belongs to an enemy sex," she counsels Juliette concerning a man, "a sex bitterly at war with your own . . . that you ought never let pass an opportunity for avenging the insults women have endured at its hands, and which you yourself are every day on the eve of having to suffer" (p. 527). Asked whether she ever likes men, Clairwil responds that she uses them, "but I scorn and detest them nevertheless: I'd not be adverse to destroying every last one of those by the mere sight of whom I have always felt myself debased" (p. 277). She proves her loathing in practice. Excited by lust while she and her friend enjoy a bout of torture, she replies to Juliette's offer of a girl to kill with this stern declaration:

> I've nothing against giving a woman an occasional pummeling, but as for total material dissolution, you understand . . . I'd have to have a man. Only men rouse me to serious cruelties; I adore revenging my sex for the horrors men subject us to when those brutes have the upper hand. You can't imagine with what delight I'd now murder a male. Any male at all. My God, the tortures I'd inflict upon him; the slow, winding, obscure path I'd find to bring him to his final destination . . . Alack, 'tis plain to see, your mind has yet to reach full flower, you haven't any man about for me to kill. (pp. 294–95).

With such a teacher, Juliette seems en route to reversing the last social convention and moving into a world where women enslave their men.

Like Claire, Clairwil works against the control of her Saint-Preux, metamorphosed into the monstrous Saint-Fond, in whose power Juliette remains.[44] When Juliette reverentially refers to Saint-Fond as "the Minister," Clairwil counters with her own title for the two grand libertines; "those two scoundrels," she contemptuously calls them. Far from envying Juliette's position in Saint-Fond's entourage (as Juliette had feared), she downgrades her friend's function: "You collaborate in them [Saint-Fond's debaucheries], and that is laudable," she declares patronizingly, "were I needy I'd do the same, and I'd do it happily, for I positively worship crime. But I also know, Juliette, that by laboring much in behalf of others you have, so far, labored little on your own . . . so let me encourage you and steel you to more considerable undertakings, if indeed you really wish to be worthy of us" (p. 285). Juliette had seen herself as a grande dame, exulting in her triumphs over respectable court ladies. Clairwil reduces her to the reality of a procuress.

Clairwil leads Juliette to new depths of cruelty. She massacres men simply because they are men or because they resemble

---

44. Philippe Sollers has noted the connection between the names of Rousseau's *Julie* and those of Sade's *Juliette* in "Sade dans le texte," *Tel Quel* 28 (1967), 45–46.

Jesus Christ, son of the male God whom she despises. She entertains Juliette at enormous affairs of cannibalism, bestiality, and lust, and to the vast number of sexual positions, so dear to Saint-Fond, she adds a vast number of bodies. Juliette and she raid whole monasteries, sullying three hundred in a night of debauchery. Always Clairwil surpasses Juliette in capacity; always she is in the vanguard of filth.

Delbène had taught Juliette the link between lust and crime, but Clairwil urges her now occasionally to sever the two, to be wicked without the spur of lust, to kill without orgasm. She explains her prompting by lauding the gratuitous and purposeless crime, but she does not indicate why she alone of Juliette's mentors should so insist on this point. Perhaps her care derives from the passionate and libidinous nature of women in the traditional male mind; to combat this image she may be fashioning a woman who is above all intellectual and criminal.

Yet Clairwil too is ambiguous. Having broken every taboo and committed every crime, she is zealous in her preaching of the gospel of libertinism and excited by her image of whore and female revolutionary. But like Juliette she exists in the phallocracy:

> I live in the name of nothing but the penis sublime; and when it is not in my cunt, nor in my ass, it is so firmly anchored in my thoughts that the day they dissect me it will be found in my brain. (pp. 492–93)

Despite the similar terminology, there is a difference here. Juliette is made to accept the phallus as a religion, while Clairwil holds it as an obsession, part and parcel of her fascination with and detestation of male power. Debarred from possessing the symbol of potency in a phallic world where in spite of all reversals Saint-Fond and not Clairwil may aspire to rule and corrupt his country, Clairwil lodges the penis in her brain. By doing so she suggests that, although she may lack opportunity, she has at least the mental power, imaginative daring, and insatiable cruelty associated with the male. Clearly it is the penis as talisman she

179

covets: her ecstasy over it is most ferocious when she can sever it from its origin and form it into a pure symbol. When chance shows her the biggest penis she has ever beheld, she is quick to possess it, reducing the man and aggrandizing herself in one slice of cruelty.

Like Saint-Fond and Noirceuil, Clairwil is a verbose philosopher. She stresses the same points as they do but she goes further in her investigation of women. Not content like Saint-Fond with praising prostitution and denigrating virginity and modesty, she raises the whore into a goddess:

> Woman has one innate virtue, it is whorishness . . . woe unto her whom a thoughtless and stupid virtuousness ever keeps prisoner of dull prejudices; a victim of her opinions and of the chilly esteem she hopes for, almost always in vain, from men, she'll have lived dry and joyless and shall die unregretted. Libertinage in women used once to be venerated the world over; it had worshipers everywhere, temples even; I become more and more a zealot in that cause. 'Tis my creed, my whole concern and ambition; so long as there is breath in me, I shall be a whore, I proclaim it, I swear it. (p. 492)

Clairwil is an atheist, Saint-Fond a Satanist, and the two argue their viewpoints. Where Saint-Fond confesses to believing in an "eternal and universal evil," Clairwil holds to the "certitude of nothingness." In the debate Saint-Fond is initially given the upper hand, but Clairwil obtains the last word, which suggests a sort of triumph. The novel itself is ambiguous and fails to give a clear victory to the woman.[45] Saint-Fond's philosophy is borne out by the close of the book when the virtuous Justine goes to an inhuman death by lightning, but Saint-Fond and Clairwil are equally destroyed before the finale, succumbing to the fate reserved for libertines who fail to believe or act to the prescribed limit.

Clairwil has an uphill struggle to educate her pupil, who yet insists on her desire to follow and learn. She tries hard to impose

45. Mario Praz discusses the problem of Sade's own point of view and concludes that the "ravings" of all the characters "are evidently the outpourings of Sade himself," *The Romantic Agony* (London: Oxford University Press, 1970), p. 171.

her own savage hatred of men on Juliette, but, although her friend does not lack cruelty, she fails in particular fury. Well after her meeting with Clairwil, when Juliette thinks of her fortune, she sees it in terms of Saint-Fond, from whom, she declares, she can get anything. When she sorties into vice on her own to burn down the cottage of her poor neighbors, she is accused by Clairwil of failing in imagination; she has omitted to complete her crime by having it ascribed to the blameless man. The crime itself is hidden; when Juliette makes an open attack in the streets, she does so in male dress and her victim is female.[46]

In her efforts to influence Juliette, Clairwil is little aided by the society of libertines; in fact she commonly finds it a hindrance. Beyond Saint-Fond and Noirceuil, she has to battle with a whole host of conventional misogynists, all flourishing in this world of seemingly overturned conventions. In the club of criminal friends, a group of libertines who meet to indulge in all varieties of crime and sex, Clairwil and Juliette are faced with the traditional contempt of women. In spite of the distaste of Noirceuil for the club where, he alleges, "everything has fallen into the hands of a sex whose authority I dislike" (p. 208), the president's seat is occupied by a misogynist male, Belmor. Women are indeed given place "to butcher men," but they pay for their pleasure in subjection to a harangue by Belmor, whose philosophic length outdoes even such masters as Noirceuil. This harangue, unanswered in the text, centers on women, for whom the new president feels a mingling of loathing and contempt.

Belmor begins by declaring that friendship between a man and a woman is as inappropriate as impossible.:

if . . . she be regarded in the role of a friend, her duplicity and her servility, or rather her baseness, scarcely favor the perfection of the sentiment of friendship; friendship requires openness and equality; when one of two friends dominates the other, friendship is destroyed; now, this preponderance of one of the two sexes over the other, fatal to friendship, exists necessarily where two friends are of unlike sex; thus, woman is good neither as a mistress nor as

46. Barthes has noted how rare is transvestism in Sade and how little it is used as a source of illusion, "L'Arbre du crime," *Tel Quel* 28 (1967), 26.

a friend; she is only where she belongs when in the servitude where the Orientals keep her. (p. 505)

Like other Sadian libertines he undergirds his philosophy with a wealth of geographic and historical examples:

the inferiority of female to males is established and patent . . . respect for women increases the farther the principles animating a given government depart from those of Nature; so long as men remain obedient to her fundamental laws, however, they are bound to hold women in supremest contempt. (p. 506)

Nature, Belmor argues several pages later, gave muscle and intelligence to men "to rule that weaker and deceitful sex, to force it into our desires' service; and we totally forget her intentions when we accord some independence, let alone some ascendancy to beings whom she made to be absolutely in our powers." The debasement of women is both mental and physical, and the president is especially eloquent when he describes the filthiness of a woman in childbirth.

To this rancorous address there is no reply and indeed it is lent force by authorial footnotes proclaiming with scientific seriousness that a woman is as far from a man as an ape, or that she "is simply man in an extraordinarily degraded form" (p. 511). Clairwil is disapproving but gives no answer, and she disports herself with the men as soon as the harangue finishes. The only qualification to it all comes from the peculiar sexual habit of the speaker; he desires a child to be bled in such a way that his blood flows over the sexual parts of the woman. Clearly he simulates menstruation and negates childbirth, and the fact suggests that his disgust of women, while genuine, is also lubricious and envious.

Clairwil teaches Juliette much and, as the pupil progresses, a new equality enters the relationship. When Juliette tumbles from Saint-Fond's favor for a momentary reluctance to starve France, she is ready in many ways to graduate from the school of Clairwil. But she never achieves her mentor's ferocity and, when she wanders off to remake her fortunes in the provinces, she carries with her Clairwil's indomitable spirit but little of her special antagonism to men. Perhaps it is as well, for she can rise—initially at least—only through men.

Juliette storms the provinces as successfully as she had Paris some years before. Here success is ratified by a man, the Comte de Lorsanges, who unwittingly marries her. Tiring quickly of the bourgeois joys he offers, she kills him and abandons their daughter to a libertine friend. Wealthy and free, she sets out on her travels through France and Italy, encountering on her way a whole circus of monstrous and bizarre libertines. The novel shifts from bildungsroman to picaresque, and the change of genre indicates that she has achieved some stature.[47] The effects of her education, not the education itself, become the center of interest.

Occasionally Juliette tries her hand at teaching in the manner of Clairwil, reprimanding with murder the faulty learner. One pupil is appreciated as long as she plots the slow death of her mother and daughter; when the pupil expresses some weakness for an illegitimate child, however, she is killed in turn by her pitiless mentor. Later, in Rome, Juliette discovers a more likely student in the Princess Olympia Borghese, already much advanced in lust and crime, but still ignorant of their lewd connection. But by this time it is clear that teaching is not to be Juliette's vocation, and, although she inspires passion, she rarely provokes the awe she had felt for Clairwil. Significantly too she never even tries out her pedagogy on a man; the hierarchy of education remains undisturbed.

Fortunately for the libertines of Italy, Juliette does not search long for a suitable proselyte, nor pine excessively for Clairwil. Captured by a brigand, she waits in terror for her fate—revealing that she is yet of weaker stuff than the fearless Clairwil. But destiny in the Sadian world is vicious, and the wicked must flourish. The brigand's ferocious wife-cum-sister turns out to be none other than Clairwil herself!

The reunion of the two friends is warm and savage, cele-

47. R. F. Brissenden discusses Sade's novels in terms of the eighteenth-century "sentimental" theme of a young lady's entrance into the world, *Virtue in Distress*, p. 284.

brated in a welter of voluptuous slaughter. When Olympia Borghese arrives as the new captive, happiness is complete; she is introduced to Clairwil as "the friend who assumed the place you had occupied in my heart, to the extent that another could replace you there" (p. 814). It is a graceful compliment to the two women Juliette will later betray.

Together the three women set out to ravage the countryside. Under Clairwil's tutelage and during her years of independence Juliette has progressed in vice to a point close to her mentor. She wishes now to exploit sexually only those men whose death she also desires, and she has learned to use sex politically. If as a woman she cannot come directly to power, she can manipulate those in power; so she overawes the Grand Duke of Tuscany and the Kings of Naples and Sardinia, preaching her political philosophy of license, republicanism, and francophilia, and showing these powerful men none of the reverence so evident in her dealings with Saint-Fond. In addition she uses the man she has in tow as a procurer for her own pleasures, as she herself had formerly been used by her master, and she is as ferocious to male weakness as Saint-Fond had been to female. When she learns this man has been concerned for her honor, she is appalled and speedily arranges his death.

Although the women cohere in their vicious aims, the trio is not a stable Sadian figure and its cracks soon show. Libertine and cruel in the extreme, Olympia nonetheless lags behind Juliette. To her two "friends" she appears somehow faltering and timid, guilty of insufficient imagination. So they plan for her a dramatic death: she will end her life plunging into the volcano of Mount Vesuvius. Her death is for Juliette delicious to contemplate, for it makes "a mockery of every sentiment of trust and friendship" (p. 1015).

By this point in the novel, with all obstructions between them removed, Juliette and Clairwil seem to approach the equality their friendship had promised. They talk to each other rather than harangue and they plot deeds together. Juliette is at the height of her iniquitous powers, free of any man's control and looking back on a ravaged Italy; Clairwil is, as always, confident and superb. There seems no reason why her dream of a ferocious life of man-slaughter should not come to pass.

3

But the reader should be suspicious. Except for the hapless Justine, the auditors of Juliette's tale are male, and we can expect the story to tend to their entertainment. In addition, the central misogyny of Belmor, supported in footnotes, does not suggest Sade contemplates so misanthropic an end. The signs are all disquieting for the admirers of Clairwil.

Before Juliette had gone into provincial exile from Saint-Fond, she had briefly met a woman named Durand, a sorcerer and poison-vendor. She is a forbidding personage, nearing fifty and possessing a decidedly masculine appearance. Tall, commanding, and Roman-featured, she is as awesome below as above; her vagina—that hated organ in the Sadian sexual economy—is obstructed and she has an outsize clitoris, even sperm.[48] If she is not a man, she is certainly the next best thing. Indeed she seems a kind of fearful male dream of a woman, stripped of her otherness, yet not completely endowed with male power. The almost heterosexual relationship she sets up with Juliette as the third of her "female" mentors in large part destroys the educative effect of Clairwil, reducing Juliette again to an adjunct agent.

In Paris Durand had prophesied the coming death of Clairwil. When she meets up with Juliette and her friend again (she has secretly been trailing them on their travels), she speedily ful-

48. Sade's use of the same terms for male and female sexual phenomena bears witness to the eighteenth-century debate between the ovists and the spermatists concerning women's part in procreation. In the *Encyclopedia* there was a discussion over whether the female emission was seminal and the equivalent of male ejaculation. The contemporary debate may help to explain Sade's bizarre descriptions of female orgasm. Leo Braudy has noted that later pornography has become fixated on the eighteenth-century belief that both men and women ejaculate, "Fanny Hill and Materialism," *Eighteenth-Century Studies* 4, no. 1 (Fall 1970), p. 26.

fills the prophecy she herself made. To glut her passion, she poisons Juliette's mind against Clairwil, ultimately manipulating her into killing her old friend to avoid her supposed plots. Juliette murders Clairwil, exclaiming, "Infamous creature! Thou whom I loved sincerely, in whose arms I surrendered myself in such candid good faith!" (p. 1028). For Clairwil she abandons her principle never to kill a thorough libertine and savage, a principle that had saved such ogres as the cannibal Minski.[49] Perhaps, however, the action is true to a deeper impulse, for the deaths of Clairwil and Olympia suggest that Juliette does not carry the saving principle to her own sex; it is the male libertine alone who is sacred.

Of course Durand has deceived her. When Juliette learns of Clairwil's innocence and Durand's treachery, she transfers her affections indelibly to the woman who has already once controlled her mind, and she avows to Durand: "I worship you to the point where, had this crime to be committed all over again, I would commit it unprompted" (p. 1035).

Juliette's passionate declaration to Durand is only the first of a long series of expressions of love and awe. Such overwhelming and self-abasing emotions have largely been absent from the more political—and lately more equal—relationship of Juliette and Clairwil. To find their equilvalent we must return to the old liaison with Saint-Fond.

Early in their friendship when Clairwil had invited Juliette to form with her an anti-male alliance, Juliette had hardly replied; now she reacts enthusiastically to Durand's proposal of a union which is, however, indiscriminately offensive. "I shall swear an oath to adore you everlastingly," exclaims Juliette so slavishly that even Durand seems taken back. She replies quickly, "I have no wish to tyrannize over you, Juliette"; yet she insists on being the only friend and accomplice, while leaving Juliette free to pursue her cruel pleasures wherever she wishes. Saint-Fond too had

---

49. Jean Biou discusses the anomaly of the death of Clairwil in "Deux oeuvres complémentaires," p. 110.

demanded unique reverence while licensing Juliette to follow her lusts elsewhere.

Through a series of tests, Juliette finds Durand true to her, and her worship of her new friend grows apace. They will be inseparable for life, Juliette avers, and Durand even persuades her to dismiss her entourage of libidinous women, boasting, "Think not that you shall ever regret having lost everybody else, for in having me you shall have more than a whole world" (p. 1057). Sure of their alliance, Juliette exults, "Our strength is in our union and nothing will dissolve it" (p. 1040). Clairwil is superseded: "Next to you, Clairwil was a mere child," Juliette declares to Durand: "you are what my happiness demands, you are the woman I have been seeking, never leave me again" (p. 1041).

But Clairwil is not the only "mere child" beside Durand. When Juliette and her friend set up in Venice to whore and poison, they pass as mother and daughter. It is not a stray pretence, for Durand is old enough to be Juliette's mother, almost her grandmother, and she has a magical motherlike quality that sets her apart from ordinary women. On her side Juliette is innocent of her own mother's murder and it is her father who suffers a ritualized and lengthy death. (Juliette's supposed father proved a fraud and the true one appears early in the book only to be assaulted, raped, and killed by his daughter, who goes on to abort their incestuous child.) Later Juliette will roast her only daughter alive and connive at the death of her only sister. Certainly the mother is conspicuously absent from this list of sacrificed relatives and it does seem that Juliette has retained a certain respect for the maternal principle.[50] In Durand she appears to find it embodied.

50. Pierre Klossowski, however, finds the key to Sade's work in his implacable hatred of the mother. He states that Sade frequently describes scenes where mothers are humiliated and murdered before their children. See *Sade mon prochain* (Paris: Editions de Seuil, 1947). Certainly Sade degrades the mother as he degrades the father and child, but in *Juliette* the mother seems the least persecuted of the family members. For a full discussion of Juliette's relationship to the family and her contradiction of all its codes, see Nancy K. Miller's "*Juliette* and the Posterity of Prosperity," *L'Ésprit createur* 15, no. 4, pp. 413–24.

187

MANIPULATIVE FRIENDSHIP

Because they were more or less equal toward the end of their friendship, Clairwil and Juliette had little to teach each other. With Durand, however, Juliette falls back into the role of pupil. From her friend she learns the ultimate lesson she needs—that, since all life's necessities are pleasure-producing, death itself may yield voluptuousness. Sensual excitement, which Juliette had seen leading to cruelty, may also promote "an eager expectancy of death." All of life, including its ending, has now been sexualized, and Juliette can have little else to learn from any libertine.

With Durand, Juliette loses something of her bold antagonism toward men; her presence becomes less awful and her speech less disconcerting. In Italy she had used and abused kings at will. Now with Durand she relapses into the postures abjured since the days of Saint-Fond. To a man who demands it she shows the "deepest respect." She ministers dutifully to all his perverse needs, although in the end she rallies to poison him with one of Durand's concoctions.

The union of the two friends fails when Durand, like Juliette before her, seems to waver in crime. When the authorities of Venice order Durand to cause a plague, she at first demurs. Her reluctance is noted in silence and swiftly punished. Her dead body is displayed to a fearful Juliette, who obeys with alacrity the command to flee the city. Friendless but wealthy, she returns to Paris to a waiting Noirceuil.

During her exile Noirceuil has grown tired of seconding Saint-Fond and he is about to tumble him from office into the grave. He is eager to take Juliette back into favor, content merely to warn her against any further show of weakness. He ratifies their renewed association with a bizarre quadruple marriage, in which on one day Noirceuil weds his two sons, once as husband and once as wife, and Juliette marries her daughter dressed as a man, then takes another girl as husband.

After the marriages have been celebrated, the adjuncts to the ceremonies are assaulted, tortured, and killed, with the usual orgiastic frenzy. Noirceuil has sodomized one son as his wife, while eating the heart out of the other. Reluctant at first to sacri-

188

fice her only child, Juliette finally agrees to her roasting. The action is the culmination of the Sadian fury at social bonds and taboos. Noirceuil and Juliette emerge seemingly freed from all relationships and all restraints. Yet this nightmare exists to ensure the final sustained relationship of dominant male and obedient female. In the carnage the patriarchal relationship of Juliette and Noirceuil remains intact.

The lustful mockery over, *Juliette* winds down to a gentle close, almost approaching the conventional happy ending. Durand helps the mood by opportunely arriving to announce that she was hanged in proxy only. When she agreed after all to infect the citizens of Venice, she was pardoned and rewarded. She has now returned to Paris, rich and affectionate. Inspired by the relaxed and lyrical mood, she indulges in a maternal dream: to die "in my cherished Juliette's arms" (p. 1192).

The book closes on the hierarchical family trio of Noirceuil, Durand, and Juliette, static beside the earlier unstable trio of libidinous women.[51] As the new ruler of France in place of the ousted Saint-Fond, Noirceuil enters on a glorious path of vicious luxury and national devastation; Juliette will be his helpmate, Durand her duenna. Having started her on her rise and saved her life when Saint-Fond coveted it, he now emerges her protector forever. Once the scourge of Italy and tentative champion of her sex, Juliette settles down in comfort and silent contentment with Noirceuil and Durand. She has abandoned her search for a pupil of her own and her child is dead; she has achieved no equal friend. Her status is then fixed as perpetual daughter, object of parental affection and care, breeding neither children nor proselytes.

Her reduction is noted in the text. Although her own verbal account breaks off, the author-narrator declares that she

51. M. Tortel has noted the respect Juliette has for Noirceuil and Durand, although she has felt at least the equal of all the other characters. Noirceuil alone has caused her to sacrifice her daughter, while Durand has made her kill Clairwil. Tortel concludes by wondering whether the true hero of the novel is not the couple Noirceuil-Durand, "Interventions sur la communication de Jean Biou," *Colloque d'Aix-en-Provence, 19 et 20 fevrier* (Paris: Armand Colin, 1968), p. 113.

flourishes for another ten years. This is hard to grasp, for the great libertines have always lived through speech as well as action, their vicious exploits played out in word and body. Juliette's silence seems to remove her from the libertine ranks and reduce her to the condition of her ill-fated and virtuous sister, Justine. As Justine is smitten by a force of lightning, silenced by a stroke of the divine pen through her mouth, so Juliette is silenced by the human pen of the male narrator.[52] Virtue and vice fall together in this world, which, in spite of reversals, remains cloven by gender.

Sade, who fantasized incest and nuptial sodomy, appears then to stumble at female friendship, unless it is parental and manipulative. Durand manipulates Juliette into killing Clairwil, and the murder is in turn a further drastic controlling of a female friend. Clairwil, who promised a political tie founded on achieved equality, reciprocity, and shared distrust of men, gives way to Durand, who reduces Juliette to a daughter and almost a wife. By the end of the novel, manipulative friendship and subservience within heterosexuality seem alone left to the Sadian woman. Ultimately the "divine marquis" proves himself human and a man. Although coached in flying by Clairwil, Juliette—Apollinaire's new woman "who shall have wings"—never quite leaves the ground; the phallocracy, for all its lewd gyrations and insulting naughtiness, leaves the patriarchy intact and Juliette and her friends within.

52. Writing is allowed only to the male author, so Clairwil's dreams of a perpetual crime which would continue corrupting even when she slept—evil writing or Sade's own work—is not fulfilled. Sollers discusses writing as the ultimate crime in Sade dans le texte, pp. 49–50. For the association of writing and maleness, sperm and lightning, see Barthes, Sade, Fourier, Loyola, pp. 32–38; Godelieve Mercken-Spaas's "Sade and Rousseau: the Self and the Other," paper read at NEMLA, Spring 1977; and Nancy K. Miller's "Juliette and the Posterity of Prosperity," 423–24, which deals in detail with the silencing of Juliette. Pierre Klossowski sees the lightning that strikes Justine less as an image of male destruction than as a symbol of purity and anger, acting to consecrate virginity, Sade mon prochain, p. 108.

CHAPTER FOUR

Political Friendship

Mary Wollstonecraft's *Mary, A Fiction* (1788)

IN HER POLEMIC, *A Vindication of the Rights of Woman,* Mary Wollstonecraft exalts friendship, severing it cleanly from love and endowing it with all virtue. It is, she announces, "a serious affection; the most sublime of all affections, because it is founded on principle, and cemented by time." Love and friendship cannot coexist within a person, she argues, since "even when inspired by different objects they weaken or destroy each other, and for the same object can only be felt in succession." Love is selfish and sexual, while friendship is just and pure: "The vain fears and fond jealousies, the winds which fan the flame of love . . . are both incompatible with the tender confidence and sincere respect of friendship."[1] So in Wollstonecraft's emotional economy the battle of sexual infatuation and friendship is joined, for each threatens the other. Love or infatuation may thrive on battle, but friendship should be calm and sure; by contesting, it becomes dangerously vulnerable.

For Wollstonecraft friendship is further menaced by the faulty, paltry upbringing of women. Taught to dress, paint, sing, and lisp, they are raised as objects of sexual infatuation, not subjects of friendship; imprisoned in perpetual childhood, they are denied the maturity required for a reasonable relationship with

---

1. *A Vindication of the Rights of Woman,* ed. Carol H. Poston (New York: Norton, 1975), p. 73. Wollstonecraft is of course concerned with friendship not only between women, but between men and women as well.

their own sex. Wearily she summarizes the dilemma of women deeply in need of friendship yet rendered incapable of it:

> I know that a little sensibility, and great weakness, will produce a strong sexual attachment, and that reason must cement friendship; consequently, I allow that more friendship is to be found in the male than the female world, and that men have a higher sense of justice . . . how can women be just or generous, when they are the slaves of injustice? [2]

Certainly Wollstonecraft is dubious about female friendship. Yet her strictures imply the idealist. Her harshest criticism betrays her vison of the just and generous friend, while her lament declares the liberating power of a relationship that alone can free women from a round of slavish dependence and stolen mastery. Ratifying and nurturing the reason essential for the free woman, friendship in her view is able to bestow the true consequence women yearn for in their amorous struggles with men. But first it must descend and engage in battle.

1

Mary, A Fiction, Wollstonecraft's first novel, was written in 1787, several years before *A Vindication of the Rights of Woman* and before Wollstonecraft had developed and refined her ideas about women and their social situation. It is almost a case study of the difficulties of female friendship, although the focus is less on friendship itself than on its contrast with sexuality, and less on social than on psychological problems. Mary, the heroine, sees sexuality both as a social demand of the male world and as an inner threat. She tries to establish a friendly relationship but her efforts are flawed. Trapped in adolescence and haunted by sexual dread, she has neither the maturity nor the self-awareness to be a friend; she mistakes benevolence for justice and self-interest for generosity. The novel fascinates through its depiction of the heroine and her emotional etiology. Beyond Mary's obsessive

2. Ibid., p. 189.

fears and desires beckons a tantalizing ideal of friendship to which she never quite lets herself be drawn.

As Wollstonecraft's "Advertisement" declares, the heroine of *Mary, A Fiction* will be the subject, not the object, of the action; agent and lover, not victim and beloved. So she will differ from Clarissa, whose distasteful virtue the author finds passive and negative.[3] But to present such a figure is difficult, as the first pages show. Wollstonecraft starts by describing Mary's unloving parents, and, since a daughter—far more than a son who escapes to school or to tutors—will be conditioned by these parents, Mary is in a way already condemned. Admittedly she will act because she must if she wishes to find love, but with such parents she will retain the lineaments of the victim nonetheless.

Mary's parents consist of a passive, vain mother and a vicious, debauched father. There is no tender nurse or kindly older friend. In her last novel, *The Wrongs of Woman*, Wollstonecraft will provide a sensitive and cultivated uncle to account in part for her heroine's taste and sensibility.[4] In *Mary, A Fiction*, the heroine's singular virtue springs from neglect and unhappiness—neither nurture nor nature seems to play much part in it.

The first female relationship in the novel is between Mary and her mother. In depicting the latter, Wollstonecraft benefits from her chosen method of third-person narration, for, without implicating her generous and sensitive heroine—on whose behalf she is flauntingly partisan—she can be scathing and scornful of

3. *Mary, A Fiction*, ed. Janet M. Todd (New York: Schocken Books, 1977), p. 3. References in the text are to this edition. Until recently, most critics of Wollstonecraft ignored *Mary, A Fiction* or, repulsed or embarrassed by its sketchiness and abruptness, have commented unfavorably on it, J. M. S. Tompkins was one early critic who noted but did not investigate the "suggestion of richness and depth in the book that is never wrought out, of impulse, struggle and attainment which, however poorly conveyed, are felt to be real," *The Popular Novel in England 1770–1800* (1932; Lincoln: University of Nebraska Press, 1961), p. 345.

4. Nancy K. Miller comments on the avuncular relationship in the feminocentric novel: "The component of authority (severity) is deleted in favor of compassion and protection. Adoptive 'parents' supply the unconditional love and approval that natural parents withhold in the name of the family." "Female Sexuality and Narrative Structure in *La Nouvelle Héloïse* and *Les Liaisons dangereuses*," p. 634.

the fashionable lady whom she harshly reduces to a "mere nothing." Superficially Mary is the antithesis of her mother, and the author demands that in the contrast between the two we contemplate the callow, selfish, and frivolous against the thoughtful, serious, and benevolent, the bad against the good.

Certainly the mother is trivial beside her exemplary daughter, but her triviality seems to mask something equally suspect and less socially approved: the hunger of a sexual woman in a world where overt sexuality is male and brutal, where female desire must be covert and displaced. She exists in a lonely world, for, in spite of Mary's castle and lineage, her parents are in reality hopelessly bourgeois: there is no aristocratic divorce for them and they are rarely interrupted by the social forms that give variety and substance to upper-class life. They must exist together forever in isolation. The father is no company. He lives a sensual life, given to immoderate dinners, whose "cumbrous load" he somnolently digests through the afternoon. The sexual encounter he then requires comes as a kind of dessert, and, since he is a gourmand in women, he leaves his wife for more appealing fare. The sexuality and the eating are both immoderate, self-indulgent, and repulsive, and the reader is meant to cringe from each in the same way; the wenching is as inelegant as the gluttony. The mother of course can indulge neither in culinary nor in adulterous pleasures. The convention that allows her husband to cast a lewd eye on his pretty tenants decrees that she must be chaste—in body at least. So we might assume that her sexuality will find vent elsewhere, but we are allowed to feel no pity for the displacement; when the author calls the novels she reads "those most delightful substitutes for bodily dissipation," we must condemn not commiserate. Indeed so harshly is she treated that she is denied degradation only to enhance her vapidity: "to make amends for this seeming self-denial [her chastity], she read all the sentimental novels, dwelt on the love-scenes, and, had she thought while she read, her mind would have been contaminated" (p. 8).[5]

5. Wollstonecraft constantly worried about the escapist content of female fiction and she castigated novelists for providing it. In the review of Charlotte Smith's *Emmeline, the*

POLITICAL FRIENDSHIP

In the daughter we see a very different creature, insistently endowed with sensitivity, intellect, and benevolence. Yet, for all the author's insistence, we cannot help distinguishing a rather pathetic young girl, whose adolescent rhapsodies do not impress merely because we are told they should.[6] Instead, her sweet, touching songs and her raptures over the morning insinuate a hidden truth: that below the neatly antithetical surface the women may be remarkably alike, that the repressions and emotional excesses of both may have a common source, and that Mary does well to cry—as she repeatedly does—that she is her parent's child. Certainly both women are alone, and both are great readers.

Like her mother Mary begins by searching for an object of love, but, unlike her mother, she searches in life and finds her object not through romance but through benevolence. Mary's benevolence is one of the reiterated goods of the novel: it is constantly praised in abstract and painted in action. Mary succors the poor, gives to the needy and wipes the tears of the unhappy. The lavish praise for her benevolence should not however obscure its link with the romance of her mother. Judging according to her own needs, the mother romantically creates husband, handsome son, and enamored lover. She pours affection on her lapdogs because she admires the picture of her own devotion and enjoys the luxury of petting them in French. Mary is not so selfish, but her benevolence is clearly streaked with narcissism.

Mary cries for her vicious father most intensely when she contrasts him with her own virtuous self. She is touched more by the picture of her own goodness than by her father's sorry moral

Orphan of the Castle, she attacked the silly romantic plots that "tend to debauch the mind, and throw an insipid kind of uniformity over the moderate and rational prospects of life"; in the review of *Mount Pelham* she criticized "the varnish of sentiment" that hid the "sensuality" of what elsewhere she termed romantic unnatural fabrications and "whipped syllabubs." See *A Wollstonecraft Anthology,* ed. Janet M. Todd (Bloomington: Indiana University Press, 1977), pp. 217–19.

6. In her novel Wollstonecraft is acutely concerned with her heroine, whose self-pity at times does duty for her own. Frequently it seems that Wollstonecraft's own experience underlies Mary's responses and that to understand the novel one must look to the author, not the text.

state. Later she is said to feel especially gratified in her benevolence not when the people she helps are improved but when she suffers through helping—when she feels, for example, "pinched by hunger" after giving away her food. Indeed, all her sacrificial kindness cannot disguise the fact that she is unloved by her parents and in turn fails to love. So she chooses benevolence while living intensely in a compensatory world of imagination and books. This other world in turn impinges on her reality, for it allows her in her actual benevolence to feel uniquely virtuous and sensitive. The narrator joins her in this makebelieve, asserting that "the poor adored her" and providing her on the whole with appreciative, loving, and unthreatening objects of care.[7]

One of them is her dying mother, for, as she approaches death, the distance between her and her daughter is traversed, and Mary manages to relate to her. Sickly and weak, her mother at last can become a needy object, and the daughter's self-esteem is gratified by the apology her dying parent is forced to make. She is reaffirmed in her benevolent and forgiving character.

The bond between mother and daughter, then, is deep and unstated, a matter of narcissistic attitude and fearful sexual interest. On the surface, however, there is until death no relationship. So Mary is constrained to seek her absent parent elsewhere. But her search is complicated by the parent's legacy: she seeks and demands love because no one has loved her, but her search is confused by the sexual fears and desires derived from her family. She runs into friendship both to avoid the sexual love she shrinks from and wants, and to compensate for her parents' neglect. It is not a strong basis for the just and generous friendship so yearningly depicted in *The Rights of Woman*.

7. Mary's situation is well described by Lacan when he writes of those who, experiencing no love in early life, link themselves with the imaginary rather than the real; consequently they come to experience a gap or space where they should have a sense of self. To fill it they image themselves as they see themselves through others in contrast or comparison. This analysis may explain Mary's concern to distinguish herself in virtue from her father and in intellect from Ann. See *The Language of the Self: The Function of Language in Psychoanalysis* (New York: Dell, 1968), p. 9. The concept of the gap (béance) in Lacanian psychology is discussed in this volume by the translator, Anthony Wilden, pp. 98–99.

The main female relationship within the novel is between Mary and her friend Ann, and to it all other ties are mere prologue and epilogue. As with her mother, so here with Ann, the third person narrative method fails to create distance from Mary, serving rather to shut out the other. The narrator's emotional commitment to her heroine keeps Ann silent and largely unknown throughout her history.[8]

What attracts and then repulses Mary is Ann's air of sadness, which makes her "interesting." While staying with an uncle, Ann had fallen in love with a cultivated young man who promptly forgot her when she returned to her impoverished parents. But his image is indelible in her mind and she grows melancholy. Because she has associated with him she has taste, and because she is now sad she is solitary. Mary too is cultured and solitary, snd she feels mightily for her friend who seems so remarkably like herself. The resemblance is, however, false: Ann's love for solitude is circumstantial, not natural; her taste imposed, not achieved.

The relationship of Mary and Ann is made in spite of the world. Conventional people scoff at it, while the parents, by marrying Mary off, do their best to destroy it. An equal relationship of female friends could possibly triumph over the hostile forces, but the relationship is not equal, partly because Ann is stated to be unworthy—and in love with a man to boot—and partly because Mary seeks a situation of benevolence rather than friendship.

As in her earlier life, Mary luxuriates in her nurturing function with Ann. She enjoys denying herself, revels in "the luxury of doing good," and seems infatuated less with her friend— although this is repeatedly asserted—than with her own benevolent image. In addition, she carries on living through reading and continues to indulge in rhapsodies of devotion and self-pity. Above all her sexual feelings and fears grow apace.

8. The narrator is strident in her advocacy of Mary, seemingly fearful that we will sympathize with Ann and divide an emotion destined for Mary alone. So she frequently intrudes to demand we confine our feeling solely to the heroine.

POLITICAL FRIENDSHIP

In the first stage of her relationship with Ann, Mary is both attracted to and repulsed by the emotional closeness she offers. She seems to yearn for rapport and yet spurn it whenever it is feasible. As her fears overwhelm, she turns abruptly from her friend to enter her own lonely psychic space, furnished with symbols of her erotic longing. Her state is embodied in a harsh sexual landscape to which she withdraws to read and fantasize:

> One way home was through the cavity of a rock covered with a thin layer of earth, just sufficient to afford nourishment to a few stunted shrubs and wild plants, which grew on its sides, and nodded over the summit. A clear stream broke out of it, and ran amongst the pieces of rock fallen into it. Here twilight always reigned—it seemed the Temple of Solitude; yet paradoxical as the assertion may appear, when the foot sounded on the rock, it terrified the intruder, and inspired a strange feeling, as if the rightful sovereign was dislodged. In this retreat she read Thomson's Seasons, Young's Night-thoughts, and Paradise Lost. (p. 18)[9]

Her growing sexuality is hard, lonely, and private, expressed in vicarious emotions and displaced fears. Its narcissistic nature is established when in the text this passage of erotic scenery is juxtaposed with a description of Mary's self-gratifying yet self-denying benevolence. The relationship with Ann has clearly not eradicated the patterns of childhood.

The second stage of Ann's friendship with Mary follows the sexual awakening in the Temple of Solitude. Describing her on Mary's behalf, the narrator looks through a male lover's eyes: "This ill-fated love has given a bewitching softness to her manners, a delicacy so truly feminine, that a man of any feeling could not behold her without wishing to chase her sorrows away" (p. 23). Toward this femininity—so desirable for a man—Mary is

9. Ellen Moers has noted in this description an early appearance of the erotic female landscape common in female fiction of the nineteenth century; she finds it again in the section on the Red Deeps in George Eliot's *Mill on the Floss*. She notes that in both books the landscape has nothing to do with the plot of the novel or the rest of its geography, but "surges up, a kind of vision, when the heroine is alone," *Literary Women: The Great Writers* (New York: Doubleday, 1976), pp. 254–55.

however ambivalent. Ann is "truly feminine" not only in her delicacy, but also in her taste for the pretty over the great, for harmony over genius and speculation. So Mary is both attracted and repelled by the feminine ideal Ann embodies: as an object of desire she fascinates, as an equal companion she repels.

While Mary's relationship with Ann thickens, the primary link of mother and daughter breaks in death. At this point a curious incident occurs. To avoid litigation over property, the father plans to marry Mary off to the fifteen-year-old son of the other claimant. The ceremony takes place in dramatic circumstances. Ann is suddenly rendered helpless and dependent on Mary through the eviction of her family; at the same instant, Mary's dying mother insists that her daughter's marriage take place before her death. The combined catastrophes numb Mary and she sleepwalks through a service that will bind her for the rest of her days. It is a typical scene. The economic and familial have come together to undo Clarissa and Suzanne before her. As for the feminine penchant for sleeping through crises, it has been noted in the fiction of Richardson, Diderot, and Cleland; clearly it is a convention that ignores the author's gender.

Mary's marriage can be variously interpreted. Through giving herself socially and sexually to a complete stranger, she ensures her continued suffering. Perhaps in this she follows the masochism that has led her to hurt herself in serving others and love a person already in love. Perhaps agains she affirms in her action her relationship with her will-less mother at the moment of death, for, if we regard the mother instead of Mary, the marriage may be viewed as a symbol of her power over her daughter's entire life. Through marrying, Mary forfeits the chance of an equal relationship with man or woman, and condemns herself to the social system her mother has long suffered under and supported.

After the marriage, the new husband wanders off to tour the Continent and Ann moves in with Mary. Of course she disappoints at first, for, still lovesick, she cannot completely attune her moods and wishes to her friend's. She wants "to be alone" when

Mary seeks company and she is discontented when her friend feels close. Mary is quick to condemn: "She had not yet found the companion she looked for," and she judges harshly: "Ann and she were not congenial minds" (p. 28).

In much the same way as the mother-daughter bond was established in death, the relationship with Ann enters a new and deeper phase when Mary realizes her friend is dying. Ann's consumption halts the disintegration of the friendship and prevents Mary—and her partisan narrator—from turning from her. As Ann hastens to death we enter the third phase of the relationship.

Through dying, Ann can become an object of "pure" affection for Mary, who now gives vent to the emotion she has long repressed. When Ann coughs, Mary "would then catch her to her bosom with convulsive eagerness, as if to save her from sinking into an opening grave" (p. 29). Her love pours out, since all sexual possibilities are stanched and no equality can occur—it is love as benevolence. As earlier, this benevolent love is sweetest when most tormented: Mary loves Ann because she is dying.

As she becomes increasingly wrapped up in her friend, Mary grows more and more hostile to the male world, more and more obsessed by her fears. The boy-husband is a dim character in the novel—much later we learn from an outsider that he is good-natured and weak—but to Mary he looms as ogre, both mentally and physically repulsive: "An extreme dislike took root in her mind; the sound of his name made her turn sick" (p. 29). The physical reaction is excessive, suggesting the physical horror he especially threatens. Significantly, the husband is due back when the doctors predict Ann's death; he will intrude on Mary when she is most solitary and vulnerable.

The contrasting relationships between Mary and Ann, and between Mary and her husband, are expressed in their differing methods of communication, although they are linked by their common ending in silence. Mary and the husband—whose name she never utters—communicate through the formal letter. They write coldly and distantly; yet their words bind them and rivet their bond, as surely as their signatures at their marriage. The letters dictate movements and attitudes, acting as weapons in the contest each joins with the other. But it is a contest Mary must lose; consequently her letters most clearly fall from formality, edging toward the hysteria below: "I am her only support," she writes to her husband about Ann, "she leans on me—could I forsake the forsaken, and break the bruised reed—No—I would die first!" (p. 34).

In contrast, the friendship with Ann, although starting in formal letters, diverges quickly into informality and spontane-ousness; finally, living together, the two women dispense with the written word altogether and express feelings directly through speech and gesture. When most intense, when Mary's friendship with Ann occupies her heart and resembles a passion, the rela-tionship is displayed mostly through the convulsive hug or tearful glance.

As she sinks toward death, Ann's inadequacy as a person and friend dims and we hear far more of Mary's love. To her husband she describes this love as "like a maternal one" and cer-tainly the mother haunts the relationship. Tending and caring for Ann, Mary plays the mother to her. Her own mother had never been maternal, instead making a mother of her daughter; so when Mary cares for Ann, she reenacts the contradictory and un-satisfactory relationship with her mother. Like the mother, the dying Ann becomes pitiful and open to benevolent love. She is not "the companion" Mary sought and Mary herself has given up the search. Indeed we could say that her mother's neglect has prevented her from ever beginning it.

To halt Ann's decline, Mary takes her to Portugal to the sun. She chooses Portugal because it is farthest removed from her hus-band—rather as she chooses to love the sickly and poor Ann, the antithesis of the wealthy and healthy man. In Portugal, however, Ann's condition quickly worsens. Mary devotes herself entirely to her, sleeps with her, supports her, comforts and entertains her. Only now, when Ann is completely enveloped by Mary, are we allowed a glimpse of Ann's view of her friend. In Mary, Ann concludes, love and pity were closely allied. It is as true a perception as any authorial one, but it should be more strongly stated: in Mary, love *must* be allied to pity if it is not to threaten.

3

When Ann dies, Mary declares she "has no other friend." Yet through her suffering and dying, Ann has provided Mary with a new relationship which in a way extends and provides the epilogue for their friendship. At the hotel in Portugal, Ann and Mary meet the sickly and sensitive Henry. Although a man, Henry is worlds away from the threatening husband and is instead akin to Ann, of whom he seems a purer and worthier version.[10] Like Ann he is marked by a pensive melancholy arising from disappointed love, and, like Ann again, he is clearly dying. He has turned his back on physical passion and is as asexual as the dead woman he supplants.

Mary attracts Henry first of all in the role of Ann's friend. As in *Julie*, the display of female friendship seems profoundly moving to the man. Henry is struck by the way Mary attends her friend and entranced by the affection she shows her, mingled as it is with horror for the absent husband:

[Mary] exclaimed, "I cannot live without her!—I have no other friend; if I lose her, what a desart will the world be to me." "No other friend," re-echoed they, "have you not a husband?"

Mary shrunk back, and was alternately pale and red. A delicate sense of propriety prevented her replying; and recalled her bewildered reason . . . she made the intended enquiry, and left the room. Henry's eyes followed her. (pp. 44–45)

Later he declares his feeling: "I would give the world," he exclaims rapturously, "for your picture, with the expression I have seen in your face, when you have been supporting your friend" (p. 48).

10. Patricia Meyer Spacks describes Henry as "the ideal of a man with woman's virtues, capable like Mary herslf of loyalty, fortitude, and endurance, devoid of aggressive and obvious male pride," *Imagining a Self: Autobiography and Novel in Eighteenth-Century England* (Cambridge: Harvard University Press, 1976), p. 71.

POLITICAL FRIENDSHIP

Having once been betrayed through love as infatuation, Henry is now ready to choose love as exalted friendship. Mary is attracted by Henry's choice and the melancholy that attends it; like Ann's earlier sadness, it suggests a committed heart and promises pain. As Ann's sadness was for her "interesting," Henry's illness and melancholy are now "pleasing," for they allow Mary to tend and comfort him. The purity of her heart, of her affection, is stressed; this will be a pure female love as friendship, a higher version of the friendship of Ann and Mary. But through choosing a physically sickly and dependent person— however strong in spirit and emotion—Mary is again playing the role of benevolent nurse and mother, eschewing the more strenuous one of equal friend and companion.

As the mother haunted the friendship of Mary and Ann, lending her personality and function to both young women in turn, so Ann haunts the friendship of Mary and Henry. We have seen how Henry resembles and seems to extend Ann; Mary too assumes something of the character of her dead friend. At one point indeed Ann seems to draw Mary into the death she has suffered: in her last days, Ann had breathed painfully and when she dies, Mary finds herself suffocating. Furthermore, she feels deadened by grief and numbed into a senselessness that is the shadow of Ann's. From this deathlike state she is rescued by Henry's compassionate tears. He delivers her from the dead Ann, but he himself is captivated by Mary's deathlikeness which to him betokens strong feeling. Although Ann seems to have lost Mary to her rival—without Henry, she "had sunk into the grave of her long-lost friend"—in fact Ann has ratified and blessed the new union.

Henry welds Mary to him through his confession of his life's story. Like Mary he is "dead to the world" and the two of them exist together in a kind of emotional limbo. When once Henry suggests Mary may be happy, she is shocked and insulted at the idea: "her feelings were so much in unison with his, that she was in love with misery."

Like Mary again, Henry feels threatened by sexual intimacy. The woman he loved forfeited his "esteem"—through a sexual slip, it is suggested. In revenge, he fashions a fantastic woman endowed with sensations "which the gross part of mankind have not any conception of" (p. 59). In Mary, passionate in friendship and repulsed by sexual marriage, he finds his fantasy embodied. She in turn encounters neither a sexual nor an equal companion, but a parent and a child. She will care for Henry and he will treat her as "a darling child." When he requests her to "rely on him as if he was her father," the substitution dazzles her: "If she had had a father, such a father!" she exclaims, and the thought is so overpowering that it momentarily "unhinged" her mind (p. 61).

Mary throws herself passionately into a friendship in which she can be both child and benevolent parent. It is her culminating relationship, and at night she dreams variously of her mother, Ann, and Henry, all somehow fashioned into a pure and worthy whole. With Henry she seems to enter on earth into the pure and passionate heaven she once imagined, where love exists without the alloy of "earthly infirmities."

As Mary's love for Henry burgeons, so her feeling for the dead Ann grows. The friend who had earlier been uncongenial and inadequate becomes now essential to her peace, and the flawed friendship is exalted into a relationship of perfect harmony. "I could not exist," exclaims Mary, "without the hope of seeing her again—I could not bear to think that time could wear away an affection that was founded on what is not liable to perish" (p. 67). The love of Henry now does double duty for male and female friendship: "had Ann lived, it is probable she [Mary] would never have loved Henry so fondly" (p. 81).

After Mary returns to England, she awaits Henry in Ann's house. When he arrives, he is clearly dying. Like Ann he catches a cold with Mary and thereafter rapidly declines; like Ann, too, he comes closest to Mary as he approaches death. Earlier the relationship had been strained, expressed in a cold and formal letter from Henry. When Mary sees him dying, however, she forgets her displeasure, revealing her tenderness now in caressing speeches and abrupt emotional exclamations. At the end she enacts again the dying scene she has played earlier with Ann and her mother. Certainly love for Mary seems death-ridden and closeness contingent on pain and coming separation.

With the deaths of Ann and her extension, Henry, we are left with the conventional union of husband and wife, yoked unhappily together. The book opens with the misalliance of Mary's parents and ends with her own, resulting from it. The long struggle, marred from within and without, for an equal relationship in friendship is over, but the author stresses that it is not wasted:

> It was an advantage to Mary that friendship first possessed her heart; it opened it to all the softer sentiments of humanity:—and when this first affection was torn away, a similar one sprung up, with a still tenderer sentiment added to it. (p. 98)

The relationship with the husband breaks the pattern of female friendship extended by Henry, and brings Mary face to face with the powerful male world, from which she has so long recoiled. The author's consolatory words are at this point belied by the action: because Mary has run to other relationships to compensate for absent parents and to escape the male sexual threat, friendship has not been strengthening to her; in no way can it be described as an "advantage." The end of the novel leaves us with a fearful picture of Mary, hysterically terrified of a relationship that implies so much that she has long shunned.

Even before the husband appears, she suffers his power. Because a husband controls his wife's fortune, Mary finds herself relatively poor when she refuses to return to the family home. In this state she cannot give so grandly as in the past and she learns something of the limits of the benevolence her two friendships have reinforced. A poor woman she once helped but can help no longer loads her with abuse when her allowance stops; Ann's mother is ungrateful once she understands she will receive no more benefits from her guest.

Most striking, however, is the husband's physical power. Dreading "sensuality," Mary sickens at his very name. Later she controls herself sufficiently to write to him, but, when he replies in person, she faints. In their life together, her sexual horror is overt:

> She tried to appear calm; time mellowed her grief, and mitigated her torments; but when her husband would take her hand, or mention any thing like love, she would instantly feel a sickness, a faintness at her heart, and wish, involuntarily, that the earth would open and swallow her. (p. 110)

For the child Mary, the male sexual act was aggressive, perpetrated by her father on the body of the female. Nothing in her short life has severed sex from the fear of male aggression, or associated it with love, and her masochistic and narcissistic affections have been her retreat from this sexual dread.[11] Her final retreat in death is one that has repeatedly beckoned to her.

The book ends with an affirmation of the sexless, deathly friendship with Ann-Henry:

> [Mary's] delicate state of health did not promise long life. In moments of solitary sadness, a gleam of joy would dart across her mind—She thought she was hastening to that world *where there is neither marrying,* nor giving in marriage. (p. 111)

Love and death are one, and both, it seems, are celibate.

On the surface of *Mary, A Fiction,* Wollstonecraft contrasts sexual desire and pure friendship, as she would later do in *A Vindication of the Rights of Woman.* Yet the two texts do not tally. Certainly the later one is wistful, but it does not hint at obsessional depths below its words as the novel does. In *Mary, A*

11. In her discussion of the psychology of women, Marie Bonaparte, an early Freudian analyst, has some interesting observations on female sexual fear. She believes that women are especially prone to masochism through their dread of male penetration and she describes a progress in fear close to that illustrated by Wollstonecraft's Mary. See "Passivity, Masochism and Femininity (1934)," *Women & Analysis,* ed. Jean Strouse (New York: Dell, 1974), pp. 279–88. Bonaparte does not, however, discuss the other intuition of Wollstonecraft's novel, that it is women's social situation, their dependence on men and male values, that allows the sexual fear to grow. In the Wollstonecraftian world women do well to fear the sexual act as both real and symbolic aggression.

Fiction, the obsession and fear mark the text, both when friendship is extolled and when marriage and "sensuality" are condemned. Why should the two works differ so widely?

Possibly because theory and practice are distinct. In representing rather than describing, the novelist cannot so lightly gloss over difficulties; the polemicist always has an easier ideological time of it. Yet Wollstonecraft wrote her polemical work *after* the novel, when she had fully encountered the problems she later appears to ignore. Certainly it is strange that she should exalt in the one work the friendship she has earlier shown to be inadequate.

More probable is that in *The Rights of Woman* she turned from *Mary, A Fiction* and developed her theory of friendship away from its obsessions. The different genesis of the two works, as well as her later reaction to her novel, seems to bear this out. Where the novel derives from Wollstonecraft's fear that female friendship cannot easily be realized in the world except to isolate and warp, *The Rights of Woman* springs from a courageous conviction that it must exist and benefit. In her later work Wollstonecraft attacks, not retreats, and her prose is aggressive, not fearful. The implication of friendship becomes an act of will in the face of difficulty, not an obsessive cry.

Years later, the new will-ful Wollstonecraft was ashamed of her first novel, which she dismissed as "a crude production," one she would not wish in the way of people whose good opinion she valued. No doubt she regretted the "crude" techniques of narrative and style of *Mary, A Fiction,* but she may also have been uneasy at the aching pessimism she betrayed. She may too have felt wary of the kind of pain she had caught in her novel. A narcissistic one, it gazed on and embraced itself, and demanded that the reader join, not combat, the questionable embrace.

By the time Wollstonecraft wrote *A Vindication of the Rights of Woman*—and later *The Wrongs of Woman*—she had made the pain general and she was ready to formulate a theory of female friendship as political pact rather than pathological state. The power of equal female friendship, only hinted at in *Mary, A Fiction,* then, is wistfully but willfully imagined in the later

207

books. Its antithetical context of sexual infatuation, now clearly embodied, will always remain to vex but not destroy.

Mary Wollstonecraft's *The Wrongs of Woman* (1798)

The Wrongs of Woman: or, Maria is Wollstonecraft's last work on friendship. It was left unfinished in 1797 when she died in childbirth. The truncated state of the book mirrors th'e unfinished nature of the vision: as in *The Rights of Woman*, we see a potential rather than an actual relationship. The intricate roots of friendship, not its flowering, are anatomized.

Like *Mary, A Fiction*, *The Wrongs of Woman* is a third-person novel, but it encloses lengthy first-person narratives. Since she will speak for herself, Maria needs little of the special pleading Mary required, and her friend Jemima, who also speaks, can be probed in a way Ann never was.[12] The monologue technique eases equal friendship; at the same time it stresses the single self and denies immediate interaction. It ensures that friendship will flourish, but only in the future, and it requires that the relationship be studied primarily in the characters and previous lives of the friends.

Maria and Jemima fall neatly into the humorous eighteenth-century dichotomy of reason and sensibility. Since the age decreed reason for the man and sensibility for the lady, the sentimental Maria is in many aspects the very model of femaleness, while the controlled and hard Jemima is branded an unsexed woman, a monster. The motive of the book, however, is the impurity of these characterizations; Maria's melting sensibility is vulnerable, Jemima's rational hardness brittle. As the two women implicitly approach each other through the static narratives and the fragments of the text, they come to suggest the political bonding and psychological wholeness their explicit stories deny.

12. The author is further shut out from her book by the circumstances of publication. The manuscript of *The Wrongs of Woman* was edited and issued by her husband, William Godwin, whose prose surrounds and influences the text.

1

The Wrongs of Woman is set in Gothic fashion in a madhouse, to which Maria, a sensitive and romantic soul, has been confined through the machinations of George Venables, the wicked husband she once loved but later tried to escape. With his act, he has neatly parted her from baby daughter and fortune, providing on the way a forceful symbol of male power and female weakness. The weakness is psychological as well as social, for, cocooned in the asylum, Maria falls in love again and glories in the female emotionality that helped bring her to the madhouse. Her story tells of a progress in sensibility that is not the least of woman's wrongs.

The heroine is first discovered in the novel limp with sorrow, occasionally toughening herself against the hysteria and childlike passivity her Gothic predicament suggests.[13] When in the asylum she focusses on her husband's cruelty, she comes closest to abjuring passivity and achieving some fortitude of mind; when she regards only herself and her sensations, she becomes inept: "to the master of this most horrid of prisons, she had, soon after her entrance, raved of injustice, in accents that would have justified his treatment."[14] Again, she tries to console and stiffen herself by books obtained from another inmate, but her sentimental habits prevail and she discovers "tears of maternal tenderness" obscuring the "reasoning page"; she is moved only when the tale she reads speaks directly to her own sorrow. Literature is twisted by emotion and, as in *Mary, A Fiction,* it replaces action instead of promoting it.[15]

---

13. Wollstonecraft too struggles against the Gothic elements she has invoked. She insists she is merely a plain speaker, but she uses the elaborate Gothic language of the day to attract to her subject and she is to some extent trapped within its conventions and implications.

14. *The Wrongs of Woman,* published as *Maria or The Wrongs of Woman,* edited by Moira Ferguson (New York: Norton, 1975), p. 25. Page numbers in the text refer to this edition.

15. The susceptible state of Maria is well pictured in *A Vindication of the Rights of Woman,* which tells how the romantic tendencies of women are fostered by loneliness and novel-reading and how their judgment is warped by romantic inclination.

Unfortunately, however, it goes beyond mere passive corruption. Unable to concentrate on the books, Maria comes in time to think on their owner, a "gentleman" prisoner about whom she knows nothing but for whom "her heart throbbed with sympathetic alarm." Immediately her affections are engaged and she is sexually alert. The leaves of the book awe her and the words once repellent grow "sacred." Avidly she reads the marginalia and is seduced by the handwriting: "fancy, treacherous fancy, began to sketch a character, congenial with her own, from these shadowy outlines" (p. 34).

Her infatuation with this phantom grows until she dreams at night of her child, but wakes to desire only the young annotator. Once when she misses seeing him she is momentarily checked by the thought that women "who have no active duties or pursuits" easily grow romantic. The asylum, it seems, is a metaphor for more than the external tyranny of men.

The closeness of such romantic indulgence to actual madness is suggested by a contiguity in the text, for her musing precedes the entry of a "lovely maniac." The singing of the maniac is beautiful, conjuring up for Maria the image of the man who haunts her mind. Interrupted by a fit of madness, the image is dashed. The ambivalence of the moment is caught in Maria's observation: " 'Woman, fragile flower! why were you suffered to adorn a world exposed to the inroad of such stormy elements?' thought Maria, while the poor maniac's strain was still breathing on her ear, and sinking into her very soul" (p. 37). The music of passion is allied to the music of madness, and both fall into her soul like poison. Indeed her traditional and degrading metaphor reveals the taint.

At a crucial moment in her romantic descent, Maria receives from the man she yearns to love a copy of Rousseau's *Julie*. Judging from female fiction of the late eighteenth century, this was a most potent book, one that had inflamed and corrupted a generation of modest young girls.[16] Certainly its effect on Maria is elec-

16. The corrupting power of books was a commonplace of eighteenth-century thought. At the beginning of the century Mary Delariviere Manley in *The New Atalantis* has a young lady seduced after reading Ovid and Petrarch; at the end, Charles Lucas in

trifying and it concludes the work her own temperament had begun. Thoughts of active escape and struggle are stilled.

Quickly the stranger is clothed in the glory of Rousseau's passionate hero, Saint-Preux:

> the personification of Saint Preux, or of an ideal lover far superior, was after this imperfect model, of which merely a glance had been caught, even to the minutiae of the coat and hat of the stranger. But if she lent St. Preux, or the demi-god of her fancy, his form, she richly repaid him by the donation of all St. Preux's sentiments and feelings, culled to gratify her own, to which he seemed to have an undoubted right, when she read on the margin of an impassioned letter, written in the well-known hand—"Rousseau alone, the true Prometheus of sentiment, possessed the fire of genius necessary to pourtray the passion, the truth of which goes so directly to the heart." (p. 38)

Saint-Preux and the stranger are welded into a single object of infatuation, which pushes from her mind all thoughts of her own escape and her daughter's fate; if she does remember the child, it is "to wish that she had a father whom her mother could respect and love." So the link of mother and daughter fails and Maria chooses Saint-Preux, the passionate destructive element of *Julie;* in her comments on the book, she makes no mention of Julie as mother and friend.

When Maria finally meets the stranger, Darnford, he has already been elected her lover through the mediation of Saint-Preux and enough of Maria's temperament is known for her emotional course to be planned. Yet she has struggled momentarily for control and read for restraint, and, like Mary before her, she is endowed with intellect, however unnurtured. Clearly she is a complex character, worth investigating; she demands this investigation when she writes her history. The work is designed for her lost daughter, but presented to Darnford; its end well fits its plot.

Two main movements mark Maria's history, one circular

The Infernal Quixote corrupts his heroine with Wollstonecraft's *Vindication of the Rights of Woman,* while Mary Hays's heroine in *Memoirs of Emma Courtney* is sexually awakened by a reading of Rousseau's *Julie.*

and repetitive, the other linear and developmental. The circular binds her to male relationships within the patterns of youth; the linear tends toward freedom and maturity. The two contrary movements struggle throughout the narrative, breeding a tension that converts simple reminiscence into psychic drama.

Maria sets the context for her repetitive fate by describing her birth "in one of the most romantic parts of England." Throughout *The Rights of Woman,* Wollstonecraft had used "romantic" for uncurbed sensibility approaching madness, an irrational disregard for actual surroundings. In the novel the word "romantic" certainly binds Maria, becoming almost synonymous with mental imprisonment. Even the obnoxious husband throws it at his wife, and it is one of the few external judgments on her we are allowed.[17] Slicing through the thick of her narrative, it destroys the magic of self-representation and catches her in an inescapable repetition.

Maria's romantic transfiguring of nature echoes in the novel. When she is trapped in a marriage so ghastly we forget her own part in its making, we are reminded of the romantic child by the rapture over nature. Returning to her original home, she had retreated into her childhood and her old enthusiasm blossomed forth. The rhapsodical emotion is so acute even in memory that Maria is overcome when she thinks on it, and she must pause to feel again what she describes. Later in her history when she has resolved to escape her gross and grasping husband, she again turns enthusiastically to the nature long ignored; the sudden joy transfigures all and the air, she declares, "never smelled so sweet."[18] Later still, when Darnford's presence has made heaven

17. In the female first-person narrative, written by male authors, the heroine is constantly described from without; she relates the compliments she receives and is much concerned with her social effect. Maria is rarely commented on and she seems little aware of her theater, except in one histrionic moment when she casts off her ring before her husband and friend.

18. Marriage is also described romantically in terms of sudden changes in nature. Maria sees her awakening to Venables' true character as the discovery of "a wasp in the rose-bush" or the entry of the demon into paradise. These images suggests Maria's entrapment in the conventional perception of stationary females and active men.

of an asylum cell, the dead nature around her is revitalized: "The air swept across her face with a voluptuous freshness that thrilled to her heart, awakening indefinable emotions . . . Maria was happy" (p. 37). In all these cases the change suggests escape: it is not the child but the wife who returns home; the abandonment of the husband, although a noble act, is not simply a matter of female will; and love does not conquer imprisonment but obscures it.

As we read the history, we can perceive the relationship with Darnford as an echo of the earlier one with Venables. The repetition is underscored by Maria's repeated error. Inclined to view benevolence as the prime virtue, she had judged Venables on a single benevolent act and found him worthy of love; she makes the same mistake with Darnford and only later learns that "a fondness for the sex often gives an appearance of humanity to the behaviour of men, who have small pretensions to the reality" (p. 143). She ascribes her errors with Darnford to her imprisonment and resolves "to eradicate some of the romantic notions" springing from "adversity." As we have seen, however, the "romantic notions" antedate this adversity and are strongly rooted.

Beyond the textual repetition looms an intertextual one, the threatening shadow of *Mary, A Fiction.* In the events of the later book we retreat into the earlier world and Maria is partially formed in the debilitated mold of Mary.

Like her predecessor, Maria is flanked by a tyrannical, self-indulgent father, a passive mother, and a favored eldest son. Unloved and romantic like Mary, she turns from the unnurturing family to the first person to heed her, George Venables, son of a neighboring merchant. On first sight his family appears in a haze of romance, resplendent in "white robes and waving plumes," streaming through the gloomy church and her dreary life, diffusing light into both. The son is worthy of such kin: "Finding his attainments and manners superior to those of the young men of the village, I began to imagine him superior to the rest of mankind" (p. 79).

As in the early novel, the mother dies as the daughter mar-

213

ries, the contiguity of events suggesting that Maria moves from one loveless relationship to another and that the early one mars the later. Like Mary, Maria is devoted to her dying mother and she shows "unceasing solitude" in spite of rebuffs. Dying, her mother murmurs: "A little more patience, and I too shall be at rest!"[19] In the ending segment of the novel, these words are repeated by the suicidal Maria; in the repetition, she harshly reveals her inheritance from her unloving and passive mother and demands our attention to the circularity of her fate, the textual and intertextual determination.

As in *Mary, A Fiction,* so in *The Wrongs of Woman* marriage begins the heroine's real suffering. With it her history degenerates into self-pity, the drug of the miserable. Since we have already seen this here and in the earlier novel, it is hard to disapprove Maria's miserable question: "Why was I not born a man, or why was I born at all?" When she interrupts her story, reduced to nothingness in writing, she enacts her legal interruption in marriage, a state where "the very being . . . of the woman is suspended."[20] The suspension echoes the deathly ending of *Mary, A Fiction.*

Yet *The Wrongs of Woman* transcends its predecessor by modifying the circling narrative with a contrary linear movement. In this Maria develops rather than repeats; moving from a spiral of romanticism and illusion, she severs in part her links with the earlier Mary and approaches the freedom of response her childhood patterns seemed to deny.

As we have seen, the mother's death links the novels, but in the later one there is no dwelling on it, and the mother—like the "artful kind of upper servant" who quickly replaces her—is seen as a type more than an individual. For Maria both women come to display the wrongs of women and the difficulty of meaningful

19. The last words of Wollstonecraft's own mother were "A little patience, and all will be over!" The last written words of Wollstonecraft herself were "I must have a little patience."

20. William Blackstone, *Commentaries on the Laws of England* (Chicago: Callaghan, 1889), I, ii, 442.

female bonding. To the very end the insipid mother prefers the undutiful son to the dutiful daughter while the servant rejects women for the men who can raise her in society. Maria understands all this, and she is bitter rather than contemptuous when the servant tries to seduce her brother as well as her father: "By allowing women but one way of rising in the world, the fostering the libertinism of men, society makes monsters of them, and then their ignoble vices are brought forward as a proof of inferiority of intellect" (p. 88). Whether this is the perception of the young or of the older Maria, it indicates progress from Mary's self-pity and lonely righteousness.

Mary, A Fiction is further spurned in the treatment of benevolence. Like Mary before her, Maria adds a general benevolence to her particular infatuation, and she too is especially pleased when made to suffer in her generosity. The older narrator has moved to judge this phenomenon and she has perceived that benevolence does not always spring from pure motives. Where the young woman is won by a benevolent act in Venables, the older understands that this act can be self-indulgent or calculating as well as principled:

> My fancy had found a basis to erect its model of perfection on; and quickly went to work, with all the happy credulity of youth, to consider that heart as devoted to virtue, which had only obeyed a virtuous impulse. The bitter experience was yet to come, that has taught me how very distinct are the principles of virtue, from the casual feelings from which they germinate. (p. 85)

Benevolence is still a virtue, but impulsive benevolence is less so.

Even the pejorative word "romantic" can yield some development, some hope of escaping "the magic circle"[21] of female imprisonment, for it is precisely from her "romantic" conception of her miseries that Maria comes to feel for other women. In extreme fashion she paints herself as sexual victim to her husband;

21. The phrase was used by Wollstonecraft's friend Mary Hays in her polemical novel *The Memoirs of Emma Courtney* (1796; New York: Garland, 1974) to describe the external and internal constraints of women.

so she can lament that all women, rich and poor, have been forced to view their sexuality as a commodity. All have to some degree become "outlaws of the world." When Mary in *Mary, A Fiction* saw the world in ruins, she never understood so clearly her own ruined state.

Above all Maria turns from Mary in purposing to escape her loveless marriage and avoid the melancholy ending of *Mary, a Fiction,* which she had once sought:

> I had no longer the cruel task before me, in endless perspective, aye, during the tedious for ever of life, of labouring to overcome my repugnance—of labouring to extinguish the hopes, the maybes of a lively imagination. Death I had hailed as my only chance for deliverance. (p. 113)

Mary had welcomed death as a release from the sexual man she hated, but Maria is made of sterner stuff, and she shrinks "from the icy arms of an unknown tyrant." The choice of phrase associates death with tyrannical, sexual men; her accepting it would be accepting the male world she is fighting. Instead she breaks from both death and husband, wondering that she could ever have been so blinkered as to accept either. "Had an evil genius cast a spell at my birth," she demands in exasperation, "or a demon stalked out of chaos, to perplex my understanding, and enchain my will, with delusive prejudices?" (p. 114)

Maria does not always change so dramatically, but she does come to understand the roots of certain instinctive feelings. When she has escaped her husband's house, she goes into hiding alone and has much time to think on the female predicament. She concludes that women's compassion and benevolence are both strengths and weaknesses. The landlady who fears to hide her is weak because she cares what her brutal husband thinks and feels, but the caring is also her only strength. So the romantic sensibility for which Maria has so often been blamed may, if purged and strengthened, become women's glory. True fortitude and true sensibility are not necessarily antagonistic, for both require an unselfish commitment to others. When Venables catches up with his wife, he shows his ignorance of this, mistaking her dislike of resistance for weakness: "he thought my indulgence and compassion mere selfishness, and never discovered that the fear of being unjust, or of unnecessarily wounding the feelings of another, was much more painful to me, than any thing I could have to endure myself" (p. 129).

More pessimistic but equally perceptive is Maria's musing once Venables again controls her. Women, she then accepts, have suffered but without the ennobling so often assumed for suffering. Instead they have been indeliby scarred and degraded by their misery: "the evils they are subject to endure," she concludes sadly, "degrade them so far below their oppressors, as almost to justify their tyranny." It is a bitter reflection, which she takes care to apply to herself.

As she progresses in suffering, then, Maria comes to accept her kinship with all oppressed women; she notes their common degradation and their inevitable spurning of the female union that might have liberated them. She perceives these attitudes in the landlady who rejected her but lovingly endured her husband's brutality, and in the French maid who by male command betrayed her to the asylum. Finally she hints that she sees it within herself. After she has related her abduction by her husband, the narrative breaks off abruptly, leaving the text to indicate what she will not say: that in choosing the romantic figment, Darnford, she is following again her own misdirection and female conditioning.[22] Like the landlady and the maid, she spurns female bonding and runs to the "oppressor," who alone answers her

22. Marilyn Butler states that *The Wrongs of Woman* begins as a conventional love story requiring sympathy for the lovers, but falters mid-way: "At first the victimized heroine's love for her fellow-prisoner, Henry [Darnford], is presented as 'natural' and the innately virtuous emotion . . . but the apparent tendency of the whole was to be that a woman had better not trust in love . . . ," *Jane Austen and the War of Ideas* (Oxford: Clarendon Press, 1976), p. 46. This is certainly a persuasive view, for Maria's ambivalence about romantic love is shared by the author, who seems to value it highly in many comments and who provides copious excuses for the excesses of her heroine. Yet, the action is unambivalent throughout and the novel seems intended as the history of a woman's growing disillusion with a love she wished to exalt.

degradation. The line of development in the narrative is forced at last into circularity.   .

2

The kinship Maria rejects is with Jemima, the attendant at the asylum, and it is with her name and with Darnford's that Maria's narrative ends. To Maria, Jemima holds out her friendship and the reasonable self-control it brings. Maria's failure to accept it is the signature of her female upbringing.

Jemima comes from the very lowest class and has suffered under different conventions. She has had no education to make her sensitive and vulnerable, and, because she is more than a simple child, she appears unfeminine. From her alienated state she becomes superficially strong, and it is the sane, brave aspect of Jemima that we first see: "A woman entered . . . with a firm, deliberate step."

Early in the story Jemima is characterized by the narrator. Cut off by misery which had almost "petrified the life's-blood of humanity," she is allowed only a first name. She is reduced from a human to an almost bestial level: "hunted from hole to hole, as if she had been a beast of prey, or infected with a moral plague" (p. 28). Interestingly, this description foreshadows the account of Maria, who alone and outcast termed herself "an infected beast" and a "felon." Women are linked across class, then, but less in solidarity than in hopelessness.

Deprived of the nurturing and constricting family which has fostered Maria's sensibility and romanticism, Jemima is devoid of both qualities. In their place she develops the faculty of survival, and self-preservation becomes her aim and sole concern. Under a life of hardship Jemima develops the strenuous competence Wollstonecraft wished all women to obtain, but this competence has been bought at too high a price. Maria, so thoroughly "a woman," is right to awaken the sensitive woman in Jemima, "long estranged from feminine emotions."[23]

23. In the treatment of both Maria and Jemima, an ideological shift can be discerned from *Mary, A Fiction*. In the early, more Christian and pessimistic book, character ap-

218

POLITICAL FRIENDSHIP

When Jemima and Maria meet, we immediately see that the female friend can deliver the power of reason, thwarted in the middle-class woman. Maria is attracted, discerning in the attendant "an understanding above the common standard." When she resolves to make an ally of Jemima, the resolution strengthens at once; after it she pauses before she speaks, conquers her disgust of the food she is given, and tries to eat calmly. With Jemima's help, she takes the first step toward the active fortitude she requires if she is ever to break from the asylum.

Jemima persuades Maria to take the linear course, but her influence is constantly bent into circularity. She brings books to mitigate the grief and Maria feels only their sentimental encouragement; she brings writing materials, which Maria uses to set down her story for Darnford; she entertains by chatting of the gentleman prisoner, whom Maria transforms into a prince of reveries. She inspires Maria to some calm, but her patient progresses unguided from calmness to the euphoria of love.

With Darnford, Maria discovers a paradise in the asylum, one from which she may be ejected but from which she will not escape, and it is toward escape that Jemima would push her. So in this false Eden Jemima dwindles from inspiring friend to go-between. She is absent when Maria first sees Darnford and absent again when they become lovers.

Yet, Jemima is not without weapons in her struggle with Darnford and the infatuation he brings. Her most potent one is the traditional female narrative. When Maria has lost all sense of the wrongs of woman and has allowed her asylum cell to grow a paradise, Jemima deploys the female confession which has so often controlled female relationships. She aims not only to influence Maria but also to edge herself toward the feeling woman who attracts her. Already she has felt the melting magic of Maria's emotion and, contemplating her, she has shed a "tear of pleasure"—"the first tear that social enjoyment had ever drawn from her."

pears fixed in the patterns of youth; in the later, more rationalist and optimistic work, changing circumstances seem able to change or release character.

POLITICAL FRIENDSHIP

The author has prepared us for Jemima's narrative, which shocks nevertheless. It opens abruptly and bleakly:

"My father," said Jemima, "seduced my mother, a pretty girl, with whom he lived fellow-servant; and she no sooner perceived the natural, the dreaded consequence, than the terrible conviction flashed on her—that she was ruined." (p. 52)

And of course she was. A few days after the birth of Jemima she dies, leaving her child to the baby-farm, that most notorious of eighteenth-century institutions. There unwanted babies were expected to die or acquire the deformities required for begging. Jemima does not die, and she suffers only mental deformity. She grows into a drudge and slattern, brutally treated and constantly taunted with her illegitimate birth. Her starvation diet forces her to steal, and she quickly adds the epithet of "thief" to that of "bastard."

Jemima is the "mark of cruelty" until her sixteenth year, when "something like comeliness appeared on a Sunday." Automatically she is raped by the nearest man, who thereafter procures her frequent submission with threats. The result is inevitable. Thrown out pregnant, she is forced to take refuge with beggars, and, although feeling some tenderness for her unborn child, she gives herself a painful abortion. Later she becomes a professional thief and prostitute. She is despised by all, moved from street to street, and regarded as a monstrous blot on society.

The brightest period in this grim life occurs when Jemima finds refuge as the kept mistress of a licentious but cultivated "gentleman," in whose house she learns some book knowledge and refinement of manner and speech. Such acquirements, however, serve only to embitter her when, on his death, she is ejected as a moral outrage by his relatives and forced again to become a beggar and washerwoman. Similarly in *Fanny Hill,* the male knowledge and refinement Charles gives Fanny helps her in no way to success—it is the knowledge of vice and cunning alone that causes her to prosper.

By now Jemima perceives it is primarily her sex rather than her lowly social condition that oppresses her and keeps her a permanent outcast from the society she wants to enter. As she comments justly:

A man with half my industry, and, I may say, abilities, could have procured a decent livelihood, and discharged some of the duties which knit mankind together; whilst I, who had acquired a taste for the rational, nay, in honest pride let me assert it, the virtuous enjoyments of life, was cast aside as the filth of society. (p. 65)

The remainder of the narrative drags Jemima through the vicious institutions that oppress the female poor in particular; she goes to prison, the pauper hospital, and the workhouse. In such surroundings, her character deteriorates, and she becomes indifferent to others, even at times malevolent. She "hated mankind" and with womankind she has forged no bonds. Finally she is taken on by the master of the workhouse as an attendant at his private asylum. She is chosen primarily because she seems to him emotionally and morally dead.

Jemima represents the specific horror of being deprived of a family. Because she has no mother (and no kindly relative like Maria), she can never be a child: "I was an egg dropped in the sand; a pauper by nature, hunted from family to family, who belonged to nobody—and nobody cared for me. I was despised from my birth" (p. 56). She does not have the first primary link and so she cannot easily make others; plaintively she asks, "Who ever risked any thing for me?—Who ever acknowledged me to be a fellow-creature?" She has never been loved or befriended and in turn, like Mary, she finds it difficult to love; unlike Mary she is denied a middle-class benevolence, and all her dealings with her fellows are abrasive. When she gets one chance of a domestic haven, therefore, she has no fellow feeling for the pregnant girl she displaces. Ejected from the house on Jemima's insistence, the girl in despair drowns herself. Through the act she renders Jemima truly bestial: "I was famishing; wonder not that I became a wolf!"

221

Often in fiction, the poorer, darker, lower-class woman is given sexual feelings, whereas the richer, paler, middle-class heroine is bound fast in her purity. Such seems the case from Henry Fielding's *Tom Jones* in eighteenth-century England to George Sand's *Indiana* in nineteenth-century France.[24] But Jemima has as little basis for sexual infatuation as for friendship. Anxious only to preserve herself, she has no time for romantic or sexual entanglements, and she sees sexuality only as a weapon and commodity. Maria, the middle-class woman, with indulged sensibility and satisfied material needs, can alone have such longings.

Because Jemima has entered the world of struggle where only reason and cunning prevail, she has suppressed the sensibility which could only harm her. She is then a defective woman, a monster who grows from a child with an old face to a woman with no womanly feelings. Yet these feelings have been numbed rather than killed, and they may be awakened.[25] At the end of Jemima's narrative, Maria, who had earlier seen only a potential ally in her attendant, is moved to clasp her hand. It is the first act of spontaneous kindness Jemima has experienced and she is overcome; she hastens from the room "to conceal her emotion."[26]

Jemima compels the reader to regard the miseries of lower-class women. But within the novel she has recounted her history to move Maria, and she momentarily succeeds. When the history stops, Maria's "thoughts take a wider shape" and she remembers her kinship with other women, lamenting now "that she had given birth to a daughter."

24. For a treatment of this contrast in *Indiana*, see Leslie Rabine's "George Sand and the Myth of Femininity," *Women & Literature* 4, no. 2 (Fall 1976), 2–17.

25. The progress of Jemima to insensitivity and alienation resembles the experience of negation described by R. D. Laing in *The Politics of Experience*: "Nothing, as experience, arises as absence of someone or something. No friends, no relationships, no pleasure, no meaning in life, no ideas, no mirth, no money" (New York: Ballantine Books, 1967), p. 38. Jemima is conscious of others only as terms, as madwomen or masters, for example.

26. Jemima's narrative has been much admired for its audaciousness and originality. Philippe Séjourné considers it truly innovative in its depiction of brutality. See *Aspects généraux du roman feminin en Angleterre de 1740 à 1800* (Gap: Louis-Jean, 1966), p. 181.

At this point the male and female relationships collide. Jemima's friendship acts centrifugally; it reaches out to the daughter who becomes a link between the two women, and Jemima even searches for the child, proposing to become a "second mother" to her. The male relationship is centripetal, however; it moves inward, excluding other women and the daughter. When Jemima reports that the child is dead, Maria remembers this exclusion: "for a while, she indulged the superstitious notion that she was justly punished by the death of her child, for having for an instant ceased to regret her loss" (p. 73). Indeed it is a superstitious and ridiculous notion, but there is an element of truth within it.

Ultimately the breaking of the bond of mother and daughter throws Maria back to Darnford. Jemima had appealed to her through their common femaleness, ratified by her narrative and the lost child which both had sought. The narrative past and the daughter seemingly dead, Maria reverts to her infatuated state, revelling in her new emotions to avoid succumbing to the old ones of guilt and sorrow. When she gives her lover the memoirs intended for her child—memoirs that might better have gone first to Jemima, the seeker of her daughter—she rejects her new female friend and the struggle she demands. She writes her account to Darnford and breaks the symmetry of friendship; her history becomes less a binding confession than a love letter.[27] Except for her own impulsive melting, it seems that Jemima has ultimately spoken in vain.

3

Clearly Maria chooses infatuation over female friendship, then, but her choice is immediately called in question. The asylum disintegrates into uproar as the keeper absconds, and it is Jemima, the unromantic active woman, touched by new sentiment,

27. Darnford too has a narrative. It is spoken to Maria, who fails to understand it. Only the reader learns that Darnford is a conventional womanizer, whose shady activities hardly give him time to acquire the literary sensibility with which he seduces Maria.

223

who takes control of their destinies. It is she alone who helps Maria escape.

Outside, Maria remains incorrigible. She searches for Darnford and the two set up house together. Inevitably life proves different from her fantastic picture of it. Where Jemina helped her always to better her condition and control her fate—to resist indulged grief or escape the asylum—Darnford seems to worsen both. With him Maria loses her former female acquaintances and she sacrifices money which could have meant freedom later; she "wished," she said, "to be only alive to love."

Jemima's relationship with Maria after the escape is puzzling. She lives with the couple, but, while her friend is infatuated with Darnford, she refuses to be considered an equal. She will, she declares, remain only if she can serve as housekeeper. Such determination may reflect her inadequate pride, for through hardening herself she has managed to preserve her life, not establish self-esteem. It may, however, arise from her understanding that the infatuated Maria can have no equal friend.

Yet it is at this time, living with Jemima and Darnford—appreciating the one and learning the limits of the other—that Maria really begins to understand the nature of infatuation and appreciate the joys of affection and friendship. Her experience in the asylum with Jemima initiates this change, fostered now by her disappointing life with her lover. In time she comes to echo *The Rights of Woman,* opposing friendship and affection to sexual and romantic infatuation. But the elaborate literary language and natural images distinguish the passage from the earlier book and suggest the romantic route Maria has traveled:

> The real affections of life, when they are allowed to burst forth, are buds pregnant with joy and all the sweet emotions of the soul; yet they branch out with wild ease, unlike the artificial forms of felicity, sketched by an imagination painfully alive. The substantial happiness, which enlarges and civilizes the mind, may be compared to the pleasure experienced in roving through nature at large, inhaling the sweet gale natural to the clime; while the reveries of a feverish imagination continually sport themselves in gar-

dens full of aromatic shrubs, which cloy while they delight, and weaken the sense of pleasure they gratify. . . . Maria found herself more indulgent as she was happier, and discovered virtues, in characters she had before disregarded, while chasing the phantoms of elegance and excellence, which sported in the meteors that exhale in the marshes of misfortune. The heart is often shut by romance against social pleasure; and, fostering a sickly sensibility, grows callous to the soft touches of humanity. (pp. 143–44)

Nature is restored to naturalness, and the balmy and aromatic air Maria had often inhaled in romantic moments is discovered to asphixiate. Jemima's prostitution and Maria's indiscriminate romance come together and both become travesties of human relationships.

Maria progresses some way, then—haltingly, for her progress is always threatened by circularity. She learns what Jemima has known throughout, that reason and self-preservation are a woman's first duty, rather as Jemima learns through Maria that self-esteem—and the affection and emotion it allows—are her second. But at the end of Wollstonecraft's continuous fragment, neither woman has moved sufficiently toward the strength of the other to become the androgynous ideal of womanhood. When the book disintegrates into discrete paragraphs and hints, all of these suggest further sorrow for Maria.

Darnford, it seems, must prove false. The bleakest of the hints reads: "Divorced by her husband—Her lover unfaithful—Pregnancy—Miscarriage—Suicide." The most extended paragraph, however, the one printed last, continues from these hints and provides an ending that consists of a female tableau of Maria, her daughter, and Jemima.

The paragraph is eloquent in echoes, as the dying Maria exhorts herself in her mother's words to "have a little patience." She has, however, come far since she sat at the bed of her unmotherly parent. She has learned to love her baby unselfishly and unromantically and to befriend and appreciate the active and unsentimental Jemima. So the mother is not all-powerful. As Maria repeats the potent dying words, a "new vision swam before her."

It is Jemima leading the child once believed dead. With her own confession, Jemima has appealed to Maria and moved her momentarily from selfish infatuation to social concern. Jemima refers to this change when she reminds her friend of her own history, demanding to know whether Maria would leave her daughter in the world "to endure what I have endured."

Through Jemima's exhortation and demand, Maria rejects the indulgence of easeful death as she has now rejected the indulgence of infatuation. She chooses to live for her child—to live for and with, not through, another human being. The steps toward her choice are of course missing, but the choice continues the novel's tentative development, striking at the circularity that has impeded it.

Jemima and Maria have moved toward each other in friendship, learning to combat their natures, conditioned by neglected childhood and reinforced by dreary maturity. The sentimental Maria has grown more self-reliant and the hard Jemima more self-respecting; both have learned the necessity and limit of responsibility for others. We can expect that Jemima, who has saved Maria and rescued her child, will now accept the equality she once rejected, and we can hope that Maria, twice deceived, will not again mistake a shallow libertine for a demigod. Admittedly neither woman reaches psychic health—the faint ideal of the novel—but treatment has begun. Perhaps complete fitness will only be experienced by the child, for whom Maria and Jemima will be joint mothers; like Claire's daughter in *Julie,* she seems fatherless, the progeny of friendship rather than marriage. Perhaps again it is left to us, the readers, to learn the route to health, so finishing the unfinished text and befriending its author.

Madame de Staël's *Delphine* (1802)

1

Delphine opens with the heroine's words, "I shall be extremely happy, my dear cousin, if I can promote your marriage with M de Mondoville." After a thousand pages of unremitting anguish over M de Mondoville, she finally writes: "on earth or in heaven, you shall know me happy." The rhetoric of happiness is shunted to the periphery of this long, obsessive novel to clear the center for Staël's real subject, the inevitable misery of the passionate, superior woman. Delphine falls in love with Leonce de Mondoville and from then onwards knows hardly a moment's peace. Throughout the scattered episodes of the book she repeatedly declares her desire to unite with him; yet, as Leonce comes forward, she persistently prevents him. Her writing and action seem at odds: one is directed toward the fulfillment of passion, while the other busily blocks it. The passion is Leonce; the blocks are the women friends who excuse Delphine from passion.[28]

Staël published Delphine in 1802, a period of reaction and empire, but set it in the early 1790s, a time of action and revolution. It is an epistolary novel, written when third-person narration had carried the day. The oppositions in period and form are paralleled by oppositions in the novel, which in turn account for the strange tension of writing and acting. The book presents the story of an unconventional, superior woman who pursues a passion opposed by the conventional, inferior society which ultimately defeats her.[29] But another story is told beside the first—of an unconventional, superior woman who both desires and fears to be conventional and inferior, who internalizes society's conventions and opposes them at the same time. The novel is then both

---

28. Most critics see Delphine simply as a defense of the passionate woman. Georges Solovieff, for example, describes the novel as supporting women and passion and presenting in the heroine a woman who acts freely in the face of a society that does not allow originality, Madame de Staël: Choix de textes thématique et actualité (Paris: Klincksieck, 1974), p. 24. The most comprehensive account of the novel is in Madame de Staël, Novelist: The Emergence of the Artist as Woman (Urbana: University of Illinois Press, 1978) by Madelyn Gutwirth, who argues that Delphine is a defense of the stereotyped image of femininity; Delphine both validates this image by the intensity with which she lives it, and shows its nonviability by her fate.

29. Jean Starobinski argues that, in Staël, superior faculties always lead to a sense of imcompletion; if the surest happiness is in autonomy, the Staëlian heroine is not made for happiness. She will always search for another as intermediary to plenitude, and, when love fails, she will enter a state of living death, "Suicide et mélancolie chez Mme de Staël," Preuves, 190, no. 16 (1966), 41–48.

revolutionary and reactionary, in keeping with the two periods it inhabits. Its dual nature is intimated again in its women: Delphine, the seemingly unconventional, is kept from convention by women who are themselves either sincerely or hypocritically conventional.

In her own account and the accounts of friends, Delphine combines sensibility and grace, genius and beauty. Indeed in her virtues she is almost supernatural, an angel among mortals; a dying friend clutches at her to intercede before God and she plays the priest with éclat at two death scenes. When still a child, she was married to a fatherly husband who formed her mind androgynously; so she avoided the duplicity of the clever woman, whose female upbringing teaches her to hide her cleverness, and the emptiness of the pretty fool, educated only in coquetry. Regulating her conduct by her own judgment, Delphine has, by the time her husband dies, no need of any man to rule her mind, and, considering all subjects by her own information, she declares herself free from the arbitrary opinions and rules of society. She is enthusiastic, generous, liberal, and ardently religious but not dogmatic.

Conventional society—almost a character in this novel—is unappreciative, even contemptuous, of such youthful goodness, and Delphine at first returns the feelings; she has, she believes, the qualities for autonomy—for happiness within the self without social approval. Yet her rejection is superficial, a verbal repulse that carries only moderate conviction, and, when society seduces with more subtlety, she responds ambiguously. Although she scorns many of society's cruder values—female stupidity and the inexpiable sexual sin for women, for example—she is drawn to its ideal of sacrificial femininity, of the woman's subservience to the man she loves, however spectacular her own gifts and accomplishments may be. And she yearns for passion, whose social dynamics require the woman to repudiate her autonomous self. When Leonce arrives, he intensifies Delphine's conflicting tendencies. To pursue him, she will chase society's ideal of dependent femininity, while ignoring its derision of female excellence. The ambivalence and fatedness of Delphine's passionate pursuit is represented in Leonce, who is object of a passion that is both conventional in its subjection of the woman and unconventional in its illegal intensity. While he seems to free Delphine from social constraint, he is also the embodiment of constraint—he is perfect but for one fault, an excessive concern for honor, reputation, and public opinion. Answering Delphine's deep social need for loving and being loved, then, he also functions as society's revenge on the woman who insisted she scorned its power.

Delphine, the unconventional, is fated to love the conventional Leonce by all the laws of irony: she opens the book by giving half her fortune to a relative who marries the man she herself will later adore, and she declares when she hears of him that she should not love such a man since it would mean "to bow submissive to public opinion," because he is the foremost among its slaves.[30] In his turn Leonce writes to his tutor before meeting his future beloved; "I dreaded the idea of conceiving a passion for a woman, whose ideas should not accord with mine respecting the importance I attach to public opinion." Naturally the course of true love between such beings is not smooth. Delphine continues to regulate her conduct by her heart and conscience—helping her friend Thérèse and then pitying a fanatical suitor, both at the expense of her own reputation. On his side Leonce will marry another because he does not look beyond reputation to reality; when he learns his mistake, he will rush futilely for a sword he cannot honorably wield.

Delphine and Leonce are socially neurotic in complementary ways. But more distressing is their complementary psychological neurosis. Before Leonce meets Delphine, he writes: "Is not a man the natural protector of his mother, his sister, and especially his wife?" And he is quick to perceive her as dependent: "Though the extent of her understanding gives her an independence of sentiment, her disposition stands in need of support: her looks be-

---

30. Mme de Staël-Holstein, *Delphine* (London: G. and J. Robinson, 1803), I, 100. Names anglicized by the translator have been kept in French in the quotations. References in the text are to this three-volume edition.

tray a trembling sensibility, which seems to implore some aid against the troubles of life" (I, 128–29). And speedily Delphine seeks his protection, in spite of the independence she had once vaunted. When he demands that a woman hide any opinion that might arouse passion, the intelligent and fervent Delphine meekly responds that indeed "it does not become a woman to take part in political discussions; her situation in life screens her from all the dangers attendant on them, and her actions can never give either importance or dignity to her words." Her passionate progress is punctuated with verbal obeisance: "I seem born to obey him as much as to adore him," she avers; "all my value is derived from Leonce." It seems an admirable match of master and slave.

Delphine's self-abasement and reduction are extreme. Socially she sinks through passion until she becomes an outcast. When she is rebuffed at a party for continuing to love the married Leonce, she flees in terror "alone on foot, in the wind and rain," unaided by her wealth, position, or intellect. Physically she follows the route of the pathetic heroine of passion, moving through fever, delirium, and semimadness. Psychologically she shifts from the independent woman to the dependent beloved in a direction that leads toward death: "Yesterday I experienced an unknown emotion in my heart, which enfeebled my reason, my virtue, and all my strength," she once admits to Leonce, "and I experienced an inexpressible desire of reviving your life at the expense of my own, of shedding my blood, that it may quicken yours, and of restoring some warmth to your trembling hands with my last breath" (II, 103). Caught later in one of the book's grotesque repetitions—seated by a loving Leonce in the church where he had married another—she declares: "I besought the Almighty that I might die in that situation; it was full of delight." Such passion can be fulfilled only in a woman's death, viewed by a man.[31]

31. There are many foreshadowings of Leonce's final experience of Delphine's death. At one point, for example, he notices that Delphine's "hair fell down her shoulders, a deadly paleness was spread over her face, yet was there a grace, a charm in it, that I had never witnessed before" (II, 196).

But this reductive movement is not for lack of female effort. Although every word of Delphine leads her to passionate dependence and death, her actions struggle against them. With the often unwitting help of female friends, good and bad, she stealthily opposes the political, social and psychological institutions of passion, marriage, and female decorum which Leonce represents. Although her later words deny it, her actions suggest that women can indeed aim at autonomy and avoid the traps they had at first no hand in setting. Among these women helpers, these female obstacles to union with Leonce, there is first of all Thérèse, a lesser copy of the brilliant Delphine, who intrudes her passionate troubles so seductively they undermine her friend's love; then Matilde, cold, pious bride of Leonce to whom Delphine is obsessively generous; Mme de Vernon, Matilde's mother, the rapturous sentimental friend of Delphine and villain of the piece; and finally the selfish Leontine de Ternan, aunt and sinister image of Leonce, with whom Delphine constructs the last external obstacle.[32]

2

Thérèse is pretty, impulsive, passionate and sensitive; with something of Delphine's natural gifts, she has received no guidance in reason and no education in judgment. Her marriage to an older man stultified where Delphine's liberated. So she is torn by a blend of uncontrollable impulse and restraining Catholicism, society's meanest weapon in this anti-Catholic novel. More passive and unstable than Delphine, more selfish therefore, she inspires both liking and pity in her friend, but little passionate attachment. She reverses the effect of Leonce, whose life she blights.

Thérèse compromises herself with M de Serbellane, a man gratifyingly sensitive to Delphine as well. Her husband discovers

32. There are several other female friends in the novel. They represent the various destinies of women, but they are less central to the action than the four I am selecting. The most interesting is Delphine's ill-favored sister-in-law, Louise, who enjoys a vicarious love life through the detailed letters of her beautiful relative.

his wife's liaison, provokes a duel, and is killed by the lover. Fearing that the scandal will allow the relatives of her hated husband to take her child, Thérèse begs Delphine to hide the reason for the duel. Delphine agrees and pays for her agreement by herself appearing compromised.[33] The sensitive Leonce does not wait to sift the truth, but damns the woman he has just learned to adore.

"She thinks that morality is all-sufficient, and that established prejudices, and the arbitrary rules of decorum admitted in society, are to be treated with contempt, when virtue is not interested in them," wrote Leonce before the Thérèse affair broke, and he added ominously, "but a regard for my happiness will correct her of that fault" (I, 191). Although passionately in love and knowing that women in society must guard appearance above virtue, Delphine has let her name be sullied at the crucial moment. In a way Leonce is right not to pry into the apparent scandal, for it is the appearance that is the scandal.

In this episode Delphine clearly pits female friendship and male passion. In spite of the constant rhetoric of passion; she chooses friendship. She bolsters her choice by making passion indulgent and friendship heroic. Although passion requires ultimately that she lose her self, it appears selfish to Delphine because she desires it; requiring the sacrifice of passion, friendship must then be selfless. "If there be a duty which I hold peculiarly sacred, it is that of inviolably keeping my friend's secret," Delphine declares, and she vows she will not sacrifice to Leonce "the duties of kindness, generous kindness," which have during her whole life, been the object of "daily worship." Thérèse and female friendship are valorized like religion and social convention are for other women; so the sacrifice Thérèse inadvertently demands easily replaces the sacrifice of autonomy Leonce's passion

---

33. This seemingly noble motive is somewhat undercut by the child's later history. She is first abandoned by her mother, who enters a convent, and then by Delphine, who does the same. She ends up with the ugly nun Louise, who helped educate Delphine inappropriately for her social role and who wears the nun's habit, so feared by the child since her mother's desertion.

232

requires. The exalted resolves and the parallel in sacrifice suggest that, when Delphine supports the other woman, it is less an impulsive gesture of injudicious friendship than the deeply motivated recoil of an endangered spirit.

Once marriage to Leonce has been obstructued, however, Delphine can in her discourse luxuriate in dependence and subservient femininity. She would, she insists, have been a devoted wife to Leonce had they married; consulting him on everything, she would have made his wishes and thoughts her own. The love that has been sacrificed for friendship and independent judgment now becomes the whole of life and with Byronic fervor Delphine cries that women exist only for love: "in the destiny of women, society has allotted but one hope: when the lot is drawn, and has proved a blank, all is over." Since she has not married the man she loves, she has lost her reason for living, her ambition for excellence. She will, she vows, grow ordinary and conventional, suppressing in herself all that distinguished her: "natural thoughts, impassioned movements, generous flights of enthusiasm." In all this self-abasement she forgets that her superiority and excellence not only attracted but also repulsed: if they pulled Leonce toward her, they also prevented his possessing.

The sacrifice once made, the friendship that provoked it loses much of its meaning. Intimacy with Thérèse had countered intimacy with Leonce and, when this subsides, the friends grow cool, no longer confidential or even affectionate. But it is not the end of Thérèse's interference. When a new understanding has grown between the lovers, rethreatening possessive intimacy, Thérèse is there again to damage and obstruct.

"There are only two asylums on this earth for our sex," Thérèse informs Delphine, "love and religion." After the dramatics of love, although free to marry Serbellane, Thérèse is drawn to religion, the major social institution for restraining women. She enters a convent and begins her novitiate. Meanwhile Delphine, pulled by Leonce into a chaste and passionate friendship, has come to move and live entirely for him, eschewing or courting society at his will. But inevitably Leonce desires more

233

and it is at this dangerous juncture that Thérèse reenters to warn the reckless lovers.

She comes also to ask forgiveness of Leonce for blighting his life, a humbling feminine act that much moves him. Her submissive stance he finds delicious: "in his whole life he had never felt so much respect for any woman," as he felt for her "at the very moment when she conceived herself to be performing an act of humility" (II, 166).

Beyond their mutual delight in female abasement, Thérèse and Leonce are strikingly alike. Both are caught in society's institutions: the convent and marriage, legal religion and legal love. Both are much concerned with public opinion and will by the end have sacrificed love to it. Above all, both are extremely selfish. Leonce urges Delphine to give up her life to him, becoming his emotional or physical mistress, while, for the sake of her own soul, Thérèse insists Delphine abandon Leonce. Since passion for Leonce must lead to sexual fall, Thérèse herself will be implicated as the obstructor of the marriage; so her soul will be endangered.

Between the poles of selfishness, Delphine has little to choose and, vacillating, she moves at last toward the least dangerous. Protesting and weakening, she yet resolves to give up Leonce for Thérèse. But this time she pleads not morality but will-lessness for her extraordinary retreat. "I am like one bewildered," she laments, "Thérèse disposes of me, without any exertion of my own will to guide me." And the reputedly courageous and obstinate Delphine is reduced to admitting, "I had not the courage to refuse her." Something beyond passion for Leonce or compassion for Thérèse seems to prompt her, and Leonce approaches the truth when, looking at Thérèse, he asks Delphine, "Are you in league with her?"

Matilde, wife of Leonce and immediate obstacle to Delphine's union, is a severer version of the religious Thérèse. She is the conventional woman exaggerated into caricature, representing both the spiritual fanaticism and the social rigidity of Cathol-

234

icism.[34] By nature harsh, she has been trained in religion, so that her harshness might be deflected and controlled. In a man, her mother admits, so stern a character might have led to great things, but in a woman it could only be unfortunate, so she must be tamed into narrowness, toned down into submission. In the eyes of society Matilde makes a reputable wife—faithful, loyal, and adequately loving—while her unkindness to other women elevates rather than mars her reputation.

With such a woman Delphine should have had little to do. But Matilde is a relative, her mother is Delphine's dearest friend, and Delphine is neurotically generous. So the book opens with the twenty-one-year-old Delphine's extraordinary gift of half her estate to the eighteen-year-old Matilde, to effect her match with the yet unknown Leonce. She gives because she enjoys giving and because she yearns to be loved—by everyone, even the closed Matilde who can never return her affection. And indeed Matilde is immediately wary of the female bond Delphine seems to impose with her gift; she tries to extricate herself by turning the generous present into a duty, making a free act into conventional obligation or delicacy. Instead of the thanks Delphine happily awaits, she receives only religious reproof from the woman she has helped.

Leonce marries Matilde in error and pique. When he awakens to his mistake, Delphine insists he rest within it. Matilde must always exist between them; when divorce seems possible, she pleads the conventional woman to the conventional Leonce: "from the dependence of our situation, and the weakness of our hearts, we cannot go through life alone" (II, 25–26); Matilde must be supported forever. Yet with all her caution Delphine is drawn to Leonce, and even after Thérèse has done her best to separate the lovers, the two spring back together. Matilde must act directly to sever them.

Long after all have gossipped their fill about it, Matilde is

34. According to Gutwirth, Matilde represents the *caveats* of society in their strictest and least attractive form. *Madame de Staël*, p. 112.

unaware of the love between Leonce and Delphine. When she does learn of it, however, she demands instant action: Delphine must quit Paris and bury herself where Leonce will never find her. And she demands more: the going, she declares, "is not enough . . . you will have done nothing for my happiness, if Leonce could suppose you leave him at my entreaty." On this request for secrecy as well as flight, Delphine indulges in a rare sarcasm: "I thank you for esteeming me so highly, as to suppose me capable of so many efforts" (II, 313). As with Thérèse, such selfishness is compelling and Delphine bows to it.

At once her passion is marked by this submission to a female will. She grows restrained with Leonce, in prelude to the silence of her going. She is heartbroken of course and yet at the same time Matilde's command and discovery—which she herself effected—have come as a kind of relief, an exit from the guilt she never quite admits but cannot cast off. Technically she is innocent, where female chastity is virtue, and she can justify at length her covert love. And yet, as she awaits Leonce's daily visits, she is uneasy, naggingly aware of the woman and wife she is wronging. The self-esteem of perfect rightness is damaged in these transactions and the self-consequence she has nurtured is lessened. Matilde's cruelty erases the tentative guilt and Delphine can again soar above a narrow world. As she once surpassed Matilde in feeling, so now she excels her in suffering, a sad but adequate preeminence.[35]

Like Thérèse, Matilde reenters Delphine's life after long absence. Delphine has become a nun as Matilde becomes a mother. And here the narrator and Delphine become accomplices, for Delphine's decision is rushed and Matilde hangs onto life after bearing her child. She dies a month after Delphine's vows, obstructing again by living too long.

35. Gutwirth notes the lack of sympathy Staël allows Delphine to show in this scene and relates it to the author's peculiar hatred for Matilde. She notes too the power of Matilde's accusations which suggest a moral ambiguity that the righteous Delphine cannot bear, since she believes in her own moral freedom. Delphine must escape this ambiguity by running into actual death or into the death of the cloister. *Madame de Staël*, p. 139.

3

Matilde and Thérèse impede Delphine's union with Leonce. Although they prevent the happiness with him she insists she craves, they also prevent her feminine self-effacement, her capitulation to the conventional society he embodies. Yet while they act to free Delphine from institutionalized marriage and passion, they themselves are conventional women who have entered willingly the female institutions. In Delphine's history they are unwitting political supporters.

Delphine is generous but not especially loving to Thérèse and Matilde, both of whom in different ways wish her well. Yet she is both generous and affectionate to two older women who actively work against her, who manipulate and enthrall her through her love for them. Each has an emotional advantage over the younger women, coming to Delphine as surrogate mother or lover. Mme de Vernon approaches as a parent, reverenced by the orphaned Delphine, while Mme de Ternan appears as replica of the desired Leonce. Neither woman is the conventional social ideal that Matilde and Thérèse represent, for both have surreptitiously rejected this image of women. Mme de Vernon exists in a world of feminine propriety and subordination only through a studied hypocrisy; Mme de Ternan has retreated into self-indulgent authority. Although they inhabit opposite worlds—the gambling salon and the convent—the two women have arrived there by similar routes; each is embittered at the female lot and each lives now only for revenge and selfish pleasure.

The rapturous and naive affection of Delphine for the false Mme de Vernon, mother of Matilde, is one of the prime annoyances of the book. Repeatedly warned, she continues to shower money and love on the older woman and lay up obligations that can only provoke resentment. Delphine's perverse behavior is made more suspect by the past. Mme de Vernon was, we learn, disliked and distrusted by Delphine's admirable husband and is constantly and rightly reviled throughout the book by his sister. When Delphine persists determinedly in her love, then, her action

237

may be hinting at an early reluctance—even before Leonce—to rely completely on any man. Through choosing to love a woman of whom her fatherly husband disapproved, and squandering on her daughter half his fortune, Delphine may be asserting a dubious but needed independence from a man judged at last too overwhelming.

Mme de Vernon foreshadows Leonce in the response she provokes. As a woman, she cannot pose a great threat to Delphine's autonomy, but she can arouse in her a fervent and self-forgetting love. "You met a young person who loved you with her first friendship," Delphine tells her at the unmasking, "a sentiment almost as profound as the first love." And again like Leonce she constrains the loving Delphine, dampens her original sentiments, and dulls her unconventional speech: "I find it . . . impracticable to discuss with her my inmost thoughts and feelings," Delphine complains to her sister-in-law, and she discerns that her friend "takes no pleasure in long conversations: but what, more than anything else, cuts short all development in discourse with her is that her penetrating genius proceeds at once to the conclusion, and seems to disdain all the intermediate steps" (I, 20). Intelligent women, as Mme de Vernon knows, must hide their intellect if they are to succeed in a society that requires female contingency.

But her liking for results not methods, for ends not means, points also to her failing in morality, in which the steps to action and thought must always be considered. Where Leonce subordinates everything to public opinion, Mme de Vernon holds in public only to social success and in private to money. Delphine is fascinated with both people, disapproving and loving them all at once. Her choice of them hints that she will give herself completely only where she knows her love will receive some check, where the gift of herself cannot be entirely received and where she will always be disturbed by her own giving.

Delphine must study to please Mme de Vernon. Although she escapes the role of coquette with men, she must play it with her female friend, regarding her moods and adapting herself to

238

her desires. At the same time she is maneuvering into the male role of providing financial support and constant security for the impecunious Vernon. "When it has been in my power to be useful to you, you so nobly accepted the tribute of my heart, you repaid it by a sentiment which renders life so sweet to me!" exults the duped Delphine at the beginning of the novel. In much the same way Leonce pushes Delphine into contrasting sexual roles: she must be the female dependent but excel in understanding, so magnifying his conquest.

"My confidence in her is unbounded," remarks Delphine of Mme de Vernon, whom she repeatedly calls "the friend of my heart." Yet at every turn Mme de Vernon deceives her. She squeezes out vast sums of money for herself and her daughter and she cleverly ensures that the wealthy Leonce will fall to her own family. At the most propitious moment for union, she parts Delphine and Leonce by deceiving him on the Thérèse affair. To each lover she gives a false image of the other, showing Leonce a loose woman and Delphine an inflexible man, when both are filled with eager love. Later she will blame Delphine for her naïveté at this juncture, her stupid expectation that any mother will put another before her daughter.

With Mme de Vernon, Delphine again obstructs Leonce through a woman. However passionately she protests her desire to unite, she avoids it by distancing herself or approaching only through a mediator. When she chooses to send to her lover the Mme de Vernon against whom she has been amply warned, she is as effectively blocking Leonce as if she had confessed her infidelity. For Thérèse and Matilde, Delphine had actively to sacrifice herself; Mme de Vernon is helpful in making the sacrifice for her.

When she finally comprehends Mme de Vernon's duplicity, Delphine is appalled, mutilated in her mind: "on the day which disclosed to me the ingratitude of friendship, I received a wound which has never closed" (III, 294). And yet even after this she is attracted to her old friend, who can master her again merely by dying. The process is helped by the female confession, a weapon

Mme de Vernon uses with skill: her faults, she explains to Delphine, have derived from her sex, for unlike her young friend she has been raised simply as a woman, a plaything in childhood, a mistress when grown. Like her diagnosis of the social woman, her remedy is shrewd. To avoid dependence, women must act selfishly and hypocritically, above all shunning the impulsiveness and enthusiasm to which Delphine is so prone: "by being the victims of every social institution," she points out, "women are doomed to misfortune, if they suffer themselves in the smallest degree to be governed by their feelings, or lose in any way command over themselves." So she is justified: "I believed that the condition of women compelled them to falsehood" (I, 420); women are for her always right in deceiving men. It is a persuasive plea for sympathy, and Delphine gives it, of course, although her own expressed views are unmodified. She will continue to extol society's female ideal of submissiveness and goodness—but through her antisocial friend she has neatly denied herself any fulfillment of it.

Like her daughter, Mme de Vernon is in death as potently destructive as in life. Leonce has discovered the deception she practiced and is ready to abandon a wife he was duped into marrying. He rushes to Delphine only to find her beside the bed of the woman who has betrayed them both. Astute to the end, the dying Mme de Vernon fends off Leonce's reproach and instead exacts from Delphine a vow that she will hold Matilde's happiness sacred. Delphine is thus blocked again by Mme de Vernon, severed from happiness throughout the life of her daughter. Only when Matilde dies can she be released from her vow and reputably embrace Leonce. But by then she has found a successor for the wily Vernon.

Mme de Ternan is malevolent, selfish, and far more openly destructive than Mme de Vernon. A decayed beauty with none of the Vernon charm, she is hard, haughty, and coercive. She fascinates Delphine not with her wit and grace but with her resemblance and blood tie to her nephew Leonce.

POLITICAL FRIENDSHIP

Mme de Ternan acts for herself and her sister, Leonce's mother. She presses Delphine to enter her convent because she wants to live again through her and because in the young and beautiful woman she can enjoy the blighting of another life. At the same time she can console herself about her own age, knowing that youth too may be miserable. Her sister wants Delphine trapped because she is a rival for Leonce's love, in a way Matilde has never been. The two older women are then avowedly selfish and predatory, and necessarily they tinge Leonce with their faults. As they wish to imprison Delphine in the constraining religion of the convent, so Leonce would trap her in the constraining love of marriage.

Mme de Ternan is forthright and unpleasing. So when she wishes to attract Delphine with her female narrative, she fails. She will hold the young woman only by her Leonce-like appearance and by her cruelty. When Delphine yet again compromises herself through a kindly act, Mme de Ternan crudely threatens to expose her to Leonce. Delphine can win her silence only through accepting the veil.

The coercion is bare and the bewildered Delphine succumbs to it. On the surface her surrender expresses her debility, for until now she has automatically recoiled from the twin horrors of religion and force, here ferociously combined in the older nun. On a deeper level, however, her extraordinary surrender may indicate how desperate is the moment for both author and heroine. If Delphine is finally to escape Leonce, she can do so only by trapping herself elsewhere. Of the female destinies—marriage and religion—religion has claimed her at last.

Yet as Delphine moves toward her sacrifice, her choice becomes hazy and confused. In a kind of trance, she is urged on by Mme de Ternan, who before her eyes dissolves into Leonce. It is a calculated effect, for the older woman has purposely dressed more youthfully than her age, perhaps to assume the coercive power of Leonce, perhaps to torture Delphine with memory of what she leaves, so embittering the sacrifice. The ceremony of the vows becomes then a kind of wedding and funeral all in one.

241

Leonce is accepted through his aunt as a younger woman and repulsed forever by the nun who must be dead for him. "Is there not something supernatural in this shadow of himself which conducts me to the altar?" gasps Delphine as she prays confusedly to her God-lover. Religion and marriage have in part merged in the Leonce-like Leontine, and the Catholic God and the haughty lover have almost coalesced.

Mme de Ternan is, like Thérèse, severely functional in Delphine's history. Once she has prevented Leonce's union, she slides abruptly and unmissed from Delphine's life. Unlike Thérèse, however, she is never rediscovered. The most odious of the female impediments to Leonce, she has been the closest to him. When the man appears, she loses her attraction and provokes in Delphine neither pity not empathy. But, although Delphine is at last unimpressed with the older woman, and unmoved by her confession, there is much in her writing and character that modifies Delphine for the reader.

Mme de Ternan displays herself as the female model of Leonce, embittered and marred by the social scheme which Mme de Vernon earlier described. Like Leonce she yearned for a splendid public role in life, but found herself crossed not by love for a woman but by being a woman. There was no sphere for her talents beyond the coquetry her fading charms denied. Worse still, she learned that these very talents were a function of coquetry. Seeming clever when they desire to please, women grow dull when they grow gray. Even the intelligent woman, then, lives in the gaze of men; when it is removed, she becomes dull and alienated from all that she thought she was. Delphine, like the younger Mme de Ternan, lives to please and she is youthful and charming. Although she has resources and virtues far beyond Mme de Ternan's, she is inevitably tainted by the older woman's conclusions and marked by her dreary fate.

In her narrative Mme de Ternan implicitly attacks Delphine's reiterated faith in the good marriage, the right and only happy path for a woman. Mme de Ternan did marry well; she had an affectionate and reasonable husband and she bore children she wanted and loved. And yet after thirty she found her life over. She had functioned as mother and mistress and when these contingent functions were over, she was valueless. Although in her actions Delphine is not so clearly dependent on men as Mme de Ternan, in her letters she swears she lives for and through Leonce, and it is hard to avoid lightly applying even to her the general logic of Mme de Ternan's female progress. On the eve of Delphine's final failure to obtain the happy marriage to Leonce, then, Mme de Ternan both obstructs and consoles. She obstructs forever the union that at last might have occurred, while hinting that the obstruction might still be as well.

When all external obstacles are past, Delphine at last confronts Leonce alone. For him she agrees to abrogate her vows in the new revolutionary France, but he cannot accept her action and is shattered to hear a passerby call her a runaway nun and their union a scandal. Seeing his grief Delphine swears she will die rather than become his wife, finally thrusting between them her own words.

It seems the start of a new verbally ferocious Delphine, continued in the strange incident of the sick child. When Leonce is captured by the revolutionary French, she pleads his case to the magistrate. The magistrate's wife enters and mentions their ailing child, whereupon Delphine seizes the moment and threatens him with its death if he refuses to free Leonce. Overwhelmed, the hapless magistrate capitulates. It is an active, supremely unfeminine Delphine who speaks here, in authority and cunning a mingling of her two perfidious female mentors, Mme de Vernon and Mme de Ternan.[36]

Throughout the novel, Delphine has spoken raptures and supported her feminine dependence while acting to maintain her independence. Now, however, action and expression seem to have changed places. While her expression grows self-assertive,

36. On this incident, Gutwirth comments that, although scarcely Madame de Staël's intent, it reflects the darker side of a human nature that takes only itself as arbiter of right and whose will to power is so thwarted that it is tempted to arrogate divine attributes of destructiveness to itself. *Madame de Staël*, p. 149.

her action moves toward the self-abasement she had earlier fought, and she at last acts out the female role of Leonce's dreams. She stays with him in prison, and when the magistrate is overruled she prepares to follow him to death. As he nears it, she takes poison—proving her passion through the ultimate sacrifice of self. The suicide—at first glance a romantic act of love—is also the end of a movement to self-abasement, an act of despair. Delphine dies the death of woman, giving Leonce the exquisite pleasure of knowing the extent of her love and sacrifice.[37] She becomes a corpse moments before his own death, a monument to the supreme immolation of the female, while he is left to die the public death of male honor.

Delphine is ultimately an ambiguous novel, built on antithesis as well as single thesis. The struggle of an independent, superior woman for her love against the institutions of society, it is also the suffering of a divided soul pulled toward independence on one side and love and society on the other. In her preface, Staël suggested that events of her book had little importance in themselves and were intended more as occasions for emotional display. Yet it is less in these passions alone than in the dialectic of events and expressed passions that the poignancy of the novel lies. In this dialectic the ultimate opposition appears to be not vice and virtue, society and love, or even Delphine and Leonce against the rest, but Delphine and her female friends against Leonce and the social image of woman he implies. The politics of revolution and reaction is, then, not merely a context of the book but also an ironic commentary on it. The Bastille has fallen and men have been forced through the gates, in much the same way

37. Owing to the outcry that met this episode and owing to her own changed views on suicide, Staël later supplied another ending for her novel. In this Leonce and Delphine go to Mondoville together, but Leonce hesitates to marry a runaway nun. Delphine fades and dies, while Leonce joins the war to let himself be killed. For a discussion of Staëlian suicide see Starobinski's "Suicide et mélancolie," p. 46, and Staël's own *Reflexions on Suicide*, 1812. Delphine's death has been further explored by Godelieve Mercken-Spaas in "Death and the Romantic Heroine: Chateaubriand and de Staël," forthcoming in *Pretext/Text/Context: Essays on Nineteenth Century French Literature*, ed. Robert L. Mitchell (Columbus: Ohio State University Press).

as women in this novel leave their social prison through female friends. And yet women remain imprisoned in the image of the prison, an image which the book's rhetoric does much to sustain. Like many sufferers from the old regime, Delphine edges her way toward an unwelcome freedom. But, despite female friendship, she ends her life with Leonce alone, reinstated in a cell she has voluntarily entered.

CHAPTER FIVE

Social Friendship

Jane Austen's *Mansfield Park* (1814)

JANE AUSTEN'S FANNY PRICE, a poor relation in all her aspects, enters the gentry through the family of her aunt, Lady Bertram. She anticipates the uprooting of marriage which a young girl usually suffers by moving to Mansfield Park at the age of ten, a frightened little child with a sweet smile but plebeian manners. Over the next eight and a half years she is ignored, despised, and used for errands by aunts and female cousins alike. At the end of this purgatory she emerges triumphant, routing both the persecuting aunt and the indifferent cousins. She routs too the charming Crawfords, who have played havoc with the Bertrams; rejecting Henry, she spurns the man her cousins desire, and, repulsing Mary, she dismisses the woman Edmund loves. Discovered at the very center of Mansfield Park, Fanny Price closes its doors to all aliens; she marries Edmund, its true son and her true brother. Her impressive but incestuous achievement has cost her female friendship, a strangely threatening potential in this novel of family love.

One of fiction's most ambiguous characters, Fanny Price has been revered and hated by critics; for some she is the arch prig-pharisee, for others the truly Christian heroine.[1] Preaching virtue,

1. Roughly, her critics may be divided into three groups. First, there are the hostile ones who find her distasteful or nauseating. These can be exemplified by Reginald Farrar in a 1917 article reprinted in *Discussions of Jane Austen,* ed. William Heath (Boston: D. C. Heath, 1961), p. 86; D. W. Harding in a 1940 essay, "Regulated Hatred: An Aspect of

she often appears viciously mean-spirited; emotionally powerful, she frequently thrives on weakness. The author exaggerates the contradictory impression by energetically supporting her in both her nobility and her meanness. This union of author and character threatens her textual opponent Mary Crawford and her extra-textual readers, who find they must believe in Fanny or be damned with Mary.

Much of Fanny's meaning in the novel derives from her peculiar tie with Mansfield Park. Living at its heart, she acts out the moral, hierarchical, domestic, and feminine codes it enshrines, the traditional ideal of the inherited estate.[2] Although he owns the house, Sir Thomas diverges from its lofty standards when he lets ambition silence him or when he confuses manner with morals in bringing up his daughters. Fanny, who owns

---

the Work of Jane Austen," reprinted in *Jane Austen: A Collection of Critical Essays*, ed. Ian Watt (Englewood Cliffs: Prentice-Hall, 1963), p. 175; C. S. Lewis in "A Note on Jane Austen," in *Jane Austen: A Collection of Critical Essays*, p. 31; Lionel Trilling occasionally in his famous essay *"Mansfield Park"* from *The Opposing Self*, reprinted in *Jane Austen: A Collection of Critical Essays*, p. 128; Marvin Mudrick in *Jane Austen: Irony as Defense and Discovery* (Princeton: Princeton University Press, 1952); and Kingsley Amis in "What Became of Jane Austen?" *Jane Austen: A Collection of Critical Essays*, p. 144. Second, there are the approving critics, who find Fanny the true embodiment of the ideals of the novel. Among these are Henrietta Ten Harmsel in *Jane Austen: A Study in Fictional Conventions* (London: Mouton, 1964); W. A. Craik in *Jane Austen: The Six Novels* (London: Methuen, 1965); Marilyn Butler in *Jane Austen and the War of Ideas* (Oxford: Clarendon Press, 1975); A. Walton Litz in *Jane Austen: A Study of Her Artistic Development* (New York: Oxford University Press, 1965); Joseph Wiesenfarth in *The Errand of Form: An Assay of Jane Austen's Art* (New York: Fordham University Press, 1967); and Alistair Duckworth in *The Improvement of the Estate: A Study of Jane Austen's Novels* (Baltimore: Johns Hopkins Press, 1971). Third, there are the ironic critics who consider Fanny intentionally flawed, an ironic creation of Austen. They include Kenneth Moler in *Jane Austen's Art of Allusion* (Lincoln: University of Nebraska Press, 1968); and Thomas R. Edwards in "The Difficult Beauty of *Mansfield Park*," *Nineteenth-Century Fiction* 20 (June 1965), 51–67. An immensely stimulating discussion of the character that cuts across the categories is Avrom Fleishman's *A Reading of "Mansfield Park": An Essay in Critical Synthesis* (Minneapolis: University of Minnesota Press, 1967).

2. For the traditional significance of Mansfield Park, see Alistair Duckworth's *The Improvement of the Estate*, in which he calls the estate a "metonym for other inherited structures—society as a whole, a code of morality, a body of manners, a system of language," p. ix. In *"Mansfield Park"* Lionel Trilling calls it "the Good place," Yeats's home "where all's accustomed, ceremonious," p. 137.

nothing and is last in all hierarchies, may disobey Sir Thomas and yet obey a deeper rule, so in time aligning the two.[3] In a way she *is* Mansfield Park, and her qualities of diffident strength, feminine stillness, silence, and propriety are its standard. The problem of the book, then, is why this standard must be inimical to women's friendship. Why must Fanny marry Edmund and break the hearts of both Crawfords? Why must Mary leave Mansfield forever?

The questions require some digging among all the women who surround Fanny; none is rejected quite as crushingly as Mary but all in their way contribute to her supreme rejection. First, of course, there is the mother, Mrs. Price, who doesn't much care for her daughter and who very readily packs her off to a wealthier home. Then there are Mrs. Price's two sisters: the odious Mrs. Norris, who carries Fanny to Mansfield for the pleasure of demonstrating her own importance, and the indolent Lady Bertram, the mistress of the house, to whose whims all cater. Among the younger women is Susan, another Price daughter, separated from Fanny and the reader for most of the novel; the privileged cousins Maria and Julia, who throw some used toys Fanny's way and then grow tired of her; and finally the outsider Mary Crawford, who aspired to be the sister the cousins never were. Clearly they are mother and sister types, those who may dominate Fanny and those who may equal her. Yet there is something miscellaneous about these groupings, and they fail to account for Fanny's disparate attitudes, her extreme hostility and moderate liking. Among the "mothers," for example, she passionately resents Mrs. Norris and indulges Lady Bertram; among the "sisters," she warms to Susan and determinedly shakes off Mary Crawford. Other groupings seem required and they emerge when the relationships are divided according to variety of influence.

3. Janet Burroway argues that Fanny is morally committed to the hierarchy which assigns her its meanest position and that the absoluteness of her commitment brings her to a crisis in which she must place herself mentally and morally above her master, "The Irony of the Insufferable Prig," *Critical Quarterly* 9 (1967), 129.

SOCIAL FRIENDSHIP

Within society women relate to each other either vertically or horizontally. Vertical relationships are pedagogical, structured on the mother and daughter tie; by argument and example the older woman may instruct the younger in social customs or female lore. Socially approved but largely ignored by men, these unions educate the young girl for marriage and a life of social propriety. When adulthood is reached they should be gently relaxed or transformed. Horizontal friendships are a more difficult matter, sometimes starting in benevolence but requiring at one point intellectual equality and some parity in status. Rarely instructing directly, they can subtly influence, and, although they may help toward marriage, they need not. Less concerned with propriety, they pry the young girl from her family by suggesting other modes and manners, opening without excessive danger the big world beyond the paternal home. Unlike vertical friendship, they intensely interest men, who may enjoy their moderate warmth—the raptures in social friendship are left for vertical friends—or fear the independence they bring. Divided along these lines, Fanny's relationships group themselves more meaningfully. The few women she can stomach, Lady Bertram and Susan, come happily together, while the women she spurns, Mrs. Norris, the cousins, and Mary Crawford, are strangely united. Although both groups of women differ enormously from Fanny, one approaches her through instruction, the other in status. We are left then only with the mother Mrs. Price, whose vertical, instructive relationship begins all the trouble.

1

Mrs. Price refuses to teach Fanny directly and her refusal forces her daughter to look elsewhere for guidance, first to her brother, the favored William, and then to his extension, her cousin Edmund. Such displacement ensures that Fanny will define herself throughout by a male image of womanhood and look for no open female counsellors. By default, then, Mrs. Price has taught her daughter. In addition, she cannot help but instruct through example, and she does so both times she enters the plot, at first when we hardly glimpse her with the young Fanny and her copious siblings, and at the end where we see her receive again her grown-up daughter.

Another Fanny, Mrs. Price has married "to disoblige her family." She moved down society's ladder, disobeying the social advice to sell her beauty dearly. The outcome was of course disaster and, with nine children and an oafish husband, Mrs. Price grew ready to court the family she had defied and find in her sisters the only hope of her children. The lesson is taught the young Fanny, much affected by her mother's misalliance. She shows herself aware of it when she marries upward again and holds fast to her genteel adopted family.

After eight years away, Fanny returns happily to her mother's home. Agitated by Sir Thomas's blame and Edmund's momentary defection, she has prepared for herself an idyllic picture of her Portsmouth family, eager and waiting to receive her:

> It seemed as if to be at home again, would heal every pain that had since grown out of the separation. To be in the centre of such a circle, loved by so many, and more loved by all than she had ever been before, to feel affection without fear or restraint, to feel herself the equal to those who surrounded her. . . . (p. 370)[4]

And it has the paradoxes of a dream, for Fanny wishes to be both first and equal, to be loved without provoking love. She wants to enter her old home, both as the long-lost daughter, special from separation, and as the delicate lady, special from status. The mother who receives her will replace the unloving mother who dismissed her and will fall on her as maternal and affectionate friend.

All these dreams the homecoming shatters; the passage describing the shattering wonderfully conveys Fanny's mind, while testifying to her feelings for the mother and the beloved brother, the pair who had long shut her out:

4. Page numbers in the text refer to *Mansfield Park, The Novels of Jane Austen*, ed. R. W. Chapman (Oxford: Clarendon Press, 1934).

She was at home. But alas! it was not such a home, she had not such a welcome, as—she checked herself; she was unreasonable. What right had she to be of importance to her family? She could have none, so long lost sight of! William's concerns must be dearest—they always had been—and he had every right. Yet to have so little said or asked about herself—to have scarcely an enquiry made after Mansfield! It did pain her to have Mansfield forgotten; the friends who had done so much—the dear, dear friends! But here, one subject swallowed up all the rest. Perhaps it must be so. The destination of the Thrush must be now pre-eminently interesting. A day or two might show the difference. *She* only was to blame. Yet she thought it would not have been so at Mansfield. No, in her uncle's house there would have been a consideration of times and seasons, a regulation of subject, a propriety, an attention towards every body which there was not here. (pp. 382–83)

Priggish humility and genuine disappointment combine as Fanny discovers a respectable source of grief—the overlooking of Mansfield Park—to justify her own wounded self-consequence.[5] At the same time, she shows how ambivalent is her love for the favored William, the boy who has entered Portsmouth and Mansfield and been welcomed in each, the child who alone provoked her and her mother's love. For William, both mother and daughter had in a way been rivals; when Edmund supplants him, Fanny will again rival a woman who dares to love him.

In Portsmouth Fanny is full of Mansfield Park. Although she has rarely been favored there or given much love, except from Edmund, she now uncritically embraces it. When she ritually blames herself, she even echoes Mrs. Norris, coercing the hated aunt of the house to attend her in her alien world. Before the totality of Mansfield Park—"her uncle's house," as Fanny reverently terms it—the defective mother clearly cannot stand. Shorn

5. Fanny does the same maneuver when jealously watching Mary Crawford on a horse with Edmund: "if she were forgotten, the poor mare should be remembered." David Ellis has discussed Fanny's tendency to incorporate unworthy feelings into feelings of which she will have no reason to feel ashamed, "The Irony of *Mansfield Park*," *Critical Review* 12 (1969), 109.

of her friendly image and denying her daughter the status of long-lost child, as well as the privileges of the mansion, Mrs. Price is harshly judged "a dawdle, a slattern, who neither taught nor restrained her children, whose house was the scene of mismanagement and discomfort from beginning to end, and who had no talent, no conversation, no affection towards herself" (p. 390). It is a severe indictment of a mother not actively cruel, but Fanny cannot compromise, and the untidy Mrs. Price, lacking proper respect for Mansfield and the daughter who serves as its ambassador, must be condemned. For the rest of her stay Fanny will fastidiously avoid the food, as if fearing to be trapped in this disorderly domestic hell.

Fanny then vehemently rejects the mother who first nonchalantly rejected her. Yet she has grasped much from Mrs. Price about the evils of poverty and the need of genteel family and proper marriage, and she has been scarred by her mother's indifference into complete allegiance to Mansfield Park. From now on there will be no wavering, no sentimental reference to a "home" elsewhere. And indeed it was for this she went, for Sir Thomas had determined that in her crowded house she should understand the value of elegance and propriety. In her own mind now Mansfield is her home and she returns to it whole-hearted and dedicated. She finds it her true parent as Sir Thomas finds in her a true daughter. Fanny reenters the house vindicated, to triumph and possess. She rushes into the maternal arms of Lady Bertram, a second, more acceptable mother who in her own quiet way also instructs her niece.

Lady Bertram, the sister of Mrs. Price, is transfixed in her first description:

> She was a woman who spent her days in sitting nicely dressed on a sofa, doing some long piece of needlework, of little use and no beauty, thinking more of her pug than her children, but very indulgent to the latter, when it did not put herself to inconvenience, guided in every thing important by Sir Thomas. . . . (pp. 19–20)

252

She is a caricature whose only action is the captivating of a baronet at the beginning of the novel. And even this is made passive when qualified by the "good luck" of the enterprise. Yet Fanny is less harsh on her lazy aunt than on the worn and faded Mrs. Price and, where she cannot even respect the unfortunate sister, she loves the fortunate one. She does, however, recognize a bond between mother and aunt, for both are "easy and indolent" and both would equally have flourished in affluence and do-nothingness. If Mrs. Price is condemned, it is because she made an imprudent marriage, while Lady Bertram is saved through honoring her family and ensuring her own comfort.

The novel closely links Mrs. Price and her sister. Both are beauties who cannot create beauty, Lady Bertram in needlework and Mrs. Price in her squalid home. Both are unmothering mothers, although Mrs. Price has an edge over her fortunate sister here; she does not wait till her son nears death to show him affection. Similarly, although both women are selfish, Lady Bertram excels for, with her social status, she can demand constant service. Finally the sisters join in being husband-centered. If in beauty, wealth, and indolence, they begin the same, they grow apart in marriage. Mrs. Price becomes slatternly with her coarse sailor, while Lady Bertram grows even more rarified and refined beneath the well-bred stillness of Sir Thomas.[6]

In their contrasting fates, Lady Bertram and Mrs. Price are examples for Fanny, who learns through them she must hold to a family and marry into the elegance she values. Indeed, even before she visits Portsmouth she grasps that order, elegance, and fastidious femininity require male money and principle. Lady Bertram obtained both in Sir Thomas; only Edmund of the next generation can give as much. Lady Bertram succeeded with an adroit use of passivity; Fanny may imitate her.

6. Both women also draw their principles from their men. Where Lady Bertram, following her husband, is aghast at Maria's sexual fall, Mrs. Price echoes her husband's conventional male response—"I'd give her the rope's end as long as I could stand over her"—with the conventional female one—"so very shocking"—after which both husband and wife turn indifferently away.

Lady Bertram is mysteriously weak and avoids all exertion. Fanny too is sickly for no clear reason and almost as helpless as her aunt. If Lady Bertram cannot pour her own tea, Fanny cannot mix her own wine and water, or even live enough to want it if Edmund is not by. Lady Bertram cannot choose between whist and speculation and appeals to Sir Thomas to decide which will amuse her most; Fanny thinks she wishes to write to her brother but can look for neither paper nor pen and must wait for Edmund to draw the lines. This shared helplessness is appealing in both women; Lady Bertram captured a baronet beyond the claims of her fortune, while the penniless Fanny rivets the noble-named Edmund with her state. Prostrate on the sofa with a headache caused by picking roses, she sweetly urges him to investigate her oppression and become responsible for her comfort. At the end, when Fanny "captivates" him, his love is "founded on the most enduring claims of innocence and helplessness" (p. 470). Sir Thomas could have said the same when he married his pretty vegetable.

Lady Bertram and Fanny share much then, but it is not until the niece is richly courted that the aunt sees any kinship. Usually she is indifferent to Fanny, careless of the riding Edmund wanted for her and selfishly ready to scotch her single outing. She gives her niece no support against a loveless marriage, and indeed the only advice of eight and a half years together occurs when Lady Bertram observes that it is every young woman's duty to accept an unexceptionable offer. She sweetens her rule with a promised present, a puppy from the litter of the supine pug, symbol of the luxurious and sensuous indolence Fanny could enter with her match.[7] The niece has not courage or respect enough for the aunt to object—as she does to Edmund—that women do not always

---

7. Although declared capable of mothering a litter of puppies, Pug is an animal of uncertain gender, male in one sentence, female in another. Lesley H. Willis has argued that Pug's varying sex reflects her/his owner's incapacity to perform any specific parental function apart from biological motherhood. See "Object Association and Minor Characters in Jane Austen's Novels," *Studies in the Novel 7*, p. 113.

like the unexceptionable, and that Henry Crawford's money is no objection, but his morals are.[8]

At the end of the novel Fanny and Lady Bertram move to a union through Edmund, true son of Sir Thomas, as Fanny is Lady Bertram's true daughter. When her real daughters go and her eldest son approaches death, she turns to Fanny in a single energetic act:

> By one of the suffering party within, they were expected with such impatience as she had never known before. Fanny had scarcely passed the solemn-looking servants, when Lady Bertram came from the drawing room to meet her; came with no indolent step; and, falling on her neck, said, "Dear Fanny! now I shall be comfortable." (p. 447)

Suddenly attractive, Lady Bertram again reinforces in her own selfish terms the message that intense needs attract most— Fanny catches Edmund by requiring more care than others. At the same time the aunt suggests the only development her niece is to experience in the book. From this greeting Fanny may learn what all insist upon in the closing pages: that she may now bring comfort as well as demand it.[9]

Toward the end of the novel, Fanny brings comfort also to Susan, a girl largely unsuspected until her sister discovers her on the Portsmouth visit. There deprived of her favorites—Edmund and William—Fanny has time to look about her and find the dissatisfied Susan. No raptures follow, for Fanny keeps her passion for the men, but the sisters do connect, and their connection is imaged as they sit together by the empty fire. In Mansfield Park, Fanny had sat fireless in her room and in this cold atmosphere

8. Female solidarity crosses books when the very different Emma echoes Fanny Price by declaring that, "A woman is not to marry a man merely because she is asked or because he is attracted to her."

9. Norman Page has noted the frequency of the word "comfort" and its cognates in *Mansfield Park*, which he feels provide a clue to the essential nature and role of Fanny, *The Language of Jane Austen* (New York: Barnes & Noble, 1972), pp. 39–42.

had grown the moral fiber Sir Thomas learns to appreciate. Not surprisingly, Susan enters the novel to continue the worthy Price line at Mansfield. At the end she succeeds Fanny as resident niece and becomes daughter of the house as her sister arrives as daughter-in-law.

Susan is tied to Fanny through her distaste for her sloppy home and a yearning for the genteel things of life. Together the two sisters fashion a common dream of Mansfield Park, shorn of its loneliness and cruelty. By allowing Fanny to help her and encourage her reading, Susan enables her sister to move nearer the adulthood she eschews in other ways and prepares her to enter Mansfield as comforter and moral leader. By smoothing the coarseness of Susan's manner and speech, Fanny improves her to a state where she may enter a genteel household without unduly embarrassing anyone. Such pedagogy nudges the male-centered Fanny into female territory, for, in teaching Susan, she passes on some of the direct training she has received only from Edmund.

In many respects Susan is a modified Fanny. Allowed some of the naughty Mary's spirit, she retains much of her sister's morality. So attractive is the little we know that it is difficult to avoid seeing in her the only hope of the silent and serious house she enters, the only possibility of any airing of its claustrophobic rooms—that is, if Lady Bertram can coax another Price child to wait on her and if a reformed Tom Bertram can avoid following Edmund and seeing in his cousin his only comfort.

Fanny is not close either to Lady Bertram or to Susan, but she learns indirectly from the one and directly teaches the other, and ties are formed. Perhaps it is the most that can be expected after her experience with Mrs. Price, whose ability to hurt her daughter is clear from the hostility she provokes. Urged too soon into symbiosis with a man, Fanny it seems has made the best of her situation and formed some tenuous ties with women who may help her and be helped, but who do not insistently approach her either in person or in predicament. In their different ways both are children—Susan in years and Lady Bertram in intellect—and they do not engage all the faculties of an adult. Such women may benefit Fanny in a mild, unthreatening sort of way. It is the best that vertical friendship can do in this unfriendly world.

2

Fanny is, then, not equipped to meet women as her equals or form alliances with them. Damaged in childhood, she has made Sir Thomas and his son her reason for being, and their place has become sacred. Defining herself in their terms, she refuses to move from Mansfield or accept an adulthood that requires some journeying from home. At the same time she refuses for Edmund who, wickedly attracted to alien ways and values in Mary, comes precipitously home to learn how comfortable a sister-wife may be. To close the doors so finally on herself and Edmund, to imprison both in the stasis of the original family, Fanny must be ruthless toward women, and in her quiet subtle way she combats all the females who would pry open the house—Maria, Julia, Mrs. Norris, and Mary Crawford. To her victorious fight with them she brings dependence, the weapon honed and used by Lady Bertram, and her own peculiar power, the neurotic diffidence that passes for femininity.[10]

Maria and Julia are the Miss Bertrams who, Sir Thomas early and erroneously asserts, can never be their cousin's "equals." They enter the novel at once as foils to their lowly relative. As a child the natural Fanny cries and blushes, while her cousins deny their spontaneous reactions of pleasure and pain; their assumed manners restrain them but do not relieve their feelings or dictate real decency. Fanny consoles herself in gentle na-

10. Karen Horney's psychological analysis may be relevant here. She has argued that some people respond to a difficult environment by adopting a self-effacing posture. They try to overcome feelings of inadequacy by winning the approval of others and displaying themselves as good, loving, and submissive. Such people—and Fanny is surely close to them—tend to see a providential order in the world which rewards virtue. See *Neurosis and Human Growth* (New York: W. W. Norton, 1950), pp. 214–38. Avrom Fleishman considers that Fanny compensates in moral aggressiveness for the psychic costs of her submissiveness, *A Reading of "Mansfield Park,"* p. 45.

ture; the cousins are first introduced cutting out "artificial" flowers and they have no joy in nature unless it indicates wealth. In her lowliness, the humble Fanny tempts Aunt Norris into gratifying her cousins at her expense and flattering them away from the virtuous and humble. At the end, her innocent presence undoubtedly helps to exile Maria, the most favored one, and Mrs. Norris is not far from the truth when she bitterly exclaims that Fanny is to blame for the downfall of her contrasting cousins.

Certainly, as the author insists, Maria and Julia deserve little of Fanny's attention for they have never much cared for her, never eased her childhood or taken any pains to give her pleasure. But the converse is also true, for Fanny has rarely tried to approach and engage her cousins.[11] The consciousness of the book is hers; consequently the reader is often in her mind, well aware she understands the needs of the other woman. Yet her cloistered virtue will not walk out to encourage theirs, nor will she overcome her prim diffidence enough to enter their distress. On the bewildering Sotherton trip, for example, she sees Maria jealous and miserable but cannot exert herself to aid her; later when Maria flirts outrageously with Henry Crawford, the watching Fanny makes only a single, indirect effort to caution her. During the play, she is again a watcher, voyeur of moral slips; she never interferes, never warns or supports, instead withdrawing to criticize and jeer with Edmund. Fully comprehending Julia's jealousy, since she is wracked with it herself, Fanny makes no link through suffering: "Fanny saw and pitied much of this in Julia; but there was no outward fellowship between them. Julia made no communication, and Fanny took no liberties. They were two solitary sufferers, or connected only by Fanny's consciousness" (p. 163). The hidden thoughts, open only to us, allow Fanny all the credit of perceptive sympathy, although she says not one word of comfort to the miserable Julia.

11. Although less warm to her cousins than to her sister, Fanny is more lenient to them than to any outsider; when Maria is rude to Mrs. Norris, for example, Fanny is not especially shaken. After the sisters leave Mansfield Park on Maria's wedding trip, Fanny grows fonder of them: they are said to be missed by "their tender-hearted cousin" and, when the ball is planned, Fanny's reaction is again "tender regret" that they are away—a regret undoubtedly due in part to her fear of being forced to lead the dance.

Distinct from her cousins in status, morality, and emotion, Fanny is yet oddly connected with them in matters of love, both in her pursuit and in her pursuing. When she grows interesting to Henry Crawford, she displaces Maria and Julia in love—as later she will in family. Henry's suit of Fanny renders him unkind to the cousins who had courted him: "They will now see what sort of woman it is that can attach me," he sneers, "that can attach a man of sense. I wish the discovery may do them any good. And they will now see their cousin treated as she ought to be, and I wish they may be heartily ashamed of their own abominable neglect and unkindness" (p. 231). It seems almost a challenge to the jealous Maria to use her arts against him.

When she does, she is destroyed and, in her destruction, she is again subtly tied in love to her despised cousin. Fanny's is the only reaction to Maria's fall we see closely and it is extreme:

> The horror of a mind like Fanny's as it received the conviction of such guilt, and began to take in some part of the misery that must ensue, can hardly be described. At first, it was a sort of stupefaction; but every moment was quickening her perception of the horrible evil. . . .
>
> Fanny seemed to herself never to have been shocked before. There was no possibility of rest. The evening passed, without a pause of misery, the night was totally sleepless. She passed only from feelings of sickness to shudderings of horror; and from hot fits of fever to cold. The event was so shocking, that there were moments even when her heart revolted from it as impossible— when she thought it could not be. A woman married only six months ago, a man professing himself devoted, even *engaged*, to another—that other her near relation—the whole family, both families connected as they were by tie upon tie, all friends, all intimate together!—it was too horrible a confusion of guilt, too gross a complication of evil, for human nature, not in a state of utter barbarism, to be capable of! (p. 344) [12]

Deeply impressed in mind and body by an evil that is complicated and clearly sexual, Fanny sees Maria sucked into the physi-

---

12. Avrom Fleishman has commented on the power of this passage and noted "the suggestions of incest" that "lurk" in it. *A Reading of "Mansfield Park,"* p. 65.

cal abyss of the Crawfords. The horror of the sexual fall, strong enough to bring on shuddering and fever, obliterates Fanny's own incipient sexuality, her slight movement toward the fascinating Henry. At the same time it scotches the hint of incest with which Fanny's love for the brotherly Edmund has been tinged. The passage, stressing familial sexuality and sins against blood, certainly fits incest more than ordinary adultery. Yet it is the adulterous Maria who provokes it. After such an outburst there is no room to doubt Fanny's purity, if we ever did, and when the erring daughter is denied Mansfield Park, to guard the purity of the niece, we are forced to concur. As the wicked elopement of Henry and Maria frees Edmund for Fanny, so the horror of Maria's sexual sin frees the union of Edmund and Fanny from any taint.

Maria, the favored, has fallen and dragged her sister Julia part of the way down; the poor niece is thus warmly welcomed to an alliance that would have found little favor before. It has been well for Fanny that she did not befriend her cousins more or strengthen their defenses with her own stiff morals.

With Maria goes Mrs. Norris, and the author takes grim joy in contemplating the mutual torment of the exiled pair.[13] The aunt's fate is just, for she has throughout the novel tormented her unfavored niece. "It is all her fault," she exclaims at one point and her words echo in Fanny's prose, rebounding on the aunt when Sir Thomas turns to her his icy gaze.

Still and quiet, like Mansfield Park itself, Fanny irritates Mrs. Norris. Always scheming and bustling, talking incessantly and fidgeting about, the aunt is appalled by the immobile and delicate niece. While Mrs. Norris can stride along in any weather and discommode two houses at once, Fanny is overcome by the slightest exertion, the merest hint of upheaval.

13. Nina Auerbach notes that in Austen's novels women together lead a purgatorial existence. The colony of Maria and Mrs. Bertram seems a fate worse than the death or transportation usually suffered by fallen women. *Communities of Women* (Cambridge: Harvard University Press, 1978), p. 47.

No doubt Fanny's link with the other aunt exacerbates the difference, for Lady Bertram is the powerful sister on whose successful alliance all the scanty importance and fortune of sister and niece depend. Certainly it must exasperate the active and bustling Mrs. Norris that she has always to attend her indolent sister, and in the weak Fanny she may be glad to relieve her exasperation, as in the young and lively Maria she may live once more her own expectations of fortune. When the strong Mrs. Norris sees Fanny at the same game as her fortunate sister—when she finds Edmund preoccupied with his cousin's headache from a walk she ordered or when Sir Thomas warms to his shivering niece and commands the fire Mrs. Norris had denied—she has reason to sulk and punish Fanny for the inequities of all their fates.

But Mrs. Norris dislikes Fanny not only because they differ so markedly but also because they coincide, because they are in a way equals in status and aim. Long ago she was angry at the first Fanny for her inadequate marriage, exaggerating her own middling match, and she is now prepared to condemn the daughter whose lowly state extends her own. Ultimately both Mrs. Norris and Fanny must be judged poor relations; both exist to amuse the stupider Lady Bertram and both must tremble at the frowns of Sir Thomas.[14] Both live to ease the family, promote its joy and comfort it in distress. But no family needs two dependent comforters. When Sir Thomas is absent, Mrs. Norris bustles for his children and practises consoling the bereaved widow should he die. When he lives, she finds her comfort unnecessary and her bustling inappropriate. The quiet Fanny who has shrunk from all her functions inherits her place and administers real comfort in the social and sexual disaster her aunt's bustling has helped to cause.

14. Mrs. Norris's favorite phrase is "between ourselves," which, as Mary Lascelles has pointed out, is pitiably at variance with her actual impotence. See *Jane Austen and Her Art* (Oxford: Clarendon Press, 1939), p. 164. Thomas R. Edwards has also noted her "yearning for intimacy with Sir Thomas's power." "The Difficult Beauty of *Mansfield Park*," p. 56.

SOCIAL FRIENDSHIP

Like good and evil angels, Fanny and Mrs. Price fight for sway in Mansfield Park. Initially Fanny's coming to the house is Mrs. Norris's idea, although her aunt contrives her niece shall never disturb her. Perhaps she pushes the proposal so she may obtain someone as low as herself in the social scheme. Certainly it is no part of her plan that Fanny enter Mansfield as real daughter, and much of her contriving over the next years is to keep Fanny out, to urge her away from the family. In this aim Sir Thomas is at first unwittingly helpful:

> "There will be some difficulty in our way, Mrs. Norris," observed Sir Thomas, "as to the distinction proper to be made between the girls as they grow up; how to preserve in the minds of my *daughters* the consciousness of what they are, without making them think too lowly of their cousin; and how, without depressing her spirits too far, to make her remember that she is not a *Miss Bertram*. I should wish to see them very good friends, and would, on no account, authorize in my girls the smallest degree of arrogance towards their relation; but still they cannot be equals." (p. 11)

Stripped of its judicious constraints, this is Mrs. Norris's plan, but it goes strangely awry. She flatters and spoils Maria and Julia so thoroughly that they disdain to remain Miss Bertrams. Neglected and despised, Fanny assumes the quiet, sober virtues Sir Thomas wished of his house. In the end she becomes a Mrs. Bertram to confound them all.

Mrs. Norris is active in excluding Fanny. She keeps her from her own White House, whose spare bed is retained for the "friend" who never comes. Instead her niece is confined to the white attic of Mansfield Park, a room that fits her state—somewhere between the family and the servants. When she grows up a little, she takes over the East room, vacated by the sisters and filled with the discarded bric-à-brac of the family. But it encloses as well the noble profile of Edmund, and to this icon Fanny may repair for comfort and spiritual sustenance. Soon the room grows powerful in its own right, shrine not only of Edmund but of Fanny herself; fireless and disdained as it is, it draws into it all who would inherit or possess the house properly.

To it comes Mary Crawford, momentarily made gentle by its influence, and Edmund, troubled by the tangle of his conscience. To it comes also Sir Thomas and when, repulsed by Fanny's only disobedience, he yet lights a fire in its cold grate, he shows his understanding of the room's significance, his approval of its humble pedagogy. Mrs. Norris of course is absent, although her harsh command that no fire be lit has made the room sacred with suffering, and has allowed the atoning gesture of Sir Thomas. So it is just that here she should be broken, rebuked by the man she reveres before the niece she despises. For the hierarchical Sir Thomas, such criticism is a noble but humiliating reversal; it becomes the main station on the route to Mrs. Norris's downfall.

In other matters too Mrs. Norris tries and fails to guard Fanny's lowly state. When there is talk of riding for health, she adamantly opposes Fanny's having a proper lady's horse like her cousins; when Sir Thomas proposes a carriage to carry his niece to the parsonage, Mrs. Norris counters it as far as she can, then mars its tribute by declaring it ordered for Edmund, not his cousin; when Sir Thomas asks pointedly for Fanny, Mrs. Norris insists it is she herself who is wanted. In family events she maneuvers to exclude Fanny, urging that she stay with Lady Bertram when the others plan an outing, and advising Sir Thomas not to waste a ball on an indigent niece. At the same time she pushes Fanny physically from the house, demanding constant errands from her and insisting she stay out if caught in the rain.

Finally Mrs. Norris works to keep Fanny from the family by imposing an incestuous image on her marriage into it.[15] Like Sir

15. In *"Mansfield Park: Freedom and the Family,"* R. F. Brissenden draws attention to the extremely significant role that incest plays in the novel. He considers that the alliance between Edmund and Fanny has distinctly incestuous overtones and that these give it its underlying power. He notes that incest is again involved in the play *Lovers' Vows,* performed at Mansfield; in it Henry Crawford plays Frederick, the illegitimate son of Agatha, who is played by Maria. The theatrical "son" is therefore seducing the theatrical "mother" when the real father arrives. *Jane Austen: Bicentenary Essays* ed. J. Halperin (Cambridge: Cambridge University Press, 1975), pp. 165–67. It is worth noting that several women writers of the age show some fascination with incest, for example, Fanny Burney in *Evelina* and Charlotte Smith in *Emmeline.* It is of course a common theme among male writers: Henry Fielding in *Tom Jones,* Daniel Defoe in *Moll Flanders,* and Matthew Lewis in *The Monk* are obvious examples.

Thomas, she is aware that Fanny would enter and possess the house most thoroughly by marrying one of its sons. At the beginning of the novel Sir Thomas, still unchastened by misfortune, expresses this very fear to Mrs. Norris, who forthrightly replies:

> You are thinking of your sons—but do not you know that of all things upon earth *that* is the least likely to happen; brought up, as they would be, always together like brothers and sisters? It is morally impossible. I never knew an instance of it. It is, in fact, the only sure way of providing against the connection . . . breed her up with them from this time, and suppose her even to have the beauty of an angel, and she will never be more to either than a sister. (pp. 6–7)

Her determined speech ensures that cousinly love will seem incestuous until purged by Maria's fall.[16] Fanny marries her cousin at last and continues in purity. She has attracted Edmund not with the beauty of an angel as Mrs. Norris feared, but with the sweetness of the angel in the house.

Fanny has cried often for herself, but when Mrs. Norris is sent from Mansfield Park, she sheds no tears. The two women have fought for position—as they must, being two poor hangers-on—and one has lost. Both in their different ways influenced and coerced others, Mrs. Norris openly and violently, Fanny quietly and furtively. Inevitably Fanny has won, for her weapons of helplessness and stillness are powerful in the house of Lady Bertram. At the same time her ideals of quietness, isolation, propriety, and withdrawn suffering agree with Sir Thomas's final image of what Mansfield Park should embody. Mrs. Norris, who welcomes strangers into the family and pushes her nieces into external mercenary marriages, becomes the evil component of the house. She leaves Mansfield Park to the stasis of a single family,

16. Sir Thomas hints at the incestuous vision when he grows satisfied he has been "bringing up no wife for his younger son," while Edmund, thwarted in outside love, rushes back to Fanny exclaiming "my only sister." Mary Crawford—who may have her own motives—again suggests it when she declares that Fanny and Edmund have the same look.

presided over by Sir Thomas, who is anxious only "to bind by the strongest securities all that remained of domestic felicity."

Mrs. Norris had to go, for she was clearly threatening in a book devoted to Fanny's triumph. A potential equal, she could— if both had been of good will—have gently led her niece from Mansfield to return or not as Fanny chose; malevolent, she can only alienate entirely. Both Edmund and Sir Thomas come to see her horror and both apologize to Fanny for her meddling aunt. Neither, however, understands until much later the more insidious threat of Mary Crawford, Fanny's other potential equal. Only Fanny is aware that Mary threatens her future by meddling with her love, as Mrs. Norris had tried to do, and endangering the closed world of Mansfield Park by opening its son to other manners and morals. To preserve the beloved Edmund, embodiment of the house for her, Fanny vigorously repulses Mary, denying her the friendship which neither inclination nor experience dictates. In spite of her subtlety, Mary is at the close as decisively exiled as the obnoxious aunt.

"I would not have the shadow of a coolness arise," whispers Edmund to Fanny one day, "between the two dearest objects I have on earth." With the usual male delight in female friendship, he has watched the apparent sprouting of affection between his cousin and his beloved, gladdened by their mingling of domestic purity and sexual charm. His approval should strengthen the friendship in Fanny, who is usually devoted to his taste. But instead she is horrified at it—it becomes for her his only error, his one fall from godlikeness. Here alone Fanny moves away from Edmund and here, consequently, best reveals herself. Entering a relationship she knows nonexistent but which she lets others believe real, she avoids horizontal friendship altogether and escapes the threat she sees in equal women. Watching her maneuver we can discern the shadow of her indifferent mother and come to appreciate the fearful determination in her denial of friendship.

Mary Crawford is a lively, witty, active young woman, intelligent and susceptible like Fanny, but adaptable and socially poised as well. She charms almost everyone, disarming the handsome Maria and Julia and interesting both brothers. Even Mrs. Norris enjoys her, for the diplomatic Mary is always ready with the right phrase, taking pains to ease sociability. When Mrs. Norris looks sour, Mary cheers her by remembering the favored niece; when Maria swells at the sight of her fiancé's estate, Mary is quick to encourage her pride. Only Fanny stands aloof from the flattering word, repulsed by her affability and easeful gestures.

Yet Mary, intrigued by the furtive and prickly Fanny, woos her constantly and intensely. She praises her to Edmund, his father, and to her own brother and sister. Frequently she invites Fanny to visit and, on the rare occasion when Fanny does, finds her arrival "delightful." In social trials she shields Fanny from the worst assaults, giving sympathy against the persecuting aunt and active help against the demanding cousins. So pressing is her suit in word and deed that at one point "a sort of intimacy" occurs between the two women, but it is, the narrator assures us, "an intimacy resulting principally from Miss Crawford's desire of something new, and which had little reality in Fanny's feelings" (p. 208).

As Edmund remarks, Mary's kindness to Fanny is invariable, but it is not always disinterested. Praising Mary, the author hints at the mixed motive of some of her benevolence when she comments on "the really good feelings by which Mary Crawford was almost purely governed." The incident of the necklace can illustrate. When Mary offers Fanny a present of Henry's necklace, she is both friendly and deceitful. The gift is meant to charm Fanny, but may well be intended for Edmund's eyes as well. Certainly it is Edmund, not Fanny, who welcomes it. In addition, since she believes that Henry merely flirts with Fanny, she is in a way pimping for her brother with her gift. Yet when flirtation moves to courtship she continues to befriend the dowerless Fanny and she welcomes her wholeheartedly as sister-in-law.

Mary is also mixed in her presentation of herself to Fanny as friend. Very often she appears attuned to her; appalled, for example, at Mrs. Norris's unkindness, she enters immediately into Fanny's dismay. At other times, she is less sympathetic; uneasy at Fanny's stilted rhapsodies on nature, she answers them flippantly, and she is equally flippant when faced with Fanny's mountainous respect for the church and its clergy. On such occasions, she seems an inappropriate candidate for Fanny's friendship, unless strenuously reformed. Yet she remains the only one provided by the society of the book.

On the other side, Fanny's feelings for Mary are rarely ambiguous. From the beginning of their acquaintance she has rejected Mary Crawford as harshly as she later rejects the brother. She is always mindful of the other woman's faults, invariably thinks the worst of her, and goes beyond all others by naming her "ungrateful" and "cruel." She sees Mary Crawford as mercenary and debauched because lively and speculating, and she can give her little credit for the sincere affection the relatively humble and impoverished Edmund has inspired in her. After the ball when Mary seems disconsolate, Fanny will not try to console, although she knows of Edmund's love and could soothe Mary with it. In company Fanny refuses to laugh at the other woman's wit or smile at her sallies, and she is mortified when forced in any way into her debt. In return for praise and support, Fanny at worst scoffs at Mary, at best forebears dispraise, and she is aghast when a bond of gratitude seems possible between them; bitterly she laments that "it was Miss Crawford to whom she was obliged, it was Miss Crawford whose kind exertions were to excite her gratitude" (p. 194). That Miss Crawford can exert herself at all seems odious to the debilitated Fanny; that she can oblige is truly horrifying.

But Fanny need not have worried, for when the novel concludes she has defeated Mary as lover and friend. Withholding her liking, she denies friendship and, clutching Edmund, she scotches love. If the victory had seemed destined for Mary, daring, strong, and often generous beside the timid, sickly, and occasionally mean-spirited Fanny, by the end the mistake is clear.

Mary loses so devastatingly because she is caught in the contrasts that undergird the book and overdetermine its conclusion. No horizontal friend has been meant for Fanny and anyone who presumes becomes a foil. The contrasting qualities Mary represents are not to mingle with Fanny's or modify her character; they are simply to be repudiated. If she is to win Edmund, Fanny must bring to him her femininity—her lowliness and purity—intact.

Fanny has learned the message of Lady Bertram, that helplessness can attract where bustling energy merely repels. Such helplessness is conventionally the mark of a kind of domestic femininity that Sir Thomas and Mansfield appear to require.[17] In this Fanny excels, and it forms the basis of her relationship with Edmund. Always too delicate or too sensitive and emotional for action, she constantly needs reviving by her cousin who must act and speak for her. Tears spring quickly and easily to her eyes while her blushes impede her speech. Her helpless femininity is quite explicit in the novel: in one place, she is described as "so truly feminine," in another, she is said to have "that sweetness which makes so essential a part of every woman's worth in the judgment of man" (p. 294). In Henry Crawford's eyes, Fanny's femininity appears so idealized that she has "some touches of the angel" in her. She is truly a man's woman and the "judgment of man" is implied in most of the eulogistic comments on her. Sir Thomas praises her for being gratifyingly free from that independence of spirit which is so offensive in a young woman and, when she does—just once—oppose, it is to remain in the family, to stay forever a dependent. At the end of the novel when the union with Edmund is fulfilled, Sir Thomas understands that her feminine virtue is born of her lowliness. Femininity has come easy to the poor and passive Fanny.

17. In *Mansfield Park,* there are two separate codes of femininity, only one of which is named and supported. The first, embodied in Mary Crawford and the Bertram sisters, leads to coquettish behavior and an emphasis on female accomplishments; as Kenneth Moler has noted, this code was much attacked by pedagogists in the late eighteenth century, especially by Hannah More. See *Jane Austen's Art of Allusion,* pp. 124–26. The second code results in the passive, virtuous, serious, and wifely woman, like Fanny Price, close to the Hannah More model.

SOCIAL FRIENDSHIP

In femininity Mary is Fanny's antithesis, far more even than the disobedient daughters of Mansfield. She is, we are clearly told, "not truly feminine." When Edmund is presented as blind to her real character, he appreciates her femininity; he thought Miss Crawford "perfectly feminine, except in the one instance" (p. 64). The instance is crucial, of course, for it is blame of her uncle, blame which hints at a distaste for unworthy or imposed male authority. When Edmund's eyes are opened to Mary's real character—when he comes to share Fanny's vision of his former beloved—he perceives her drastic failure: she has, he confesses, "no feminine . . . no modest loathings." To preserve the femininity of Fanny's Mansfield Park, Mary must go, condemned unheard to spinsterhood.

With Mary, sexual passion leaves the house too. Both Crawfords have suggested this dangerous unfamilial element, unsettling to the confined, constrained inhabitants. The Bertram sisters, who first found Henry unhandsome, speedily responded to his devastating sexual power, while Edmund, grave at Mary's flippancies and risqué remarks, soon danced attendance on her charm. Even Fanny has been touched by the Crawford enchantment. Rigidly opposed to Henry and his approach, she yet warms to his reading, transfixed by the seductive melody of his voice. In Mary too she glimpses an enticing sexual power. She visits the other woman unintentionally and appreciates Mary's powerful riding, symbol perhaps of her unfeminine force and sexual vitality. Timid on a horse, Fanny is afraid of falling or straying too far; she neither owns the animal nor makes it her own. But Mary is immediately at ease, riding actively and fearlessly and exciting Edmund with her skill. During one such show, a deserted Fanny watches the lovers playing with the horse and understands the sexual pull. When Mary leaves, Fanny reinherits the horse but there is no hint she will ever ride it with skill. As Edmund remarks to her, she rides only for health, Mary Crawford for pleasure.

But Mary is inadequate in more than female dependence and helplessness; she fails the test of class. In *Clarissa* the marauding aristocrat Lovelace menaced the bourgeois world of the Har-

269

lowes with his undomestic, sophisticated power. In *Mansfield Park*, the classes are less delineated, but the Crawfords certainly share more of the aristocratic ways than the grave Sir Thomas and his younger son.[18] Through her class, Mary is again opposed to the lowly Fanny.

Where the Bertrams are proper and correct, a trifle stuffy and unbending, the Crawfords are unceremonious, putting everyone at ease with their familiar speech and intimate manners.[19] If Mary Crawford has the quick snobbishness of the aristocrat—arrogantly disdaining lower naval ranks—the politer Sir Thomas has a deeper need to distinguish his state. He is, for example, concerned how the lower-middle-class Fanny will relate to her cousins, and he takes pains to separate himself from the aristocratic Mr. Yates, to whom he is unremittingly hostile. Finally, although the Bertrams and the Crawfords are gentry and possess landed estates, Henry seems surer of his money than Sir Thomas, less tied to his property and less dependent on business interests. Nothing West Indian can threaten his status and he feels no urge to work to safeguard his wealth. Certainly the differences between the two families, landed gentry both, are slight, a matter more of manner than of substance; yet they are enough to tinge with class Mary's pursuit of Edmund and make it hint at Lovelace's aristocratic stalking of Clarissa.

Fanny of course is free from aristocratic and libertine associations. From her lowly class she can outdo even the bourgeois Sir Thomas in rigidity and propriety; at once poor and pure, she can purge Mansfield Park of the flaws of wealth.[20] Indeed Fanny's

18. Although in *The Country and the City* (Frogmore: Paladin, 1975) Raymond Williams has warned us how difficult it is to oppose the Bertrams and the Crawfords socially, Avrom Fleishman has persuasively argued for cultural links between the Crawfords and the aristocracy. For a discussion of the social context of *Mansfield Park* see *A Reading of "Mansfield Park,"* pp. 40–41. The hostility between gentry and aristocracy is investigated by R. W. Chapman in *Jane Austen: Facts and Problems* (London: Oxford University Press, 1949), pp. 197–99.

19. Colloquialisms pepper the Crawford speech, contrasting with the slow abstractions of Sir Thomas. For a discussion of the verbal differences between the two groups see Norman Page's *Language of Jane Austen*.

20. The problem of Fanny's innate goodness has been touched on by many critics, some of whom regard it as a product of her early home, while others see it derived from

class position is essential to the proper functioning of the house, the fulfillment of its ideals, for, in spite of his occasional mercenary practice Sir Thomas values her qualities of responsibility, thrift, struggle, and morality, none of which can easily be instilled into affluent children. So three of his offspring fail him, repudiating at once his principles and his position. Lured into the aristocratic ways of wealth, Tom becomes a spendthrift, Maria a libertine woman, and Julia a noble wife. Edmund alone—although sorely tempted to marry beyond his means and manners—is saved for Mansfield. He is saved by Fanny, who purifies both him and his father's house. Genteel because she inhabits Mansfield Park and virtuous because she has known something worse, she is the only proper wife for Mansfield's only proper son.

So Fanny Price wins her lover. Throughout her successful course she has feared friendship, which might pull her from the familial marriage her whole being desires, and she uses the complementary woman as foil not instructor. Her stance is explicable for, out of the family, marriage may lead to the Price misalliance and Mary may teach of an open world best ignored. It is also exonerated, since her neurotic reaction coincides with the feminine ideal of passive and moral behavior. But what surprises is the author's seeming complicity in this neurosis, this denial of social female friendship. At every turn "my Fanny" is lovingly supported while just as insistently Mary is abandoned. Mary may smile kindness but a sly author is there to make faces behind her back; Edmund may be infatuated but the author and Fanny will sneer at our morality if we dare to be so too.

On all counts Mary is made suspect. Her health is scoffed at, while her wit and sociability affront the quiet and furtive Fanny.

her training in Mansfield Park. The debate can be broadened by comments in *Patriarchal Attitudes* (New York: Stein and Day, 1970) in which Eva Figes associates qualities like thrift, self-control, and duty to oneself with the rise of capitalism, arguing that these are male virtues since women, no longer the breadwinners, represent sloth and pleasure, the temptation to spend "which by the nineteenth century had actually become the vernacular for ejaculation," p. 79. Certainly Fanny, the patriarchal woman, is associated with poverty, thrift, and self-absorption, while Mary, with her sexual and social charm and her desire to spend a large income, represents the subversive female threat.

Her repartees are bunched together—"something clever to be said at the close of every air"—and hidden from us, so that, although they cannot please they may declare their artifice. Her ingratiating speeches, useful at Sir Thomas's sombre ball, are again condensed, forced to declare their insincerity. Even her beauty somehow seems dishonest, a sort of conspiracy between her harp and the sunny day. Finally her good nature is shattered in the unlikely letter where she wickedly speculates on her lover's inheriting title and fortune. Nothing in her earlier speech and act has prepared us for this heartless young woman who wishes a man dead that she may have his money, while none of her socially shrewd actions has suggested she would write cynically to the serious Fanny. When Fanny celebrates her victory, she reveals to Edmund this letter, written only for herself; the letter and its unkind and unremarked divulging seem collusion of author and heroine. By both, Mary is reduced to her beauty and her £20,000, a predatory monster lurking in wait for wealthy sons.

In contrast, Fanny is enlarged by the author who first dramatically rescued her. When first pressed to act, she is saved from complying as Mrs. Norris suddenly lashes out against her; further coerced, she is again prevented as Sir Thomas abruptly arrives. The hated necklace which she cannot politely spurn proves too large for William's cross and only Edmund's valued chain fits. Always she speaks "gently," and, like Wollstonecraft's Mary, she is "little" in a harsh and threatening context. Insistently the author demands attention for her because she feels acutely and, when anyone dares disrespect, the author leaps to defend her. A flustered and miserable Julia, newly escaped from the horrible Mrs. Rushworth, snaps at her cousin, "you always contrive to keep out of these scrapes" and provokes the comment: "This was a most unjust reflection." The author wrings still more from the incident by adding, "Fanny could allow for it, and let it pass." In Portsmouth again the author may convey the awfulness of Mrs. Price and Fanny's awareness of it without in any way tinging the heroine's character with impropriety: "She might scruple to make use of the words, but she must and did feel that her mother was a partial, ill judging parent, a dawdle, a slattern . . ." (p. 304). Indeed, why should Fanny openly criticize when the author will do it for her and spare her virtuous propriety?[21]

The prize is marked for Fanny. Edmund marries his cousin and keeps her forever in the shadow of a Mansfield Park purified by her presence. A proper conclusion certainly, it is nonetheless darkened by hints of what might have been. Against Fanny's own conviction, the author admits Mary could be improved with a principled husband; if so, she might also grow with a principled friend. When Fanny rejects her, she abandons another woman to the sorry effects of upbringing and hardens her in a mold she might have escaped. On the other side, if Fanny can blossom a little with Henry Crawford and thrill at his spoken charm, she might more safely have opened to his sister and learned to appreciate more fully the Crawford wit and vitality. The friendship that is rejected, then, carries with it the hope of mutual development, social, intellectual, moral, and sensual.[22] Discarding it, Fanny retreats to her lonely room in Mansfield Park, wrapping herself round in Edmund's profile and shutting the windows against the unfeminine and the unfamilial.

Fanny has been scarred by Mrs. Price into dependence on men and instructed in helpless femininity by Lady Bertram. The vertical ties she sometimes tolerates image the male hierarchy to

21. I am aware that the case may be overstated. Toward the end of the novel, when Fanny seems reasonably settled, the author slightly withdraws into archness: "It would not be fair to inquire into a young lady's exact estimate of her own perfections," she comments coyly, and she remarks that, like all other young ladies, Fanny would prefer to be sought by an agreeable suitor than have him driven off by her vulgar relatives. On the other side, Mary is not invariably condemned by the author, although she is so by Fanny. She is allowed genuine feelings and a possibility of improving, if well husbanded.

22. Of the ending of *Mansfield Park* Darrel Mansell writes: "The Virtuous have withdrawn and have huddled together in a moral haven that is marked off by prim boundaries from the world outside," *The Novels of Jane Austen: An Interpretation* (London: Macmillan, 1973), p. 145. The sombreness has been wittily captured by Marvin Mudrick, who asks "What imagination will not quail before the thought of a Saturday night at the Edmund Bertrams, after the prayer-books have been put away?" *Jane Austen: Irony as Defense and Discovery*, p. 179. His sentiment is echoed by Kingsley Amis, who concludes that "to invite Mr. and Mrs. Edmund Bertram round for the evening would not be lightly undertaken," "What became of Jane Austen?" p. 142.

which she and Mansfield Park adhere; partly through them she achieves the claustrophobic family she values. She works too by denying the horizontal friends who might air the stuffiness. Although at one time sanctioned by the upright Sir Thomas and his son, friendship with Mary is abjured by Fanny, who outdoes the men in orthodoxy; with her experience she can admit no compromise. So she eschews the social friendship that might connect her to a wider society, create alliances beyond Mansfield—in the white house with Mrs. Norris or in the parsonage with Mary— and reveal to her other less "feminine" ways of behaving, other pleasures beyond Mansfield propriety. And the novel concurs, catching her possible companions in pejorative contrasts and weighted comment. At the end Mrs. Norris suffers a harsher fate than Austen usually inflicts on unworthiness, while the charming Mary Crawford goes down in one of fiction's most decisive defeats of friendship.

Jane Austen's *Emma* (1816)

Like Fanny Price, Emma Woodhouse in a way marries her older brother. With Edmund, Mr. Knightley has watched his future bride grow and develop, has corrected her conduct and fashioned her taste. Again like Fanny, Emma avoids the uprooting Mrs. Elton declares to be "quite one of the evils of matrimony": married, Emma will rest in her father's house and continue the duties she has long fulfilled. The denouement reasserts the family, merely redefining its borders. Yet there the resemblance to *Mansfield Park* ends. Hartfield House, Emma's home, is far from Mansfield, a feminine preserve of heartfelt warmth, with no man as its verbal and physical head. Emma too is no Fanny. Favored child of a doting, demanding father, she is Highbury's first lady, "the princess paramount."[23] Her position, like Fanny's, marks her character: where the lowly Fanny is self-effacing, the proud

23. Sir Walter Scott, reviews of *Emma* in *Quarterly Review* (1815), reprinted in *Discussions of Jane Austen*, ed. William Heath (Boston: D. C. Heath, 1961), p. 8.

Emma is self-assertive, openly ordering others and insisting on her own high, single status. If the two women initially recoil from a world beyond the defining family, the recoil is differently motivated. With the help of men, Fanny avoids being a female friend; with the help of women, Emma tries to avoid being a wife. Where Fanny remains firm in her exclusion of women, supported by her author and vindicated by her plot, Emma is trounced by her author until she discovers herself and achieves approval.[24]

Although symbolized by wifehood, her achievement is defined by women, first the vertical friends, Mrs. Weston and Harriet, whom she should outgrow and whom she naughtily uses to play the wife, and finally the horizontal companion, Jane Fairfax, the equal friend, sanctioned by society and the novel, whom Emma first rejects as improperly close to her. Through these three women, the novel investigates social friendship, picturing its abuse as well as its use, admitting its necessary limits in an ordinary world of marriage and subordinate women, and indicating its potential to help a young girl discover herself and a world beyond the family. If in *Emma* the most promising friendship is cut short, it is so not by the repulsion that blocked Fanny's friendship in *Mansfield Park*, but by the author, who laughingly dispatches friend Jane to Yorkshire and sends Emma home.

---

24. Emma has provoked almost as much conflicting criticism as her predecessor Fanny Price, and it can only be faintly suggested in a footnote. The critics of Austen's novels in general, mentioned in the section on *Mansfield Park*, also treat the character of Emma: A. Walton Litz, Alistair Duckworth, Darrel Mansell, Joseph Weisenfarth, and Kenneth Moler, among others, while Marvin Mudrick is again provoking and illuminating. Other studies concentrating on Emma include F. W. Bradbrook's *Jane Austen's Emma* (Great Neck: Barron's Educational Series, 1961); Joseph M. Duffy, Jr.'s "Emma: The Awakening from Innocence," *Journal of English Literary History* 21 (March 1954), 39–53; Lionel Trilling's "Emma and the Legend of Jane Austen," *Beyond Culture: Essays on Literature and Learning* (New York: Viking Press, 1965); Malcolm Bradbury's "Jane Austen's *Emma*," *Critical Quarterly* 4 (Winter 1962), 345–46; Edgar F. Shannon, Jr.'s "*Emma*: Character and Construction," *PMLA* 71 (September 1956), 637–50; and Mark Schorer's "The Humiliation of Emma Woodhouse" in *Jane Austen: A Collection of Critical Essays*, ed. Ian Watt (Englewood Cliffs: Prentice-Hall, 1963).

1

Emma's mother, we are told, possessed excellent qualities, and her excellence strengthens the potential of her daughter, the cleverest of a simple family. But the mother dies too soon to furnish anything but genes, and her place is taken by a comfortable governess. Miss Taylor—soon to become Mrs. Weston—avoids the maternal role; together, she and Emma live with the "intimacy of sisters."

Mrs. Weston adores her charge and thoroughly approves her ways.[25] She exults at Emma's "loveliness" and exclaims at her intellect and good heart. In return Emma rejoices in her friend, exhilarated to find their relationship untouched by marriage:

> there was not a creature in the world to whom she spoke with such unreserve, as to his wife; not any one, to whom she related with such conviction of being listened to and understood, of being always interesting and always intelligible, the little affairs, arrangements, perplexities, and pleasures of her father and herself. She could tell nothing of Hartfield, in which Mrs. Weston had not a lively concern; and half an hour's uninterrupted communication of all those little matters on which the daily happiness of private life depends, was one of the first gratifications of each. (p. 117)[26]

Yet the relationship is not equal. If Emma is merely Emma where her governess is always Mrs. Weston, the address reflects only age. Although few allude to Mrs. Weston's initial status—established at Hartfield, she shares its dignity—yet, like the vulgar Mrs. Elton, we remember it through Jane Fairfax, who often refers to the lowliness of the governess. Indeed Emma herself once points to it when offended that anyone could suspect

25. Only through a contiguity in the text is Mrs. Weston even linked to judgment. When Frank Churchill—the man with whom Emma might be in love—runs off to London merely to have his hair cut, Mrs. Weston uncomfortably remarks: "All young people would have their little whims." The criticism might apply to Emma, who will be lenient to Frank because she has learned he admires her "extremely." Often Mrs. Weston represents an escape from the judgment of self and others; after her embarrassment with Mr. Elton and her unkindness to Robert Martin, Emma yearns for the "refreshment" of her friend.

26. References in the text are to *Emma*, ed. R. W. Chapman (London: Oxford University Press, 1952).

her governess of being unladylike, and Mrs. Weston seems to recall it when she gently remonstrates with Emma for mentioning Jane's social predicament. Mostly, however, both women ignore the unpalatable, and, when the poor Jane is to marry the wealthy Frank, the former governess observes, "It is not a connexion to gratify." Certainly she speaks from sadness that Emma is not the connection, but she may also show a happy assimilation of status. Ironically it jolts the reader and momentarily reveals the governess in the married lady.[27]

The inequality between Emma and Mrs. Weston subtly emerges even when their relationship is most highly praised:

> It had been a friend and companion such as few possessed, intelligent, well-informed, useful, gentle, knowing all the ways of the family, interested in all its concerns, and peculiarly interested in herself, in every pleasure, every scheme of her's;—one to whom she could speak every thought as it arose, and who had such an affection for her as could never find fault. (p. 6)

A pleasing picture, but Mr. Knightley—the voice of truth and conscience in the novel[28]—continues painting it less rosily. Descanting on Emma's position as the spoiled child of the family, he declares to Mrs. Weston: "You might not give Emma such a complete education as your powers would seem to promise; but you were receiving a very good education from *her,* on the very material matrimonial point of submitting your own will, and doing as you were bid" (p. 38). Mrs. Weston has put up with too much, has played the wife, not the governess, to her charge. When later Frank Churchill perceptively appeals to Emma through praising Mrs. Weston, he thanks her for reversing roles and forming the merits of her governess. His compliment uncom-

27. Kenneth Moler notes that Miss Taylor's situation in life almost exactly parallels that of Jane Fairfax, *Jane Austen's Art of Allusion,* p. 183.

28. In *Jane Austen's "Emma"* (Sydney: Sydney University Press, 1968), J. F. Burrows has argued that Mr. Knightley is not always the standard of the novel, but most critics seem to agree with Mark Schorer, who calls him "the humanely civilized man" and asserts that "if we are to see Jane Austen's values as they positively underlie her drama, we must look at him," "The Humiliation of Emma Woodhouse," p. 110. Certainly a man named Knightley living at Donwell is not to be lightly faulted.

fortably echoes Mr. Knightley's gentle reproach, that the roles have been oddly confounded.

In her marriage, Mrs. Weston plays an even more dangerous part in the grown Emma's life. Strenuously declaring she will never wed but stay always the favored child, Emma yearns to know the adult world of marriage. So she welcomes the weddings of people close to her—those of her simple sister Isabella to Mr. John Knightley and later of her governess to Mr. Weston. The latter, Mr. Knightley declares the most natural thing in the world, quite independent of prompting, but Emma insists she has made it and is part of it. Through Mrs. Weston she can experience the matrimony which fascinates her, while avoiding its threat to her status as first lady and grown-up child.

Emma is not entirely blind to the limits of her friendship with Mrs. Weston. Early in the novel she commiserates with her father over her lost governess: "you would not," she urges Mr. Woodhouse, "have Miss Taylor live with us forever and bear all my odd humours, when she might have a house of her own?" (p. 8) Yet the dangers of a woman's playing "husband" to another female or of experiencing vicarious wifehood through her may escape Emma. Mrs. Weston is rebuked by her pupil's heap of ignored reading lists, her excessive self-confidence, and her narcissistic isolation. The governess has been too obliging and only the event can tell whether her wifeliness will corrupt. Certainly in society her docile admiration can endanger.

Mrs. Weston helps her new stepson Frank fool Emma into believing herself courted. Openly prompting the match, she unwittingly directs it as well. When Emma and Frank talk of Jane's humble status, Mrs. Weston interrupts to remind them she is present, and she provokes a heartfelt tribute from her old pupil: "I certainly do forget to think of *her* . . . as having ever been any thing but my friend and my dearest friend" (p. 201). Frank appreciates the quick compliment, but his admiration deceives. At the time this admiration seems to rise wholly because he values his new mother and likes the display of female friendship; later, when we learn he admires the lowly Jane, herself destined to be a governess, it appears to spring from his feelings for her. Emma is fooled and Mrs. Weston, unawares, has assisted in the fooling. At the same time she has again allowed Emma to approach matrimony without commitment and compromise. Although unsuspicious of her unimportance, Emma never hazards all herself with Frank or endangers her proud autonomy.

With Harriet, too, Mrs. Weston is wrongly approving. When she is questioned by Mr. Knightley on the propriety of friendship between Emma and the lowly, silly Harriet, she gently replies: "perhaps no man can be a good judge of the comfort a woman feels in the society of one of her own sex, after being used to it all her life" (p. 36). Putting sex before class, she finds the relationship right, especially since it fills the void her marriage has caused. Judging in terms of her own association with Emma, she even forces the censorious Mr. Knightley to withhold his strictures and concentrate on the earlier tie. When he contemplates this, his admiring feelings resurge and Harriet is for the moment forgotten.

As a friend Mrs. Weston is defective and delightful, then, neither quite equal nor wholly subservient, contributing to Emma's pride, her comfort, and her imaginative life. Although she encourages Emma to move from the family toward the outsiders, Frank and Harriet, she does this so unwisely that Emma speedily returns, too easily confirmed in her family role of mistress of her father's house.[29]

With Mrs. Weston, Emma cannot travel far, hardly past her own childhood grounds. If then she is to stray into new experience, her governess must inch back, leaving to another the post of friend. And, fortunately, this happens. When Mrs. Weston

29. Quoting the opinion of an anonymous nineteenth-century critic, Lionel Trilling discusses the relationship of Mrs. Weston and Emma in terms of the platonic idea that the giving and receiving of knowledge, the formation of another's character, is the strongest foundation of love. He sees the relation of Harriet and Emma as a perversion of the relation of Mrs. Weston and Emma, "Emma and the Legend of Jane Austen," p. 54. Certainly there is much positive in the friendship of Emma and Mrs. Weston, but it is also true that its consequence as well as its contradiction is to be found in Harriet and her mentor.

marries, she adopts a ready-made family of father and son, Frank. The son's interest in Jane Fairfax soon pulls another person into the Weston orbit, and Jane, a young and attractive woman, begins to displace Emma for the Westons. After visiting her prospective daughter-in-law, Mrs. Weston is compelled as usual to describe her meeting to Emma. The visit to Hartfield is, the author tells us, a duty to Emma as well as a pleasure to herself. It is lightly done, but certainly there was no mention before of duty in Mrs. Weston's dealings with the house. Possibly she remains embarrassed that Frank has apparently rejected Emma and, as his new step-mother, feels she should smooth what he has ruffled; yet possibly too she is enjoying a new family relationship.

The process of slight withdrawal is crowned with the birth of a baby girl to Mrs. Weston. As Emma observes, the baby will be a tie even "dearer than herself." She is right, and the final scene of the two women bears her out. The news of the engagement of Mr. Knightley and Emma delights Mrs. Weston, rendering her truly one of the happiest of woman. But the author adds slyly, "If any thing could increase her delight, it was perceiving that the baby would soon have outgrown its first set of caps" (p. 468).

2

Emma, who loses her governess, fills her place with a girl she herself can tutor. Harriet Smith is younger than Emma, lower in class and stature, stupider and sweeter; she has some taste, much gratitude, but little understanding. Although she leads Emma from her family she does so ambiguously; in many ways she seems a new Mrs. Weston, less familial however, and less worthy.[30] She never lives at Hartfield like her predecessor, but she stays there to be influenced by its ways.

30. Emma early on foresees that Harriet will be a very useful walking companion for a young lady who cannot properly and pleasantly walk out alone. The two will, however, walk when and where Emma wishes—her friend is described as "a Harriet Smith . . . whom she could summon at any time to a walk." Marvin Mudrick finds Emma and Harriet "the most unexpected companions in all of Jane Austen's work" and he stresses the fascination and inadmissible love Emma feels for this pretty girl only she and Robert Martin ever admire, *Jane Austen: Irony as Defense and Discovery*, pp. 189 and 203.

Emma tries to shape Harriet in every particular—physically, emotionally, socially, and intellectually. When she organizes her courtship, for example, she discerns that the vicar Mr. Elton has in mind for a wife someone resembling herself, although she is unaware how far he presumes. So, while insisting that all men must admire a short, plump, fair girl like Harriet, she intrudes her own image in her drawing: " 'Miss Woodhouse has given her friend the only beauty she wanted,'—observed Mrs. Weston. . . . 'The expression of the eye is most correct, but Miss Smith has not those eye-brows and eye-lashes. It is the fault of her face that she has them not' " (p. 48). It is not long since we learned of Harriet's fairness and the admirable hazel eyes of Emma.[31] "You have made her too tall, Emma," says Mr. Knightley more bluntly, and Emma knows that she has—indeed she went to some pains to lend Harriet some of the height and elegance we assume in her own person. The changes serve their purpose, for Mr. Elton declares the portrait the image of the subject; it is only later that Emma learns that the subject for Mr. Elton has always been herself.

In her emotional shaping, Emma is more successful and more dangerous. She insists on absolute affection from Harriet and when her friend receives a marriage proposal from Robert Martin the farmer, Emma cleverly forces her to refuse by placing it in the scale with her own friendship. Soon the poor Harriet is exclaiming, "I would not give up the pleasure and honour of being intimate with you for any thing in the world" (p. 54).

In social manners Emma bends the pliable Harriet, teaching her the polite forms, when to feign openness and when to be reserved, how to behave in courtship and in disappointed love. In her pedagogical discourse, Emma acts the governess, openly imposing courtesy and consideration. "It is not worth while, Harriet," she chides primly on one occasion, "to give Mrs. Ford the trouble of two parcels" (p. 235). When she preaches self-command, she is equally blunt, and the adult Harriet is pushed back

---

31. In *Emma* fairness seems associated with insipidity rather than with conventional purity, and the dark heroine triumphs through wit and understanding, not sensuality. Like Emma, Jane Fairfax has dark eyes.

281

into the schoolgirl. But she is a schoolgirl with a difference, for her giggles have been cured; in fact Mr. Knightley declares the conquest of giggling Emma's primary success with her pupil.

Her least success is certainly with Harriet's mind. The reading is never accomplished and the student sometimes even fails in proper response. When Emma wishes to arrange her friend's views on marriage and the glories of affluent spinsterhood, for instance, she is unexpectedly opposed:

> I am sure I should be a fool to change such a situation as mine. Fortune I do not want; employment I do not want; consequence I do not want: I believe few married women are half as much mistress of their husband's house, as I am of Hartfield; and never, never could I expect to be so truly beloved and important; so always first and always right in any man's eyes as I am in my father's. (p. 84)

This heady mixture of reality and fantasy does not convince Harriet, who dilutes it by exclaiming: "But then, to be an old maid at last, like Miss Bates!" A woman is but a woman, it seems, whatever her station, and an old maid cannot be glossed.[32]

Emma tries then to teach Harriet manners, attitudes, and propriety so that she may be genteel without being well-born or rich—may remain gratifyingly lower-class, yet marry above herself. But her attempt is ultimately vitiated by the friendship that allows it. Emma offers Harriet a vertical relationship across class which no intellectual similarity justifies, and the impropriety colors all her pedagogy. It is this example that Harriet learns when she thinks it no shame to act proudly before the high-born Mr. Knightley.

Emma's "infatuation about the girl" disturbs Mr. Knightley; yet she is not always blind to Harriet's defects, nor impressed with her own handiwork. Indeed she sometimes fails to give her simple friend her due. She judges Harriet rather shallow, for ex-

32. Later Harriet appears won by Emma's discourse when she dramatically exclaims, "I shall never marry." But the context works against this rash decision: she will be single because she loves hopelessly, not because she can live without love. Interestingly, she loves the man before whom Emma's independent resolves eventually fall.

ample: her nature was not, Emma surmises, "of that superior sort in which the feelings are most acute and retentive" (p. 138). She is not shaken in her opinion even when Harriet persistently and unreasonably regards the lost Mr. Elton. At a social gathering later, Emma again waxes condescending, even contemptuous, toward her protegée, whose entrance she nonetheless relishes:

> Emma watched the entrée of her own particular little friend; and if she could not exult in her dignity and grace, she could not only love the blooming sweetness and the artless manner, but could most heartily rejoice in that light, cheerful, unsentimental disposition which allowed her so many alleviations of pleasure, in the midst of the pangs of disappointed affection. There she sat—and who would have guessed how many tears she had been lately shedding? To be in company, nicely dressed herself and seeing others nicely dressed, to sit and smile and look pretty, and say nothing, was enough for the happiness of the present hour. (p. 219)[33]

When Harriet speaks, however, she is quick to mention the false Mr. Elton, and the impression so confidently conveyed is pushed slightly askew. We perceive that Harriet's face has been reflected in Emma's mind—so notoriously prone to alter with its own lighting; of Harriet's real countenance and feelings we have scarcely a hint.[34]

In her relationship with Harriet, Emma makes three main

33. Harriet here is close to Lady Bertram in *Mansfield Park,* but she will capture no baronet, nor, as D. W. Harding has pointed out, will she fulfill the theme, represented by Fanny Price, of the child brought up in humble circumstances whose inborn nature fits her for better things; in *Emma* the humble girl remains insignificant at the end. "Regulated Hatred: An Aspect of the Work of Jane Austen," 166–79.

34. Emma also judges Harriet verbally deficient, and in this judgment the reader must concur. Harriet is either tongue-tied or given to a disorderly speech which mirrors her mental confusion amidst colored ribbons and rival husbands. On this verbal inadequacy Emma's teaching makes little mark: at the very end of the Elton affair, Harriet shamefacedly approaches Emma with a box labelled "Most precious treasures," containing a "small piece of court-plaister" and the "end of an old pencil," both sacred from Mr. Elton's touch. Although Harriet is embarrassed at having held them so long after his marriage, she is happily unaware of the childishness of the label and the irony in Emma's request for the court-plaister. Not since Catherine Morland in *Northanger Abbey* has an Austen female been so clearly in need of linguistic and literary training.

mistakes, the novel suggests. First, she believes she can confer status in the way a man confers it. Her belief is aided by the delicious inequality between herself and the humble Harriet, an illegitimate girl of unknown parentage; with her, Emma is always Miss Woodhouse. Because Harriet is connected with her, Martin the farmer is no longer good enough—he is, Emma declares to an astonished Mr. Knightley, an insufficient match for her "intimate friend." When the intended suitor, Mr. Elton, returns with his dreadful wife, Emma is sure Harriet would have been a better choice; though not wise or refined herself, she would have connected him with those who were. Emma confuses the social powers of the sexes and assumes that she can confer status on the woman she picks. Mrs. Weston, it is true, gained some gentility from Hartfield, but its influence is not enough to raise Harriet Smith. At the end of her course in social awareness, she is merely uneasy in all society. As Mr. Knightley remarks to Emma, "Till you chose to turn her into a friend, her mind had no distaste for her own set" (p. 63).

Second, Emma insists on regarding Harriet almost as her wife—far more than she ever could her older governess. She assumes compliments addressed to her friend and when she muses affectionately she falls into the tender, belittling language of a man for his pretty, muddle-headed wife: "Dear Harriet!" she exclaims to herself, "I would not change you for the clearest-headed, longest-sighted, best-judging female breathing" (p. 269). Gratitude toward husbands unites many Austen heroines— Marianne Dashwood, Elizabeth Bennet, and Fanny Price—and the joy of Harriet, Mr. Knightley remarks, is her gratitude. She is "pleasantly grateful" for being admitted to Hartfield and flattered by the attentions of the superior Miss Woodhouse. And Harriet happily understands the limits of lordly affection. A sick woman must not impose; when she falls ill at Hartfield, she is eager to be gone to her motherly headmistress, and cause no trouble to her friend.

Harriet's wifeliness pleases Emma, who declares her to be precisely the person she wants. Yet this "marriage" of intelligence and simplicity echoes—perhaps painfully—Emma's past. In her simple sister Isabella, united to the clever John Knightley, she has seen an intelligent man pick a stupid woman over a sensible one, Isabella over herself, and look for sweetness and smallness in a wife.[35] Emma and the Harriet she both loves and despises become the model for this flawed marriage. To Mr. Knightley she descants on this feared state of things, declaring that handsome faces, not well-informed minds, please most men: "I know that such a girl as Harriet is exactly what every man delights in—what at once bewitches his senses and satisfies his judgment" (p. 64). And Harriet is exactly the friend Emma desires.

The third error with Harriet occurs when Emma tries, more drastically than with Mrs. Weston, to live through her. Where the governess had allowed her to enjoy marriage, Harriet enables her to experience the zest of courtship. Her penalty for such vicarious living in both cases is the threat of abrupt isolation, but her bonus is the imaginative pleasure of seeing from the outside while yet the mind and heart are stirred. The friend, forced to stand in for the self, provides both emotional and ocular rewards. By hazarding Harriet in the matrimonial game, Emma can enjoy the play while keeping herself safely in reserve. At the same time her independent status—social, intellectual, and sexual—is not bruised or endangered. By fashioning Harriet's life Emma may be the true "imaginist," the artist she never quite becomes in painting or music.

Certainly Emma is central to Harriet's affairs.[36] Mr. Elton is to be seduced by the picture painted in Emma's own image and

35. Isabella was not, we are told, "a woman of strong understanding or any quickness," while her husband is described as a "very clever man" (p. 92).

36. Marvin Mudrick notes that Harriet seems a kind of proxy for Emma, *Jane Austen: Irony as Defense and Discovery*, p. 203. Discussing this use of Harriet, Joseph M. Duffy argues that Mr. Elton must replace Robert Martin as suitor since he is not an impossible candidate for Emma herself and since, as a clergyman, he avoids "the force of Martin's sexuality implied in his occupation [farming]," which must disturb Emma, "Emma: The Awakening of Innocence," 45–46. Darrel Mansell again considers Harriet to have been sent out as an advance scout for a proper husband for Emma and he notes the close connection between the two women, both of whom in a way end by marrying the same man—Robert Martin seems a yeoman version of Mr. Knightley, *The Novels of Jane Austen*, pp. 181–83.

she will write out Harriet's riddle—always intended for herself. Even the female intimacy—usually dismissed by Austen when the woman weds—must here remain intact. The marriage with Mr. Elton would, Emma announces to Harriet, "confirm our intimacy forever."

But as Emma approaches Mr. Elton through Harriet, so she is herself approached through her friend. Mr. Elton is warm in praise of her "fair friend—her fair, lovely and amiable friend," divining that such compliments to Harriet will please Emma. When the vicarious becomes authentic and Emma recoils from Mr. Elton, Harriet sheds her attractions, dwindling into "a very good sort of girl" for people undiscriminating about birth. For both in different ways Harriet inverts desire. For Mr. Elton she reverses the image of Miss Woodhouse, whose high birth and wealth attract, while for Emma she opposes Mr. Elton, the presumptuous and violent lover.

Frank Churchill, the second candidate for Harriet, comes forward when Emma herself loses serious interest in him or when she perceives he has lessened in devotion to her. Condescendingly she joins the two—Harriet is just the wife Frank needs since she is stupid and placid enough to tolerate his boorish ways. Like the marriage of Mr. Elton and Harriet, the union of Frank and Harriet will allow free rein to the vicarious and serve female intimacy: "When we cease to care for each other as we do now," Emma muses, "it will be the means of confirming us in that sort of true disinterested friendship." But Emma cannot deceive herself here as thoroughly as with Mr. Elton. While she overtly wishes Harriet to be Frank's choice, she yet delights to hear Harriet mentioned by Frank only as "Miss Woodhouse's beautiful little friend." The possessive and diminutive both satisfy. This time Emma approaches a man knowing he must at his sanest level prefer her, although wisely she never tests him. When she learns that Frank really values Jane Fairfax, she thinks immediately of herself before lamenting poor Harriet.

The final mismatch with Mr. Knightley fulfills the underlying pattern of relationships, but certainly contradicts the pattern

Emma intended. Harriet herself initiates it, for once abjuring her subservience, and Emma unwittingly fosters and promotes the match against her own interests. It is a culmination in both women's lives. Emma moves through it decisively into her own relationship, while Harriet at its close quits the domain of Hartfield.

When Harriet announces her interest in Mr. Knightley, Emma is jolted into self-knowledge: "It darted through her, with the speed of an arrow, that Mr. Knightley must marry no one but herself!" (p. 408). Through Harriet Emma recognizes the only man who will allow her to grow into marriage, while leaving her in the independent importance of Hartfield.[37] With Mr. Knightley, then, Emma has no longer any need to live through another female or to lavish affection on a woman falsely judged the male ideal of wifeliness. A woman of sense herself, she has, contrary to her fears, attracted a man of sense. With Mr. Knightley, the dread behind her vicarious living is stilled. She marries a brother-father and retains her position in her father's house.

In her attachment to Mr. Knightley Harriet too changes. She starts out at Hartfield totally subservient to Emma; gradually through the novel, she learns some of her mentor's independence, first by turning the manipulative weapons on their owner and then by assuming the matchmaking herself. In both cases the result is dismaying. When Harriet recognizes the coolness between Emma and Jane Fairfax, she understands she can please Emma by denigrating Jane. Since Emma is sensible enough to know Jane surpasses her in music, Harriet cleverly turns the musical superiority into a compliment to Emma on the superior status she cherishes: Jane plays better than Emma, Harriet hints, because she will have to teach. Again, Harriet controls Emma with Mr. Knightley, although she does so less consciously. By construing Emma's words on Frank into encouragement for a match between herself and Mr. Knightley, she can protest when Emma appears amazed and even coerce her friend into some kindly sentiments about this dismaying alliance.

37. Emma seems to perceive the advantages of Mr. Knightley at once, even before she admits she can marry him and before he proposes setting up at Hartfield.

Her most alarming change is, however, in self-esteem. Hopeful of Mr. Knightley's affection, Harriet turns on her Pygmalion, and the experience shatters Emma. After so long reiterating that her friend is always right, Harriet has learned through two blunders to exclaim: "Dear Miss Woodhouse, how could you so mistake me?" and turn away. It is the first time Emma has been accused of error and the first time Harriet has moved from her. When Emma goes on to doubt she could ever have encouraged Harriet in her arrogant affection, Harriet retaliates: "Oh! Miss Woodhouse, how you do forget!" The humble Harriet is lost in the presumptuous woman who insists on inappropriate equality. Bitterly, Emma contemplates her handiwork as Harriet smugly declares that now if Mr. Knightley chooses her "it will not be any thing very wonderful."

Like Frankenstein, Emma has created a monster she heartily wishes destroyed, but which instead seems about to take from her all she values. Unlike Frankenstein, however, Emma stays somewhat responsible for her creation and she learns from her error:

> Who had been at pains to give Harriet notions of self-consequence but herself?—Who but herself had taught her, that she was to elevate herself if possible, and that her claims were great to a high worldly establishment?—If Harriet, from being humble, were grown vain, it was her doing too. (p. 414)

Like the monster, Harriet is a product of isolation and fear, created to fill the needs of her creator alone. She exists against the social order of things as the monster had contravened the natural. Inevitably both monsters assert themselves and the assertion rebounds on their creators. As a result, the monster's self or the creator's selfishness must be destroyed.

"I have often thought it a very foolish intimacy," remarks Mr. Knightley of the friendship between Emma and Harriet, and he is proved right. Emma considered that she had done nothing which "woman's friendship and woman's feelings would not justify." But friendship cannot justify, for it requires a larger degree of intellectual and social parity than Harriet provides. Unlike a

288

man in marriage, Emma cannot confer status on a friend, and intellect cannot be imposed. Harriet, humble or presumptuous, remains an inappropriate companion.

Nor can womanly feelings absolve her. In the Austen world a woman develops in the proper marriage, but she can do so only within a context of candor. Intense feelings for another woman, especially an inferior, can only lead in marriage to a conflict of roles and to secrecy and restraint. The "wilful intimacy with Harriet Smith" becomes for Emma "the worst of all her womanly follies," for it strikes at her womanly fitness for marriage. Toward the end of the novel, when she desires complete openness with Mr. Knightley, she is held back through loyalty to Harriet, and the restraint pains her.

Emma of course inhabits a comedy and she is saved from the worst effects of her "wilful intimacy." Robert Martin, the farmer once despised, conveniently proposes again, and Harriet, exiled from Hartfield, readily accepts him. The match delights and relieves Emma, while it reasserts her gentle contempt for her too tractable and unredeemably lowly friend. Through her marriage, Harriet becomes wife to Mr. Knightley's tenant and lover of three men in a row. In the social and emotional hierarchy, she is again lowered and Emma may once more condescend—but now from a safe distance: "She must laugh at such a close—such an end of the doleful disappointment of five weeks back! Such a heart—such a Harriet!" (p. 475) As is proper, the relationship subsequently declines. The intimacy between Harriet and Emma "must sink; their friendship must change into a calmer sort of goodwill."

Like the other vertical friend Mrs. Weston, Harriet teaches Emma little about society beyond Hartfield, but she does instruct her in the dangers of entering it in camouflage. At the same time she makes Emma aware of the perils of her privileged family position and her overconfidence in it. She has, then, indirectly helped her patron; but in the process she has harmed: by taking the place of the proper friend. Harriet's occupation of the spare room at Hartfield prevents its being offered occasionally to Jane.

Emma and Jane Fairfax head different scales in Highbury, of social status and worth. Since eminence in the second scale should justify it in the first, Emma is naturally resentful, and she regards the elegant and accomplished Jane with a bitterness in no way lessened by her own security.[38] Jane is not from Hartfield— scarcely indeed from Highbury—and she hardly ever enters the domain of Emma.[39] To approach her then, Emma must herself move from Hartfield, stepping from the familial pedestal that protects and isolates her. It is worth the effort, for Jane alone of Emma's female companions promises horizontal equal friendship. But it is a painful act.

We hear much of Jane—as we do of Harriet—mainly through Emma, who ascribes to the other woman faults of coldness and reserve remarkably like her own.[40] The author adds a less than candid sketch of her past life. Jane grew up, she tells us, within a kindly and educated family, valued by parents and daughter alike. "Living constantly with right-minded and well-informed people, her heart and understanding had received every advantage of discipline and culture" (p. 164). A real child of her family, Emma could not boast as much.

For a friend Emma protests she does not want, Jane connects Emma with a wide variety of people, each of whom assists and impedes the relationship. Frank Churchill, Jane's secret betrothed, fascinates her, especially when he speaks of Jane. Indeed the quick intimacy of Frank and Emma—like that of Elizabeth

38. Jane is preeminent too in heroine material, and several critics, most notably Wayne Booth, have argued that Austen can only keep the reader's sympathy for Emma by never showing the inside of the more clearly sympathetic Jane. *The Rhetoric of Fiction* (Chicago: University of Chicago Press, 1961), p. 249.

39. In "Emma Woodhouse and the Charms of Imagination," Susan J. Morgan discusses the social meaning of Jane Fairfax, who arrives in Highbury with real burdens and conflicts. *Studies in the Novel*, 7, no. 1 (Spring 1975), 33–48.

40. Mark Schorer has noted that the Jane we see through Emma's eyes is complacent, cold, and tiresome, whereas in fact she is a woman capable of rash behavior and genuine commitment to passion; it is Emma who is complacent and possibly cold. Jane then stands as "a kind of symbolic rebuke to Emma's emotional deficiencies." "The Humiliation of Emma Woodhouse," p. 107.

and Wickham in *Pride and Prejudice*—seems partially to spring from a shared obsession with someone else. But Frank also serves to separate the two women, for when Emma fashions an image of Jane—as she had of Harriet—Frank finishes and ornaments it, so blinding Emma to her model. Like Harriet, Frank manipulates Emma through her displayed dislike of Jane; once Harriet praised Emma by slighting Jane's proficiency at music, now Frank turns her elegant pallor into a compliment for Emma.

Through Harriet Emma upsets the Eltons; in revenge Mrs. Elton takes Jane, and the patronage of such a woman makes friendship between Emma and Jane doubly impossible.[41] Yet indirectly Mrs. Elton benefits Jane, and Emma through her. With her constant prodding she forces the reticent Jane to the bitter expression Emma would have welcomed but could not encourage. Compelled to speak of governessing, Jane breaks through her reserve and lashes out at employment agencies as "offices for the sale—not quite of human flesh—but of human intellect." Mrs. Elton's further prodding allows Jane to control Frank with her only weapon, the miserable independence of the governess. Frank is abruptly called to matrimony when Jane threatens to go to work for Mrs. Elton's friends. Her action slaps the face and wounds the friendship of Frank and Emma, and sets both people to right thinking.

Finally Emma and Jane are connected through Mr. Knightley, who is deeply involved with both women. Repeatedly he declares that Jane and Emma should unite, and to the possible union he brings the weight of his moral and social authority. Edmund was wrong to push Fanny toward the unworthy Mary Crawford, but Mr. Knightley, it seems, understands his women; he has chosen the heroine and knows her worth. His admiration of Jane, however, angers Emma before she knows herself to be

41. The resemblances between Emma and Mrs. Elton have been discussed by, among others, Yasmine Gooneratne in *Jane Austen* (Cambridge: Cambridge University Press, 1970), pp. 149–51; Mark Schorer in "The Humiliation of Emma Woodhouse," 106–7; Marvin Mudrick in *Jane Austen: Irony as Defense and Discovery*, p. 194; and Darrel Mansell, who calls Mrs. Elton "a caricature who serves to show up the thin, delicate imperfections of the heroine," *The Novels of Jane Austen*, pp. 157–60.

loving and beloved, and, with Frank's pretended scorn and Mrs. Elton's patronage, it is one more obstacle to friendship.

The fear that Mr. Knightley loves Jane starts Emma on her path to self-knowledge. Only when Harriet declares herself does Emma understand her own heart, but already her extravagant hostility must hint the truth. At the mere suggestion of Mr. Knightley's interest, she exclaims, "Jane Fairfax mistress of the Abbey!—Oh! no, no;—every feeling revolts" (p. 225). The match would be, she asserts, "shameful and degrading." Yet the woman in question is one whom Emma has declared to be all that is elegant and accomplished, and her only disadvantages have been the reserve Mr. Knightley esteems in moderation and her loquacious aunt. Certainly Emma's own unconscious desires intrude here to make the horror, and the match further repulses by its uniting of social status and worth, a combination which threatens to top Emma herself. "A Mrs. Knightley for them all to give way to!" she muses bitterly.

With Jane we come to one of the fascinations of *Emma*, the question of why the two women will not be friends. The reasons are often and clearly stated, but they never entirely convince and, when looked into, grow surprisingly complex. In a way Jane provides a key for much of the novel; in the repudiation of her, Emma explains her vicarious living, her denial of wifehood and of horizontal friendship, her fear of growing up.

All in Highbury agree that Jane and Emma should be friends. Mr. Knightley approves it and Isabella wishes it. Jane, she declares, is "so very accomplished and superior—and exactly Emma's age." Aware of the expected, however, Emma cringes from it, turning elsewhere for companionship, to the older Mrs. Weston and the younger Harriet, and she gives to Frank a straightforward history of the nonrelationship with Jane:

we have been children and women together; and it is natural to suppose that we should be intimate—that we should have taken to each other whenever she visited her friends. But we never did. I hardly know how it has happened; a little, perhaps, from that wickedness on my side which was prone to take disgust towards a girl so idolized and so cried up as she always was, by her aunt and grandmother, and all their set. And then, her reserve—I never could attach myself to any one so completely reserved. (p. 203)

Emma is jealous of Jane because she is adored by the Bateses; she dislikes her because she has long been too reticent. Yet Emma is only intermittently envious of Jane and her feeling for the Bateses is shot through with ambiguity. At the end Jane blames an engagement for a reticence we learn has always marked her.

Emma's cruelest act in the novel is toward Miss Bates, Jane's adoring aunt. With her foolish old father Emma is unfailingly kind and patient; yet toward the garrulous Miss Bates and her mother, gentlewomen in reduced circumstances, she feels constantly irritated. For this inconsistency there are several reasons. First, Miss Bates is both like and unlike Mr. Woodhouse. Both center the world on their young charges, but Miss Bates hurts Emma's pride by insisting on Jane. Both aunt and father are lovingly coercive, and Jane and Emma are inflated and reduced by their oddities. Emma pities Jane her imprisonment with the kindly, silly Miss Bates, while her own servitude and self-restraint go unremarked. Perhaps then some hidden resentment of her exacting father is visited on the unfamilial Miss Bates.

But it is not only to Mr. Woodhouse that the annoying Miss Bates relates; she approaches Miss Woodhouse herself. When Emma fearfully designs herself for spinsterhood, Miss Bates provides the model of her future. Emma quickly distinguishes herself, of course, but the distinction, as we have seen, does not convince. Again, Miss Bates threatens through her loquaciousness. Certainly it is for this that Emma so memorably slights her on Box Hill, and she often reacts in horror at the flood of verbiage. "One is sick of the very name of Jane Fairfax," she complains, and it seems that Miss Bates's prosing has drowned the putative friendship. Yet, when Emma tries to explain to Mr. Knightley her dislike of Jane, the author conveys it in rushed, exclamatory speech which contrasts severely with the ordered indirect mode of Mr. Knightley and the restraint of which Jane Fairfax is accused:

she could never get acquainted with her: she did not know how it was, but there was such coldness and reserve—such apparent indifference whether she pleased or not—and then, her aunt was such an eternal talker!—and she was made such a fuss with by every body!—and it had been always imagined that they were to be so intimate—because their ages were the same, every body had supposed they must be so fond of each other. (p. 167)

It is the hurried discourse of embarrassment and it resembles nothing so much as the spurting, gushing manner of Miss Bates, whose image truly seems to haunt Emma.[42]

Although the subject of her aunt's garrulity, Jane herself guards her speech. Like Frank Churchill, she is known in Highbury mainly as a letter-writer. Consequently she has all the importance of script and all the advantages of its formal conventions. She may control her readers with her rhetoric while remaining herself hidden and uncontrolled. But Emma is known only through speech and, for Highbury at least, she is denied written dignity, confined to the less ordered medium. Both Frank and Jane sport with others through their concealing letters and both succeed in their social game far beyond Emma.[43]

When Emma ponders her antagonism toward Jane, beyond what even her reserve demands, she herself is most eager to admit jealousy. Constantly Jane's superiority of mind, her accomplishments, and her elegance intrude on Emma, who laments her own inconstancy as a child, recognizing that, although she intermittently aspires to these things, she has them not. The elegant woman cannot be offensive and snobbish, as Emma is at times,

42. A further reason for Emma's negligence of Miss Bates is that, as David Lee Minter argues, she embodies a refusal of Emma's own demand that self and life compel abundance and style to cohere, "Aesthetic Vision and the World of *Emma*," *Nineteenth-Century Fiction* 21 (June 1966), 53–54. Darrel Mansell makes a similar point when he states that Miss Bates opposes the early Emma in her willingness to embrace the whole world; as the ideal receptor of unmediated reality, she has no particular aesthetic vision and she suggests reality itself, the simple world Emma disdains for her own romantic one, *The Novels of Jane Austen*, pp. 168–69.

43. Robert Martin also offends Emma with his encroaching letter. As she manages to avoid Jane's letter by a social maneuver—although she suffers the contents paraphrased—so she parries Martin's by disputing its authorship.

and the accomplished woman always plays well and finishes her paintings. The jealousy is admitted, then, and it is well-founded; yet when Jane and Emma actually meet, we see little of it:

> when the due visit was paid, on her arrival, after a two years' interval, [Emma] was particularly struck with the very appearance and manners, which for those two whole years she had been depreciating. Jane Fairfax was very elegant, remarkably elegant; and she had herself the highest value for elegance. Her height was pretty, just such as almost everybody would think tall, and nobody could think very tall; her figure particularly graceful . . . and then, her face—her features—there was more beauty in them all together than she had remembered; it was not regular, but it was very pleasing beauty. Her eyes, a deep grey, with dark eyelashes and eye-brows, had never been denied their praise; but the skin, which she had been used to cavil at, as wanting colour, had a clearness and delicacy which really needed no fuller bloom. It was a style of beauty, of which elegance was the reigning character, and as such, she must, in honour, by all her principles, admire it:—elegance, which, whether of person or of mind, she saw so little in Highbury. . . .
>
> In short, she sat, during the first visit, looking at Jane Fairfax with two-fold complacency; the sense of pleasure and the sense of rendering justice, and was determining that she would dislike her no longer. (p. 167)

Curiously the passage denies the reasons both women give for failing in friendship. Jane's past coldness is independent of the engagement she blames and Emma shows that she gladly admires excellence. The friendship seems set when Emma starts to scheme for Jane's marriage and confirmed when she admits that Highbury holds no man worthy of her.

But the first impressions are not supported and both women soon fall into the roles they earlier chose. Emma grows irritated with praise of Jane and envious of her musical powers; Jane is found to be "so cold, so cautious," judged disgustingly and suspiciously reserved. For her own shift in feeling Emma takes the blame, perhaps preferring responsibility to rejection, but Jane's restraint has clearly caused it. Emma is prevented from committing herself "by any public profession of eternal friendship" and the relationship is stripped of promise.

It is a sad failure. Yet, considering how silly such professions in the Austen world are—Isabella Thorpe vowing to Catherine Morland in *Northanger Abbey* for example—and the mess Emma makes when she organizes her friends, perhaps we should rejoice that no relationship is made at this point. Emma is not yet mature enough for horizontal friendship, and any other kind must be again a dangerous parody.

But at first we see only the bitter sadness of the missed opportunity. When Emma invents the Dixon scandal, she aims not only at maligning Jane but also at discrediting the female friendship Jane had and which she is denied. As she tells the story, she knows she is being disloyal to Jane and the bonding of women she represents: "She doubted whether she had not transgressed the duty of women by woman, in betraying her suspicions of Jane Fairfax's feelings to Frank Churchill. It was hardly right . . ." (p. 231). Learning that Mr. Dixon wishes to hear Jane play above her foster sister Miss Campbell, his betrothed, she mocks Frank's disclaimer of jealousy in words that again devastate friendship:

> "How did Miss Campbell appear to like it?"
>
> "It was her very particular friend, you know."
>
> "Poor comfort!" said Emma, laughing. "One would rather have a stranger preferred than one's very particular friend—with a stranger it might not recur again—but the misery of having a very particular friend always at ahnd, to do everything better than one does oneself." (p. 202)

Miss Campbell cannot have valued a superior woman because Emma has balked at doing so; equal friendship, denied to her, must not flourish elsewhere.

Curiously, the scandalous story touches Emma even more nearly when Miss Campbell is seen in another light, and the analogy may provide a key to much of Emma's fearful action in the novel. Jane and Miss Campbell are more than friends, they are foster sisters. Like Emma with her married sister Isabella, Jane surpasses Miss Campbell in beauty and accomplishments. The spiteful story Emma concocts links Jane and her foster brother-in-law, whose marriage to Miss Campbell Emma assumes Jane could not welcome. It is strange since she herself has rejoiced in her own sister's happy marriage.

Emma, we have learned, is piqued by the indifference of her brother-in-law John Knightley; possibly she resents more than she expresses. Possibly again she displaces her envious resentment of Isabella onto Miss Campbell through Jane. Certainly in his marriage John Knightley seems to fulfill or perhaps cause the fear Emma displays in the novel, that sensible men take silly wives and reject worthy women.[44] Harriet is another Isabella, simple and kindly, just the sort of woman to catch the man Emma should have caught. In Harriet's romances we have seen the shadow of Emma's desire, and in this configuration of Miss Campbell and Mr. Dixon there may be a deeper shadow of Emma and John Knightley, dispelled only at the end when Emma takes as husband her brother-in-law's older brother, wresting him from the simple, wifely Harriet.

Unlike Emma, the hidden Jane cannot be probed in herself or in her relationships, and we learn only that she does not respond to friendship because she is not open. She divulges neither her romantic yearnings nor her family secrets, and she never courts intimacy. Yet the openness in romance has been improper in the friendship of Harriet and Emma, who speak of far more than they should. Both grow in reserve as they grow in experience. In other Austen novels, too, increased reserve marks the heroine's maturation, however it might blight the impetuous friendship of the young girl: Catherine in *Northanger Abbey*

44. John Knightley is said to be no great favorite of his sister-in-law. "Nothing wrong in him escaped her. She was quick in feeling the little injuries to Isabella, which Isabella never felt herself. Perhaps she might have passed over more had his manners been flattering to Isabella's sister . . . ." (p. 93). I am aware that I may be making more of the relationship than the text warrants, and that Emma was probably twelve when Isabella married, but it does seem reasonable to look in Emma's past for the roots of her decided views on marriage.

learns to withhold herself from Isabella, and Elizabeth Bennet in *Pride and Prejudice,* once blithely open to Charlotte about Darcy, grows quiet as she grows up. In both cases, the involvement with a man requires the change. Catherine and Elizabeth are reserved when their hearts are really engaged and complete female candor seems the first sacrifice to adult heterosexual union. Jane Fairfax's early reserve may express a certain maturity beyond her years, the result perhaps of her orphaned state. Her later reserve suggests engagement; it appears excessive because she must hide her state.

Horizontal social friendship in this world is never infatuated. Jane cannot be an intimate vertical friend because she has a commitment that in her society must deny all others and Emma will not go to school to her. She cannot be a socially sanctioned horizontal friend because most of the time Emma does not desire it and because she herself is marred by furtiveness.

Toward the end of the novel, Emma begins to modify her amicable aims and look less coldly on Jane. The thaw, never to be reversed, gets properly under way when Jane at last may grow open. It is a painful process and both women have much to learn.

Emma begins by being wounded in her zeal. Penitent and embarrassed by her earlier ill-will, she tries to enter the Bates domain. Fittingly she approaches in writing, Jane's medium, and fittingly she is rejected. It is not long since she has wounded Jane in a game of letters. Emma has responded to Frank's creation of the charged word, "Dixon," the name of Jane's supposed lover, and, although Emma is of course the one fooled, it is Jane who is immediately hurt. The two women are separated in writing and it is no wonder a letter fails to bring them close.

Jane's spurning of the letter saddens Emma—"it mortified her that she was given so little credit for proper feeling, or esteemed so little worthy as a friend"—but it does not discourage her, and her good will, shocked from hierarchical benevolence into real concern for an equal, survives the repulse and even the final awakening. She is angered at being duped by Frank and

Jane, of course, but after some hyperbole (the secret engagement was "a system of hypocrisy and deceit—espionage and treachery") she settles into a more modest and subdued style, pronouncing fairly on Jane, the woman whom she has wronged and who has wronged her: "If a woman can ever be excused for thinking only of herself, it is in a situation like Jane Fairfax's" (p. 400), she concludes. It is not warm and tender but it is just, and Emma seems worthier of Jane here than she has ever been before. She is also more socially aware. Until now Hartfield had been her world, and Mrs. Weston and Harriet both judged in its context. She had visited the poor of course and known of genteel deprivation in Miss Bates, but she had never understood the threat of poverty or social insecurity. With Jane Fairfax she momentarily comprehends both and appreciates the proper selfishness to which they must lead. It is not much perhaps, but it is enough to make her a better, more sympathetic mistress of Hartfield.

In the end Emma accepts what Mr. Knightley has insisted all along, that Jane was indeed marked for her friend:

> She bitterly regretted not having sought a closer acquaintance with her, and blushed for the envious feelings which had certainly been, in some measure the cause. Had she followed Mr. Knightley's known wishes, in paying that attention to Miss Fairfax which was every way her due; had she tried to know her better; had she done her part towards intimacy; had she endeavoured to find a friend there instead of in Harriet Smith; she must, in all probability, have been spared from every pain which pressed on her now.—Birth, abilities, and education, had been equally marking one as an associate for her, to be received with gratitude; and the other—what was she? (p. 421)

Emma harshly rejects the wifely, subservient Harriet and spurns the vicarious living she allows. Jane is brought forward as a friend equal in worth and accomplishments, equipped with a mind Emma could not have subverted or inhabited. Through Jane, Emma would have reached outward beyond the narcissism and obsessions of Hartfield, and the good in Mrs. Weston's influence would have been confirmed and extended, where Harriet had encouraged only the worst. Certainly Mrs. Weston takes pains to enter the relationship of Jane and Emma, to give her blessing on her proper successor, and Jane approaches Emma first through the mediation of the old governess. Mrs. Weston tells of Jane's contrition to Emma and becomes intermediary in the first sincere dialogue between the young women.

As the novel concludes each woman advances swiftly toward the other, assuming something of her peculiar attributes. The change, long coming, has already been foreshadowed when at her dinner party Emma maintains restraint to create for others the image of friendship—"the appearance of goodwill highly becoming to the beauty and grace of each" (p. 236)—and at Donwell where Jane, for once unreserved, bursts out "Oh! Miss Woodhouse, the comfort of being sometimes alone!" (p. 288). By the end of the book Emma knows that not all should be said, and her engagement to Mr. Knightley is, before Mrs. Weston's delivery, to be kept as mum as ever Jane's has been. Her motive differs, but the reticence is Jane's. Similarly Jane replaces her reserve and coldness with a sudden gushing warmth: "I know what my manners were to you," she hurriedly confesses, "so cold and artificial." Her candid accent is Emma's. Ultimately, however, it is not restraint or speech—any more than the hated letter—that draws the women together, but silence and expansive gesture, the true Austen mark of deep feeling. Jane's blush and hesitation in the passage conquer and Emma's seizing of the hand ratifies.

As both Jane and Emma come to see, friendship between them could have been good, equal, decorous, and decently close. Certainly it is the highest relationship available to unrelated women within the female conventions of Austen's world. If such horizontal doings appear attenuated, they glow beside the vertical, intimate, and hierarchical friendship which corrupts and mocks marriage, and beside the isolation of the exclusively familial woman. Although they may ultimately strengthen a woman's ties with her family, they offer too the only route to a wider social awareness that can make these ties positive and voluntary.

The good friend for Emma should have been worthy of admittance to Hartfield, but should not have lived there.[45]

Much of *Emma* is concerned with defining equal social friendship between women, not—like *Mansfield Park*—with avoiding it. Yet it shies away from the final statement. As in *The Wrongs of Woman*, we have the introduction of two friends but not the friendship. "And the next news," remarks Emma ruefully to Jane, "will be that we are to lose you—just as I begin to know you." So Austen chops off the relationship at its inception, leaving to the reader fine and positive feelings but little experience. In spite of the euphoria of the ending, we must perceive that what could have been the most fulfilling female friendship in all her novels never took place.

45. Susan J. Morgan discusses the hopeful effect of *Emma* in terms of Jane, who guarantees that life will not fail Emma. In Jane, Emma has found someone worth knowing and has discovered that to see people as they are can be a greater joy than seeing them as she wants them to be, "Emma Woodhouse and the Charms of the Imagination," pp. 47–48.

PART II
The Literary and Biographical Contexts

CHAPTER SIX

The Literary Context

RICHARDSON, CLELAND, DIDEROT, Rousseau, Sade, Wollstonecraft, Staël, and Austen all in their different ways represent their literary time. While some excel in their craft and some miss excellence, each dips into a stock of literary conventions that are shared by all the authors of the period. Like the gynocentrism of the novel, female friendship is a literary given of the eighteenth century. But, while women's prominence in the novel may reverse their social obscurity, fictional friendship remains incidental. The other woman enters the orbit of the heroine as rival, confidante, stepmother, or youthful bosom friend. The plot tells of "faithless Men, and ruin'd Maids"[1]—adjectives may be exchanged but are rarely discarded—and the fictional world is at its center severely heterosexual. Yet, as we have seen, incidental may become central when investigated or may at least fight for preeminence. This ambiguity of female friendship marks the mass of fictional works.

Sentimental Friendship: Eliza Haywood, Charlotte Lennox, Mme de Grafigny, Fanny Burney

In the eighteenth century, female friendship was caught in the cult of sensibility, a movement that washed a whole era in its tears. A complex phenomenon with firm philosophical roots in Locke and Shaftesbury, it affirmed a belief in the innate goodness

---

1. The phrase is Eliza Haywood's in *The Fair Hebrew: or, a True, but Secret History of Two Jewish Ladies* (London: J. Brindley, W. Meadows, et. al., 1729), p. 33.

305

and natural virtue of humanity, with corruption entering only through circumstance and society. To the sentimentalist, feeling was paramount and justified itself, without recourse to action; taste, refined sensibility, and goodness became inextricable. In the novel, sentimental notions demanded exemplary protagonists—usually women, since, passive and socially impotent, they were *par excellence* the carriers of the new cult. Paradoxically, fictional realism was also required, for the exquisite feelings of the heroine had to be probed by the novelist and experienced by the reader. This virtuous heroine in realistic settings can best display herself through letters in which she may act and prove her emotion. Because the letter demands a correspondent and because women correspond with men at their peril, there must be female friends. The confidante enters, then, as a necessary fictional device in the sentimental work.

But other factors influence sentimental friendship as well. The growth of the novel is generally linked to the growth of the bourgeois family in eighteenth-century Britain and France, the spread of isolated units containing at their core leisured women with little to do but read and flaunt their leisure and chastity. Certainly in the novel the middle-class family is prominent. The heroine may still be of noble birth—for worth and aristocracy always form a heady combination—but more frequently she may with Clarissa represent the middle class against an unfamilial and libertine nobility. As such a representative, she must abide by the patriarchal customs of her class, remaining chaste, private, and isolated from outsiders who might damage her worth. But if she has to repress sexual, sensual, even social feelings, she must also cultivate the sensibility essential for the fictional heroine.

The conflicting demands of bourgeois femaleness in the novel can in part be reconciled through a friend, a woman similarly placed, similarly constricted, and similarly yearning. With her the heroine can unleash the pent-up emotions that no other outsider ought to receive. If such a friend can be found within the family, then the tie becomes deliciously sentimental, combining the joys of friendship and sisterhood. Certainly the intensest

306

ecstasies in many sentimental novels occur not when the hero approaches but when a long-lost sister is recognized in a dearest friend. Like lovers of another convention, these siblings often intuit each other long before discovery, but in the proof and sanction of their love, friendship reaches its apotheosis. Where nothing can be discovered, no blood link proved, the sentimental friendship often appears curiously aimless, forced to turn from the heights. Anna Howe is saddened she can never be Arabella, while Clarissa is left lamenting that friend and sister do not coincide.

Sentimental friends lead conventional lives in fiction. They must cry and confide a lot, protest and embrace, in short, exist so intensely that their friendship acquires many of the signs of love. Their relationship is close, even suffocating, prying, exacting, hortatory, and eulogistic. But because all runs on so extremely, the least check confounds; instead of cool courtesy, bitter hatred must supplant the euphoria and the sentimental novel is thus as rife with rivals as with bosom friends.

One of the most popular and prolific novelists of the earlier eighteenth century, Eliza Haywood, spans the extremes of sentimental friendship, creating intense comrades and noisy rivals. Sometimes the women are sisters, one of whom is all goodness, while the other yearns to betray this paragon. Or they may be unrelated except through jealousy, trapped by a man who ultimately will wound them both. Occasionally, however, the women may avoid rivalry or purge themselves of it; if so, they may turn from men and come to look to each other for affection and comfort.[2]

Lasselia is an example of Haywood's intricate plots of jealousy. In it the heroine first meets a rival in her aunt, who is out-

2. Oddly enough, in her courtesy books, Haywood ignores or slights friendship. In *The Husband* and *The Wife,* she contents herself with coldly advising a man not to be too free "in his Wife's presence with any of her female acquaintance" and a woman not to choose prudes and coquettes for friends, *The Wife* and *The Husband. In Answer to The Wife* (London: T. Gardner, 1756).

307

raged to find her royal lover turning a lascivious eye toward her pretty niece. But Lasselia protests she would die rather than injure her aunt and proves it by entombing herself in the country to avoid the king's embrace. The aunt is left incredulous, "Can you for no other Motive than my Repose," she exclaims, "be content to bury any part of your Time in a Solitude so remote from all those Gaieties your Youth has been accustom'd to?"[3] But in the lonely country Lasselia is tested in friendship once more and comes off less handsomely.

Attracted to a new woman friend, she has a more dramatic encounter with the husband. As he steps forward, "three Drops of Blood fell from his Nose, which stain'd a white Handkerchief she happen'd to have in her Hand."[4] Presaging future union, the incident repeats the nosebleed scenes of *Clarissa, Fanny Hill,* and *The Nun:* it occurs before another woman, and, although the blood is the male's, the female as ever receives the stain. Lasselia indeed becomes a mistress and fails in friendship.

Rivalry marks the episode as well as the central action of *Lasselia,* and wickedly inspires two sisters. The hero prefers the younger but is destined for the older, who, piqued by rejection, grows passionate and vindictive, degrading herself so far that she imposes her love on the man. A shocking act, severely punished in literature, it elicits an infuriating response: "all that can be conceived of Scorn, Contempt, and Detestation, were to the Life display'd in his expressive Eyes." It is too much for the sister, who counters with a penknife. Clarissa too had used such a weapon but she had pointed it toward herself, directing onto her own body the anger against the man. Although she is of course easily disarmed, the sister's act remains unredeemable, for she has sinned against the double codes of sentimental friendship and femininity.[5]

---

3. *Lasselia: or, the Self-Abandon'd* (London: D. Browne, 1724), p. 10.
4. Ibid., p. 14.
5. Ibid., p. 65. In *Placentia and Philidore,* Haywood provides a more Clarissa-like use of the female weapon. Placentia threatens to kill herself, not her lover, with a penknife.

But Haywood is not always embroiled in rivalry and in her pages women are found sustaining and confiding in each other as often as hating. In *The Surprize* the heroine, learning she is encouraging the suit of a man formerly her friend's lover, resolves at once to dismiss him to save her friend. "Never Woman gave a greater Proof of her Friendship to another," exults the author, "than she did in discarding Bellamant."[6] In *The British Recluse* two women come together to recount their histories of *"ill requited Love"* and to create a deep friendship: "The meeting of these two Ladies was something particular for Persons of the same Sex; each found, at first Sight, so much to admire in the other, that it kept both from speaking for some Moments."[7] It is almost the classic meeting of long-lost sisters and it is no surprise when they are proved, if not blood-sisters, then sisters in misfortune, rejects of the same man.

In *The British Recluse,* the friendship is the pretext of the narrative each woman unfolds, but it also modifies the response. When in one story the false lover follows his betrayal with advice on the handling of men—"whatever in our Days of Courtship we profess," he tells his former beloved, "the Excess of any Passion is ridiculous to a Man of Sense," and "had your Passion, at least the Show of it, been less Violent, mine might have had a longer Continuance"—he reduces the woman to the ranks of passionate females who must be condemned.[8] We avoid being trapped in the man's rhetoric primarily through the compassionate female listener. Her presence also controls the response within the text, allowing the speaker to generalize and embrace all women in her male-inflicted woes. At the same time, she can forthrightly tell her troubles and reenact her own frenzy.

At the end of *The British Recluse* neither woman is cured of her passion for the philanderer, but each is comforted and supported by the other. So it is a mildly happy ending when the two

6. *The Surprize; or Constancy Rewarded* (London: J. Roberts, 1724), p. 24.
7. *The British Recluse: or, the Secret History of Cleomira, Suppos'd Dead* (London: D. Brown, 1723), p. 9.
8. Ibid., p. 75.

friends unite their lives and set up housekeeping together: "There grew so entire a Friendship between these Ladies, that they were scarce a Moment asunder." They settle near London and there "they still live in a perfect Tranquillity, happy in the real Friendship of each other." [9] It is a conclusion that neither parodies the heterosexual one nor merely escapes tragedy. As usual at the end of Haywood's breathless novels, we are left wishing that the author had paused to probe and expatiate on a relationship we are allowed only to glimpse.

The dream of a separatist future, realized at the end of *The British Recluse*, haunts Charlotte Lennox's *Euphemia*, which encloses another portrait of sentimental friends. The novel is a series of letters, mostly between Euphemia and her friend Maria and they serve to convey Lennox's high conception of a female friend, defined as "a witness of the conscience, a physician of secret griefs, a moderator of prosperity, and a guide in adversity." [10]

Such amiable perfection struggles in a society where the primary tie must be marriage, and Maria—who judges Euphemia above the married state—is doubly angered that an unworthy man has wrested her paragon from her: "she, of whom hardly any man can be worthy, must follow one, who assuredly cannot be ranked among the best, to the wilds of America." [11] In her letters the voyage out becomes a dreaded route from sensitive female friendship to a tearless male world reeking of gross sexuality.

Against marriage presses the female tie. "There is no friendship in the world of so much use to me as yours," sighs Maria, "it is my defence in all my contests." [12] Euphemia is clear in preferring her friend to her unsentimental husband and even Maria shows her choice when, as friend and lover depart, she mourns Euphemia's going the most. The lover accepts such pref-

9. Ibid., pp. 137–38.
10. *Euphemia* (Dublin: P. Wogan, P. Byrne, et. al., 1790), p. 170.
11. Ibid., p. 107.
12. Ibid., p. 186.

erence, and like Saint-Preux enjoys the female devotion. When Maria obtains a miniature of her beloved friend, he ties it round her neck and then obsequiously tiptoes away to avoid marring the exquisite sensibility of the moment.

The end of the novel partially unites the two friends. Maria marries her lover somewhere along the way, but the marriage passes almost unnoticed in the text; Euphemia remains tied to her unworthy mate. Yet Lennox does her best for the sentimental heroine in her realistic world, providing her with a son who supersedes his father and an independent legacy to educate him. The friendship continues to provide the emotional fulfillment. Certainly it is a bizarre ending, unlikely to appeal to a male author, but it allows Lennox a compromise of friendship and marriage in which a female relationship can at least move and breathe.

In the novels of Haywood and Lennox, friends seem there for the asking, and a woman must only vibrate with sensibility to attract a confidante to her bosom. The tension is not within the relationship but between it and the outside world of men and marriage. The French writer Mme de Grafigny is, however, less optimistic about things in France, and in her *Peruvian Letters* she depicts her South American heroine searching French womanhood for the sentimental friend of her heart. When she tries with one woman, she finds her neither fellow nor rival in the Haywood manner, but simply an inadequate friend. The novel is, then, sentimental in the heroine's aspirations, not in its picture of friendship.

Despite her sheltered life as a virgin in the Temple of the Sun, the Peruvian Zilia is intellectually curious and she seeks someone to discuss religious doctrine and debate the niceties of the Trinity, as well as enter into her deepest feelings. She tries hard to find this exemplar in Celina, but she is soon judged a sad and trivial product of French female upbringing, talking solely of family and light feelings, while showing little loyalty to her new friend. When Celina warms after a period of coldness, Zilia wea-

311

rily comments, "I am so happy in the appearance of her friendship, that I do not examine too deeply into the reality of it."[13] By the end of the novel, an acculturated Zilia is ready to find a companion only in her husband and prepared to agree with her cool friend who believes "the sentiment of friendship" rare among women: "Men embrace it between each other with ardour," Celina declares, "women with caution."[14]

The search for the correct female friend forms part of the far more complicated plots of Fanny Burney, the main painter of sentimental female friendship in England and France in the late eighteenth century. Although less perfect than *Evelina*, her first, triumphant novel, her later works more engagingly depict female relationships, and both *Cecilia* and *The Wanderer* deeply probe the dangers and rewards of female ties. If in the main Burney paints with dark colors, the sombreness conveys regret for a lightness she rejects from both fear and principle. Haywood and Lennox find friendship an asylum in a predatory world; Mme de Grafigny wishes it were so but cannot discover it. Burney seems close to Richardson in seeing it not only rare but dangerously tempting.

In *Cecilia,* the heroine's path is strewn with uncomfortable women. She inherits some from childhood and has no strength to repudiate the legacy; others she takes to meet her psychic needs. Lonely and rich, she wants mother-figures to guide her (feeling betrayed when they prove flexible), and daughters to call forth her benevolence. Like Wollstonecraft's Mary, similarly rich and isolated, she seems unable to find and like an equal.

In Mrs. Delvile, the parent of her lover, Cecilia discovers a kind of mother. Initially the older woman repels with her haughtiness, but later she is won by Cecilia's exemplary resignation to her will. Certainly Cecilia's position is unconventional: she will inherit a fortune on marriage only if her husband agrees to take her name, so playing the woman. It is a humiliating con-

13. *The Peruvian Letters* (1747; London: T. Cadell, 1774), I, 151.
14. Ibid., II, 25.

dition no man of metal seems ready to meet, and Mrs. Delvile is heartily opposed to her son's marrying so ignominiously. Finally she comes to accept a clandestine marriage, but it is to Cecilia as penniless orphan not mastering heiress. For her condescension, she sinks in Cecilia's esteem, and her raptures over her new daughter-in-law fail to impress: "Your mother, in her tenderness forgot her dignity," Cecilia remarks icily to her lover.[15] Little mitigated by Mrs. Delvile's approval, the antisocial, secret marriage still horrifies, and Cecilia repeats its shocking facts, as fascinated and appalled as the Sadian heroine exulting over her intricate incest.

In the young daughterlike Henrietta, Cecilia tries to unite friendship and benevolence, as Wollstonecraft's Mary and Austen's Emma also try. Henrietta interests through her youthful need, her melancholy state, her loveliness and "the uncommon artlessness of her conversation," all of which excite in Cecilia "a desire to serve, and an inclination to love her."[16] But the friendship is a disturbed one. Cecilia soon discovers that her friend and she crave the same man, and their joint infatuation disperses for a while their dream of living together. They cannot unite, muses Cecilia, unless they are both rejected. The man determines their relationship and rules their affection.

A striking example of this male ordering of friendship occurs when, after a long absence, Cecilia and Henrietta reencounter each other in front of a male visitor. At once they dissolve into the raptures of sentimental friendship, but are interrupted by the man commenting rudely: "The young ladies . . . have a mighty way of saluting one another till such time as they get husbands: and then I'll warrant you they can meet without any salutation at all."[17] The quick put-down, so reminiscent of Lovelace's insistent belittling of female friendship, chills Cecilia, and she immediately checks "the tenderness of her fervent young friend."

Toward the end of the novel after the two women have lived

15. *Cecilia or Memoirs of an Heiress* (London: J. M. Dent, 1893), III, 282.
16. Ibid., I, 249.
17. Ibid., III, 125.

for a time together, Cecilia is abruptly isolated and plunged downward. Burney is adept at such dramatic reductions, which deprive her characters of all props of money, caste, and gallantry. Impoverished and alone, Cecilia is finally driven insane—headed, it seems, for the exemplary, eulogistic death of Clarissa. But women novelists are less prone to kill their heroines, and, when the mandatory delirium is past, Cecilia is en route for the happy ending. Awakening from her healing sleep, she first encounters Henrietta, who has rushed to her bedside and answered her friend's madness with her own frenzied love. Lost friendship appears to lead both women to insanity; psychic health requires a reunion.

Although decently happy, the ending of *Cecilia* is marred by the heroine's earlier suffering. No wedded bliss can compensate for such degradation. The bliss is further diminished when Henrietta is ejected, packed off with an old lover of Cecilia's. While rich and powerful, the heroine could entertain and support her friend, but seemed unfit for her male lover; shorn of money and weakened into dependence, she is a proper wife, and the symbol of her earlier independent power must be dismissed.[18] As Clarissa well knew, when women grasp a legacy, they somehow dissolve it. Severely qualified as the rhapsody of marriage is, then, it is no accident that the novel's last word should be "resignation."[19]

Many of the motifs of female friendship recur in Fanny Burney's final, little appreciated novel, *The Wanderer; or, Female Difficulties,* which presents her most ambiguous and complex

18. In *Imagining a Self,* Patricia Spacks discusses Cecilia's development from security to insecurity, her progress in renunciation. "She must learn to give up, yielding her money as sign and symbol of larger relinquishments," p. 181.

19. Defending the muted ending of *Cecilia,* Burney wrote "the hero and the heroine are neither plunged in the depths of misery, nor exalted to UNhuman happiness." And she asks, "Is not such a middle state more natural, more according to real life, and less resembling every other book of fiction?" Quoted in Joyce Hemlow's *History of Fanny Burney* (Oxford: Clarendon Press, 1958), p. 150.

portrait of female relationships.[20] Like Cecilia, the heroine of this work is degraded to the depths of society, severed from friends and relatives, and deprived of all signs of domestic worth. Like Cecilia again, she treads a bitter path through defective women who fail her at every turn and, worse, humiliate her with a nastiness not seen in fiction since the whores baited the saintly Clarissa. But at the end her suffering is rewarded and she receives the sentimental prize denied Cecilia—a sister-friend.

The story of *The Wanderer* is Burney's most improbable; it concerns Juliet, a young woman whose name we learn only in the third volume and whose circumstances are divulged even later; indeed her tale is so complex it is little wonder she refuses to tell it. Reduced initially to the denuded state of Cecilia toward the end of her novel, Juliet must prove over and over again the difficulties of females. Her sorry lot is darkened by disjunction of character and circumstance: socially anomalous as a lone woman, she must strive for self-respect and independence. "Is it only under the domestic roof,—that roof to me denied!—that woman can know safety, respect, and honour?"[21] she cries at one point, and the answer is for her certainly yes; teaching a little music, sewing a fine seam, and companioning the old and irascible do not ward off destitution, and more public, less feminine efforts appall. In this difficult context, then, Juliet must discover the limits and strengths of female association.

The heroine enters two contrasting relationships, both extreme in their way. One is with the extraordinary Elinor, a woman deeply impressed and impeded by French and feminist sentiments; the other unites her with the gentle Aurora, a young

20. Thomas Babbington Macaulay exemplifies the negative opinion of this book: "In 1814 she [Burney] published her last novel, *The Wanderer,* a book which no judicious friend to her memory will attempt to draw from the oblivion into which it has justly fallen," *Edinburgh Review* (January 1843). Burney's modern biographer, Joyce Hemlow, calls the book "intolerable" and remarks that "every reference to *The Wanderer* must serve to poke it further into the shadows," *The History of Fanny Burney,* pp. 338–39.

21. *The Wanderer; or, Female Difficulties* (London: Longman, Hurst, et. al., 1814), IV, 253.

girl who remains always sweetly amiable and feminine. Juliet is bandied about between these extremes, confounded by the one, comforted by the other, but she never wavers in her allegiance. She may sometimes benefit the wild Elinor, but her heart is always Aurora's and it is for her she sheds the most copious and delicious tears.

Elinor is mocked from the start as "the champion of her sex," a fierce Wollstonecraft who insists like the older sister in *Lasselia* on forcing her love on a man. She is most feminist when most demented, hysterically asserting "rights . . . which all your sex, with all its arbitrary assumption of superiority, can never disprove, for they are the Rights of human nature; to which the two sexes equally and unalienably belong."[22] To prevent our accepting such assertion, it is given a bizarre context. Elinor is threatening murder and suicide, wielding not the feminine penknife but a real pistol; yet like her predecessors she is easily disarmed and all her exotic suicide attempts fail. Violence—both verbal and physical—should be masculine.

Nonetheless, Elinor impresses in spite of coercion from her context. Indeed the novel's horrifying picture of female degradation in Juliet strengthens Elinor's rhetoric (even as Elinor's grotesqueries underscore Juliet's stress on feminine propriety):

> Why, for so many centuries, has man, alone, been supposed to possess, not only force and power for action and defence, but even all the rights of taste. . . . Why, not alone, is woman to be excluded from the exertions of courage, the field of glory, the immortal death of honour;—not alone to be denied deliberating upon the safety of the state of which she is a member, and the utility of the laws by which she must be governed:—must even her heart be circumscribed by boundaries as narrow as her sphere of action in life. . . . Must every thing that she does be prescribed by rule? Must every thing that she says, be limited to what has been

22. Ibid., I, 399. It is notable that, in spite of her eccentric behavior, many of the characters persist in speaking well of Elinor. Indeed there seems a discrepancy between her action and the response to it, which might indicate Burney's ambivalent feelings about her. Similar ambivalence occurs in the presentation of the "masculine" Mrs. Selwyn in *Evelina*.

said before? Must nothing that is spontaneous, generous, intuitive, spring from her soul to her lips?[23]

Nothing destroys the power of this, but Burney clearly worries about its effect. Elinor, so fitted in principle to bond with Juliet against the vicissitudes of female fate, is rendered friendless, coupled in rivalry not love.

In a world where femininity is virtue and the heroine seeks only to embrace it, the feminist Elinor is ridiculous, mocked by her exaggerated actions, her uncontrollable passions, and her desperate shiftings from principle to love. As the book proceeds, she disintegrates, appearing only in quixotic episodes. Maddened by rejection, for example, she "rent open her wound, and tore her hair; calling, screaming for death, with agonizing wrath."[24] She seeks death as she had sought a man, parodying the passive exemplary ending Clarissa achieved and Cecilia almost suffered, but her impotent frenzy suggests only the author's sadism. Elinor is denied active love and active death.

Juliet's second friend contradicts Elinor in all her postures. Lady Aurora enters first to sustain the fainting heroine, and her other actions are as discreetly supportive. The two women join in a sentimental, tearful friendship, blessed and sanctioned by the hero and reversing the feminist alliance fitfully imagined by Elinor:

> while generally engaging to all by her general merit, to Lady Aurora she [Juliet] had peculiar attractions, from the excess of sensibility with which she received even the smallest attentions. . . . Pleasure shone lustrous in her fine eyes, every time that they met those of Lady Aurora; but if that young lady took her hand, or spoke to her with more than usual softness, tears, which she vainly strove to hide, rolled fast down her cheeks . . . ."[25]

Indeed the two women seem to vie with each other in emotional display, and the joint ecstasy often leaves Juliet literally breathless.

23. *The Wanderer*, I, 404–5.
24. Ibid., II, 445.
25. Ibid., I, 257–58.

Later in the novel we learn that all these aching raptures are justified, for Aurora is discovered to be the younger half-sister of Juliet. Sanctioned by blood, the union reaches new heights. "How you have engaged my thoughts," Aurora cries out to Juliet, "rested upon my imagination; occupied my ideas; been ever uppermost in my memory; and always highest,—Oh! higher than any one in my esteem and admiration!"[26] Expecting once to part from Aurora, Juliet watches her in her sleep: "in looking at her, [Juliet] thought she contemplated an angel. The touching innocence of her countenance; the sweetness which no sadness could destroy; the grief exempt from impatience; and the air of purity that overspread her whole face, and seemed breathing round her whole form, inspired Juliet, for a few moments, with ideas too sublime for mere sublunary sorrow."[27] The blood link demands the loverlike language. When friend and family unite, the bond is mystical, sensuous, and delicious.

In *The Wanderer,* friendship reaches new heights in sisterly love. Yet in its success it reveals its flaws. If the novel supports the display of friendship, it seems to vitiate its substance. Elinor, though given room to show her force, is rejected, and Aurora herself is more a rapturous shade of Juliet than an equal. Women in both *Cecilia* and *The Wanderer* may console each other and compensate for loss, but they can rarely spur to action. Both heroines ultimately act alone, if they act at all, and come to grief in solitude. The most promising tie of Juliet with Elinor is rejected in ridicule, although their union might have released the androgynous power Wollstonecraft described. Certainly Juliet could have used such a union as psychic model when she sought her own feminine strength. As it is, Elinor is cast out and the feminine left to grow effeminate.

Sentimental friendship in the novel is extreme and radical in expression but limited in action. In the works of Richardson,

26. Ibid., V, 261.
27. Ibid., V, 331. *In La Destinée féminine dans le roman européen du dix-huitième siècle 1713–1807,* Pierre Fauchery discusses the imagery and decor of sister reunions and gives a full account of the conventions marking the sisterly relationship (Paris: Armand Colin, 1972).

Lennox, Haywood, Grafigny, Burney and a host of other writers, it seems an ideal, avidly sought for its promise of female growth and autonomy. It provides a relationship into which two women can enter with passion and propriety, and it supplies a code of behavior that eases them toward each other. Yet, when it approaches fulfillment as it does in *The Wanderer,* its limitation appears. Seemingly the last bastion of the female self against the reductive claims of patriarchy, it yet fearfully retrenches when it might subvert, rendering the woman more accepting, not more desperate. In the structure of the novel, too, sentimental friendship defuses. The heroine avoids working out her difficult tie with the man who will define her, but instead flees him or simply accepts him on the final page. Left with an impotent friendship, the two women may become not androgynous but schizophrenic, while the model of the female alliance remains the duplication of sisters.

Erotic Friendship: Seigneur de Brantôme, Anthony Hamilton, Henry Fielding

The eighteenth century is marked by the eroticizing of the non-physical, and the language of passion conveys the religious experience of Methodists and mystics—Charles Wesley and Madame Guyon, for example—as well as the emotional raptures of literary young women. Yet, as we have seen, if the language of erotic love marks friendship, the experience rarely troubles it in female literature, and the raptures, although passionate and prolonged, are insistently "chaste" and "virtuous." A few male authors keep the amorous language and add the content; others reverse the paradigm, abandoning the erotic language of friendship to seize an erotic content. In their works, lesbian love, taboo in genteel and female fiction, is unveiled to shock.[28]

---

28. Some "chaste" depictions do, however, flirt dangerously with the erotic. In *Pamela,* for example, the relationship between young and older women, a staple of pornography, does suggest more than a sentimental interest. Mrs. Jewkes, the substitute for the lecherous Mr. B., imprisons Pamela for her master and, when Mr. B. seems dilatory,

THE LITERARY CONTEXT

From classical times lesbianism has been satirized, attacked, and exploited, and the eighteenth century continues this tradition. The aggressive aim marks the medical manuals and cautionary anecdotes, while the exploitative motive surfaces in exotic travellers' tales, pornographic jaunts, and gossipy court histories. In most of these, lesbianism is incidental, thrown in to make the harem more sultry, the Indian custom more strange, or the convent more enticing; only in *The Nun* does it receive extended serious treatment.[29]

In the eighteenth century, medical books were often heady fiction. They display a high degree of imaginative power and they relate their awful anecdotes with conspicuous art. One popular book that touches lesbianism takes pains to shock: M. Tissot's work on masturbation, translated into English and expanded by A. Hume as *Onanism: Or, A Treatise upon the Disorders Produced by Masturbation: or, the Dangerous Effects of Secret and Excessive Venery.* Discussing the "crimes of one's fellow creatures," it is a compendium of horror stories, all of which convey

she sneers "If I was in his place, he should not have his property in you long questionable" (New York: Norton, 1958), p. 129; while in *Sir Charles Grandison,* Harriet is pursued by a "Miss Barnevelt, a lady of masculine feature," who studies Harriet with the eyes of a lover, *The History of Sir Charles Grandison,* ed. Jocelyn Harris (London: Oxford University Press, 1972), I, 42–43.

29. Several pornographic or semipornographic works have lesbian episodes, the seventeenth-century *Satyra Sotadica* by Nicholas Chorier, and *Vénus dans le cloître, ou la religieuse en chemise* by Jean Barrin, for example, both of which have many eighteenth-century adaptations. A later example is *Histoire de Dom B . . . Portier des Chartreux* by J. C. Gervaise de la Touche (Rome: Philotanus, n. d.), a work read by Diderot. In it Suzon tells of her convent seduction by a more sexually knowing sister, Monique. Like the Superior in *The Nun,* Monique comes at night to the younger woman's bed. There, as in *The Nun,* she encounters a sexually naive Suzon, who interprets the orgasmic gyrations as illness. Unlike Diderot's heroine, however, Suzon is immediately and clearly awakened to sexuality. According to David Foxon, an English translation of this book was seized from Thomas Read, printer, in a drive against pornography. *Libertine Literature in England, 1660–1745* (New York: University Books, 1965). An odd use of lesbianism to shock occurs in the satire *The Toast, an Epic Poem, in Four Books* by Sir William King (1732). According to notes in the copy in the Bodleian Library, Oxford, the author was inspired by a private grievance over a lawsuit with Lady Frances Brudenall, who appears as the lesbian Myra in the poem: "she had been guilty of all kinds of Pollution, unsated by her male Gallants she daily practised that unnatural Act the *Spaniards* call *Donna con Donna,*" p. 18.

a host of secret masturbators to their appointed ends of blindness, madness, lethargy, palsy, paralysis, and death.[30] One chapter devotes itself to the effects of masturbation on "the fair sex," among whom, it laments, the evil has progressed further than with men. In passing it notes "another kind of pollution," originating with Sappho and common among licentious Romans. Women who indulge in this vice are both mental and physical monsters, explains Tissot, shocking their fellows by a "semi-resemblance to man."[31] The picture he paints of their vice truly horrifies but fails to enlighten:

> Some women who were thus imperfect, glorying, perhaps, in this kind of resemblance, seized upon the functions of virility. The danger of this kind of pollution is not, however, less than that of the other sorts of masturbation: the effects are equally shocking, all these paths lead to emaciation, languor, pain, and death. . . .
>
> Women have been known to love girls with as much fondness as ever did the most passionate of men, and conceive the most poignant jealousy, when they were addressed by the male sex upon the score of love.
>
> It is time to conclude these shocking details, I am weary of detecting the turpitude and misery of humanity.[32]

We learn much of Tissot's bizarre vision of lesbianism here, but little about the love between women.

A less secretive work which excites its readers with glimpses of lesbianism is the seventeenth-century *Lives of Gallant Ladies*, written by Pierre de Bourdeille, Seigneur de Brantôme.[33] The

30. *Onanism: Or, A Treatise upon the Disorders produced by Masturbation* (London: J. Pridden, 1776).

31. In his monumental *Medicinal Dictionary* (1743–45), Robert James agrees with Tissot (and disagrees with Diderot) in assuming that lesbianism must derive from physical defects. Consequently he describes huge clitorises and gives case histories of lesbians impersonating men.

32. *Onanism,* pp. 46–47.

33. Pierre de Bourdeille, Seigneur de Brantôme, *The Lives of Gallant Ladies,* trans. Alec Brown (London: Elek Books, 1961). The edition and the introduction by Martin Turnell also deserve attention, for Turnell asserts that Brantôme deals very fully "with sexual perversion in women," and the edition keeps most of such naughty scenes in French.

book was much read in the eighteenth century for its peep-shows of court life and its prolonged lubricities. Interestingly, Brantôme is closer to Diderot than to Tissot and the other medical writers in viewing lesbianism less as physical monstrosity than as emotional perversion, and he agrees both with Diderot and with Cleland and the pornographers in assuming that female love flourishes when heterosexual love is denied—in convent, school, or harem. Lesbianism is, he declares grandly, "merely the apprenticeship to the great business with men." Yet his anecdotes do not always support his smugness and he ascribes the evil variously to the Italianate degeneracy of the times and to female narcissism.

Lesbianism appears to intrigue more than shock Brantôme, but his attitude is shifting. Of young lesbians he writes:

> they confessed to their lovers that nothing had so debauched them and stirred them up to love-making as the *fricarelle,* which they now loathed as having been the sole cause of their debauchment. And yet, notwithstanding, whenever they met, or found themselves with other women, they always took a little snack of this fricking, just because thereby they could get great appetite for the other way, with men.[34]

So powerful is erotic play among women that it has "debauched" them; yet they indulge in it solely to warm themselves for men. They loathe the practice, but use it to stir themselves to respectable lust.

Certainly Brantôme seems unsettled by the effects of erotic love between women; it excites them ungovernably, he announces, and leads them to scorn marriage and embrace whorishness. While he lends his prose to the lubricities of lesbian love, he also repeats the horrific tales Tissot was to enjoy many years later. Lesbianism, he insists, can cause killing cancers: "It is said that many women have lost their lives from engendering in their wombs growths caused by movements and by frictions which are far from natural."[35]

34. Ibid., p. 132.
35. Ibid., pp. 133–34.

Clearly Brantôme is dubious of a relationship, physical or emotional, that excludes men. Again mingling fascination and contempt, he writes of a female community in which women "tell each other stories, quite as good as ours and exchange tales about their love-making, including the most secret things, and then roar with laughter and make fun of their gallants whenever they make a mistake or do anything ridiculous or silly."[36] Like lesbianism, this community cannot be left exclusive, and Brantôme quickly adds that women also steal each other's lovers to gain secrets with which to mock their female friends. Lesbianism must give way to heterosexual passion, and female community to female rivalry.

The eighteenth century did not have to rely solely on a distant age for its court entertainment. At the beginning of the period, Anthony Hamilton provided his spicy anecdotes of high places, entitled *Memoirs of Count Grammont.*[37] From this we learn such snippets as the Countess of Castlemaine's habit of taking her rival Miss Stewart to sleep with her. The King, Charles II, usually found the two women in bed together, but Hamilton does not give us the sensations of the royal voyeur.

More detailed but just as unanalysed is the tale of Miss Hobart, maid of honor to the Duchess of York. Accused time and again of loving women, and ridiculed and mocked in ballads, she persisted until she provoked more general blame in the affair with Miss Temple, another maid of honor. For this lady's attention Miss Hobart unwisely rivalled a man and found herself utterly confounded in the combat. Soon she became a monster for the woman she had loved. Strangely, however, through all the fracas Miss Hobart retained the support of her mistress, the Duchess of York.

Hamilton is less physically detailed than Brantôme, but the episode of Miss Hobart intrigues more than any of Brantôme's explicit episodes. In neither author, however, do we have any

36. Ibid., p. 420.
37. *Memoirs of Count Grammont,* ed. Sir Walter Scott (London: Routledge and Sons, 1905).

sense of a relationship beyond physical desire or any hint of the pain of social rejection.

Something of this suffering can be surmised from the still skeletal account of women lovers in *The Female Husband* by Henry Fielding. This purports to relate an actual law case, tried before Fielding's cousin; in the tale, the case history becomes a moralistic warning to women against the dangers of unrestrained carnal appetites. Fielding is much concerned with purity—of both body and prose. In his narrative he asserts his language is chaste while castigating his lewd subject. The disjunction between prose and topic, propriety and pollution, becomes his contrast between decent marriage and indecent lesbianism, between himself and the improper Mrs. Hamilton.

Since modesty forbids description, we are left much in the dark about the woman and there is no psychological probing of her plight to compensate. The story is a bald, episodic one with a cautionary hero. It tells of Mary Hamilton, a virtuously reared young lady, corrupted by the evils of sex and Methodism. Taking up with a Methodist sister, Hamilton is inducted into lesbian licentiousness and drawn to "impurity." When the friend later chooses a man, Hamilton is as frantic and frenzied as the fondest husband, and she is in no way calmed when her friend eulogizes wedded love. Dejected and rejected, she accepts her nonconformity, dresses as a man, and sorties out for erotic adventure, inevitably to be undressed, unmasked and unwelcomed. It is a strange and masochistic odyssey.

Her first adventure is not planned. As a pretty young man, she provokes interest in a male Methodist, who quickly assaults her. At first she responds by crying out like a woman, but, abruptly remembering her dress, she throws off female conditioning and at once assumes male ways. She hits her assaulter a mighty blow on the nostrils so "that the blood issued from them with great Impetuosity."[38] There is no escaping nosebleeds, it

---

38. *The Female Husband: or, the Surprising History of Mrs. Mary, alias Mr. George Hamilton* (1746; facsimile Liverpool University Press, 1960), p. 37.

seems—whether of male or female provenance—wherever sex and innocence are involved, but here the usual pattern is neatly reversed. The male assaulter bleeds while the woman inflicts the injury. Momentarily he is put into the female position and made to bleed for his fall.

Confirmed in her disguise, Hamilton now embarks on a series of misadventures, declaring love to an assortment of unlikely women, all of whom must ultimately find her out. At the end she enters her most intense relationship, with a naive young girl for whom she feels, the author tells us, as much infatuation as ever man felt for woman. The love is mutual, but based on illusion, for never since her first encounter has Hamilton entered an openly lesbian relationship. Yet, however deceived, the women seem set for moderate happiness.

But society, repeatedly affronted, cannot let the couple be, and Hamilton's idyl is destroyed when she is exposed by the people she had earlier fooled. Dragged before the Justice, she is found an impostor, although her wife declares her a proper husband. Her doom is decided when "something of too vile, wicked and scandalous a nature" is discovered in her trunk and she is hauled off to prison, attended by the jeers and insults of the mob who delight in abusing both her and the woman she loved.

Inevitably the sentence is harsh. Hamilton is condemned to public and severe whipping through four market towns of England; afterwards she is to be imprisoned. The story breaks off there, ending with Fielding's indignant snort that all this severity did not lead to decency. In gaol, she is discovered offering a bribe to her keeper to procure her a young girl.

With Diderot's *The Nun*, *The Female Husband* is one of the few literary works of the eighteenth century to concentrate on erotic female love. It is distinguished from *The Nun* by its bareness, a characteristic of many works which treat lesbianism and avoid pornography. What makes it peculiarly dull, however, is less its stripped state than the heavily pious morality that obstructs rather than explains the events, and a trivialization that renders the painful curiously comic.

THE LITERARY CONTEXT

The effect can best be appreciated if the work is contrasted with an episode in Jane Barker's *A Patch-work Screen,* a tale likewise bare of analysis and detail. It tells of a woman who marries a man only to learn that the servant is his mistress and the mother of his children. Through a neurotic process never investigated, the wife dwindles into the "perfect Slave" of her illegitimate rival, doing the household chores each day while the "vile Strumpet" lolls upstairs with the husband. At night all three bed down together. At last, finding his children excessive, the husband wishes to abandon his strumpet and retain his wife. But instead of rejoicing at this desire, the persecuted wife roundly declares that if the mistress goes, she will go too. Disbelieving so bizarre a threat, the man ejects the mistress and finds his wife in earnest. The two women leave together and, although tempted with a pension, the wife cannot be pried from the mistress.

Like *The Female Husband,* the tale in *A Patch-work Screen* is not analysed or even fully rendered, and the only comment on it is the fictional listener's, that "This poor Creature was under some Spell or Inchantment."[39] Yet the bare facts breed a kind of intensity lacking in Fielding's fast-moving picaresque. Nothing is suggested only to be hidden; neither is there any authorial posing. The woman is left untrivialized as well as unexplained. At the end we do not feel she would bribe the gaoler for a whore.

The decent restraint of Barker also characterizes a very different tale, born of a very different age. Chateaubriand's *Atala* was published at the end of the period, at a time when Romanticism and sensibility had softened the hard narrative lines and taken in the exotic. In the novel, the old Indian Chactas describes Indian customs in North America. Among his pictures of funeral rites, he includes two virgins embracing each other, touching breasts and interlacing naked feet. For a moment their breath and hair mingle, but then, catching sight of their mothers, they blush and part, and the episode and image are over. The sensual innocence, so far from the coy crudity of Fielding and the

39. *A Patch-work Screen for the Ladies* (1723; New York: Garland, 1973), pp. 97–106.

fearful power of Diderot, speaks of another era and another—primitive—place.[40]

In eighteenth-century literature, erotic and sentimental friendships are antithetical. In the sentimental novel language and gestures are often sexual, while content almost invariably remains chaste. By fleeing any actual erotic statement, but titillating with hints, then, the sentimental novel left overt female sexuality to pornographers and prurient moralists who could sensationalize female love and drop the sentimental garb. There is little sensuality and amorous language in eighteenth-century accounts of erotic friendship; the women are not elevated and their passion rarely reaches the mythical and allegorical level of much male love. For most writers lesbianism becomes either a quaint custom, poorly substituting for heterosexual coupling, or a grotesque madness demanding vigorous repulsion. In both cases it deserves no elevated sentiment or thoughtful analysis from the author, no tearful empathy from the reader; instead it comes to intrigue or shock, requesting of us at best little beyond a well-bred smirk.

Manipulative Friendship: P. C. de Marivaux, Henry Fielding, Choderclos de Laclos

Sentimental friendship is frequently parodied in the eighteenth century by writers wishing to mop the edges of sensibility. It is the target of Jane Austen, whose hyperbolic Isabella in *Northanger Abbey* discredits a host of gushing maidens. Charlotte Smith, too, in *Emmeline* mocks the aspiring confidante, while Maria Edgeworth in *Moral Tales* harshly disillusions her heroine about sentimental friends; peered at closely, they prove uncultured and their Welsh cottages dirty. Beyond these outright attacks, sentimental friendship is more subtly endangered if its conventions are

40. *Atala.René* (Paris: Garnier-Flammarion, 1964), pp. 90–91. Several English editions omit the paragraph hinting at lesbian love.

manipulated for selfish ends. When Rousseau's Claire bends Julie to her will, or Juliette tortures her sister Justine after telling her female tale, and lives to flourish, the whole edifice of friendship is disturbed. The mocking Austen and the subverting Sade unite to insist that sentimental female friendship is dangerous, but they are differently provoked: Austen responds to the hint, however muted, that such friendship can disrupt society and give undue power to women, while Sade is angry that it helps society repress, that it reinforces impotence.

Manipulative friendship thrives on the display of sentiment. It is rich in tears and long embraces. Sometimes its distorting effects are intended and the woman glories in her control over her friend. Laclos' Mme de Merteuil in *Dangerous Liaisons* is such a woman. At other times, the display and distortion may be so hidden we are never quite sure they are delivered. This is the case with Fielding's Amelia. Usually, however, manipulative friendship treads between the extremes, subtly coercive and covertly predatory. Such friendship is imaged mainly in male literature with a female narrator and one of its first and finest examples is Marivaux's Marianne.

In the unfinished *Life of Marianne,* the fictional woman emerges from her text deeply conscious of her own ravishing pose and demeanor, caught in a web of narcissism which constricts all her language and actions. Perhaps such a woman answers a male vision of self-mirroring women or perhaps she in a way mirrors the author, whose own narcissism is given free rein in her contrary image. Whatever the case, her manipulation of all the signs of sentimental friendship separates her from the sentimental friend; despite her effusive ties, she is never bound in friendship, and her status as single consciousness in the novel resembles her state in the society she describes.

Female friendship is so puissant in the world of *Marianne* that it threatens to overwhelm the heterosexual passion on which the book must turn. It begins in the first line, where we learn that the narrative is retrospective and, like Suzanne's in *The Nun,* designed to please, but its reader is here a woman. The coquettishness which the male novel delights to confer on women immediately marks the relationship of reader and writer, and points to the rhetorical manipulation which Marianne freely admits. The narrative situation mirrors the content: Marianne never escapes her controlling act or weakens her image, whether she fashions it in prose to move her correspondent or delivers it in tears and sighs to ensnare her friends.

The Life of Marianne is an anthology of clichés in female friendship. Its major ties illustrate the functioning of these, revealing their manipulative force. For her benefactor, Mme de Miran, Marianne falls seductively ill, for example; for Mlle Varthon, her rival, she tells her female tale. With Mlle de Tervire, the unhappy nun, she studies the limits of female benevolence.

Most sentimental heroines decline or hurt themselves, so exaggerating an inherent weakness. Marianne is no exception. She begins life as a poor orphan, seemingly set on Fanny's Hill's path to high status through seduction and vice. But she is diverted from the way by an accident in which she displays a foot so ravishing that the hero Valville is captivated. More important, she reveals an enticing sensibility that overwhelms his mother, Mme de Miran. If the book aims primarily at recounting the vicissitudes of love between Marianne and Valville, in reality it describes the love between Marianne and his mother.

Marianne cries profusely for Mme de Miran. When she kisses her hand, she bathes it with "the most tender and delicious tears I ever shed in my life."[41] The tears are a fine investment, for Mme de Miran rewards them by befriending Marianne, keeping her and promoting her in society. But Marianne goes further. She insists she loves Mme de Miran even more than her son, Valville: "I love M de Valville, but still my heart is more yours than

---

41. *The Virtuous Orphan Or, The Life of Marianne Countess of * * * * * *,* trans. Mary Collyer (Carbondale: Southern Illinois Press, 1965), p. 117. This translation, a popular one in the eighteenth century, makes a few changes in the French text—primarily to subdue Marianne's narcissism and prepare her for the *Pamela*-like conclusion Mrs. Collyer adds to Marivaux's unfinished work.

his. My gratitude to you is dearer to me than my love."[42] In return, Mme de Miran supports the unequal marriage to her son.

Marianne's *tour de force,* however, arrives when Valville halts her social rise with his infidelity. At this point she makes her greatest assault on Mme de Miran by falling violently ill. Her sickness deeply impresses her benefactor, for Marianne in utter weakness is irresistible. Soon mother and son are alienated and Marianne becomes the only child; she recovers from her illness to be the perpetual daughter of Mme de Miran.

Less triumphant is her progress with Mlle Varthon, a convent friend and rival for Valville. At first the other woman attracts her. "I seemed to find in her a person more really my companion than any other," Marianne admits. But she does not seek a companion, rather an instrument, and, although she acts the friend to Mlle Varthon, she never quite assumes the identity of one. Her avoidance becomes clear when she tells the story of her life. Instead of displaying her true wounds for the other to soothe and heal, in the way of sentimental friends, she fakes it, glossily reinterpreting the sordid: "I appeared like a noble unfortunate," she confesses as she busily creates herself "a victim of fortune, or the heroine of a romance."[43] Perhaps the adjectives should be reversed, but, either way, the portrait excludes much and we may deduce we are similarly served in the larger narrative. Certainly we may sympathize with her listener when she later complains that Marianne's story is inadequate. After such hoodwinking it does not surprise that Mlle Varthon serves Marianne in the same style, only gradually identifying herself as rival. Assuredly the two women are alike, as Marianne noted, for both are calculating and self-regarding, and neither is fooled by her "friend's" artifice.

42. Ibid., p. 209. For a further discussion of the relationship between Marianne and Mme de Miran, see Ronald C. Rosbottom's *Marivaux's Novels: Theme and Function in Early Eighteenth-Century Narrative* (Rutherford: Fairleigh Dickinson University Press, 1974), pp. 120–34.

43. *The Virtuous Orphan Or, The Life of Marianne*, p. 267. Rosbottom has noted that this is the sixth and last time Marianne recounts her entire story to an audience. By this time she is well aware of its tearjerking effect and instinctively able to adapt it to her listener. *Marivaux's Novels,* p. 128.

A sadder tie is formed with Mlle de Tervire, a nun who contrasts with Marianne in using her life story to benefit, not fool, another woman. Through Mlle de Tervire Marianne is confirmed in what she must already know, that the display of female benevolence can be a manipulative device—along with tears and languishing attitudes—to attract and control another woman. With actual benevolence, the ambitious woman had best have little to do.

Mlle de Tervire has a history close to Marianne's, but, denied her overriding selfishness, she fares worse. She and her benefactor are similar to Marianne and Mme de Miran, and both young women are in a way motherless. But their paths veer apart when Mlle de Tervire moves from the straight road of self-interest and public charity into a selfless and secret benevolence. She befriends another woman, the daughter-in-law of her benefactor and, unlike Marianne, does not discover her rival until too late. Duped, she falls from fortune and declines in a convent. Her story is intended to warn Marianne against choosing seclusion, but it also cautions against the benevolence of sentimental friendship. It is a warning that Marianne has never been in danger of needing.

Interestingly there is in this narrative another tale of an unhappy nun who in turn relates her story to Mlle de Tervire to dissuade her from the convent. Through these receding narratives we glimpse a female community across time which bequeaths female knowledge and incites to courage. At the same time we detect another kind of procession, of female predators, whose origins and motives suggest a general cause of female manipulation. Each of the nuns has been lured and flattered into the convent by other nuns, who desire only that more women share their pain. The convent system, extreme symbol in so much fiction of female social oppression, spawns women who perpetuate on others the system that crushes them.

Like so many first-person novels of the eighteenth century, *The Life of Marianne* is a disquieting book, and it is not solely the perverse modern habit of looking through, as well as with, a narrator that makes it so. Translating it, Mrs. Collyer modified

Marianne's constant self-worship and, in the conclusion she added, she removed her heroine's coquettishness, so displaying the uneasiness of at least one contemporary woman. Certainly the book disturbs, then and now, because it so powerfully paints the narcissistic female who haunts the male imagination; at the same time it distorts the close friendship between women which has come to fascinate and worry both sexes. Marianne makes us uneasy because she is totally self-directed in the way women have been taught to be and because she preys on the sentimental friendship that might modify this self-absorption.

Fielding presents a bleak picture of female relationships in his fiction. In *Tom Jones,* for example, a few maids follow a few mistresses, but nothing very equal, close, and companionable seems allowed. The nearest is the tie between Sophia, the heroine, and her cousin Mrs. Fitzpatrick. But the good Sophia never really approaches her cousin and, although moved once by her story of misery, she remains on the whole dubious. In her turn, Mrs. Fitzpatrick scorns her cousin's childish naiveté. Yet, the tale she tells might have bound the two women, for, like Maria's story in *The Wrongs of Woman* or Euphemia's in Lennox's novel, it describes a general female sorrow: the incompatible yet inescapable marriage and the misery of bearing children within it. But neither we nor Sophia are allowed real involvement. When she eats heartily midway through her narrative, Mrs. Fitzpatrick is damned beyond sentiment.

As Fielding's only gynocentric novel, *Amelia* promises a brighter vision, but the fulfillment is as grim and glum as ever. If Marivaux's Marianne is not honest with us, we feel she is at some level honest with herself; even such rudimentary honesty seems denied the heroine in *Amelia,* where the display and distortion of manipulative friendship are always covert. The woman who inhabits so secretive a book seems unconscious of her effect and she is aided in her ignorance by a third-person narrator. By letting someone write for her, she avoids the extreme narcissism of the self-representer, while her manipulation need never be delineated. The author looks lovingly at her and hides her schemes.

Amelia's use of friendship springs less from her feminine self-absorption than from her male-centeredness. Her gaze is fixed firmly on her man, and she has no eyes for any woman who cannot help him. Her story centers on marriage to the sentimental but shiftless Booth and it progresses to reaffirm married happiness. A curious female prelude opens the book, a cautionary tale in minor mode which harshly prepares for the exemplary major chords of Amelia. In this, the picture of female relationships, bleak enough, is drastically darkened.

Booth encounters the ferocious Miss Matthews when she is imprisoned for suspected murder. The lengthy list of her famous forebears—Dalila, Jezebel, and the like—leaves no doubt that Fielding is presenting his female monster, and it does not surprise when the woman emerges powerful, sexual, and predatory. She has sisters as well as ancestors, for, like the saintly Clarissa, she wields the female penknife, but, like Haywood's vicious female in *Lasselia,* she is horribly unfeminine in turning her weapon on the man. When her murder fails, she is related both to Haywood's character and to Burney's Elinor; like her literary sisters she is frustrated in violence and, finally, denied the stature of a biblical fury.

Miss Matthews is vicious from the start. She rivals all pretty women and, if she is to know a moment's peace, she must always excel her sister. She is most unkind to those who are stupidly kind to her. When, for example, her immoral life is discovered, she is appalled at the continued benevolence of one she considers her inferior. Indeed she seems especially aghast at the kindness and obligations of female relationships; even in her dealings with men, she disdains receiving. She loves only those who are indebted to her and she is never won by gifts or deeds.

Miss Matthews is monstrous and her opinions vicious. Oddly, however, when she describes the perfidy of female friendship, the deceit and betrayal habitual among women, and when before the spectacle she scoffs "such are the friendships of women," she appears less monstrous than realistic. The author who makes her vicious somehow spreads her vice over womankind and the pessimism of her portrait is allowed to taint the relationships she has repudiated. In the book, both she and friendship are condemned.

Amelia enters softly after Miss Matthews' harsh exit. Yet she too is linked with passionate literary heroines. We hear at once that, although beautiful, she has an injured nose and automatically she assumes a context of bleeding noses, female sexuality, rape, and ambiguous sisterhood. The author assures us his heroine is exemplary, but her nose hints otherwise. Certainly her friends find her suddenly unworthy and she is mocked as derisively as any fallen woman. The bloodied nose separates her from even her most intimate acquaintances, and it is his support in this hour of trial that nurtures the vast growth of her trust in Booth. The saintly Amelia remains saintly, then; yet her injury, connoting female sexuality in literature, adds earthly and earthy colors to her picture.[44]

In spite of her advertised goodness, Amelia is almost as friendless as Miss Matthews, and her story, echoing in parts the vicious tale before, underlines its harsh conclusions. Miss Matthews is alienated from her sister, and so is the good Amelia; Miss Matthews antagonizes other women and Amelia constantly provokes malice. Miss Matthews is concerned with herself and Amelia is obsessed with her own beauty. Like Marivaux's Marianne and Miss Matthews, Amelia cannot give the self she so carefully hoards. Nonetheless she does approach two other women, Mrs. Ellison and Mrs. Bennet, and, if she never quite exposes herself by entering a friendship, her doorstep conversation with them illustrates her character.

Mrs. Ellison is Amelia's landlady, and her relationship with her pretty tenant is, according to the author, formed in spite of Amelia's looks. Amelia is described as warming toward Mrs. Ellison when she compliments her beauty. Yet she reaches only a

44. Amelia's nose provoked considerable comment when the book first appeared. Dr. Johnson claimed that the "vile broken nose, never cured" ruined the sale of *Amelia*. *Johnson Miscellanies* (New York: Barnes and Noble, 1966), I, 297. More scurrilous comments in journals hinted at the sexual nature of the injury. See Frederick Blanchard's *Fielding the Novelist* (New York: Russell and Russell, 1926).

tepid level for, when the other woman offers her a free ticket to attend the oratorio with her, she firmly refuses, primly protesting to her husband: "do you believe that I am capable of any sensation worthy the name of pleasure when neither you nor my children are present to bear any part of it?"[45] No friendship could grow through such chilly propriety.

And of course Amelia is right to hold back, for Mrs. Ellison is soon proved a veritable swamp of amorousness and, worse, little better than a pimp for her noble relative. So her caution against Amelia's husband-centeredness and wifely subservience—"what, is a woman to be governed then by her husband's inclinations, though they are never so unreasonable?"—rings hollow and Amelia's defense of the unfaithful and spendthrift Booth becomes proper instead of preposterous.[46] When we finally learn just how wicked Mrs. Ellison is, we also learn we should always have suspected it. A homely woman—especially if she compliments a beauty—must be vicious.

Opposing Mrs. Ellison is Mrs. Bennet, a learned young widow in reduced circumstances. She is not as ill-favored as the libidinous Mrs. Ellison, and indeed she can in a mask pass for the ravishing Amelia. She it is who does the true office of the female friend by saving Amelia from the amorous lord, by whom she has herself been scarred. She tells her own tale of seduction and betrayal and, like countless other fictional women of her time, forces narrative into action within friendship. Warned, Amelia avoids the fate cruelly prepared for her.

Yet neither woman quite gives herself to the tale. As she strays into acres of unnecessary detail, Mrs. Bennet is uncomfortably aware that she speaks to exonerate herself as much as to caution Amelia, while her listener, although approving, never pities the speaker so intensely that she forgets herself. Among all the horrors of Mrs. Bennet's history, it is only when it touches herself that Amelia requires hartshorn and water.

Mrs. Bennet is a complex character. Although divided in

45. *Amelia* (London: G. Bell, 1914), p. 189.
46. Ibid., p. 265.

motive in her tale, she proves trustworthy and she resembles the classic sentimental friend in enjoying the homage of a man for the woman she admires. She is rewarded with marriage to Amelia's milk-brother, a union that ties her to Amelia certainly, but also yokes her to a social inferior. Indeed the marriage to the kindly but illiterate soldier seems part of the book's insistent aim to mock Mrs. Bennet for her unfeminine learning. Against this mockery Amelia is unsupportive.

Both Mrs. Ellison and Mrs. Bennet are lesser mortals, looser in morals than Amelia and more conspiring. But Mrs. Bennet is saved for a middling future because she has been useful to Amelia, while the false friend is left to die of drink. Mrs. Bennet and Amelia, both pretty women, approached each other when in common danger, although their eyes were never quite off themselves, but, when prosperous, they fall away. In Fielding's world only the attractively miserable seem in want or in need of friends. Amelia holds to her husband, using other women only when he falters in his mastery.

Marianne and Amelia toy with sentimental friendship, avoiding commitment. Marianne languishes and cries but always orders the response; Amelia calls forth the female tale, while withholding total sympathy. In this hollow world, the villainous Miss Matthews cannot entirely repulse, for she fits action with attitude. She scorns the codes of female friendship with refreshing honesty.

But manipulative friendship can also be honest, or rather it may be blatant, rather than covert. Mme de Merteuil in Choderclos de Laclos' *Dangerous Liaisons* flaunts her control of other women and glories in her manipulative skill. The novel she inhabits also seems straightforward in its ideology, a clear warning against female friendship. The Preface declares that young people may here learn "that the friendship which seems to be granted them with such facility by persons of bad morals is never anything but a dangerous snare, as fatal to their happiness as to their virtue"; the book ends with the deceived woman exclaiming,

"What mother could see, without trembling, anyone but herself talking to her daughter!"[47]

Yet, strangely, between the clear negative extremes, the picture of friendship is more hopeful than in either *Marianne* or *Amelia*. It includes bonding for comfort as well as battling for hegemony. Mme de Merteuil lives within a web of rivalry, but it is a web that darkens rather than destroys the tenuous lines of support joining the virtuous woman to her friends.

Dangerous Liaisons describes a pair of active libertines, Mme de Merteuil and the Vicomte de Valmont, who exultantly prey on their society. At the outset Valmont is bent on seducing the pious Mme de Tourvel, and his seduction gets under way with a benevolent act, much like Lovelace in *Clarissa* or Venables in *The Wrongs of Woman*. Initially Mme de Merteuil is driven more by revenge than love of pleasure and power. She desires to hurt a faithless lover through corrupting his betrothed, the young Cécile, whose virginal charms have been preferred to her own sophistication. She also begins cleverly: by parading her friendship for the girl and displacing the mother as her confidante.

At first Mme de Tourval seems bound in a triangle of female friendships. She corresponds with Cécile's mother, Mme de Volanges, and visits an old friend, Mme de Rosemonde. Mme de Volanges proves a good confidante for her, a wise counsellor who may presume on her age and higher social class to warn her of the specious Valmont. Good and supportive as she is, however, the bond of friendship cannot withstand infatuation. Mme de Tourvel's hidden inclinations contradict her friend's warnings and she loosens the bond. For her new confidante she chooses Mme de Rosemonde, a comforting and loving being who avoids the virtuous severity of the true mother. She is a devoted friend certainly, but most important she is the aunt of Valmont.

For Mme de Tourvel, then, friendship is subtly dictated by her seducer. It is openly disturbed when Valville cunningly uses the aunt to obtain his end. He has understood Mme de Tourvel's

47. *Dangerous Acquaintances* (*Liaisons dangereuses*), trans. Richard Aldington (Norfolk, Conn.: New Directions Books, n. d.), pp. xi and 367.

337

stealthy move toward him, for, like Lovelace, he is keenly attuned to female ties. Obsessed at one point by the closeness of Mme de Tourvel and Mme de Volanges, he penetrates their correspondence only to be wounded by their plotting. Through the aunt, he comes to subvert as well as scrutinize the female writing.

Only when Mme de Tourvel is deceived, disabused, and dying do the three women reunite. Mme de Volanges returns in order to comfort and support her friend in her last days, and she is inexorable in reclaiming her; toward the end Mme de Tourvel lives only in her friends' letters. But she remains acutely aware of her aloneness and the expulsion she believes her due from the community of women.

In a way she is right, for she has indeed rejected and manipulated female friendship to approach a man. In addition she has more generally repudiated her own sex. When the notorious womanizer Valmont was attracted to her, she prided herself that she was not as other women, that her manifest virtue distinguished her from all his previous conquests. When Mme de Volanges warned her of her danger, she replied she was sure Valmont could not confuse her with other seducible women. The kinship of all women is the knowledge she buys with her death.

The young Cécile is far more isolated than Mme de Tourvel. She has of course her mother, but romantic convention almost demands that she deceive her. Briefly she corresponds with a convent friend, but the letters soon peter out, and she is left largely unattended to the ravages of the male world and Mme de Merteuil.

Methodically, Mme de Merteuil sets about Cécile's defloration. She will revenge herself for a past humiliation, but also perhaps gain an ally. "I am often tempted to make her my pupil," she declares, impressed by Cécile's lack of character and principles and by her "natural duplicity."[48] For a while she feels a pedagogical desire toward the girl, and she contemplates turning her into "at least a subsidiary intriguer." Ultimately, how-

48. Ibid., pp. 68–69.

ever, she is diverted from such designs by Cécile's silliness. She is, after all, a mere facile woman, Mme de Merteuil concludes, a mere "pleasure machine," and her immorality can never become systematic.

But if Mme de Merteuil decides against mental seduction, she remains devoted to a physical fall. Like Phoebe in *Fanny Hill*, she prepares her charge for the male world by arousing her sexually, while yet leaving her doubtful of the significance of her feelings. When Cécile disappoints intellectually, she hands her to Valmont, who completes the seduction in the conventional way.

Although she flirts with Cécile and pretends affection for her mother, Mme de Merteuil has no intimate female friend. When she narrates her life, she notes this lack also in her youth. Yet she sees herself penalized by her sex and she announces she will avenge the common ills of women. She knows she is supreme, but, as a female, she must constantly struggle and calculate for a supremacy casually granted to such men as Valmont. So she allies herself with "intelligent" women, whom, apart from herself, we never meet in the novel.[49] Others—those who do not understand their constriction in a patriarchal world or appreciate the need to manipulate and calculate—are despised. Ultimately, like Mme de Tourvel, she is destroyed because she does not recognize her kinship with *all* women. In the battle between men and women, every woman loses.[50]

49. Perhaps these women exist in the intertextual context. Mme de Merteuil comes close to no woman in her book, but she is inspired by reading the letters in Rousseau's *Julie*. A friendless heroine's feeling of kinship with all women is again depicted in Jane Barker's *Entertaining Novels*, where Galesia never turns to a female friend but sees herself as heir of women writers and, in moments of high drama, as champion of her sex: "I will end his Race," she threatens her perverse lover, "no more of them shall come to disturb or affront Womankind. This only Son shall die by the Hands of me an only Daughter," (London: A. Bettesworth, 1719), p. 39.

50. The debasement of all women in society is one of the themes of *Traité de l'éducation des femmes* in which Laclos blamed society for making women slaves and announced that only a social revolution would allow women to have a real education. Neither Mme de Merteuil nor Mme de Tourvel is quite the natural woman praised in *Traité*, for both are corrupted in one way or another by society. For a discussion of the work see Béatrice Didier, *Littérature française Le XVIIIe siècle III, 1778–1820* (Paris: Arthaud, 1976), p. 229.

The narratives of Mme de Tourvel and Mme de Merteuil illustrate women's need for unity in a hostile world. Mme de
Tourvel was provided with caring and supportive friends whom
she rejected and Mme de Merteuil avoided the female ties offered
her. Both women stood alone against Valmont, not so fiendish an
enemy perhaps, but one rendered omnipotent in the context of
his male society. Both women failed because they insisted on
seeing themselves as exceptional.[51]

In *Marianne, Amelia,* and *Dangerous Liaisons,* manipulative
friendship is intimately connected with sentimental. For example,
manipulative friends show the signs of sentimental friendship
while avoiding the substance. Language and gestures which
should communicate are used to hide, and the manipulating
woman acts the sentimental friend to gratify only herself. In addition, although the manipulative friend may grow from a selfish
woman or one twisted by early deprivation, she may also derive
from a failure of sentimental friendship to move outward and
confront society. The ambitious woman, intellectually alone
within her close union, is socially frustrated and turns her
strength on her female relationship. Caught in this chain of mastery, female friendship falls from an alliance of equals into the
dependence of prey and predator.

Political Friendship: Mary Delariviere Manley, Sarah Scott and Barbara Montagu, Louis Rustaing de Saint-Jury, Walter Scott

They momently exclude the *Men,* fortify themselves in the Pre-
cepts of *Virtue* and *Chastity* against all their detestable undermining Arts, arraign without Pity or Compassion those who have
been so unfortunate as to fall into their Snare; Propagate their
Principles of exposing them without Mercy————Give Rules to

51. The message is reinforced in an embedded tale of three pretty young women,
whose friendship is so intense and anomalous that they are often labelled lesbians.
Together they triumph in society, attracting men through their friendly ties. When they
cease to cohere, each tangles alone with the male world and is destroyed.

such of the *Cabal* who are not *Married,* how to behave themselves to such who they think fit they should *Marry;* no such weighty Affair being to be accomplish'd without the mutual consent of the *Society:* At the same time lamenting the custom of the World, that has made it convenient (nay, almost indispensible) for all Ladies once to Marry. To those that have Husbands, they have other Instructions, in which this is sure to be one; to reserve their *Heart,* their tender *Amity* for their *Fair Friend.* . . .

. . . In this little *Commonwealth* is no *Property;* whatever a *Lady* possesses, is, *sans ceremone,* at the service, and for the use of her *Fair Friend,* without the vain *nice* scruple of being oblig'd. 'Tis her *Right;* the other disputes it not; no, not so much as in *Thought,* they have no reserve; mutual *Love* bestows all things in *common.*[52]

This political and economic community of women is envisioned in Mary Delariviere Manley's utopian satire, *The New Atalantis.* Set in an allegorical frame, in which Astrea and Intelligence contemplate a transposed England, it describes among a myriad of groupings the Cabal, a club of women united to oppose the male world and order their own society.

Manley's women form a defensive and aggressive league, actively challenging the patriarchy they inhabit, while shielding themselves against its encroachments. They overturn many of the conventions of their wider society, scoffing at the supremacy of men and defiling the sanctity of family and family property. Although they hold to a male social structure, in couple and hierarchy, they yet escape many of its tensions; they are, it is said, uncommonly happy freed from "that rapacious sex."

Yet some jealousies and distresses still wrack the group, and they spring from its sexual doings. The allegorical watchers profess uneasiness at the erotic implications of the club, although they admit women are labelled criminal whether they seek their pleasures among or outside themselves. Certainly their gaze falls often on the bizarre diversions of the women, their jealousy when

52. *Secret Memoirs and Manners of several Persons of Quality, of Both Sexes. From the New Atalantis, an Island in the Mediteranean* (London: John Morphew, 1709), pp. 46–47, 57.

a man approaches a lover—"what happy Wretch is it upon whom you bestow my *Rites!*" one member is heard to scream— or their transvestite antics when they sally forth in male dress to seek prostitutes who will never "wound" their chastity.[53] Yet even the erotic grows political when the disapproving Astrea descants on men "Who *Arbitrarily* decide, that Woman was only created (with all her *Beauty, Softness, Passions* and compleat *Tenderness*) to adorn the *Husband*'s Reign, perfect his *Happiness,* and propagate the Kind."[54] Like Sade's club of libertines in *Juliette,* the Cabal's eroticism concerns power.[55]

As well as works like *The New Atalantis,* which include utopic descriptions, both England and France have straightforward female utopias. *A Description of Millenium Hall* emphasizes common property and shared emotion, but, unlike *The New Atalantis,* it eschews eroticism. A popular novel-manual by Sarah Scott and Barbara Montagu—two ladies who lived out a version of their fictional ideal in their own lives—it tells of a community of women which is simultaneously an enterprise of benevolence and a model society.

The community is described by two wandering gentlemen. They learn that it is governed by a group of wellborn and only moderately rich ladies, determined to practice seclusion and female exclusiveness. Organized around a wonderfully productive and well-managed estate, this female paradise is centered in Millenium Hall itself, the house of the ladies, who use their extra

---

53. *New Atalantis*, pp. 45 and 49.

54. Ibid, p. 58.

55. Within the Cabal, there seems no need for women to attract attention by running mad, falling ill, or bleeding at the nose. Outside, however, fictive convention obtains and in a world of seduction and rivalry Charlot, a naive mistress, displays her nosebleed before the Duke and her friend, the Countess: "some drops of Blood fell from her Nose upon her Handkerchief . . . the Omen startled her . . . she fell in a fainting Fit upon the Countess's Bosom" (*New Atalantis*, p. 79). Her friend is moved and gives some sound wordly advice, but the simple Charlot rejects it. Consequently she is betrayed by her friend and lover together. The blood has marked her womanhood and sexual fall and, as in *Clarissa*, it ultimately fails to win the woman who shares her sex or the man who controls her sexuality. Such anecdotes, with their echoing motifs, underline the sexual politics of the separatist Cabal and make it less satiric than utopian.

space to lodge and educate destitute girls of the middle class and prepare them for a life of housekeeping, nursing, or marriage. All the servants of the establishment are unfortunates: a lame cook, a one-eyed kitchen maid, a deaf dairy maid, epileptic and asthmatic musicians. Beyond the house are various other benevolent sites: a village of poor old women whose business it is to rear babies from poor families with more than five children, a home for genteel spinsters who again must assist the poor, and an enclosed area for the deformed—dwarfs and giants and the like—bought by the ladies from unscrupulous "monster-mongers" and encouraged to live privately and decently in the community.

In all the descriptions, the emphasis is on order and beauty, aesthetics with utility. The grounds and gardens are pleasant to the eye and useful as well; the old women must keep their cottages both neat and pretty; the girls in the house must wear dresses that are clean and becoming. All the women, from the elderly paupers to the governing ladies, agree in philosophy and all strive in gratitude or benevolence to live up to the ideals of the community. Here there is no hint of the ingratitude in the lower orders that Wollstonecraft had so strenuously tried to overlook in *Mary, A Fiction*.

The bulk of the novel concerns the histories of the ladies. From these the gentlemen learn that the community grew from the close friendship of two women and their unhappy experience in the world of family and marriage. These two women bought the estate and attracted other women to it, so that their friendship, once freed from patriarchal constraints, quickly widened into group affection. Each of the women's histories stresses the joy of female companionship and the hostility of the male world toward it. Although their attitudes are on the whole Christian and conventional, far from those of Wollstonecraft's Maria (women usually suffer to preserve their character, for example), the ladies do seem to foreshadow Maria's hostile attitude to unhappy marriage, which no amount of Christian resignation can palliate.

The male narrator listens respectfully to all the histories but

343

is intrigued by the ladies' attitudes to matrimony. As he notes, they are preparing girls in their own house for marriage, while their own histories argue forcefully against it. To his questions, one spokeswoman answers by upholding propriety, while justifying her own withdrawal. Matrimony, she asserts, is absolutely necessary to the good of society as a general duty. But "as, according to all antient tenures, those obliged to perform knight's service, might, if they chose to enjoy their own fire-sides, be excused by sending deputies to supply their places; so we, using the same privilege substitute many others, and certainly much more promote wedlock, than we could do by entering into it ourselves."[56] Her companion, less conciliatory and diplomatic, roundly declares that to marry appears to her more an effort of courage than "to face the enemy's cannon."[57]

Millenium Hall is not a politically radical work. Its principles are benevolent and Christian, and their expression a welfare state of hierarchical happiness. Yet in its pitting of the calm female paradise and the bustling male hell outside, of the sceptical gentleman observers and the active committed ladies, it suggests that a community of women who have suffered authority might be worthier of wielding it than privileged men. For all its conservative stance, then, *Millenium Hall* supports the radical opinion that society's salvation might be in female government.

---

56. *A Description of Millenium Hall, and the County Adjacent: Together with the Characters of the Inhabitants, And such Historical Anecdotes and Reflections, as May excite in the READER proper Sentiments of Humanity, and lead the Mind to the Love of VIRTUE* (London: J. Newberry, 1762), pp. 144–45.

57. *Millenium Hall*, p. 145. James Lawrence's *Empire of the Nairs*, another English utopia, which impressed the poet Percy Bysshe Shelley, also treats women and marriage. Using many of Mary Wollstonecraft's arguments, its main purpose is to undermine European conventions of marriage. The most interesting argument is that they force women to develop a solely sexual and negative charm, since the preservation of chastity is their only concern; without marriage women would be free to grow intellectually and socially. More sexually radical than *Millenium Hall*, *The Empire of the Nairs* is politically more conservative. If the first ruler of the Nairs was an heroic woman, her successors are men and, although there is some companionship among equal women, the closest bond is maternal. *The Empire of the Nairs; or the Rights of Women. An Utopian Romance* (1801 in German; 1811 in English; New York: Scholars' Facsimiles & Reprints, 1976).

THE LITERARY CONTEXT

A very different utopia is envisioned in a strange French book, *The Military Women* (*Les Femmes Militaires*), ascribed to Louis Rustaing de Saint-Jury.[58] It tells of a newly discovered island where men and women have overturned the conventions and constraints of Europe to establish a genuine equality. The ideal they represent is androgynous, for, although female prowess is vaunted, so is male gentleness; the sexes dress similarly and both are marked by noble pride and modesty. Because men and women are physically and mentally equal, they share all social functions. They alternate in the rule of the country, the duke chosen by the women, the duchess by the men; women go to war beside their brothers and are distinguished for their daring and strength. Interestingly, this social importance is won less by confounding the sexual difference than by holding fast to it. In government and war the women shine because they act in unison. They vote as a block and strive together against the men for command.

Like *The New Atalantis*, *The Military Women* is both satire and utopia. The agile and warlike island women laugh at the bedecked European female, ablaze in fantastic coiffure, powder, and patches. They ridicule too the custom that demands women obey and please the man, and they judge such debased creatures mere captives and animals. Above all, they mock women's sexual subservience. Unlike the Cabal of *The New Atalantis*, the island society is not openly erotic; marriages are regulated by parents and state, and the coquettishness of the Europeans both amazes and disgusts.

The narrative joins two cultures by thrusting a trio of Europeans, two women and a man, into the island city. There the group is disrupted when Frederic is urged to comply with native custom and take one of the women to wife. Choosing Saphire, he inevitably rejects Susanne, whom he mistakenly believes indifferent to him. True to the conventions of Europe, the woman

58. *Les Femmes Militaires, ou Relation Historique d'une Isle Nouvellement de'couverte* (Paris: Didot, 1739). I am indebted to Jean-Marie Goulemot for bringing this book to my attention.

thwarted in romance seeks another excellence, and Susanne becomes a militant leader among the island women, rising abruptly to the supreme position of duchess.

But a European upbringing will out, it seems, and Susanne is bound still by the sexual jealousy of romantic convention. So she uses her power to remove Frederic and Saphire from the island forever. Since Frederic is the consciousness of the book, we leave with him and can only speculate on the future progress of the foreign duchess, fearless because rejected and powerful because vengeful. The island city is perhaps not irreparably damaged, but the European cliché of the slighted woman is forced upon the female utopia.

In confronting two ways of organizing society, *The Military Women* also confronts two systems of female bonding. The Europeans allow friendship between two women but it is quickly disrupted by rivalry and sexual jealousy; the island establishes women in groups without a splintering into pairs, and the women in these groups remain supportive to each other and powerful within society. A similar message, more covertly delivered, emerges from *The New Atalantis,* where the Cabal flourished except where women insisted on exclusive devotion, while women who tried to bond or aid each other outside conspicuously failed. In *Millenium Hall,* female friends who try to forge sentimental ties in the outside world are parted, slighted, and forbidden each other's company; in the separatist society of the female estate, however, the bonding is general, firm, and politically potent. It is an interesting point, rarely made in the less satiric and utopian fiction of the period, and its closest counterpart is the brothel society of *Fanny Hill.*[59]

In *The New Atalantis, The Military Women,* and to a lesser extent in *Millenium Hall,* female bonding on the whole avoids

---

59. Nina Auerbach describes a community of women as a rebuke to the conventional ideal of a solitary woman living for and through men. She argues that the communities of women which have haunted our literary imagination from the beginning are emblems of female self-sufficiency. *Communities of Women,* p. 5.

the sentimental signs of friendship, as do the more realistic novels which combine women politically. Like Wollstonecraft's pair, Maria and Jemima, the women are joined by situation or blood as much as by inclination, and they act together and for each other through extreme necessity. They unite, aid, even sacrifice themselves with hardly a rhapsody or a tear and they neither fool nor are fooled in motives. Steering away from the sentimental, they avoid the manipulative as well.

Walter Scott's *Heart of Midlothian* is a final example of such a cool female relationship.[60] It presents a union forged in blood, piety, and duty, devoid of heady companionship or violent affection. It relates the entwined stories of step-sisters, Jeanie and Effie Deans, daughters of a Scottish cowfeeder. The younger, Effie, is pretty and spoiled, inevitably courting sexual ruin; she bears a baby to an elusive but noble lover and is charged with murder when the child disappears. The older, Jeanie, is good and pious, and she enters her sister's tale first as destroyer—for she will not tell a lie to free her—and then as savior, for it is her political act of accosting the Queen that obtains the pardon. Politics and blood, not sentiment, unite the sisters. Freed, Effie does not wait to embrace her sister-savior and fall on her bosom, instead eloping before Jeanie even returns from London.

The second act of this chilly relationship occurs when Effie—now translated to nobility—descends on Jeanie, her lowly unacknowledged sister, in the full panoply of Lady Staunton. So inspiring a figure is she that Jeanie does not know her at once, overturning the sentimental convention that demands instant recognition from sisters. A few scenes of impulsive affection follow, but, as the stay lengthens, the sisterly tie is frayed. Effie's departure, when it comes, is friendly, but it relieves both women.

The unsentimental, political relationship of Jeanie and Effie occurs in a book where men are united by something more than kinship and piety. Effie's lover is saved from death by his friend, an older man who has strangely influenced him and to whom he

---

60. *Heart of Midlothian* (New York: Holt, Rinehart, and Winston, 1969).

is tied by a desperate affection. The man, who dies of his heroic act, is effusively praised and his friend always remembers him with gratitude. Jeanie's political act saves her sister but neither woman seems vastly tied to the other. They share childhood memories and a father, nothing more. The man, saved by his friend, is prepared to hold that friend in first place; the woman, saved by a sister, always puts her lover first.

Oddly enough, *The Heart of Midlothian*, so different from the utopian books of the early eighteenth century and the later *Wrongs of Woman*, bears out the conclusion of both, that the low-keyed bonding of women from need leads sooner to political action than the intense sentimental tie which dissolves in swooning rapture and escapist reverie. The women of Richardson and Lennox may dream of confronting the institutions of a patriarchy that nullifies them, but often feeling substitutes for action; the codes of sentimental friendship, which so successfully free emotion and encourage intense uniting, also sap political energy. Jeanie, the female soldiers, and the governing ladies interest less than Clarissa or Juliet, and it is not for these heroines that the eighteenth-century female reader cried. But it is they and their dry-eyed sisters who act decisively in fiction.

Social Friendship: Daniel Defoe, Susan Ferrier, and Mme Riccoboni

Of all the shifting categories of friendship, social friendship shifts most. Frequently it overlaps with sentimental and political friendships, taking an exemplary heroine and smoothing the rubble from her path. Yet ultimately it differs from both, for, although it may unite its friends in sentimental codes, it can also exist without them, basing itself on money and self-interest quite as well. Although it acts, it does not, like political friendship, oppose or confront society; rather it helps the woman to flourish within it, to exploit perhaps but not to subvert. Since it helps a woman inside the family, the father's or the husband's, it strengthens patriarchy, as Emma Woodhouse comes to understand. Yet it remains a female bonding, limiting women's dependence on men and qualifying the feminine role of virtuous passivity. Fanny Price sees only this aspect and flees.

Defoe's heroine in *Moll Flanders* easily accepts society. She wishes only to enjoy it as speedily as possible and is ready to trample on all decent female codes to do so. She enters life with hardly a female mentor, but is quick to learn unaided, and is soon teaching another woman how to trap a husband. She is concerned too about her female readers, urging them, for example, not to comply too quickly with men: " 'Tis nothing but a lack of Courage, the fear of not being Marry'd at all," she scolds. "This, I say, is the Woman's Share." She goes on to explain: "She is always Married too soon who gets a bad Husband, and she is never Married too late who gets a good one; In a word, there is no Woman, *Deformity, or lost Reputation excepted,* but if she manages well, may be Marry'd safely one time or other; but if she precipitates herself, it is ten Thousand to one but she is undone."[61] The advice is sensible, down-to-earth, socially apt, and unsentimental. Moll will enter no rapturous liaison inside or outside her text.

When she prospers in marriage, Moll has no call for friends; so she finds herself alone after each escapade. Over and over again she laments this solitariness in crises, an evil almost equal to poverty for women who cannot, like men, flourish alone. In her later years, aging and faded, she leans most heavily on other women, especially the "governess," who aided her in an early misadventure, then dropped from sight as Moll prospered, only to reappear when she tumbles again into poverty. With this help, an older Moll takes to stealing, and the two women flourish through mutual trust. When Moll is caught, the governess stands by her, works unceasingly, and sustains her as all seems lost. The association lasts until Moll sails for Virginia and renewed prosper-

61. *The Fortunes & Misfortunes of the Famous Moll Flanders* (New York: W. W. Norton, 1973), p. 60.

ity. Yet, although her friend cries for her as for a child (she has long been called Mother), Moll feels no tug to rest with her; given choice she always takes a male protector, never thinking to reject the male world. Society is for Moll to prey on, not oppose.[62]

Moll Flanders presents a businesslike, self-interested relationship, the furthest removed from sentimental ties. Helped by women, Moll can help herself through men, and she crowns her misdeeds by respectable marriage. Like Fanny Hill, she brings her own wealth to the union, so limiting its harsh patriarchal statement, but she must in the end exclude the women who bolster her wicked independence.

Other novels do not exclude the sentimental so dramatically, but they may stress its difference from the social by contrasting the two types of relationships. When this happens, the sentimental tie must prove false and unworthy, while the less euphoric social tie will be found true. Austen's *Northanger Abbey* is an example. The hyperbolic, sentimental friendship of Isabella and Catherine harms Catherine, but the social friendship of Catherine and Elinor enables her to catch a husband and establish her social self.

The same contrast is even more stark in Susan Ferrier's symmetrical novel, *Marriage,* in which the heroine, Mary, inspired by the rapturous siblings of sentimental convention, courts a long-lost sister Adelaide. She desired, the author declares, "to throw herself into her sister's arms, and tell her how much she loved her." Sadly, this extravagant longing burns only in her own breast:

62. The predatory nature of Moll—with its relationship to her circumstances and social codes—is discussed by Paula Backscheider in "Defoe's Women: Snares and Prey," *Studies in Eighteenth-Century Culture,* V, ed. Ronald C. Rosbottom (Madison: University of Wisconsin Press, 1976), pp. 103–20. Katharine Rogers comments on Moll's relationship to men in "The Feminism of Daniel Defoe," *Woman in the 18th Century and Other Essays,* ed. Paul Fritz and Richard Morton (Toronto: Samuel Stevens Hakkert, 1976), pp. 3–24.

she followed her sister's steps as she quitted the room, and, throwing her arms around her, sobbed in a voice almost choked with the excess of her feelings, "My sister, love me!—oh! love me!" But Adelaide's heart, seared by selfishness and vanity, was incapable of loving any thing in which self had no share; and, for the first time in her life, she felt awkward and embarrassed. . . . Adelaide could only wonder at her sister's agitation, and think how unpleasant it was.[63]

Even the fervent Mary is cooled by such frigidity, reduced to seeking a mere social friend. Fortunately she discovers an excellent example in her common-sensical cousin, Lady Emily.

Where Mary is good, rapturous, pious, and priggish, Emily is playful, abrasive, sceptical, and sprightly.[64] Although she comes to admire Mary's goodness, she despises do-gooding and mocks conventional femininity. She refuses to play the prim role of Mary or the coquettish one of Adelaide. "I defy any one," she declares with pride, "to say that I am fascinating." Certainly one could wish that Wollstonecraft's Mary had lighted on such a friend. Yet the novel casts Emily as the defective woman, sensible but unprincipled. Under Mary's quiet influence, she must gain this chilly principle and freeze into femininity; when at the end she marries Mary's stupid brother, she prepares to "hang up" all her smart sayings in her brain. Austen once described how in a niece the "delicious play of Mind" would be "all settled down into conjugal & maternal affections".[65] Lady Emily seems destined to congeal in much the same way.

In other respects Austen is pertinent to this novel—in her

63. *Marriage, A Novel,* ed. Herbert Foltinek (London: Oxford University Press, 1971), pp. 228–29.

64. Concerning the complementary relationship of Lady Emily and Mary, Nelson S. Bushell conjectures "that together they approximate a projection of the author's own contradictory nature," "Susan Ferrier's *Marriage* as Novel of Manners," *Studies in Scottish Literature* 5 (1968), 226. In his introduction Herbert Foltinek again comments on the pair, noting that Lady Emily's piquant observations on Mary's conduct often deflate her unwordly saintliness, p. xiii.

65. *Jane Austen's Letters to her Sister Cassandra and Others,* ed. R. W. Chapman, 2 vols. (Oxford: Clarendon Press, 1932), II, 478–79.

time Ferrier was termed a Scottish Jane Austen—and her book shares much with *Mansfield Park*. The same figures people it and the same actions mar the propriety it approves. Mary has the principled and proud humility of Fanny and both are humble relations in a fashionable world. Adelaide, the image of Austen's Maria, refuses friendship and marries a fool for money, later eloping with the man she always wanted, Lord Lindore. With him and her mother—in the role of Mrs. Norris—she is exiled for life. As Lord Lindore is to Lady Emily, so Henry is to Mary Crawford in *Mansfield Park* and certainly in relationship, wit, and lack of principle, Lady Emily seems cast as the sprightly Mary. Like her, Emily befriends the virtuous heroine and loses her heart to the hero. In their struggle for this man, both lively women are worsted, for the "better" character must prosper.

But the books are distinct, too. Although she cannot have the hero, Emily is allowed to marry satisfactorily—as if Mary Crawford had kindly been given Fanny's brother to wrap up the plot. Equally different is Mary's freedom to return Lady Emily's friendship, improve her, and mildly love her, even though, like Austen's Jane Fairfax and Emma, the two women end up strikingly apart. Ferrier takes pity on the witty woman, then, and grants her social salvation in marriage; friendship, though prudently severed, has been allowed to contribute to this happy state. In capitulating to friendship, Ferrier has softened Austen's bleaker, more powerful novel, modifying her severe, unfriendly vision.

Finally, some novels of social friendship neither ignore nor oppose sentiment, but coopt it. The social tie of mistress and maid, for instance, may be seasoned with sighs and hyperbole, while still benefiting at least the mistress. In the ambiguous alliance with Defoe's *Roxana*, Amy the servant constantly proves she can ease Roxana's life; at the same time she is exuberantly loyal and affectionate. In Lennox's *Euphemia*, a devoted governess lavishes her savings on her mistress's child and follows her to an uninviting America, while the French writer Mme de Riccoboni in *The History of Miss Jenny Salisbury* forges a similar bond for a faithful maid; to comfort the orphan, the servant plays the roles of both mother and sentimental friend.[66]

Like the close tie of mistress and maid, the main female alliances in Riccoboni's novels are again social and sentimental, moving ultimately into the heroic. Female rivalry—a convention so constant it structures fiction from Haywood to Austen, lightly touching even *Clarissa*—is here overthrown. The female characters aid each other in society, smooth and support like other social friends, but in crises they shine beyond their sisters, doing great deeds silently. In *The Life of Marianne*, two women who love the same man fight to the end; in Ferrier's *Marriage*, one struggles and surrenders, while in Haywood's *Idalia* the heroine gives up her lover quite wholeheartedly. Riccoboni goes further in showing a woman renouncing a beloved for a friend.

Since the main female tie of *Jenny Salisbury* is heroic, it requires some equality if the heroism is not to seem merely self-destructive. And indeed the hierarchical union of the poor Jenny and the rich Lady Anglesey does grow more equal: "Let us from this moment banish all distinction between us," proposes Lady Anglesey, opening heart and house to her friend; "let us live like two affectionate sisters and let no one who sees us together, be able to determine on which of us fortune has been pleased to shed her favours."[67]

But the picture of sentimental sisters should not deceive, for the women are not sisters and cannot give themselves entirely to rapture. Instead Jenny is dramatically tested in her friendship when she finds she and Lady Anglesey both love the same man. To give her friend happiness, she sacrifices her own, abandoning lover and friend together. She exiles herself to France, where she

---

66. On the other side are the unsatisfactory mistress-servant relationships. In *Amelia*, Amelia's maid Betty proves treacherous and is severely punished by Booth. In *Roxana*, although mistress and maid are close and affectionate, Roxana forces Amy into whorishness to reduce her to her own level and finally causes her to commit murder.

67. *The History of Miss Jenny Salisbury; addressed to the Countess of Roscommond* (1764; Dublin: A. Leathley, J. Exshaw, et. al., 1770?), II, 30.

lives out her days independently, tranquilly, and joylessly among her books.

Self-sacrifice for a friend is not rare in fiction of this period, but Jenny's lack of self-indulgence with it—if we exclude the telling of the tale—is rare. Helen Maria Williams in *Julia* has her heroine sacrificing for a cousin, but rewarding herself with the hero's and her own vast esteem. Mme de Staël's heroine in *Corinne* gives up her man to her step-sister and ends by dominating both, finally enjoying one of fiction's most self-indulgent deaths. On the other side, Burney's Cecilia is tied to her protegé neither by blood nor equal affection, only benevolence. When she finds they love in common, she ousts her friend and takes her own happiness.[68]

Heroic social friendship and its confounding of rivalry are again subjects in Riccoboni's strangely ambiguous *History of the Marquis de Cressy*, a work which varies and deepens the love plot of Haywood and Lennox. The last novel to be treated here, it is a sombre study of female friendship, which grows resonant in the general context of eighteenth-century fiction. To subvert the convention of female rivalry, it sets up unwitting rivals, while it presents its heroic ideal of social friendship only to parody it cruelly by a neurotic tie that cannot fail to taint it.

The novel tells of two friends and relatives, the older Countess who loves the Marquis de Cressy, and the younger Adelaide de Bugei, who is courted by him. Neither knows the other's state, for each has been shy of confiding her love. But the secretive Countess soon betrays herself to her beloved with passionate anonymous letters, whose origin he learns. Action follows discovery and the ambitious Marquis transfers his suit to the wealthy Countess, who has unwittingly displaced her friend. She

68. The sacrifice of a lover for a female friend also occurs in Mary Robinson's *Walsingham: or the Pupil of Nature* (1798). In the *Anti-Jacobin Review* (July–December 1798), 161, the reviewer of this novel sneers at the *"unprecedented generosity"* of any woman's yielding a lover to a friend and adds mockingly "the term *unprecedented* we mean only as applicable to fact, not as to protestation."

has then offended on two counts: she has betrayed a friend and, if not as culpable as the "masculine" women of Haywood and Burney who openly pursued their loves, she has acted unfemininely.

Rejected, Adelaide must fall into a fever. She lives but only as a prey to melancholy, bitter at the disloyalty of lover and friend. "Inhuman!" she laments, "with how much seeming sincerity did she affect to sympathize in my pains."[69] But the Countess is far from inhuman, still ignorant of her friend's love and deeply saddened by her suffering. Only when married does she come to suspect a dubious connection between her husband and her friend, and she is pained to learn that Adelaide is preparing to enter a convent. When she finally understands the full history and realizes her own shoddy happiness, she is grief-stricken, and the image of her abused friend replaces the image of her beloved Marquis in her mind: "The idea of Mademoiselle du Bugei prostrate at the feet of the altars, praying for the Marquis, drawing down from heaven benedictions on him by her pure and fervent devotions, melted her heart, and made her for ever present to her mind."[70] She reidentifies with the woman and is pulled back into the female association against which she had unwittingly but grievously sinned.

Since the Countess has betrayed another woman, however innocently, she must be punished. Her punishment marvelously fits her crime, for she is wounded simultaneously in love and friendship. Following her promise to a dying woman, she takes into her house a poor young girl named Hortensia. One of Riccoboni's most acute studies, this woman has grown from solitary youth to passionate and capricious maturity, incapable alike of tenderness or friendship. She takes what she can from the Countess and is neither grateful nor admiring. This insensitivity intrigues the Marquis, to whose charms she declares herself quite immune; piqued in vanity, he tries her by assuming a passion. As-

69. *The History of the Marquis de Cressy* (1758; London: T. Becket, and P. A. de Hondt, 1765), p. 97.
70. Ibid., p. 108.

sumption becomes reality, and Hortensia soon surveys an enamored Marquis. But what most deeply impresses her is her
triumph over the worthy Countess, whose image cruelly effaces
her lover's: "it excited her vanity, and she began to consider her
triumph over a woman so superior to her in all respects, as somewhat extremely glorious to her."[71] Perversely, this displacement
mirrors Adelaide's earlier one of the Marquis in the Countess's
vision.

Hortensia yields to the Marquis, not to love but to domin-
eer. Never infatuated, she escapes the fate of the amorous woman
and, capricious and exacting, she remains tyrant rather than slave
to her lover, even after her "fall." Caught in the horrible trap he
had himself laid, the Marquis is miserable, obsessed with a
woman he dislikes and haunted by his love for the wife he cannot approach. When inevitably the Countess learns she is betrayed by a friend as she had betrayed a friend, abandoned by a
husband who had abandoned another for her, she follows Adelaide into sickness and melancholy. So deep is her grief that, like
many other heroines of her age, she attempts suicide. But, unlike
most of them, she succeeds. Her death punishes the Marquis and
reminds him of the waste of Adelaide. Together the two women
haunt his mind and poison all his remaining days. For once
women in fiction are left to avenge themselves, and no cousin or
brother steps in to stab the betrayer.[72]

In *The Marquis de Cressy* female friendship is treated with
the high seriousness usually confined to love. A grave matter, its
betrayal leads to disaster and death. Adelaide and the Countess
owe a trust to each other that must not be slighted. They are
forced into danger when they enter as pawns into a male game.
The relationship of the Countess and Hortensia is the nemesis of
the broken friendship between the Countess and Adelaide, which

71. Ibid., p. 115.
72. In *The Novels of Mme Riccoboni* (Chapel Hill: North Carolina Studies in the
Romance Languages and Literature, 1976), Joan Hinde Stewart notes that the Countess is
one of the earliest fictional characters to kill herself for love, preceding Goethe's *Werther*
by sixteen years. The episode shocked many readers and horrified Mme de Genlis, who
blamed Riccoboni for making suicide interesting, p. 108.

it both mocks and distorts, and into it the man enters as pawn. The first relationships are thus reversed; friends become rivals and the seducing male becomes the cruelly seduced.

But the safest relationship in the novel is neither mocked nor reversed; it remains to the end to unite the author and the women she creates. Like Austen in *Mansfield Park,* Riccoboni sustains her heroine, arguing for her when appearances are awry; unlike Austen, however, she supports her in her role of friend. When Hortensia seems to choose a lover over a friend, the author angrily responds that in her choice she forgets the "tenderness and generosity of a friend, to indulge the momentary inclination of a lover—What a difference! What a loss! Whatever we may think in the delirium of passion, a lover is not worth a friend." [73] It is a heavy but perhaps just comment in this fictional world of sexual betrayals and death.

Not satisfied with supporting her heroine so strenuously, the author even interrupts her tale to champion her most odious creation when she sees her worsted by a man. The neurotically nasty Hortensia is finally renounced by her lover and the author leaps to defend her:

> [Hortensia] had failed in what she owed to gratitude, to friendship, to duty, and to herself: But had M de Cressy done her no injury? Is nothing due to a woman one has loved, or pretended to love? With whatever levity the men may treat this subject, however common the contemptible custom of abusing the fondness and credulity of a woman, let a man of honour interrogate himself; let him consult truth and nature, and then let him say if there is any occasion upon which treachery and deceit can be permitted; if he has any right to call forth in our heart that latent sentiment which perhaps might have continued for ever undiscovered there, had he not animated it by his officious ardours, to fill the soul of her with sorrow afterwards, who partook his desires only to gratify them, and yielded only to make him happy. [74]

In a fine display of female solidarity, the author transforms even the horrifying Hortensia into a social victim.

73. *The History of the Marquis de Cressy,* p. 116.
74. Ibid., p. 145–46.

Social friendship is a powerful tie in eighteenth-century fiction. As in political friendship, the partners act to benefit and sustain each other and they avoid frittering away all their good will in sentimental attitudes. Women unite in social friendship to ease each other's lives. Friends help lonely women tolerate and withstand their families or move painlessly from maid to wife. When soothing attentions are not enough, they may comfort with their own discomfort.

Yet social friends do not aim radically to change lives. Commonplace or heroic, they do not influence society and its patriarchal ways, nor do they consider why there is need of female comfort. Apparently the most equal, supportive, and stable of all the female alliances, social friendship must be judged finally an ointment for the social wounding of women, a safety valve for patriarchy.

It is fitting that Mme de Riccoboni end the survey of eighteenth-century authors, for she is representative of countless others in her treatment of friendship. More clearly than most, her works show how female relationships can nudge the romantic from center stage, while remaining incidental to the plot. At the same time her books summarize the categories of friendship, redefining and refreshing them where stagnant. Merging sentimental and social friendship in their pictures of the exemplary in action, they add the manipulative kind when women use and abuse each other. Lastly her novels exhibit political friendship when the Countess dies alone by her own hand; through this act she becomes sister or step-sister not only to Delphine and Clarissa, but to Burney's Elinor and Wollstonecraft's Maria as well, binding them all in an intertextual alliance.

CHAPTER SEVEN

The Biographical Context

IN 1773, HESTER Mulso Chapone published a series of letters to a young girl in which she advised her to select and attach to herself for life a worthy female friend. It should, Mrs. Chapone urged, be a serious tie between two devoted and faithful hearts, "desirous to perpetuate their society beyond the grave." [1] In her youth this same Mrs. Chapone had been a close friend of Samuel Richardson, the creator of two of the century's most famous fictional friends, Clarissa Harlowe and Anna Howe; it was to these creations that the devoted and faithful Ladies of Llangollen turned for inspiration before they scandalized Britain by eloping together into sentimental friendship. [2] Perhaps when the young Mary Wollstonecraft yearned for a life with her friend Fanny Blood, she had the Ladies partly in mind, for just before their elopement to Wales in 1778 she arrived there by a very different route. Led by an improvident father, she had suffered her first parting from her new soul-mate; as the Ladies started their long years together, she was dreaming passionately of a life without fathers or husbands.

Female friendship was a fascinating and inspiring theme in the eighteenth century. It was an historical phenomenon, fed by and feeding into fiction, expressing itself sometimes in companionable lives but most often in letters. In these it employed the

1. Hester Mulso Chapone, *Letters on the improvement of the mind* (London: J. Walker, 1778), p. 146.
2. For a full account of these celebrated female friends, see Elizabeth Mavor, *The Ladies of Llangollen* (Harmondsworth: Penguin Books, 1974).

language and dramatics of love, conveying friendly raptures and scenes of friendly display. When the women both lived together and wrote feelingly, the friendship might seem lesbian; sometimes no doubt it was, but not always, for the convention by mid-century was ecstasy—in friendship, family, or love. Yet, as we have seen, the times were not ignorant of lesbianism and its suspicion was met sometimes with horrified interest and sometimes with surprising nonchalance—the primary obsession was with physical virginity. As in later ages, a stereotype went with the suspicion, which the Ladies of Llangollen themselves exemplify.

After the two women had lived together for many years, the *General Evening Post* noticed them in a piece entitled *Extraordinary Female Affection,* hinting at a relationship beyond sentiment: "Miss Butler is tall and masculine," it reported. "She wears always a riding habit, hangs her hat with the air of a sportsman in the hall, and appears in all respects as a young man, if we except the petticoats which she still retains." Miss Ponsonby, "on the contrary, is polite and effeminate, fair and beautiful."[3] Yet at the time, Miss Butler was fifty-one, short and rather stout; clearly her portrait has been invaded by a lesbian cliché, based on a heterosexual model.

But such hints are the exception and, although Mrs. Thrale might snigger that " 'tis now grown common to suspect Impossibilities—(such I think 'em) whenever two Ladies live too much together,"[4] it was not altogether so, and female friendship represented for most women simply a rapturous sentimental union, springing perhaps from fear of male aggression or neglect but fed primarily by yearning for a partner in sensibility, a confidante in literature. The Ladies of Llangollen came together to admire Richardson; Mary Wollstonecraft revealed her love by imitating her friend's prose style.

Women wrote novels out of their mental image of friendship, an image deriving from past literature and their own experience.

3. Ibid., p. 74.
4. *Thraliana: The Diary of Mrs. Hester Lynch Thrale 1776–1809,* ed. Katherine C. Balderston (Oxford: Clarendon Press, 1942), p. 949.

THE BIOGRAPHICAL CONTEXT

If we can neither know the impact of the literature on them nor thoroughly appreciate their experience, we can at least learn something of their lives. So I am ending this study of literary relationships with brief speculative sketches of experienced friendships: of Mary Wollstonecraft with Fanny Blood, of Mme de Staël with Mme Récamier, and of Jane Austen with her sisters and nieces.

What, then, of the male authors? For strangely in this century the most powerful female friendships in literature were created by men—Clarissa and Anna Howe in Richardson's *Clarissa* and Julie and Claire in Rousseau's *Julie* for example. Such women sprang of course from great imaginative sympathy, but sometimes too they grew from male obsession, voyeuristic and fearful pleasure in contemplating an alliance of others. In Diderot, there seems such an obsession, both in his fiction, *The Nun,* and in his life, when he winced at his own thoughts on his beloved Sophie Volland. Rousseau and the Marquis de Sade are more opaque, usually indifferent to actual friends, and yet they seem to connect women imaginatively in unholy alliances. For Richardson, the most private of public men, there is no insistent image to investigate, for his avuncular and flirtatious letters to a host of women are little concerned with women friends. But we can at least glance at the rich milieu of friendships he inhabited.[5]

Before beginning, however, we must consider the distinction between lives and fiction, and note the material from which the lives are deduced. Inevitably the biographical sketches will be made in the shadow of the novels, but author and work should, finally, be kept separate in their analyses. The links even between such close associates as Mary Wollstonecraft and her heroine Mary should always be loose and speculative. If tightened, they threaten to simplify both living model and fictional character.

The authors discussed can be classified according to the biographical material they left and ranked by reticence. The sketches begin and end with unknowables—authors who have hidden

5. Although I have discussed *Fanny Hill,* I have omitted considering John Cleland; there is insufficient data to form any clear conception of his life and character.

themselves from their public or have avoided creating a clear self-image: Richardson and Austen wrote no confessions and never bared their souls in public letters, and neither really invites speculation. They are reticent through omission or abundance and their novels and lives do not insistently impinge on each other.

They are followed by Diderot, Sade, and Staël, whose letters more clearly create a knowable self, a consistent attitude. But this self must be sought in a welter of unorganized details and must in a way be imposed by the reader who selects. The neurosis in the novels which the authors wrote may sometimes seem close to the revelation of the personal letters, but in fiction it is always an organized neurosis. Similarly, although the conventions of female friendship in letters and in the novel occasionally coincide, fiction endows these conventions with significance in the text and uses them to structure the narrative. In her letters Staël may see herself and her friend Juliette Récamier as one; in fiction this cliché of friendship may be the psychological message of the work or it may join two systems within the plot.

Finally there are Rousseau and Wollstonecraft, both busy with revelation, both demanding a public response to the artifacts of their lives. In them especially, the border of fiction and biography, cleaner in Richardson and Austen, less so in Staël, Sade, and Diderot, almost dissolves. Rousseau created an autobiography and on his wife's behalf William Godwin wrote a biography that approaches it by enshrining a personality, a self's view of itself. In a century which developed the novel and autobiography, and took pains to confuse the two, inevitably both genres seem fiction. And indeed Rousseau's *Confessions* smacks of the novel with its plot, order, and pervasive personality. Yet it differs too, for it requires what Philippe Lejeune has called the autobiographical pact—a promise to the reader that, however falsified the facts, the narrator and protagonist are one.[6] Godwin's *Memoirs* mediates the female creation of self through a male narrator but, if it separates narrator and protagonist, it ensures that both

6. Philippe Lejeune, *L'Autobiographie en France* (Paris: Armand Colin, 1971), p. 24.

act the autobiographer; like the *Confessions,* the *Memoirs* of Wollstonecraft is intended as the record of an actual life and it exists to justify its subject.

Samuel Richardson

Samuel Richardson moved among a plethora of female friends. A successful printer until 1740, at the age of fifty-one he startled London with his first novel, *Pamela, or Virtue Rewarded,* a series of letters which captured the very accents of the smart young servant girl. After its publication he corresponded avidly with women about his own relationship with them and about his novels. The popular picture of Richardson, as he was aware, placed him at the center of a group of admiring and rather trivial ladies. But he knew their worth and in 1753 he wrote to a Dutch friend: "I am envied Sir, for the Favour I stand in with near a Score of very admirable Women, some of them of Condition; all of them such as would do Credit to their Sex, and to the Commonwealth of Letters, did not their Modesty with-hold them from appearing in it." And he exemplified, for in 1750 he composed a list of thirty-six superior women—"almost all of them of my intimate Acquaintances," he added with disarming vanity.[7] They appear as initials, but many can be translated; when they are, it is clear he spoke justly of the ability of his female acquaintances, for many were or would be outstanding women of letters. They were also intense and loyal friends to other women.

There were, for example, groups and pairs of friends often known as Bluestockings—intellectual, literary ladies who conversed much on high matters and wrote voluminously to each other. Susanna Highmore, one of Richardson's "particular favourites," patiently loved a young man of whom her parents

7. T. C. Duncan and Ben D. Kimpel, *Samuel Richardson: A Biography* (Oxford: Clarendon Press, 1971), pp. 537 and 343. Other information on Richardson's life comes from Alan Dugald McKillop's *Samuel Richardson: Printer and Novelist* (1936; Whitstable, Kent: Shoe String Press, 1960).

disapproved; she was consoled poetically in her long waiting by a friend, Hester Mulso (later Mrs. Chapone of the educational letters), a cultivated lady who was also the friend of Elizabeth Carter, a prodigy of learning and the celebrated translator of the Greek poet Epictetus. Despising men, Elizabeth Carter was clearly drawn to women, her most intimate friend being the pious and aristocratic Catherine Talbot, of whom she wrote enthusiastically, "Miss Talbot is absolutely my passion; I think of her all day, dream of her all night, and one way or other introduce her into every subject I talk of."[8] And there are others in the group, all connected by their zest for literature, their acute sensibility, their devotion to an ideal of female friendship. All were correspondents and annotators of Richardson.

Another keen correspondent of Richardson was the attractive Mary Granville Delany, whose own experience—being forced as a young girl to marry a disagreeable elderly man for whom she felt "an invincible aversion"—so closely paralleled Clarissa's intended fate. Mrs. Delany formed the center of a second web of sensitive and intellectual friends, which included Ann Donnellan, to whom she was won when she saw her devotion to another woman, and Sarah Kirkham, an acquaintance since childhood. As a young girl, Sarah Kirkham "had an uncommon genius and intrepid spirit," reports Mrs. Delany, "which though really innocent, alarmed my father, and made him uneasy at my great attachment to her."[9] In later years Sarah became exceedingly respectable, but she gave a glimpse of her earlier risqué character when she dared once to prefer the sprightly Anna Howe to the saintly Clarissa among Richardson's characters.

The main friendship of Richardson's later literary years was with the whimsical Lady Bradshaigh, whom he met in 1750 after much deliberate and fanciful delay, heightened by the lady's penchant for park assignations and humorous disguise. Richardson corresponded with her assiduously, greatly enjoying the zest

8. *A Series of Letters between Mrs. Elizabeth Carter and Miss Catherine Talbot, from the year 1741 to 1770* (London: F. C. and J. Rivington, 1809), I, 2.

9. *The Autobiography and Correspondence of Mary Granville, Mrs. Delany*, ed. Lady Llanover (London: Richard Bentley, 1861), I, 15–16.

of her style. "I love to argue with your Ladiship, and hardly with any-body else," he confessed.[10] Vital and outspoken like Anna Howe in *Clarissa,* Lady Bradshaigh often succumbed to the devilish wit and style of Lovelace, and was fascinated in a way Richardson always dreaded his readers would be. By the end of the volumes, however, she was redeemed and with Anna Howe she came to see that a Clarissa could never have been happy with a Lovelace. Yet she was unregenerate in wishing for another ending of the book, one in which the peerless heroine would not die but merely approach death. She would then recover and live on unmarried, as advisor and close friend of the married Anna. It is not the same but it comes close to Anna's own repeated wish in the novel: that she might live in retirement and friendship with Clarissa.

Richardson was surrounded by women friends. But mostly they came in later years—during and after the writing of *Clarissa.* Of his early days, the formative period of his life, there is little record, except for one hazy anecdote. His daughter remembered her father speaking often of a wild young man he knew in his youth, a man involved with two women, one of whom received his proposal but rejected it when he threw her uncle downstairs. Dismissed, he went abroad and married a foreigner. In the meantime, the first lady repented her rejection and followed him. Reencountering her, he was unwilling to offend by telling her of his marriage; so he married her as well. Soon after, he died in battle, neatly extricating himself from his kindly bigamy; according to Richardson's daughter, the two women "passed the remainder of their lives together, and loved as sisters."[11]

Denis Diderot

Richardson remains unknowable. His world can be glimpsed but his own attitudes are hidden in his mass of writing, his mounds

10. *Samuel Richardson,* p. 234.
11. Ibid., pp. 12–13.

of letters. It is very different with Denis Diderot, whose novel *The Nun* is rooted in incident and, in its strange outward portrayal of erotic female love, paralleled by the haunting picture of his private letters.

Historically, this story of an unwilling nun grew from a practical joke played by Diderot on his friend, the Marquis de Croismare. In 1758 Croismare had concerned himself with a nun wishing to leave her convent. He intervened unsuccessfully and the nun, Marguerite Delamarre, was forced to remain cloistered until her death. A few months later when Croismare decided to retire to the country, Diderot and his friends planned to lure him back to Paris and their society by sending a series of letters purporting to come from a nun who had escaped from her convent. The letters were written by Diderot. Although Croismare did not return to Paris, he grew deeply involved in the woman's plight—so deeply indeed that Diderot was obliged finally to kill her off, to release both himself and his friend from their predicament. Out of the incident *The Nun* was created.

But there is another context. Diderot created his heroine's encounter with the lesbian Superior during the fall of 1760. At the time he was much involved with Sophie Volland, to whom he wrote constantly. From these letters emerges his fear of an erotic involvement between his beloved Sophie and her married sister, Madame Le Gendre.[12] The two women live now only in Diderot's prose, which provides a poignant record of male obsession with female friendship.[13]

Diderot fell in love with Sophie Volland when she was an unmarried woman of about forty and he a married man a few years her senior. The relationship endured for the remainder of their lives, intimate, intellectual, and probably physical. Its memorial is a brilliant series of letters written by Diderot during their many separations. In these he shows himself intrigued by all

12. For a full account of Diderot's relationship with Sophie Volland, see Arthur M. Wilson's *Diderot* and Georges May's *Diderot et "La Religieuse"*.

13. No letters of Sophie Volland are extant and the available correspondence of Diderot represents only a fragment of his output of over 500 letters to her.

the female members of her family, but retaining for Mme Le Gendre a special mixture of affection and mistrust. For a part of each year, Sophie Volland went to the country, leaving Diderot desolated by the sudden absence. During one of these he conceived the idea of an erotic and overly intimate relationship between the two sisters, coming between himself and his beloved.

His obsession leaps from the letters of this period. By 1759 he is already warning Sophie Volland not to look too tenderly upon her sister or to kiss her often lest when he comes to her again he should find traces of earlier kisses on her lips. By 1760 his jealousy is rampant and, when Sophie Volland goes to the country once more, she is followed by long letters of obsessive reproach:

> Mme Le Gendre is or will be constantly with you. I have become so extravagant, so unjust, so jealous; you say so much good about her; you suffer so impatiently that one notices some fault . . . I dare not finish! I am ashamed of what is passing in myself; but I do not know how to prevent it. Your mother pretends that your sister loves pleasant women, and it is sure that she loves you; and then that nun whom she liked so much; and then that tender and voluptuous manner with which she sometimes leant on you; and then those fingers especially pressed between yours! Goodbye! I am mad.[14]

Three weeks later he is again plucking the same painful string:

> Tell Mme Le Gendre . . . , tell her that you love me to madness, and you will see that the little lie will make her go pale . . . And I will not hate her.[15]

One can only conjecture how much of this obsession informs the portrait of the lesbian Superior of *The Nun*, but in one letter the real woman and the novel are contigious: "My dear," Diderot wrote to Sophie Volland in 1760, "do not praise your sister too much, I beg you, it would be bad for me; I do not know why,

14. *Lettres à Sophie Volland*, ed. André Babelon, 2nd ed. (Paris: Gallimard, 1938), I, 112.
15. Ibid., I, 131.

but it is so. I have passed Saturday putting my desk in order. I have brought along *The Nun*. . . ."[16]

In his letters Diderot does not try to empathize with erotic female friendship, presenting it voyeuristically as male obsession. Furtively he watches Mme Le Gendre, hoping to catch her in the voluptuous gesture or the stray tender look. Unconcerned with the psychology of a woman in love, he is interested only in physical effects, the trace of a kiss, the pallor of jealousy. For it is through these signs alone that he understands the passion. Love between women becomes a male fear, a secretive physical treachery.

Jean-Jacques Rousseau

In the *Confessions* Rousseau vividly records his version of how he composed *Julie*. The book fed on its author's life and in turn fed the life. Yet the *Confessions* contains no certain clue to one of the novel's most dominant pairs, the female friends Julie and Claire, and it rarely touches on female friendship. Women are isolated in Rousseau's world, and the reader is left to bring them together.

The novel *Julie* centers on Julie; so any probing must start with the Countess d'Houdetot, whom Rousseau associated with her. A woman of nearly thirty, the Countess dramatically entered his life at a moment when he thought himself too old for love. Her entry influenced the emotion of *Julie,* but *Julie* just as certainly provoked her entry.

In April 1756, Rousseau, with his lifelong companion Thérèse and her mother, moved into a small cottage on the estate of the wealthy Mme d'Épinay. His retreat to the country was much mocked by his friends, including Diderot, who warned him he would be unable to stand the rustic isolation after the Parisian

16. Ibid., I, 106.

bustle.[17] And indeed he was lonely—even more so when Mme d'Épinay and her friends arrived at the nearby château. He felt excluded from their shifting liaisons and constrained by their style. To compensate he rambled round the countryside, open to the influence of nature and the fine summer, and amongst his reveries he found himself thinking more and more of the women of his youth, his pretty music pupils. Soon he saw himself "surrounded by a seraglio of houris," and he, an austere man of forty-five, became once more "the love sick swain."

> The impossibility of attaining the real persons precipitated me into the land of chimeras; and seeing nothing that existed worthy of my exalted feelings, I fostered them in an ideal world which my creative imagination soon peopled with beings after my own heart. . . . Altogether ignoring the human race, I created for myself societies of perfect creatures celestial in their virtue and in their beauty, and of reliable, tender, and faithful friends such as I had never found here below.[18]

But Rousseau could not ignore the human race for long:

> At the height of my reveries I received a visit from Mme d'Houdetot. . . . This visit had somewhat the appearance of the beginning of a romance . . . she arrived at the Hermitage in a pair of boots, making the air ring with her laughter in which I joined when I saw her coming. . . . It was late and she did not stay long; but our meeting was so gay that she was quite delighted and seemed inclined to come again. She did not carry out her intention, however, till the next year.[19]

During the winter Rousseau worked on *Julie,* taking great pleasure in copying out his work onto the "finest gilt-edged

17. As Jean Guéhenno points out, the mockery may also have derived from a feeling that Rousseau was deserting his friends, for he left them just as the controversial 5th volume of the *Encyclopedia* was due out. In addition he seemed to be opting for dependence at a time when they were living by their pens. See *Jean-Jacques Rousseau* (Paris: Gallimard, 1962), I, 325.

18. *The Confessions of Jean-Jacques Rousseau,* trans. J. M. Cohen, p. 398.

19. Ibid., p. 402.

paper, with blue and silver sand to dry the ink," paper fit for the two friends he had already singled out—"I could not find anything courtly and elegant enough for my charming girls." But in the spring his work was interrupted by another visit of Mme d'Houdetot: "On this occasion she came on horseback, in man's clothes. Although I am not very fond of such masquerades, the air of romance about this one charmed me, and this time it was love." Like Julie, Mme d'Houdetot—whom he soon came to call by the private name of Sophie—was not surprisingly beautiful—she was pockmarked and her eyes were too round—but she had Julie's ability to attract through her person and character. On the latter Rousseau is as eloquent as he made his fictional lover: "As for her character, it was angelic; its foundation was a gentleness of soul, but it was a combination of every virtue except prudence and strength."[20]

The connection was as inevitable as it was desired:

> I was intoxicated with love that lacked an object. My intoxication enchanted my eyes, my object became identified with her, I saw my Julie in Mme d'Houdetot, and soon I saw only Mme d'Houdetot, but endowed with all the perfections with which I had just embellished the idol of my heart. To complete my undoing, she talked to me of Saint-Lambert like a passionate lover. How contagious is the power of love! As I listened, as I felt myself beside her, I was seized with a delicious trembling that I had never experienced beside any other woman. As she spoke I felt myself moved; I imagined that I was only sympathizing with her feelings, when really I was beginning to feel as she did. I swallowed the poisoned cup in long draughts, and at first only tasted its sweetness. In the end, unbeknown to us both, she inspired me with all the emotion for herself that she expressed for her lover. Alas, it was late in the day, and it was cruel indeed to be consumed by a passion as strong as it was unfortunate for a woman whose heart was full of love for another![21]

20. Ibid., pp. 408–9.
21. Ibid., p. 410. Although in the *Confessions*, Rousseau depicts his relationship with Mme d'Houdetot as a titillating idyl in which both were restrained by the imagined presence of Saint-Lambert, a surviving copy of a letter and the draft of another suggest a

But was it unfortunate? Several times in the *Confessions* Rousseau showed that he enjoyed worshipping rather than loving a woman, desiring rather than consummating desire. Of an earlier love he wrote "none of the feelings I have had from the possession of women have been equal to those two minutes spent at her feet without even the courage to touch her dress." [22]

In addition Rousseau showed himself a voyeur in love. When a young man, he had derived much pleasure from the close association of himself, Mme de Warens, and Claude Anet. With "Sophie" and her lover, Saint-Lambert, he may well have wished to repeat his pleasure. In 1757 he wrote to Saint-Lambert, "Yes, my children, be for ever united; there is no other soul like yours, and you deserve to love each other until death. It is pleasant for me to be a third member in such a tender friendship." [23] Certainly Rousseau, like his hero, seems to have enjoyed both loving and watching love, regarding his beloved as part of himself and as part of another. This joy is the hero Saint-Preux's when he returns to Clarens to watch Julie as the wife of Wolmar.

But Mme d'Houdetot was not the only woman who bothered him that spring. Her sister-in-law, Mme d'Épinay, was Rousseau's landlady and patron, and according to the *Confessions* she figured largely in his life. On her first introduction he described her as "pleasant, witty, and talented" and he seems to have enjoyed her company. In the country, however, Mme d'Épinay grew more menacing. Kind and unsparing to her friends, she required kindness and devotion in return, and Rous-

less platonic relationship. See Guéhenno, I, 362. There has been much debate over the influence of Mme d'Houdetot on the novel. In *Rousseau: l'homme et l'oeuvre* Daniel Mornet suggests that it may be a cause of the change from erotic to moral themes from the first to the second part, since Rousseau might have desired to atone for his guilty love of his friend's mistress. F. C. Green, however, shows that Rousseau was well advanced in his novel before his passion for Mme d'Houdetot truly began, *Jean-Jacques Rousseau* (Cambridge: Cambridge University Press, 1955), p. 189.

22. *Confessions*, p. 80.
23. *Correspondance générale*, ed. T. Doufour (Paris: A. Colin, 1924–34), III, 153. Ronald Grimsley points out how passionate Rousseau's ideal of friendship was at this time. *Jean-Jacques Rousseau: A Study in Self-Awareness*, p. 89. See, for example, his eulogy on friendship in *Correspondance générale*, p. 232.

seau found he must be eternally on call: "I realized that I had hung a chain round my neck, and that only friendship had so far prevented me from feeling its weight," he lamented. He disliked their frequent meetings partly because he wished to conserve his time and partly because he felt uneasy in their intercourse:

> I dared not talk of literature since I was not a competent judge of it, or of gallantry since I was too timid and feared to be laughed at as an old beau, more than I feared death. Besides, the idea never occurred to me in Mme d'Épinay's company; not that I felt any repugnance for her; on the contrary I probably loved her too well as a friend to be able to do so as a lover.[24]

It is odd to record for posterity an idea that never occurred to him before the lady in question.

Mme d'Épinay is intimately connected with *Julie*. Accounts of her are juxtaposed so often with details of the new novel that the two seem rarely distant in Rousseau's mind. In the *Confessions*, for example, he described his copying out of the first two parts of *Julie* on beautiful paper, making an aesthetic object of his novel. Next to this he recorded the gift from Mme d'Épinay of an under petticoat of flannel "which she informed me she had worn, and out of which she wanted me to make myself a waist-coat"; the action moved him so deeply that he made an aesthetic moment of it, enshrining it in the same way as his novel: "This mark of more than friendly attention seemed to me so tender—it was as if she had stripped herself to clothe me—that in my emotion I kissed the note and the petticoat twenty times in tears."[25]

Rousseau has shadowed Mme d'Épinay in so much hysteria and obsession that it is difficult to see her clearly, to separate, for example, her ordinary jealousy from the extraordinary persecution with which he credits her; but certainly she did not look kindly on the ecstatic rambles of her protegé and relative. Whether or not she tried to suborn Thérèse to tamper with the

24. *Confessions*, pp. 382–83.
25. Ibid., pp. 407.

correspondence of Rousseau and his beloved, he was convinced that she had. He came to fear her telescopic and menacing regard, her secret vindictiveness.[26]

In this stormy phase of their relationship, when Rousseau suspected Mme d'Épinay's motives, convinced she was betraying him to Sophie's lover, he contrasts his own male transparency with her cruel female obliquity:

> Throughout the course of my life . . . my heart has been as transparent as crystal, and incapable of concealing for so much as a moment the least lively feeling which has taken refuge in it. . . . Women have all the arts of concealing their anger, especially when it is strong. Mme d'Épinay, a violent but deliberate woman, possess this power to an eminent degree.[27]

Yet her actions are hardly opaque. Showering affronts on her sister-in-law, she redoubled her attentions to Rousseau "and almost made me advances." Recriminating letters were followed by tearful reunions until neither could stand it any longer. Rousseau was dismissed from Mme d'Épinay and in time from his Sophie, and was left to wonder at the duplicity and opacity of woman. The "ideal world" was darkened and the friendship of his novel may have been dimmed in sympathy.

In his life, Rousseau inclined much to triangles, but they were male ones, two or three of their points invariably being men.[28] Perhaps this inclination derived from the death of his mother shortly after he was born, which led him to expiate an assumed guilt by constantly sacrificing and humiliating himself be-

---

26. A very different version of the relationship between Rousseau and Mme d'Épinay occurs in the memoirs of Mme d'Épinay; yet Rousseau may not have been entirely wrong in his account, for Mme d'Épinay and her friends seem to have assiduously changed evidence to support their version. For the history of the Épinay memoirs, see George Roth's *Les Pseudo-mémoires de Madame d'Épinay: Histoire de Madame de Montbrillant* (Paris: Gallimard, 1951), I, xiii–xiv.

27. *Confessions*, pp. 415–16.

28. For a discussion of Rousseau's triangular relationships, see Van Laere, *Une Lecture du temps dans "La Nouvelle Héloïse,"* p. 40, and Grimsley, *Jean-Jacques Rousseau*, p. 112.

fore another male, another bereaved father.[29] It was certainly the pattern of his youth with Madame Warens and Claude Anet. But when two women inhabited his mind—however he might ignore their interaction—a predominantly female triangle was inevitably formed; in this he could not be gratifyingly superfluous. When he loved his Sophie, the *Confessions* suggests, he shrank from an advance of his patron Mme d'Épinay far more than a repulse from his rival Saint-Lambert. Again, he feared Mme d'Épinay for her opaque and secretive nature—a characteristic with which he quickly endowed all women. When the omniscient, man-mastering woman combined with the female triangle, a terrifying configuration was formed, catching him in a fearful, unwanted structure of desire.

The Marquis de Sade

The Marquis de Sade desired a variety of women and he loved them variously. After his orgies the women he hired were left bruised and lacerated and, on one famous occasion, poisoned by aphrodisiacs. Yet he could also be romantically loyal, and the last twenty-four years of his life were passed in placid domesticity with a woman so faithfully fond that she followed him to prison and asylum. While living thus unsensationally, the prerevolutionary orgies far behind him, Sade wrote his infamous work *Juliette.* In it he describes with terrifying detail a savage world of apparent sexual and moral chaos.

If this savagery seems at odds with Sade's sexual and social docility at the time, his past experience, both active and passive, accords well with it and was certainly cruel enough to inspire it. He had just suffered decades of imprisonment, first under the Old Regime and then under the revolutionary dispensation,

29. René Laforgue advances the argument in *Psychopathologie de l'échec* (Paris: Payot, 1950), pp. 97–120. Pierre Burgelin discusses Rousseau's desire for humiliation in *La Philosophie de l'existence de J.-J. Rousseau* (Paris: Presses Universitaires de France, 1952), p. 383.

and in his last prison cell overlooking the guillotine, he had witnessed 1,800 deaths in the cause of the new virtue.[30] In addition, the ferocious female characters of *Juliette* parallel Sade's long-standing obsessions with particular women, fostered no doubt in the isolation of the prison years. Above all his ire was turned onto his mother-in-law, Mme de Montreuil, in whose family he could find the contrasting types—the loyal wife and the savage vampire—who haunted his imagination. From his experiences he may have constructed the feminine bonds and alliances that cruelly darken his novels.

As a young man in the 1760s, Sade fell in love with a young lady who returned his sexual and sentimental affection. Yet he meekly married according to his family's wishes the wealthy Renée-Pélagie de Montreuil, the daughter of the President and Mme de Montreuil. In every respect Renée-Pélagie was the wifely woman whom Sade's novels curse and torment. Not only did she tolerate her husband's bizarre sexual escapades but she toiled for his escape after they landed him in jail. When he took his mistress to his ancestral castle of La Coste, passing her off as his wife, Renée-Pélagie still stood by him, as she did again when he turned his amorous attention to her sister, Anne-Prospère.

And Sade no doubt in part returned his wife's affection. He included her in many of his theatrical exploits and during his long years in prison she frequently formed his only link with the outside world. Although he mostly saw in her the victimized wife, subservient to his pleasure, he could not thoroughly reduce her in his imagination; shut up in his cell, he was haunted with fear that she was consoling herself with a lesbian affair. By this relationship excluding the male, he was as horrified and fascinated as Diderot before him. To Renée-Pélagie, Sade was then strangely tied, both in his early manhood when he treated her perversely and in the early prison years when he combined contempt and fear. Only much later, after his decade in prison, did

30. A full account of Sade's life can be found in Gilbert Lely's *The Marquis de Sade: A Biography* (New York: Grove Press, 1961) and Donald Thomas' *The Marquis de Sade* (Boston: New York Graphic Society, 1976).

the two really repudiate each other. Her revenge is fitting on the writer who so often in his novels silenced the wifely woman for which she was the model; when Sade was taken from the Bastille she retrieved some of the fifteen volumes he was forced to abandon there—those she felt indecent she burned.

In her youth Renée-Pélagie was a stately woman, dark in eyes and hair, but her sister Anne-Prospère was fair-haired and blue-eyed. When Sade first met Anne-Prospère, she was still very much a child, but there was a mutual attraction. Indeed it was rumored that, after seeing her, Sade wished to alter the arrangement and marry her instead, but things had proceeded too far to allow so indelicate a switch. After the wedding to Renée-Pélagie in 1763, the attraction to his sister-in-law continued, and in a few years' time Sade was living with both women in his castle of La Coste. There he hired a troupe of actors to help him act out his bizarre fancies; in these theatrical entertainments both sisters are said to have participated. In his novels Sade's heroes especially relish incest, and multiple copulation is rendered more piquant when incestuous.

The peace of the seraglio of La Coste was disturbed by Sade's antics in Marseilles in 1772. On a visit there he had hired several prostitutes to engage in a variety of sexual acts, including sodomy, ostensibly punished by death at this time. Later several of the women were found poisoned with aphrodisiacs, and Sade and his valet Latour were charged with attempted murder and sodomy. Fearing arrest—quite rightly since he was sentenced to death in absentia—he and Latour fled to Savoy, leaving Renée-Pélagie to appeal his case in Marseilles. He took with him Anne-Prospère, who, onlookers reported, travelled as his wife.

Sade seems to have had an affection for both sisters and to have liked them especially together.[31] Perhaps he enjoyed con-

---

31. Richard Krafft-Ebing, the nineteenth century German author of *Psychopathia Sexualis,* considered the two sisters the inspiration of Sade's two great female creations, the virtuous and eternally submissive Justine and her sister, the evil and domineering Juliette. In this view, Renée-Pelagie appears as the meek and submissive victim, loyal in the face of incredible rebuffs; Anne-Prospère seems to have fascinated Sade sexually, while

trolling women who from their relationship might have allied against him but who served him abjectly instead. In prison he delighted in sending lubricious letters to the sisters, firmly joined now in his imagination.

The incestuous goings-on with the Montreuil daughters could not escape their mother. In prison and asylum Sade would feel women mainly through Mme de Montreuil, who looms large and fearsome from his letters. Initially Mme de Montreuil had welcomed her daughter's match with the aristocratic Sade, but as crime followed scandal, her enthusiasm waned and by the time she heard of a spurious wife at La Coste and of her other daughter's entanglement, she clearly felt the match a disappointment. For the sake of her family's honor, she paid for Sade's crimes, buying off the women he mistreated, but at the same time she relentlessly pursued the criminal. When Sade ruptured her family ties by taking Anne-Prospère to Savoy, she was outraged and swiftly organized his imprisonment there—while Renée-Pélagie worked assiduously to free him. In 1777 she again struck at him, this time more decisively. From then on until he was fifty, over thirteen years later, Sade was to know only six weeks of freedom.

In prison he consoled himself with writing and cursing the powerful woman who had conquered him; yet, when the Revolution came and the tables were turned, with Sade assuming power over the Montreuils, he either lost his enmity or enjoyed a perverse charity, for he let them go. Like the wifely woman, the masterful woman Mme de Montreuil also defeated him at last through the literary construct which paralleled her. In 1801 he was arrested for the final time, probably for publication of *Juliette*, his savage depiction of the powerful woman.

Sade was ambivalent toward women, at once loathing and exalting them. He regarded Mme de Montreuil as the embodiment of maternal female power, endowed with a mother's omnipo-

she showed herself increasingly interested as his reputation grew more sinister. Like Rousseau, who made the dark Sophie into the fair Julie, Sade reversed the coloring of his women: the fair Anne-Prospère became the dark Juliette and her dark sister the type of all meek, fair women.

tence.[32] According to Simone de Beauvoir, she became for Sade his fate, the abstract and universal justice which inevitably confronts individuals, however free they may feel. In her analysis, the vengeful Mme de Montreuil, who deflated Sade and forced him to languish in prison, defamed and dishonored him and made him doubt himself. She made him a victim. Yet for woman, the archetypal victim, Sade had nothing but horror; he despised the female genitalia and usually avoided vaginal intercourse. But, Beauvoir suggests, this very avoidance united Sade and woman, because in them he recognized his own female sexual nature and resented them for not being the men he really desired. Instead of being his complements, women became frightening and fascinating doubles.[33] The female combination of the Montreuil sisters earlier or of Mme de Montreuil and Renée-Pélagie in later years might then parallel his own relationship to his mother-in-law. The victim-wife he despised and yet relied on becomes his own displacement; the vampiric woman he applauded is sustained by the mother-in-law who, it is rumored, loved Sade while persistently tormenting him.

Mary Wollstonecraft

Richardson, Diderot, Rousseau, and Sade inevitably relate to women in heterosexual pairs and so see female friendship only from outside. They all deal with the other, the nonmale, and something of the power of their fictional friendships must derive from their alienated stance. Yet the powerful images they create—especially Richardson and Rousseau—dominated women writers and women friends throughout the century and, when such women wrote or came together, they often saw themselves

32. In his letters Sade wrote that he desired his mother-in-law to be his second mother, and the two women were associated in the cruel circumstance that he came to Paris when his mother had just died, only to be imprisoned by his mother-in-law.

33. *The Marquis de Sade: Must We Burn Sade?*, pp. 21–37. Support for Simone de Beauvoir's analysis comes from Georges Batailles, who sees Sade's language as that of the victim.

in Clarissa and Anna, Julie and Claire, creatures of the male imagination. Mary Wollstonecraft and Madame de Staël, in particular, were literary in friendship, clothing themselves in the characters they admired. Sade may have named his fictional Juliette in honor of Rousseau's Julie; life seems to have given Mme de Staël a real Juliette on the same principle.

Women friends of course inhabit a different milieu from heterosexual couples and male pairs; yet they cannot escape the conventions and constraints of their society and its literature, in which women are subordinate and men take them in rape or romantic love. Consequently the language of female friendship often seems borrowed from the literary raptures of men, and the hierarchical structure of the heterosexual couple presses against the literary friendship that opposes it. But the constraints are lighter in life than in literature; women authors, who left no truly successful image of female friendship in fiction, often made themselves into successful female friends.

Mary Wollstonecraft's novels, *Mary, A Fiction* and *The Wrongs of Woman: or, Maria,* seem to approach her life so closely that many biographers have confused them. The author herself must take the responsibility for much of this. In her first novel, *Mary, A Fiction,* published in 1786, she seems at pains to stress self-revelation; she entitled it *Mary* after herself, declared it was "drawn from nature" and in the preface lauded novels "where the soul of the author is exhibited."[34] Among these she no doubt meant hers to be placed. In the book we have a deficient mother and an inadequate friend. Her life as described by her husband William Godwin has both these characters.[35]

Wollstonecraft was not, Godwin wrote, "the favourite either of her father or mother." The father was a "despot" and the mother "the first, and most submissive of his subjects. The

34. *Mary, A Fiction*, p. 3.
35. *Memoirs of the Author of A Vindication of the Rights of Woman* (1798; New York: Garland Publishing, 1974), p. 7. The *Memoirs* is a frank, sympathetic view of Wollstonecraft. It is also a record of her view of her own life, since it is written largely from her recollection.

mother's partiality was fixed upon the eldest son."[36] The perception of this unkindness loomed large in the life of the rejected eldest daughter, and she was long in forgiving her family.

Wollstonecraft's image of her childhood with her improvident drunken father and spineless mother was unremittingly awful. Unrelieved by humor or sudden kindness, which must have been occasionally there, it is presented in a powerful image:

> Mary would often throw herself between the despot and his victim, with the purpose to receive upon her own person the blows that might be directed against her mother. She has even laid whole nights upon the landing-place near their chamber door, when, mistakenly, or with reason, she apprehended that her father might break out into paroxysms of violence.[37]

Like the heroines of both novels, the Wollstonecraft of Godwin's *Memoirs* passionately resented and desired her mother, in whom she saw both the horror of male despotism and the fascination of the passive female response. Although Mrs. Wollstonecraft raised six healthy children in an unhealthy age, Wollstonecraft regarded her as inept through and through, feckless and peevish. So she strenuously rejected the female image for herself and demanded strength instead—"Dolls and other amusements usually appropriated to female children, she held in contempt," Godwin declared—while yet she felt the lure of the feminine child.

Again like the novels, the *Memoirs* brings the daughter close to the mother only in death. The domestic chaos had been so trying that at nineteen the headstrong young woman had insisted on a kind of independence and had left as paid companion to a wealthy widow. When her mother neared death, however, she

36. Ibid., p. 7.
37. Ibid., pp. 9–10. The image suggests both the horrific situation and Rousseau's *Confessions,* for Rousseau, the man with whom Wollstonecraft admitted she was half in love, gave a similar powerful image from his childhood: "I remember once when my father was correcting him [Rousseau's brother] severely and angrily, throwing myself impetuously between them, and clasping my arms tightly around him. Thus I covered him with my body, and received the blows intended for him" (p. 21). A similar incident occurs with Julie and her parents in Rousseau's *Julie.*

was recalled to nurse her and she strenuously threw herself into the benevolent and responsible female role where alone the female stereotype and her own active desire seemed to touch. "Mary was assiduous in her attendance upon her mother," Godwin wrote.

But she wanted a reward. In both novels there is a final recognition between the two women, in which the mother asks forgiveness. In the *Memoirs* it is a little different. Although the mother was grateful at first, she quickly slipped into indifference, caring more for the absent son than for the present daughter. So Wollstonecraft was forced to make her own maternal image for herself: she drove herself into the weakness of her mother (as the fictional Mary did when nursing the dying Ann) and "by the time nature was exhausted in the parent, the daughter was qualified to assume her place, and become in turn herself a patient"; after the death she grew "eager and active to promote the welfare of every member of her family."[38] The mother's last words in life and fiction vary the same fragment—"A little patience, and all will be over!"—and are echoed by the fictional daughter. They haunted the real daughter for the rest of her days and a variation formed her own last written words. In death, fictional and actual, Wollstonecraft would approach the mother she so ambiguously despised in life.

When she was sixteen Wollstonecraft met Fanny Blood, who enters the *Memoirs* as a literary friend, the image of Goethe's heroine:

> The situation in which Mary was introduced to her, bore a resemblance to the first interview of Werter with Charlotte. . . . The first object that caught her sight, was a young woman of a slender and elegant form, and eighteen years of age, busily employed in feeding and managing some children, born of the same parents, but considerably inferior to her in age. The impression Mary received from this spectacle was indelible; and, before the interview was concluded, she had taken, in her heart, the vows of an eternal friendship.[39]

38. *Memoirs*, pp. 27–29.
39. Ibid., pp. 20–21.

Such an eternal relationship was bound to be a strain. Wollstonecraft gave all and demanded the same, while the ideal Fanny
Blood must never vary from the standard she embodied.

The ideal was exacting also to its creator. Fanny Blood had
the gentleness and feminine accomplishments—drawing, playing,
and elegant writing—that Wollstonecraft should have had if she
meant to please her mother, but she added, in her friend's view,
her own kind of intelligence. "She has a masculine understanding, and sound judgement, yet she has every feminine virtue," she later wrote of Fanny.[40] This attractive mixture was
formed in worse surroundings than the Wollstonecraft home; so
Fanny Blood became both a model and a reproach—a reproach
that would soon rebound on her as Wollstonecarft came to measure herself and her friend by other standards.

The first stage of the relationship was short, interrupted by
the Wollstonecrafts' last economic adventure in Wales. But it was
not long before the dream of a common life was partially fulfilled. After her mother's death she moved in with the Bloods and
tasted both close friendship and real poverty. The house was
drearily cramped and the family a sadder version of Wollstonecraft's own: "My mother used to sit at work, in summer,
from *four* in the morning till she could not see at night," Fanny
later wrote, "which with the assistance of one of her daughters
did not bring her more than half a guinea a week, and often not
quite that." And she added, "You may recollect that she [Woll-
stonecraft] was almost *blinded* and sick to death after a job we
did for Mrs. Bensley. . . ."[41] It is a long way even from the
skimping independence of the Ladies of Llangollen and far indeed from the affluence of the heiress Mary and her friend Ann in
Mary, A Fiction.

Inevitably closeness shifted the relationship. Initially, as
Godwin reports, Wollstonecraft had contemplated her friend
"with sentiments of inferiority and reverence." Now however the

40. *Shelley and his Circle,* ed. Kenneth Neill Cameron (Cambridge, Mass.: Harvard University Press, 1961), II, 966.

41. Quoted in Emily Sunstein's *A Different Face: The Life of Mary Wollstonecraft* (New York: Harper & Row, 1975), p. 73.

two "approached more nearly to a footing of equality."[42] In addition, Fanny Blood loved and was half-heartedly beloved by a young man called Hugh Skeys, afraid to ally himself with the impecunious Bloods but keeping Fanny always in suspense. Pining for him and weakening under the tuberculosis which was to kill her, she cannot have been quite the androgynous ideal and bosom companion Wollstonecraft willed her to be. "I am a little singular in my thoughts of love and friendship," she had written to an earlier friend, "I must have the first place or none."[43] And there may have been the kind of coldness which in fiction and life she allied to disappointed ideals. In *Mary, A Fiction,* the surface of the narrative is sometimes agitated, revealing the author's own self-pity below; when this happens Wollstonecraft often slips into a different tense—she does so when she describes Mary's sudden freezing of her friend:

> Very frequently has she ran to her with delight, and not perceiving any thing of the same kind in Ann's countenance, she has shrunk back; and, falling from one extreme into the other, instead of a warm greeting that was just slipping from her tongue, her expressions seemed to be dictated by the most chilling insensibility.[44]

Years later she wrote to her unfaithful lover in similar vein: "One thing you mistake in my character, and imagine that to be coldness which is just the contrary. For, when I am hurt by the person most dear to me, I must let out a whole torrent of emotions, in which tenderness would be uppermost, or stifle them altogether; and it appears to me almost a duty to stifle them, when I imagine *that I am treated with coldness.*"[45] Patterns like this are often longstanding and Fanny Blood, the failed ideal, may well have suffered from her friend's spurts of warmth and chill.

Soon the balance shifted even further. By now Woll-

42. *Memoirs* pp. 22 and 28.
43. *Collected Letters of Mary Wollstonecraft,* ed. Ralph M. Wardle (Ithaca: Cornell University Press, 1979), p. 60.
44. *Mary, A Fiction,* p. 16.
45. *A Wollstonecraft Anthology* (Bloomington: Indiana University Press, 1977), p. 238. Margaret George notes the parallel in her biography *One Woman's "Situation": A Study of Mary Wollstonecraft* (Urbana: University of Illinois Press, 1970), p. 44.

stonecraft had grown aware of her friend's failure of will, her feminine timidity, and it struck her forcefully in the midst of the drama of Eliza. Her sister Eliza had recently married and born a child. Depressed after the birth, she revolted from her husband and looked for comfort to Mary, whose response was overwhelming. Eliza should leave both baby and husband and flee to a female haven. It was a rash proposal, perhaps heroic, perhaps wrong-headed, an affront, as Wollstonecraft well knew, to the male world of marriage and all its conventions. But it succeeded. Unfortunately its audacious success paled beside the effort of supporting a dependent woman. To Fanny Blood she turned for comfort, suggesting she join them in their schemes of painting, sewing, or shopkeeping—the possibilities of women. But Fanny flinched from everything: "My health is so much impaired," she complained, "that I should only be a burthen on them."[46]

By the time Wollstonecraft had decided on a school, Fanny Blood had summoned the courage to join her, but her importance for her friend had diminished. Assuming his wife's disappointed, retrospective harshness, Godwin wrote:

> Fanny had originally been far before her in literary attainments; this disparity no longer existed. In whatever degree Mary might endeavour to free herself from the delusions of self-esteem, this period of observation upon her own mind and that of her friend, could not pass, without her perceiving that there were some essential characteristics of genius, which she possessed, and in which her friend was deficient. The principal of these was a firmness of mind an unconquerable greatness of soul, by which, after a short internal struggle, she was accustomed to rise above difficulties and suffering. Whatever Mary undertook, she perhaps in all instances accomplished; and, to her lofty spirit, scarcely any thing she desired, appeared hard to perform. Fanny, on the contrary, was a woman of a timid and irresolute nature, accustomed to yield to difficulties. . . .[47]

46. Quoted in Ralph Wardle's *Mary Wollstonecraft: A Critical Biography* (1951; Lincoln: University of Nebraska Press, 1967), p. 31.
47. *Memoirs*, pp. 37–38.

It is a strangely brutal judgement on a woman who had struggled against poverty and incompetence even more than Wollstonecraft herself and who was by this time deathly ill.

A softer phase followed. "I love most people when they are in adversity—for pity is one of my prevailing passions," Wollstonecraft wrote of herself.[48] And indeed, if Fanny Blood as tentative equal irritated, as object of compassion she was rivetting. Years later an acquaintance, Madeleine Schweitzer, described this intolerance with equals, this kindness with mental or social inferiors: "I was very fond of Mary Wollstonecraft, the author of *Rights of Woman,*" she wrote, "and should have liked to regard her with constant affection, but she was so intolerant that she repulsed those women who were not inclined to be subservient to her, whilst to her servants, her inferiors, and the wretched in general, she was gentle as an angel."[49]

The school was moderately successful—at least it kept the young women from penury. But Fanny Blood was deteriorating and Wollstonecraft was quite prepared to abandon everything to aid her. The procrastinating Skeys had finally proposed from Portugal, and, knowing that sun would benefit her friend, Wollstonecraft urged her to accept him. Indeed she may have pushed him into making the proposal in the first place.[50] In *Mary, A Fiction* the heroine herself takes her friend to a warmer clime; in real life the woman must attend the man. Early in 1785, having waited over a decade for her recalcitrant lover, Fanny Blood set sail for Portugal, leaving her friend more loving than ever. "True love is warmest when the object is absent," she wrote to Fanny Blood's brother.[51]

She was angry and depressed as well. Raging at Skeys for his long delay—he might "have spared Fanny many griefs the *scars* of which will *never* be obliterated"—she lamented her own deso-

48. *Collected Letters of Mary Wollstonecraft,* p. 92.
49. W. Clark Durant, *Supplement to Memoirs of Mary Wollstonecraft* (London: Constable, 1927), p. 247.
50. The suggestion is Wardle's in *Mary Wollstonecraft,* p. 38.
51. *Collected Letters of Mary Wollstonecraft,* p. 95.

lation—"My spirits are fled, and I am incapable of joy. . . . I have no creature to be unreserved to. . . . My heart—my affection cannot fix here and without some one to love This world is a desart to me."[52] When she heard Fanny was ill and about to be confined, she did not hesitate but set sail at once for Portugal. She arrived there to find her friend in labor; she died soon after in Wollstonecraft's arms.

Back in England she was haunted by Fanny Blood's death, which had so rapidly repeated her mother's. "I dreamt the other night I saw my poor Fanny," she wrote to Fanny's brother, "and she told me I should soon follow her . . . I want a friend I am now *alone*."[53] And toward the end of her life she would write rather stiltedly, "The grave has closed over a dear friend, the friend of my youth; still she is present with me, and I hear her soft voice warbling as I stray over the heath."[54] Two other tributes intervened. Her first child was named for Fanny, and she wrote *Mary, A Fiction* in memory of the bitter-sweet friendship.

After Fanny Blood's death, Wollstonecraft entered no other rapturous relationship with a woman. Something was exorcised with the novel, and the heir of the young Fanny Blood is not another woman but Gilbert Imlay, the male lover who refused like Fanny to be perfection and yet could never be pitied as she had been. So female friendship came to fulfill another need in Wollstonecraft. In her later polemical years it is with political and intellectual women—Ruth Barlow, Helen Maria Williams, and Mary Hays and their like—that she is coupled, women who were often writers themselves or who responded to her through her writings. Their image, cool and supportive, enters the moderate friendship of Jemima in *The Wrongs of Woman;* while the last Wollstonecraftian heroine, Maria, is purged of intense childhood friends.

In her life Wollstonecraft appears to have moved tentatively toward female relationships that did not repeat the one with her mother and that avoided the hierarchy society imposed on any

52. Ibid., pp. 95 and 93.
53. Ibid., p. 108.
54. *A Wollstonecraft Anthology*, p. 157.

couple. But she died before she completed her final novel and before she had time to discover whether she was ready to live in peace and intimate equality with another woman.

Mme de Staël

Like Mary Wollstonecraft, Mme de Staël was a tumultuous soul, highly demanding of men and women alike. She lived through historical and personal upheavals and her female friendships, especially the one with Mme Récamier, were central. Her relationship with her mother was unfortunate, for, again like Wollstonecraft, Staël saw herself as childhood victim, wounded by a mother who never gave her her due. Although the twenty-year relationship with Mme Récamier engrossed the adult woman and is the main subject here, the far more hidden tie of mother and daughter had set its tone. In Staël's first novel, *Delphine* (1802), aspects of both women appear, although the intensest phase of the Récamier friendship came after the novel was written, when Staël's mother was long dead.

Staël's parents, M and Mme Necker, were Protestant, bourgeois, and Swiss. On the eve of the French Revolution, Necker was chief minister of France and his wife—early love of the British historian Edward Gibbon—was hostess of a renowned philosophical salon. A handsome, respectable, and impeccably virtuous woman, she educated her precocious and affectionate daughter in the rarified atmosphere of her intellectual salon, and enjoyed displaying her product to her guests. The young Staël was indulged and flattered but, she came to feel, not really loved, and in time the witty, intelligent but plain girl grew to distrust the virtuous mother, to sense a coldness and ultimate disapproval—perhaps of her looks or manner—and to fear a sudden withdrawal.[55] In a revealing letter she wrote as a child, Staël vividly described her sense of insecurity, exaggerated in an aban-

---

55. A full account of Mme de Staël's relationship with her mother is given in Madelyn Gutwirth's *Madame de Staël* and in J. Christopher Herold's *Mistress to an Age: A Life of Madame de Staël* (Indianapolis; Bobbs-Merrill, 1958).

doned house, and she ended: "You find within yourself dear Mama, many consolations, but I find in myself only you."[56] When she came to feel that her mother had indeed withdrawn, she redirected her affection to her father and later still tried to shock or mollify her mother by a mixture of outrageous behavior and self-abasement. With a string of flamboyant lovers she sought to find the complete devotion she had desired as a child and to fill with other passion the emptiness her mother had left.[57]

When only nineteen in 1786 Staël was married lovelessly to the Swedish ambassador. Soon she took lovers and the ostentation of the scandals she provoked suggested that her liaisons served more than the instinct for love. For her grand passion she chose the unlikely Louis de Narbonne, handsome, Catholic, rather roué and aristocratic, an affront in his very being to the respectable Protestant Neckers. Narbonne entered with Staël into a passion that produced two children and a heap of ridicule on his beloved. "I live only for you in this horrible world," Staël wrote, anticipating the excess of her heroine Delphine. But in life as in literature, the implied demand was too great and Narbonne refused the ultimate devotion.

Committed by now to a creed of impulsiveness and fervor, Staël found a less consuming but still passionate successor to Narbonne in Count Ribbing, another handsome and aristocratic young man, assassin of the Swedish king by proxy, to whose ambassador she was married. In turn he too withdrew—for Benjamin Constant, who shared Staël's interest in literature and politics and matched her in neurotic demands.

To such outrageous doings, Mme Necker could not be blind. Ailing by 1794, she blamed her suffering on her daughter's

56. *Correspondance générale de Mme de Staël,* ed. Beatrice Jasinski (Paris: Pauvert, 1962), I, 1, p. 6. To this confession, Mme Necker replied, "Do not go much beyond yourself to praise and caress me. This shows a want of taste, common enough at your age," *Mistress to an Age,* p. 30.

57. Simone Balayé argues that Staël felt the absence of those she loved as a kind of mutilation, "Absence, exil, voyages," *Colloque de Coppet* (Paris: Klincksieck, 1970), p. 230. Gutwirth finds the key to this feeling as well in Staël's unsatisfactory relationship with her mother.

"guilty and public liaison" with Narbonne. His desertion she considered a punishment on Staël for her flaunted guilt. The disapproval pained Staël acutely and yet she continued to court it; as her mother lay dying the daughter took a second lover. In a way, though, she remained faithful to the standards of Mme Necker, never ceasing to exalt monogamy and marriage, and envying her dying parent in the arms of the father she herself so intensely loved. To the end she saw in her parents the self-sufficient, all-loving couple from which she would always be excluded, however passionately she loved and however deeply she demanded love. She made obeisance to this ideal couple throughout her life.

"I am continuing my *novel*," Staël wrote of *Delphine*, "and it is the story of the destiny of women presented in various ways."[58] Matilde, the anti-heroine, who in life and personality contrasts with the impulsive and generous heroine, is loyal to Delphine but has no real affection for her and, although she marries the man Delphine loves, she never appreciates her plight. She stands in Delphine's way at every turn and gives unasked a quantity of brittle, moralizing advice. Through the novel Matilde is supported by the respectable and cruel society of Paris, which Staël associated with her mother. In this character, then, there is almost a gratuitous harshness that seems to reveal a child's bitterness within the adult author. Part of the destiny of women certainly stems from their mothers, and in Matilde and Delphine, Staël may be picturing her own shadowed fate.[59]

When Mme de Staël met Mme Récamier, they were both famous, the one an author, renowned conversationalist, and notorious woman, the other celebrated for her looks, flirtatiousness, and devastating charm. The wife of a tolerant, wealthy, older

58. *Lettres choisies—1778–1817*, ed. Solovieff (Paris: Klincksieck, 1970), p. 181.

59. Gutwirth makes the parallel more fully, pointing out that Matilde echoes Mme Necker through her role not only of pious and prudish rival and critic of Delphine but also of wife to the beloved. After bearing a child, she kills herself and it through insisting upon breast feeding. Staël's "resentful jealousy of her mother, even to the conflict about nursing . . . is given its properly intemperate echo in this loaded and cruel characterization," pp. 242–43.

banker, with whom she lived in a chaste union, Mme Récamier was timid and passive beside the impetuous and vibrant Staël and they formed an attractive and complementary pair. Many worshippers came to their double shrine, including Constant, who loved both: "Nothing was more engaging than their conversation," he declared, "this strong male mind which uncovered everything, and this delicate and fine mind which understood everything."[60] It was a friendship intense and intimate, wracked by jealousy when lovers proved fickle, and darkened by misery and misfortune. Yet for Staël especially, it was a constant in her life, a rock of loyalty and anticipation that eased sometimes the hurt of her childhood emptiness. "I love you," she wrote repeatedly to Récamier, "with a love surpassing friendship."

They met in 1798. Little remains of Mme Récamier's writing about her friend, but she has left a record of the first encounter:

> One day, a day which marked a turning-point in my life, M. Récamier arrived with a lady whose name he did not mention and whom he left alone with me in the drawing-room. . . . I was struck by the beauty of her eyes and of her glance. . . .
>
> I had just read her *Lettres sur Rousseau;* I had been much moved by reading them. I expressed what I felt more by my looks than by my words; she intimidated me and attracted me at one and the same time. One immediately felt in her a person perfectly natural in a superior nature. She fixed her great eyes upon me, with a curiosity full of benevolence, and paid me compliments upon my figure which might have seemed exaggerated and too direct, if they had not seemed to escape her, which gave her praise an irresistible attraction. . . . My confusion did me no harm; she understood it and said that she would like to see much of me on her return to Paris. . . . (p. 4)

So it began, and its beginning marked its character throughout, the older Staël playing and enjoying the male social role with her

---

60. The letters of Mme de Staël are printed in Maurice Levaillant's *The Passionate Exiles: Madame de Staël and Madame Récamier* (New York: Farrar, Straus and Cudahy, 1958). Page numbers in the text refer to this work. Constant's words are quoted on p. 13.

direct compliments and invitation to further meeting, and the younger Récamier prettily embarrassed, grateful for such admiring notice. Staël always seems the warmest, the most active—although we have only her letters to judge by—and Mme Récamier appears always inclined to receive more than give; she knew herself loving to be loved and she graciously accepted homage: "You produce a supernatural impression upon my mind," wrote Staël, "You are at the forefront of my life" (p. 13).

But soon Mme de Staël would enter a new relationship—with the consul of France, Napoleon. At first she had been impressed by him, eager to play the female counsellor to his glory. But he required no such soul-mate and found the unwilling Mme Récamier more to his taste. Dislike followed indifference and by 1800 Mme de Staël was unwelcome in Paris. When she left, she began fourteen years of unequal political struggle; she was not to live in her beloved city until Napoleon himself had left it.

After her banishment Mme de Staël retreated to her family estate at Coppet in Switzerland, where later she would form a court in exile. Mme Récamier went to London. "Do you miss us, beautiful Juliette?" Staël wrote plaintively. "I hope that you have lost that singular shyness which you were feeling when you wrote to me. Did you not see clearly that I loved you and that this wit of which you accused me only helped me to understand you better and to find further reasons for being tenderly attached to you . . . ?" (p. 24).

With her friend back in Paris in 1803 Staël longed more than ever for the city. She urged Mme Récamier to intercede for her and wrote imploring letters to those well placed. But all failed, and she was answered only by a stricter exile. She set out for Germany after briefly meeting Récamier and touching her with her own grief: "I witnessed this despair, " she later wrote. "I had passionate admiration for Mme de Staël. The man who was banishing a woman, and such a woman as this, in my view could only be a despot; from that moment, I was vowed against him . . ." (p. 30).

Love on one side, admiration on the other, or some of both

on each—whatever it comprised, the friendship thickened over the next few years and from 1806, when the two women were briefly united near Paris, a new intensity crept into the letters. From this time Staël later dated their friendship. "I clasp you to my heart with more devotion than any love," she wrote to her old friend (p. 56).

Inevitably the relationship was tested. In 1805 Mme de Staël fell in love with the young Prosper de Barante, who returned her passion and even proposed marriage, until he became aware of his beloved's other lovers. With many hesitations and hedgings, he gradually retreated from the engagement, trying to substitute passionate friendship for passionate love. But he was weaned most abruptly when he encountered Mme Récamier, whose charm as usual overwhelmed. In contrast to the tempestuous Mme de Staël, she offered tenderness and peace, and her friend was well aware of the dangerous contest: "I confess that I fear that you will let him love you," she wrote sadly, "and this for me would be mortal sorrow, for two of my foremost feelings would thereby be troubled" (p. 67).

And they would often be so. Prosper de Barante was persistent and Mme de Staël felt on one occasion so pinched by jealousy that the correspondence was silenced for three months. Later when Staël's own son Auguste succumbed to the Récamier charm there was more coldness, more silence and jealousy—as there was, no doubt, when the tired and aging woman finally came to Paris only to find her old lover Constant at Mme Récamier's feet. But usually such episodes were followed by remorse, melting apologies, and stark revelation of the constant nagging fear that love again would escape: "If you should withdraw the feelings which have been my whole consolation for three years," sobbed Mme de Staël after the Prosper affair, "I would feel that life had lost for me the last charm of which I have not been robbed by exile." And she indulged in the dramatic epistolary scene so dear to female friends of the period: "I do not want to delay an hour before embracing you on my knees, kissing your pretty feet and asking your forgiveness for my touchiness. Forgive me also for thinking it possible that anyone might see you and not love you" (p. 161).

In 1807 and 1809, Staël and Récamier were united in Coppet in glorious summer months of friendship. Mme de Staël was exhilarated by the new emotion she felt:

> You have made me experience, dear Juliette, something that is quite new to me: a friendship which fills my imagination and spreads over my life an interest which one other sentiment alone has inspired in me. This year especially there was something angelic about you; that charm which deigned to concentrate on me moved my soul, and I felt cut off from some heavenly influence when you disappeared. (p. 182)

A series of tender letters followed in which Staël analyzed her heart. They form the high point of the friendship: love and friendship are intertwined and the two women although separated become interchangeable. "You have made me know all that is really sweet about love for a woman," declared Mme de Staël, "it is the alliance of two weak creatures who face their oppressors together." And the expressions of love fall thickly: "My dear friend, I have loved you for three years. It is sacred, is it not? I shall die thinking of it!" When Constant left for Paris and Mme Récamier, Mme de Staël can forget jealousy and write: "See Benjamin, dear Juliette, and see him often. It will be myself, behind your charming features, who will speak to him of me (pp. 183–85).

She had been working on her most substantial book, *On Germany,* the introduction to the French of German romantic literature and philosophy, and by 1810 she had moved near Paris for its publication. The Coppet summers with their endless talking and theatricals continued now in a rented château. All seemed sun and sentiment with the little court revolving round its two queens, Staël and Récamier, until Napoleon, skimming through the pages of the new book, sensed something subversive and un-French. Mme de Staël was re-exiled and her book ordered destroyed (the work was later printed in England). Taking an anguished farewell from Mme Récamier before her flight, she was full of memories: "It was here that you gave me those first marks of affection which have bound me to you till death" (p. 247).

Back in Switzerland she entered her last love relationship, with the young John Rocca, whom she later secretly married and whose child she bore. But she retained old friends: "never shall I feel for a woman a deeper emotion than that which will seize me when I press you to my heart once more!" she promised Mme Récamier, and the feeling must to some extent have been mutual, for, despite the clear danger of associating with the banished Staël, Mme Récamier set out the next summer to visit her lonely friend. The short stay was disastrous, for on her return Mme Récamier also found herself sentenced to banishment.[61] Staël was devastated. "I beg you not to hate me," she pleaded, "I shall have no peace until you are freed from this exile," and she blamed herself as "the scourge" of her friends (p. 282).

In exile, the friendship continued. As her mother had done before her, Mme de Staël wrote much of death, although she was, at forty-five, carrying Rocca's child, and she hinted at the dangerous escape she was soon to make from the now desolate Coppet to Sweden and England. Before she left she wrote lovingly: "Do you feel me kiss you with my face bathed in tears?" and, as she daringly crossed the border, she paused to dash an affectionate note to her old friend: "whatever happens, remember that I love you for ever" (pp. 308–10).

But time had grown short and when the longed-for event finally occurred and Napoleon fell, it was all too late. Parted for so many years from her friend and from Paris, Mme de Staël was now perhaps somewhat alienated from both. Although Mme Récamier continued in fine form, the darling of the salons, with the Duke of Wellington now in tow, her older friend was aging rapidly and felt out of place, the relic of a different age. Soon she left the Paris for which she had so long yearned. This time when

61. Since Mme Récamier had long been suspect, it was not solely her visit to Mme de Staël that caused her exile, but it certainly contributed.

she summoned Mme Récamier to Coppet, she did not come, perhaps believing her friend would soon return to Paris or perhaps understanding that their love lived best in letters. When Staël came gallantly back in 1816, she came to die. Mme Récamier visited daily and her friend was grateful: "I embrace you with all that remains to me," she wrote at the end (p. 332).

The friendship of Mme de Staël and Mme Récamier was generous and selfish in turns, riddled with the emotional peculiarities of both women and darkened by the shadow of Mme Necker. From her letters, Staël appears dominant in love, the most ecstatic in devotion; but Mme Récamier guards her secret, and, if her letters had survived, they might well have given another image. As it is, Mme Récamier seems to provoke adulation from male lovers and female friends alike, but from Staël she accepted a degree of written devotion she often feared in male admirers. And she showed a rare attachment as well, visiting her friend in exile and offering once to follow her into Sweden.

Such friendship no doubt filled many needs. Mme Récamier enjoyed admiration and was pleased to receive it from a woman so renowned. She may, too, have been happy to luxuriate in a woman's love. The pattern of her life—the hot and cold of her liaisons with men, her chaste marriage, her insistence on friendly, not passionate, love from the men she entranced—suggests a fear of male sexual passion, a withdrawing from physical commitment. With Mme de Staël she may have delighted in a passionate tie that could live mainly in sentimental prose.

On her side Mme de Staël had many needs to fill too. She was well aware of her friend's superior charms, her devastating coquetry, her calm attraction beside her own unstable bustle and jealousy. Like Fanny Blood for Wollstonecraft, Récamier was in a way the pretty daughter her mother should have had, the one who might have provoked her mother into love. Yet Staël was devoted to the charming Récamier and eager to reconcile whenever her envy overwhelmed the friendship. Perhaps she enjoyed her friend because with her she had the kind of relationship she could never acceptably have with a man—she could dominate, compliment, mother, admire, and worship all at once. Although she often chose as lovers young men who inspired something of the same treatment, it was not a socially proper response and must have disturbed both partners; with a woman she was free to indulge and she did. Their friendship was like love and their meetings delicious; Récamier was there to be pleased "after the fashion in which a flirtation or love affair begins."

In addition, Mme de Staël could, while loving her friend, see her also as a lover of others, and indeed she seemed happiest in the relationship when she could live through her pretty friend, not against her, for in competition she always lost. So, though devastated when Prosper de Barante or Auguste worshipped at the Récamier shrine, she yet insistently sent them there, knowing full well that to see Récamier was to admire her. So too she enjoyed her friend's triumphs—more even than Récamier herself. When the Prince of Prussia offered love and marriage to this French commoner for example, Staël was vain about the conquest and disturbed her friend with public boasting. In Récamier, then, Staël the intelligent, powerful, and plain woman became also the feminine, coquettish, and pretty woman, the social ideal and complete daughter. In *Delphine,* there is an ill-favored woman called Louise—a childhood name of Staël herself—who uses her friend to live the love and triumphs she can never know, and there is a pretty, naive, conventional woman who cannot follow through with passion. But the most powerful image in the novel is of course Delphine, a woman who has the perfect wit, passion, charm, and beauty of Staël and Récamier combined.

Jane Austen

Jane Austen lived in letters—just like Mary Wollstonecraft and Mme de Staël—but her older sister Cassandra shielded her from the public effect of this habit by burning the bulk of them after her death. The little that is left, the harmless residue, gives nothing much away, yet eloquently recreates a world of women, the close eager unions into which the spinster Jane Austen constantly entered. These unions included the warm, sure friendship with the unrelated Martha Lloyd, who lived with Austen in later life, finally achieving Austenhood by marrying a brother, but mostly they connect relatives, cousins, aunts, nieces, and sisters. Yet in *Emma* and *Mansfield Park,* Austen's greatest novels, there are no such female ties, but rather a strange fear of involvement in relationships which she herself seemed to have entered with joy.

Austen's early feelings for other women are hard to grasp since no letters survive, but her most ambiguous emotions were perhaps generated by her lively older cousin, Eliza, a presence in the Austen household for many years and possibly a ghost in the novels.[62] Eliza was brought up partly in France, where she married the Comte de Feuillide. During her extended stays in England she flirted with a great many young men—if her vivacious letters can be credited—including two Austen brothers, the eldest, James, and Henry, Jane Austen's favorite, ten years his cousin's junior. The young Jane must have marvelled at these antics and, when she wrote her own lively skit on romantic doings, *Love and Freindship,* she dedicated it to her cousin. Perhaps too she sometimes ached for her beloved brother who, deeply smitten by Eliza, delayed taking orders to gain her favor. After the Comte was killed in the Revolution, Henry married his cousin and lived quite happily with her until her death. By the time Jane wrote *Mansfield Park,* with its devastating attack on flirtatious women and would-be friends, Eliza was ailing—she was to die in 1813 before the book was completed. Yet youthful impressions remain, and something of the ambiguity in the two aspiring friends, the charming Mary Crawford of *Mansfield Park* and the awful Mrs. Elton of *Emma* may have sprung from the child's distrust of the exotic cousin who enjoyed the precedence her title gave her, boasted of her resources, and captivated Jane Austen's favorite brother.

When she herself grew up and became in turn a spectacle for

62. For a discussion of parallels between Austen's life and fiction, see A. Walton Litz, *Jane Austen: A Study of Her Artistic Development.*

the young, Austen entered the warmest relationship with her young nieces. With Fanny Knight especially she enjoyed a second youth, relishing her mental vivacity and entering with so much zest into her flirtations that something of Fanny and herself seems inevitably to haunt the picture of Emma and Harriet in *Emma*.[63] Sometimes the correspondence leads inevitably to fiction, as when Austen laughs at the vacillating Fanny, unable quite to make up her mind to love—"Your trying to excite your own feelings by a visit to his room amused me excessively—The dirty Shaving Rag was exquisite!—Such a circumstance ought to be in print. Much too good to be lost."[64] Perhaps it is in print—in Fanny's regard of the broken egg-shells in *Mansfield Park* or in Harriet's reverence for Mr. Elton's pencil stub and court-plaister in *Emma*.

But there is, too, a sadness in the relationship with Fanny—a knowledge that it will be loosened with marriage. "Oh! what a loss it will be when you are married," the aunt exclaims. "You are too agreable in your single state, too agreable as a Neice." Yet suddenly serious, she adds, "I do wish you to marry very much, because I know you will never be happy till you are; but the loss of a Fanny Knight will be never made up to me."[65] Fanny must marry because spinsterhood is still painful, but she will lose the warmth of close female ties and her aunt will be lonely without her.

Jane Austen had thought of her niece as "almost another Sister." And yet they were not sisters, not equals, and a generation would always separate them. This feeling of temporal isolation is especially clear in Austen's relationship with her little niece Caroline, who interested her aunt but whose loneliness could never be assuaged. In 1808 aunt and three-year-old niece were both visit-

63. Lionel Trilling has noted "the quality of intimacy" we feel with Emma and speculates that it may derive from Austen's own closeness to her heroine, "Emma and the Legend of Jane Austen," in *Beyond Culture: Essays on Literature and Learning* (New York: Viking Press, 1965), p. 44.

64. *Jane Austen's Letters to Her Sister Cassandra and Others*, ed. R. W. Chapman (London: Oxford University Press, 1952), p. 412.

65. Ibid., pp. 478–79.

ing the eleven wealthy and overpowering Knight children, and the little girl was shy and diffident before her cousins. "Little Caroline looks very plain among her Cousins," Jane Austen wrote to her sister, "and tho' she is not so headstrong or humoursome as they are, I do not think her at all more engaging."[66] But Austen was soon engaged for her, kindly drawing her brother's attention to his daughter's taste and sympathetically writing: "I believe the little girl will be glad to go home;—her Cousins are too much for her."[67]

By the time Caroline was ten, Jane Austen was nearing the end of her life, but the two came briefly together as fellow-authors. Austen was reading manuscripts from Caroline, "quite my own Neice," and welcoming a common taste in literature, a penchant for absurdity. When Anna, Caroline's half-sister, had a child, Austen laughingly told Caroline to care for herself, since she too was now an aunt and so a person of consequence; the letter ends with the greeting "my dear Sister-Aunt." In the last year of her life, she often wished for Caroline, living only a few difficult miles away, and she lamented with her the female dependence that holed them both up; like Fanny Price in Portsmouth, Caroline could move only at male convenience.

"She seemed to love you, and you loved her naturally in return," wrote the niece of her aunt many years later.[68] Jane Austen's love in later years separated her niece from the lonely Fanny Price of *Mansfield Park*. But there was more detachment from the little girl, overwhelmed by rich cousins, and no aunt could lessen the isolation, although she might understand it. It is the sadness of a tie across generations, a sadness deepened in the last years by the threat of death. For Austen died when Caroline was only eleven.

In Austen's female relationships Cassandra, the "dearest sister," must be central, and if there is any biographical clue to the

66. Ibid., p. 197.
67. Ibid., p. 205.
68. James Edward Austen-Leigh, *Memoir of Jane Austen* (Oxford: Clarendon Press, 1926), p. 91.

distrust of friendship that informs the later novels, it must be sought here. Cassandra and Jane were lifelong companions. The only girls in a large family of boys, inevitably they formed a pair. Together they were dispatched to boarding school and together they were rescued Brontëlike from neglect and fever. "If Cassandra was going to have her head cut off, Jane would insist on sharing her fate," their mother remarked of her daughter.[69]

Grown up, both sisters dabbled in love; about Jane's love life there can only be speculation, since most records perished in Cassandra's bonfire of their letters, but her sister's engagement was definite and desired, ended only by the sudden death of the young man. Jane Austen's attitude to the love of her beloved sister is unknown, but the novels are full of jealousy conquered, Fanny Price with her jaundiced look at Mary Crawford in *Mansfield Park,* Elinor Dashwood suffering with Lucy Steele in *Sense and Sensibility,* or Anne Elliot sighing over the unsuitable Louisa in *Persuasion.* Jane Austen herself had one quick engagement when she was twenty-seven, the dangerous age of the fading Anne Elliot and the desperate Charlotte Lucas in *Pride and Prejudice.* It was an overnight affair, of which she thought better in the morning—with the help perhaps of Cassandra. From then onwards neither woman seems to have been deeply tempted, for, as their mother commented, they were "wedded to each other."[70] With long visits away to relatives, the two sisters spent the rest of Jane's life together.

It was a close relationship. If either stayed away, she was missed by the other. When Cassandra went off to care for a sister-in-law less than a year before her sister's death, Jane wrote: "When you have once left Cheltenham, I shall grudge every half day wasted on the road."[71] Later their niece Anna described the sisters as she remembered them: "they were," she declared, "every-

69. Ibid., p. 16.

70. Quoted in Jane Aiken Hodge's *Only a Novel: The Double Life of Jane Austen* (New York: Howard, McCann & Geoghegan, 1972), p. 82.

71. *Jane Austen's Letters,* p. 463.

thing to each other. They seemed to lead a life to themselves within the general family life which was shared only by each other. I will not say their true, but their *full,* feelings and opinions were known only to themselves." [72] The novels, read to many, were especially discussed with Cassandra and they were referred to by the sisters like a shared past. At the end in Winchester in 1817 they were together still and it was Cassandra who at last closed her sister's eyes. When critics pity Austen her loneliness or mock her spinsterhood, they surely forget Cassandra, who after her sister's death wrote: "I *have* lost a treasure, such a Sister, such a friend as never can be surpassed,—she was the sun of my life, the gilder of every pleasure, the soother of every sorrow, I had not a thought concealed from her, & it is as if I had lost a part of myself." [73]

And yet there is an undercurrent. No sisters were closer certainly and both derived joy from their closeness. But perhaps they were too exclusive, too isolating in their mutual regard. For with their humorous, ironic eyes, they must have been a formidable pair in the ballroom or at the dinner table. Cassandra was there when Jane engaged and disengaged herself all in a night and there may have been afterthoughts. No doubt Jane Austen came to see the advantage of singleness in that age of eternal marriage, constant deliveries, and childbed death, but the life of a spinster had also its pains. Socially stigmatized, the maiden aunt might escape the frequent contempt and repulsion only to find herself regarded as a free nurse or a kind of mobile upper servant. And again as Austen ruefully wrote, "Single Women have a dreadful propensity for being poor." [74] Perhaps then, Austen somewhere blamed her powerful tie with Cassandra for her own single state and made her heroines avoid the female friendship that might deny them marriage. After her sister's death, some impulse made Cassandra write: "I loved her only too well, not better than she

72. *Only a Novel,* p. 114.
73. *Jane Austen's Letters,* pp. 513–14.
74. Ibid., p. 483.

deserved, but I am conscious that my affection for her made me sometimes unjust to & negligent of others, & I can acknowledge, more than as a general principle, the justice of the hand which has struck this blow." [75]

75. Ibid., p. 514.

CONCLUSION

EIGHTEENTH-CENTURY FICTION has women at its center, and numerous novels from *Clarissa* to *Delphine* are called by the names of their heroines. Marking these fictional women and their histories is a cluster of motifs which relate most obviously to the central romance but which achieve new meaning when analyzed in the context of female relationships. The most common and crucial motifs are the trio relating to female value: virginity (or chastity), narcissism, and money; and the other trio relating to female debility: illness, madness, and death. These and other motifs all gain significance when the focus changes from romance to friendship.

From the common property of motifs the authors select or reject on a variety of impulses. The biographical sketches have suggested that historical and personal reasons may inspire some men to write fearfully of female alliances and some women to dread the implications of commitment to women. But beyond the individual experience—a complex of psychology, class, family relationships, and so on—the two broad divisions of sex and nationality mark all the authors. It is worth investigating briefly whether these divisions correlate at all with the choice of motif and, in similar manner, whether they interact in any patterned way with the five categories of friendship.

Virginity or chastity is part of the ideology of every eighteenth-century heroine. In the tragic novels, its loss is so heinous that the fallen women can move only from one bed to another, from love to death—the path of Clarissa and Mme de Tourvel in

403

CONCLUSION

Dangerous Liaisons. In the criminal and whore histories, however—*Fanny Hill, Moll Flanders,* and *Juliette*—it is an expensive but expendable commodity. At first sight, male and female novels seem to stress virginity and chastity equally. Yet there is a difference. Male fiction often preaches that female chastity merely restrains or hides desire; once overcome, the woman is born a sexual being and nothing can reverse the change except death. Mme de Tourvel follows this common progress. In female fiction and in *Clarissa,* however, it rarely suggests repressed desire. Sometimes it may hint that a heroine has assimilated a man-made convention, as occasionally in Austen and Ferrier, but more often it indicates female integrity, a self-reliance and psychic independence that marks the Austen heroine at her best. Such resplendent chastity Clarissa displays, while Wollstonecraft's Maria in *The Wrongs of Woman* knows herself heroically chaste and self-possessed when she leaves her husband's bed forever.[1]

A bizarre motif often connected with fictional virginity in the eighteenth-century novel is the nosebleed, which the heroines often experience at violent, usually sexual crises. It is an analogue to defloration, hinting at rape, seduction, venereal disease, and all manner of psychological and sexual wounding of women. At the same time it tends to repulse and control the aggressive male in the way menstruation is reputed to do. In many cultures menstruating women are set apart as dangerous and unclean, conveyers of illness, death, and impotence. In the novels, the nosebleed seems to have the repelling function of menstruation, a substitution that may derive from the vicarious monthly bleeding some women experience; when this phenomenon occurs, the most usual source of blood is the nose.[2] The nosebleed can then

1. In "The Portrayal of Women in Restoration and Eighteenth-Century English Literature," John Richetti writes of Clarissa: "She reclaims chastity and makes it into a definitively female trait, a sign of self-possession and apartness rather than a guarantee of male dominance," *What Manner of Woman: Essays on English and American Life and Literature* (New York: New York University Press, 1977), p. 94.

2. In *Symbolic Wounds: Puberty Rites and The Envious Male* (New York: Collier Books, 1954), Bruno Bettelheim writes of the magical qualities generally ascribed to menstruation and menstrual blood. For a fuller treatment of menstruation and its mythology,

CONCLUSION

imply both female vulnerability and passive aggression. It is a show of wounding that in *Clarissa, Julie,* and *Fanny Hill* keeps the lusty male at bay. When the woman is actively aggressive, however, designing to wound rather than exhibit a wound, she displays not the nosebleed but a knife, a castrating phallic symbol that shocks as well as harms. Clarissa, Burney's Elinor in *The Wanderer* and the older sister in Haywood's *Lasselia* all astound their audience with sudden violence.

The nosebleed and the penknife function in the heterosexual plot as female wounding, both active and passive, and as agents of repulsion. In the female context, however, the nosebleed implies the female predicament—defloration, menstruation, and childbirth—and pleads with other women for a common front, a unity before the menacing male. In the tragic novels the plea goes unheeded, and Richardson's Clarissa and Diderot's Suzanne bleed in vain; in the less grim, Cleland's Fanny and Rousseau's Julie succeed in evoking female pity with their blood. The penknife is a different matter, however. It tends to repel men and women alike. While men are offended by its unfeminine aggressiveness, women take it as a kind of treachery to embattled womanhood. Where the nosebleed pleads unity, then, the penknife severs it and women are repudiated by it as much as men.

The show of blood or knife is a revelation of a kind. The woman admits either her vulnerability or her aggressiveness, which defines her as a proper or improper female in much the same way as virginity or its lack. A third revelatory motif is the female confession, which fictional heroines use to create images of themselves and so seduce others. Occasionally these seductive narratives will engage men. But most frequently they are directed at other women and the effect is often the sentimental, almost erotic involvement of the listener. Marivaux's Marianne entices an older woman into interest through her life story, while Suzanne ravishes the Superior of Arpajon with hers. The heroines of

see Janice Delaney, Mary Jane Lupton, and Emily Toth, *The Curse* (New York: New American Library, 1976) and Penelope Shuttle and Peter Redgrove, *The Wise Wound* (London: Gollancz, 1978).

CONCLUSION

Haywood and Lennox dissolve in warm tears when their friends display their hearts. In later novels, Wollstonecraft's *Wrongs of Woman* and Staël's *Delphine*, for example, the author can use the reader's expectation of the confession's power to comment on a character or situation. Maria is too romantically involved to be moved in the usual way by a female story, and Staël's cruel nun is so hard and self-centered that she fails to touch Delphine with her narrative.

In many fictional heroines of the eighteenth century, especially male-created ones, narcissism is the dominant trait. But female narcissism is a special kind, not simply a woman's love of herself, which may in time encompass love of another like herself—the genesis of lesbianism for Brantôme—but instead the love of her effect on another. The woman narcissistic in this way has little true love for herself and even less for other women.[3] She may fascinate a man and sustain a romantic intrigue—for women are licensed narcissists in love—but she cannot easily enter an equal friendship. Constantly concerned with her self-image, she can only think of charming, not of the woman charmed. In the male romantic context, then, such a woman—Diderot's Suzanne or Marivaux's Marianne, for example—may attract the reader, as she seems to do her male creator, but in the female context she offends.

Related to the narcissism of the female character is the creation of a male voyeur of friendship within the novel. Rousseau's Saint-Preux thrills at the *sight* of the two companions; when they are hidden he thinks of their closeness with distaste. Wollstonecraft's Mary is said to win her lover Henry by playing the role of female friend; he sighs for a painting of the expression she reveals when tending the dying Ann.

With virginity, money defines all women. For money female characters are locked in prisons like Clarissa, in convents like Diderot's Suzanne, and in madhouses like Maria in Woll-

---

3. Hélène Cixous writes interestingly of female narcissism as antinarcissism in "La jeune née: an excerpt," *Diacritics* 7, no. 2, (Summer 1977).

stonecraft's *Wrongs of Woman*, or thrown into prostitution like Fanny Hill or Sade's Juliette. They are sold with the estate like Wollstonecraft's Mary or constantly belittled like Austen's Fanny Price. Yet a blissful ending in these novels remains a marriage that is not probed beyond the wedding—a marriage between an impecunious or financially sacrificial woman and a very rich man.

In female friendship money continues to be influential. The business relationships of Moll Flanders are extreme in their money-mindedness, but Anna Howe and Clarissa are also sustained by their dream of the potent legacy Clarissa could have grasped; the benevolent ties of Wollstonecraft, Burney, and Staël heroines are all born of wealth. If in the romantic ending the woman may be shorn of her money to marry the wealthy man (the opposite situation makes some of the humor in *Fanny Hill*), in the happy ending of friendship, she must be left with her money. Austen's wealthy Emma is open to friendship in a way Burney's impoverished Cecilia is not at the end of her novel, while the chastened heroines of Lennox's *Euphemia* and Haywood's *British Recluse* will live within their own means, with friends.

Women fall ill in the eighteenth-century novel alarmingly often. In the romantic context, the rejected or separated woman, who has lost the meaning her male lover lent her, usually sickens; Rousseau's Julie, Cleland's Fanny Hill, and Staël's Delphine all take to their beds when their lovers leave. Sickness is a mark of female debility, a temporary surrender in the fight for love and self-esteem. It is also an excuse for inaction. Clarissa, Diderot's Suzanne, Wollstonecraft's Mary, and Cleland's Fanny Hill are all somnambulant, all paralyzed when they should act and ill or asleep when they should be most critically awake. At the same time illness is a weapon of the weak, as Nietzsche hysterically noted when he perceived "the will of the weak to represent *some* form of superiority, their instinct for devious paths to tyranny over the healthy . . . the sick woman especially: no one can excel her in the wiles to dominate, oppress, and tyrannize."[4] With her attractive illness Marivaux's Marianne in *The Life of Marianne* manipulates her lover and friend, while Fanny Price of *Mansfield Park* controls Edmund with her headaches.

In the female context illness, like the nosebleed, may again plead for solidarity and support when all effort is prevented. Through her fever Rousseau's Julie seems to beg her friend Claire to aid her. In the heavily manipulative friendships of Marivaux's Marianne and Diderot's Suzanne, it rivets the female friends to the heroines, who suck health from the women they so profoundly affect. Sister Ursule in *The Nun* declines after she has watched her beloved Suzanne recover, and in Mrs. Collyer's ending of Marivaux's *Marianne* the friendly Mme de Miran dies after Marianne grows well.

Sickness merges into madness in the common brain fever, a disease which afflicts a horde of heroines. Like sickness, madness seems an extreme metaphor of the impotent female condition; women go mad when they lose control over themselves, when their chastity (and the self-possession it implies) is shattered, as it is with Clarissa. Or when this gift on which so much store was set provokes no thanks.[5] Through the lens of female friendship, however, madness may have a different genesis: women go insane when friends fall away. In *The Wrongs of Woman* Maria nears madness when her daughter is dragged from her and before she recognizes that another woman might comfort her and sustain her failing faculties; Rousseau's Claire becomes insane when her friend Julie dies; Burney's Cecilia, shorn of all friends, grows

4. Frederich Nietzsche, *On the Genealogy of Morals,* trans. Walter Kaufman and R. J. Hollingdale (New York: Vintage Books, 1969), p. 123. Nancy Miller comments on the nameless fevers of the eighteenth-century heroine in "Female Sexuality and Narrative Structure in *La Nouvelle Heloïse* and *Les Liaisons dangereuses*," 620.

5. For an account of female madness in fiction see parts of Phyllis Chesler's *Women & Madness* (New York: Avon Books, 1972). In eighteenth-century fiction madness is of two main types: brain fever, which is a temporary surrender of rationality usually following a profound shock, and terminal insanity, a loss of faculties leading to a swift death. The good women often experience the first; the bad are reduced by the second. The lengthy female madness that is neither reversible nor fatal seems more a feature of nineteenth- than of eighteenth-century fiction.

demented in the streets; and Clarissa faces frenzy and death deprived of any close female comforter. Each woman goes mad when the solacing female presence is denied, for female friendship in these novels seems the last buttress against the irrationality always implied in the female condition.[6]

The ultimate symbol of female debility is death, and in the eighteenth-century novel women die in droves. Usually it is the good who die (apart from unnurturing mothers, who manage a deathbed repentance anyway) while the bad, like Mme de Merteuil in Laclos' *Dangerous Liaisons,* are left with smallpox or ostracism. The saintly death of heroines like Clarissa or Julie is a clean death which neither disfigures nor isolates. It is a slow refining, a gentle easing from life.[7] In the romantic plot death cleanses the heroine from the impurity of rape or seduction, while yet implying that she is powerless on earth to combat its effect. But for female friendship, it is far more powerful. The friend initially left friendless often experiences the loneliness the heroine once suffered; later she reexperiences the friend as a greater force in her life. In death Clarissa gives something of her personality and style to Anna Howe, who does the work she planned, while Rousseau's Julie pulls the loving and desolate Claire toward her own death. Mme de Riccoboni's Adelaide in *The Marquis de Cressy,* dead to the world in the convent, leads her friend the Countess to a death which will make them tormenting furies to the man who betrayed them both.

Like illness, madness, and involuntary death (a dubious category since several characters will, but do not cause their own

6. Madge Wildfire, a character in *The Heart of Midlothian* (a novel very much in the transition between eighteenth- and nineteenth-century fiction) varies the pattern. She is permanently mad from love when her lover leaves her and her baby is killed; she dies when her mother abandons her. The more traditional eighteenth-century pattern occurs in Charlotte Smith's *The Young Philosopher,* which presents another situation between mother and daughter: when the daughter disappears, the mother goes mad, although she has kept her faculties intact while losing her husband and suffering the most Gothic horrors.

7. The purity of fictional death in the heroine is similar to the purity of consumption which Susan Sontag has noted in "Illness as Metaphor," *New York Review of Books,* January 26, 1978, 10–16.

CONCLUSION

deaths), suicide is variously significant. It seems both the ultimate capitulation to a fictive society that has defined women negatively, and the ultimate heroic evasion of this society. Offensive and defensive at once, suicide can be a way of punishing a man beyond the grave; this is the partial motive of the grotesque attempts of Burney's Elinor and the dignified exit of Riccoboni's Countess. Or it can merely denote despair; Wollstonecraft's Maria in *The Wrongs of Woman* tries to kill herself because she is bereft of friends and shorn of all power, while Staël's Delphine destroys herself to complete her self-denying image of devotion. To men, then, suicide may be proof or reproof, declaring love once and for all or tormenting for inadequate love. To other women, however, it seems simply betrayal, an end of a common struggle. Few are moved by it as they are by the saintly death, and, if they arrive in time, they will do everything to stop it. The female friends in Staël's novel are absent at the end and a man gives the poison for Delphine's death. In *The Wrongs of Woman* Jemima rushes in at the ultimate moment to save Maria.

The motifs of virginity, narcissism, money, and female debility signify differently according to the focus: whether on the central romance or on female ties. They occur across the novels of the eighteenth century, whether written in English or French, by men or women. There is, however, some correlation of motif with gender or nationality, some tendency of French men to choose topics or incidents avoided by English women, for example. So the passive saintly death, exemplified most elaborately by Clarissa, seems primarily a male convention, while the active suicide is described most frequently in novels by female authors.

Similarly, although Henry Fielding created a covertly narcissistic heroine in *Amelia,* on the whole female narcissism seems more heavily French than English, and no English heroine—not even Fanny Hill—has quite the flamboyant self-regard of Marivaux's Marianne or Diderot's Suzanne. Narcissism is also primarily a male-constructed habit, and the narcissistic heroine

410

bears witness to her creator's love. When a male author dotes on his heroine, he seems to demand the same from other characters in his story, and he insists that they constantly compliment her within her text. Female authors seldom create such heroines; instead they show themselves too engaged by identifying closely with their characters—as Wollstonecraft does with Mary in *Mary, A Fiction*. They require the reader to pity and appreciate not only the heroine in the text but also the author outside.

The selection of character types also relates loosely to gender. Rivalling sisters enter male and female novels alike, but the cruel blood-sister is most often created by men. Diderot's Suzanne in *The Nun* is spurned by her sister, while Richardson's Clarissa is hated and tortured by Arabella. In the novels of Austen and Burney, however, the sister relationship seems privileged. Although the good Fanny Price in *Mansfield Park* opposes the naughty Mary Crawford, she is less hostile to her proud Bertram cousins; to her sister Susan she is simply supportive. Again in Burney's *Wanderer*, Juliette may be cool to the unrelated Elinor but she is always affectionate to her sister Arabella, even before the kinship is known. Good mothers are hard to find in any novels and inadequacy is the main maternal characteristic in male and female fiction alike.

No particular character pattern emerges for surrogate or displaced sisters in novels by men and women, but surrogate mothers tend to be especially blameworthy in female novels. Mrs. Weston in *Emma*, Mrs. Norris in *Mansfield Park*, or Mme de Vernon in *Delphine* inhabit books by women, whereas the common male type is Cleland's Phoebe in *Fanny Hill*, Diderot's Mme de Moni in *The Nun*, or Sade's Durand in *Juliette*, all in their different ways supportive and nurturing of the young girls they mother. As so often, *Clarissa* has examples of both types, and in Mrs. Norton and Sinclair the novel provides extremes of good and evil.

The parameters of gender and nationality further interact with the five main categories of friendship. Each of these has special characteristics which may variously attract or repulse ac-

CONCLUSION

cording to male, female, English, or French experience. As with the literary motifs, it is usually a matter of emphasis, a penchant for a particular type of friendship over others. In motifs and categories, exclusiveness and exclusion are rare.

On the whole, nationality crosses categories. French and English alike hail social friendship or sob over sentimental. But two categories do to some extent correlate with place: France produces more pictures of erotic and manipulative friendship than England. Both biases may derive from tradition, the influence of one or two seminal books (such as Marivaux's *Life of Marianne*) which fix a style and treatment for their successors. Again it may reflect a distinction between English and French experience. In France erotic friendship, as in *The Nun,* most commonly appears in the fictional convent, the chosen place of much eighteenth-century pornography and the obsession of Catholic writers not only as a symbol of women's suffering but also as a hotbed of female perversion and power. Over Protestant England, it would, however, have little hold. Manipulative friendship is harder to account for, but it may reflect the influence of French women in the period—court mistresses and salonistes, for example—whose importance depended on their adroit manipulation of society.

Author gender seems to divide friendship far more neatly than nationality, but the erotic and manipulative types of friendship are again the dividers. Male authors delight in manipulative and erotic female relationships far beyond their female colleagues. In their vision, female friendship dwindles into rivalry for the man. If admittedly manipulative like Sade's Juliette or Laclos' Mme de Merteuil, women live to twist and torture other women; if secretly so, like Rousseau's Claire or Marivaux's Marianne, they grow close, vampirically sucking out another woman's life.

Lesbianism, erotic female friendship, enters the novel to shock, disgrace, or titillate, severed on the whole from any emotional concern. Women have seldom written erotically about women in any age before this one; conditioned as objects of love, they were ashamed to appear its subject, abashed by aggressive

412

love itself, whether for man or woman. In addition, in the eighteenth century women authors must have recoiled from depicting a state that could so easily implicate themselves.[8] A male author like Cleland might tease with lesbianism; a woman would be indicted.

With the exception of *Clarissa,* sentimental friendship is largely depicted by female writers. In the works of Burney, Haywood, and Lennox, it allows the female author to use a romantic plot, while placing her passion elsewhere. In sentimental friendship two women can become central in fiction with propriety and safety. In *Clarissa,* however, a male author has done something more with this friendship and has succeeded in criticizing patriarchal society in a devastating way. Perhaps it is the literary androgyny of Richardson that allows this achievement and makes of *Clarissa* the century's most acute analysis of female friendship.

Social friendship cuts across sex lines but is again predominantly female-created. It admits a clear rapprochement between friendship and romance and it stresses the relative importance of women to other women within society. It allows, if it does not always deliver, the happy ending.

Political friendship, rarer than social, also boasts more female than male creators. In the utopias, it brings about the collective power of women; in other fictional societies it acts in extremity against the potent institutions of men. Under its influence Wollstonecraft's Maria escapes the madhouse and Staël's Delphine for three volumes avoids the abnegation of marriage.

The friendships of the Julies, Clarissas, Marias, and Cecilias depicted by French and English, male and female writers in the eighteenth century serve, then, a variety of functions. They balance a skewed psychology, ease loneliness, teach survival, and create power. At the same time they nudge women into development, where marriage can only bewilder or become a too sudden closing of the gulf society has formed between the sexes. Female relationships are ties between likes; in them a woman learns to

8. Jeanette Foster stresses this point in *Sex Variant Women in Literature: An Historical and Quantitative Survey* (New York: Vantage Press, 1956).

mirror herself, not a man, the traditional female role. At their worst, women in these novels spurn, manipulate, degrade, and torture other women, their only inferiors in the patriarchal structure; at their best they embody Charlotte Lennox's high ideal of a friend as "a witness of the conscience, a physician of secret griefs, a moderation of prosperity, and a guide in adversity." Or rather they embody a part of this ideal, for, in the catalogue of unfortunate virtue which is the eighteenth-century novel, they need rarely meddle with prosperity. But with conscience, secret griefs, and adversity they have much to do.

BIBLIOGRAPHY

Amis, Kingsley. "What Became of Jane Austen?" *Jane Austen: A Collection of Critical Essays,* ed. Ian Watt. Englewood Cliffs: Prentice-Hall, 1963.

Anderson, David. "Aspects of motif in *La Nouvelle Héloïse,*" *Studies on Voltaire and the eighteenth century,* 94, 1972.

Anti-Jacobin Review, July–December 1798.

Auerbach, Nina. *Communities of Women.* Cambridge: Harvard University Press, 1978.

Austen, Jane. *Emma,* ed. R. W. Chapman. London: Oxford U. Press, 1952.

——. *Letters to her Sister Cassandra and Others,* ed. R. W. Chapman. Oxford: Clarendon Press, 1932.

——. *Mansfield Park,* ed. R. W. Chapman. Oxford: Clarendon Press, 1934.

Austen-Leigh, James Edward. *Memoirs of Jane Austen.* Oxford: Clarendon Press, 1926.

Backscheider, Paula. "Defoe's Women: Snares and Prey," *Studies in Eighteenth-Century Culture,* V, ed. Ronald C. Rosbottom. Madison: University of Wisconsin Press, 1976.

Balayé, Simone. "Absence, exil, voyages," *Colloque de Coppet.* Paris: Klincksieck, 1970.

Barker, Jane. *Entertaining Novels.* London: A Bettesworth, 1719.

——. *A Patch-work Screen for Ladies.* 1723; New York: Garland, 1973.

Barthes, Roland. "L'Arbre du crime," *Tel Quel,* 28, 1967.

——. *Sade, Fourier, Loyola.* Paris: Editions du Seuil, 1971.

Batailles, Georges. *L'Erotisme.* Paris: Editions de Minuit, 1957.

——. *La Littérature et le mal.* Paris: Gallimard, 1957.

Beauvoir, Simone de. *The Marquis de Sade: Must We Burn Sade?* London: John Calder, 1962.

Bettelheim, Bruno. *Symbolic Wounds: Puberty Rites and the Envious Male.* New York: Collier Books, 1954.

Biou, Jean. "Deux oeuvres complémentaires *Les Liaisons dangereuses* et *Juliette,*" *Colloque d'Aix-en-Provence sur le Marquis de Sade, 19 et 20 fevrier, 1968.* Paris: Armand Colin, 1968.

BIBLIOGRAPHY

Blackstone, William. *Commentaries on the Laws of England.* Chicago: Callaghan & Co., 1889.

Blanchard, Frederick. *Fielding the Novelist.* New York: Russell and Russell, 1926.

Bonaparte, Marie. "Passivity, Masochism and Femininity (1934)," *Women and Analysis,* ed. Jean Strouse. New York: Dell, 1974.

Booth, Wayne. *The Rhetoric of Fiction.* Chicago: University of Chicago Press, 1961.

Bradbrook, F. W. *Jane Austen's "Emma."* Great Neck: Barron's Educational Series, 1961.

Bradbury, Malcolm. "Jane Austen's *"Emma,"* *Critical Quarterly,* 4, Winter 1962.

Brady, Patrick. "Structural Affiliations of *La Nouvelle Héloïse,"* *L'Esprit Créateur,* 9, no. 3, Fall 1969.

Brantôme, Seigneur de. *The Lives of Gallant Ladies,* trans. Alec Brown. London: Elek Books, 1961.

Braudy, Leo. "Fanny Hill and Materialism," *Eighteenth-Century Studies,* 4, no. 1, Fall 1970.

Brissenden, R. F. *"Mansfield Park:* freedom and the family," *Jane Austen: Bicentenary Essays,* ed. J. Halperin. Cambridge: Cambridge University Press, 1975.

——. *Virtue in Distress: Studies in the Novel of Sentiment from Richardson to Sade.* New York: Barnes & Noble, 1974.

Brophy, Elizabeth Bergen. *Samuel Richardson: The Triumph of Craft.* Knoxville: University of Tennessee Press, 1974.

Brownmiller, Susan. *Against Our Will.* New York: Simon and Schuster, 1975.

Burgelin, Pierre. *La Philosophie de l'existence de J.-J. Rousseau.* Paris: Presses Universitaires de France, 1952.

Burney, Fanny. *Cecilia or Memoirs of an Heiress.* London: J. M. Dent, 1893.

——. *Evelina.* London: Oxford University Press, 1968.

——. *The Wanderer; or, Female Difficulties.* London: Longman, Hurst, et al., 1814.

Burroway, Janet. "The Irony of the Insufferable Prig," *Critical Quarterly,* 9, 1967.

Burrows, J. F. *Jane Austen's "Emma."* Sydney: Sydney University Press, 1968.

Bushell, Nelson S. "Susan Ferrier's *Marriage* as Novel of Manners," *Studies in Scottish Literature,* 5, 1968.

Butler, Marilyn. *Jane Austen and the War of Ideas.* Oxford: Clarendon Press, 1976.

Cameron, Kenneth Neill, ed. *Shelley and his Circle.* Cambridge, Mass.: Harvard University Press, 1961.

Carter, Elizabeth. *A Series of Letters between Mrs. Elizabeth Carter and Miss Catherine Talbot, from the year 1741 to 1770.* London: F. C. and J. Rivington, 1809.

BIBLIOGRAPHY

Chapman, R. W. *Jane Austen: Facts and Problems*. London: Oxford University Press, 1949.

Chapone, Hester Mulso. *Letters on the Improvement of the mind*. London: J. Walker, 1778.

Charpentier, John. *Rousseau, the Child of Nature*. New York: The Dial Press, 1931.

Chateaubriand, F. R. de. *Atala. René*. Paris: Garnier-Flammarion, 1964.

Chesler, Phyllis. *Women & Madness*. New York: Avon Books, 1972.

Cixous, Hélène. "La jeune née: an excerpt," *Diacritics*, 7, no. 2, Summer 1977.

Cleland, John. Review of *Amelia, Monthly Review*, December 1751.

——. *Fanny Hill*, ed. Peter Quennell. Putnam, 1963.

Craik, W. A. *Jane Austen: The Six Novels*. London: Methuen, 1965.

Crocker, Lester. "Julie ou la nouvelle duplicité," *Annales Jean-Jacques Rousseau*, 36, 1963–5.

——. *Nature and Culture*. Baltimore: Johns Hopkins Press, 1963.

Daiches, David. "Samuel Richardson," *Literary Essays*. London: Oliver and Boyd, 1956.

Defoe, Daniel. *The Fortunes & Misfortunes of the Famous Moll Flanders*. New York: W. W. Norton, 1973.

——. *Roxana*. Oxford: Oxford University Press, 1964.

Delaney, Janice, Mary Jane Lupton, and Emily Toth. *The Curse*. New York: New American Library, 1976.

Delany, Mary. *The Autobiography and Correspondence of Mary Granville, Mrs. Delany*, ed. Lady Llanover. London: Richard Bentley, 1861.

Diderot, Denis. *Lettres à Sophie Volland*, ed. André Babelon. Paris: Gallimard, 1938.

——. *The Nun*, trans. Leonard Tancock. Harmondsworth: Penguin, 1974.

——. "Sur les femmes," *Oeuvres de Diderot*, ed. André Billy. Paris: Bibliothèque de la Pléiade, 1962.

Didier, Béatrice. *Littérature française: Le XVIIIe siècle, 1778–1820*. Paris: Arthaud, 1976.

Doody, Margaret Anne, *A Natural Passion: A Study of the Novels of Samuel Richardson*. Oxford: Clarendon Press, 1974.

Duckworth, Alistair. *The Improvement of the Estate: A Study of Jane Austen's Novels*. Baltimore: Johns Hopkins Press, 1971.

Duffey, Joseph M. "Emma: The Awakening from Innocence," *Journal of English Literary History*, 21, March 1954.

Duncan, T. C. and Ben D. Kimpel. *Samuel Richardson: A Biography*. Oxford: Clarendon Press, 1971.

Durant, W. Clark. *Supplement* to *Memoirs of Mary Wollstonecraft*. London: Constable, 1927.

Edwards, Thomas R. "The Difficult Beauty of *Mansfield Park*," *Nineteenth-Century Fiction*, 20, June 1965.

417

BIBLIOGRAPHY

Ellis, David. "The Irony of *Mansfield Park*," *Critical Review*, 12, 1969.

Ellrich, Robert J. "The Rhetoric of *La Religieuse* and Eighteenth-Century Forensic Rhetoric," *Diderot Studies, III,* ed. Otis Fellows and Gita May. Geneva: Librairie E. Droz, 1961.

Epstein, William H. *John Cleland: Images of a Life.* New York: Columbia University Press, 1974.

Fabry, Anne Srabian de. "Quelques Observations sur de dénouement de *La Nouvelle Héloïse,*" *French Review,* 46, October 1972.

Farrar, Reginald. "Mansfield Park," *Discussions of Jane Austen,* ed. William Heath. Boston: D. C. Heath, 1961.

Fauchery, Pierre. *La Destinée féminine dans le roman européen du dix-huitième siècle 1713–1807.* Paris: Armand Colin, 1972.

Fellows, Otis. *Diderot.* Boston: Twayne, 1977.

——. "Diderot's *Supplément* as Pendant for *La Religieuse,*" *Literature and History in the Age of Ideas. Essays on the French Enlightenment. Presented to George R. Havens.* Ohio State University Press, 1975.

Ferrier, Susan. *Marriage, A Novel,* ed. Herbert Foltinek. London: Oxford University Press, 1971.

Fielding, Henry. *Amelia.* London: G. Bell, 1914.

——. *The Female Husband; or, the Surprising History of Mrs. Mary, alias Mr. George Hamilton.* 1746; Liverpool: Liverpool University Press, 1960.

——. *The History of Tom Jones.* London: J. M. Dent, 1955.

Figes, Eva. *Patriarchal Attitudes.* New York: Stein & Day, 1970.

Fleishman, Avrom. *A Reading of "Mansfield Park": An Essay in Critical Synthesis.* Minneapolis: University of Minnesota Press, 1967.

Foster, Jeannette. *Sex Variant Women in Literature: An Historical and Quantitative Survey.* New York: Vantage Press, 1956.

Foxon, David. *Libertine Literature in England 1660–1745.* New York: University Books Inc., 1965.

George, Margaret. *One Woman's "Situation": A Study of Mary Wollstonecraft.* Urbana: University of Illinois, 1970.

Gervaise de la Touche, J. C. *Histoire de Dom B . . . Portier des Chartreux.* Rome: Philotanus, n.d.

Godwin, William. *Memoirs of the Author of A Vindication of the Rights of Woman.* 1798; New York: Garland, 1974.

Golden, Morris. *Richardson's Characters.* Ann Arbor: University of Michigan Press, 1963.

Gooneratne, Yasmine. *Jane Austen.* Cambridge: Cambridge University Press, 1970.

Grafigny, Mme de. *The Peruvian Letters.* 1747; London: T. Cadell, 1774.

Green, F. C. *Jean-Jacques Rousseau.* Cambridge: Cambridge University Press, 1955.

Grimsley, Ronald. *Jean-Jacques Rousseau: A Study in Self-Awareness.* Cardiff: University of Wales Press, 1961.

BIBLIOGRAPHY

Guéhenno, Jean. *Jean-Jacques Rousseau*. Paris: Gallimard, 1962.

Gutwirth, Madelyn. *Madame de Staël, Novelist: The Emergence of the Artist as Woman*. Urbana: University of Illinois Press, 1978.

Habbakuk, H. J. "English Land-ownership, 1680–1740," *Economic History Review*, 1940.

Hamilton, Anthony. *Memoirs of Count Grammont*, ed. Walter Scott. London: Routledge and Sons, 1905.

Harding, D. W. "Regulated Hatred: An Aspect of the Work of Jane Austen," *Jane Austen: A Collection of Critical Essays*, ed. Ian Watt. Englewood Cliffs: Prentice-Hall, 1963.

Hardwick, Elizabeth. *Seduction and Betrayal*. New York: Vintage Books, 1975.

Hayman, Ronald. *De Sade: A Critical Biography*. London: Constable, 1978.

Hays, Mary. *Memoirs of Emma Courtney*. 1976; New York: Garland, 1974.

Haywood, Eliza. *The British Recluse: or, the Secret History of Cleomira, Suppos'd Dead*. London: D. Browne, 1723.

——. *The Fair Hebrew: or, a True, but Secret History of Two Jewish Ladies*. London: T. Brindley, W. Meadows, et al., 1729.

——. *The Husband. In Answer to the Wife*. London: T. Gardner, 1756.

——. *Idalia; or, the Unfortunate Mistress*. London: D. Browne, 1723.

——. *Lasselia: or, the Self-Abandon'd*. London: D. Browne, 1724.

——. *The Surprize; or Constancy Rewarded*. London: J. Roberts, 1724.

——. *The Wife*. London: T. Gardner, 1756.

Hemlow, Joyce. *History of Fanny Burney*. Oxford: Clarendon Press, 1958.

Herold, J. Christopher. *Mistress to an Age: A Life of Madame de Staël*. Indianapolis: Bobbs-Merrill, 1958.

Hill, Christopher. "Clarissa Harlowe and her Times," *Essays in Criticism*, 5, 1955.

Hodge, Jane Aiken. *Only a Novel: The Double Life of Jane Austen*. New York: Howard, McCann & Geoghegan, 1972.

Horney, Karen. *Neurosis and Human Growth*. New York: Norton, 1950.

Irigaray, Luce. *Speculum de l'autre femme*. Paris: Minuit, 1975.

James, Robert. *Medicinal Dictionary*. London: T. Osborne, 1743–45.

Johnson, Samuel. *Johnson Miscellanies*. New York: Barnes and Noble, 1966.

Josephs, Herbert. "Diderot's *La Religieuse*: Libertinism and the Dark Cave of the Soul," *Modern Language Notes*, 91, 1976.

Kempf, Roger. "Sur le Corps de Julie," *Critique*, 22, October 1966.

King, William. *The Toast, an Epic Poem in Four Books*. Dublin, 1732.

Kinkead-Weekes, Mark. *Samuel Richardson: Dramatic Novelist*. London: Methuen, 1973.

Klossowski, Pierre. *Sade mon prochain*. Paris: Editions de Seuil, 1947.

Krafft-Ebing, Richard. *Psychopathia Sexualis*. Philadelphia: F. A. Davis, 1892.

Lacan, Jacques. *The Language of the Self: The Function of Language in Psychoanalysis*. New York: Dell, 1968.

BIBLIOGRAPHY

Laclos, Choderclos de. *Dangerous Acquaintances (Liaisons dangereuses)*, trans. Richard Aldington. Norfolk, Conn.: New Directions Books, n.d.

Lacombe, Roger G. *Sade et ses masques.* Paris: Payot, 1974.

Laforgue, René. *Psychopathologie de l'échec.* Paris: Payot, 1950.

Laing, R. D. *The Politics of Experience.* New York: Ballantine Books, 1967.

Lascelles, Mary. *Jane Austen and her Art.* Oxford: Clarendon Press, 1939.

Lawrence, James. *The Empire of the Nairs: or the Rights of Women.* 1811; New York: Scholars' Facsimiles & Reprints, 1976.

Lejeune, Philippe. *L'Autobiographie en France.* Paris: Armand Colin, 1971.

Lely, Gilbert. *The Marquis de Sade: A Biography.* New York: Grove Press, 1961.

Lennox, Charlotte. *Euphemia.* Dublin: P. Wogan, P. Burne, et al., 1790.

——. *The Female Quixote.* London: C. Cooke, 1799.

Levaillant, Maurice. *The Passionate Exiles: Madame de Staël and Madame Récamier.* New York: Farrar, Straus and Cudahy, 1958.

Lévi-Strauss, Claude. *The Elementary Structures of Kinship.* Boston: Beacon Press, 1969.

Lewinter, Roger. Introduction to *La Religieuse, Oeuvres complètes.* Paris: Club français du livre, 1969–70.

Lewis, C. S. "A Note on Jane Austen," *Jane Austen: A Collection of Critical Essays,* ed. Ian Watt. Englewood Cliffs: Prentice-Hall, 1963.

Litz, A. Walton. *Jane Austen: A Study of Her Artistic Development.* New York: Oxford University Press, 1965.

Lucas, Charles. *The Infernal Quixote.* London, 1800.

Macaulay, Thomas Babbington. Review of Burney's *The Wanderer, Edinburgh Review,* January 1843.

McDowell, Judith H. Introduction to abridged *Julie* by Jean-Jacques Rousseau. University Park: Pennsylvania State University Press, 1968.

McKillop, Alan Dugald. *Samuel Richardson: Printer and Novelist.* 1936; Whitstable, Kent: Shoe String Press, Inc., 1960.

Manley, Mary. *Secret Memoirs and Manners of Several Persons of Quality, of Both Sexes. From the New Atalantis, an Island in the Mediteranean.* London: John Morphew, 1709.

Mansell, Darrel. *The Novels of Jane Austen: An Interpretation.* London: Macmillan, 1973.

Marivaux, P. C. de. *The Virtuous Orphan Or, The Life of Marianne, Countess of *****,* trans. Mary Collyer. Carbondale: Southern Illinois Press, 1965.

Mavor, Elizabeth. *The Ladies of Llangollen.* Harmondsworth: Penguin Books, 1974.

May, Georges. *Diderot et "La Religieuse."* New Haven: Yale University Press, 1954.

Mercken-Spaas, Godelieve. "Death and the Romantic Heroine: Chateaubriand and de Staël," forthcoming in *Pretext/Text/Context: Essays on Nineteenth-*

BIBLIOGRAPHY

Century French Literature, ed. Robert L. Mitchell. Columbus: Ohio State University Press.

——. "Sade and Rousseau: the Self and the Other," paper read at NEMLA, Spring 1977.

Miller, Nancy K. "Female Sexuality and Narrative Structure in *La Nouvelle Héloïse* and *Les Liaisons dangereuses,*" *Signs*, 1, no. 3, Spring 1976.

——. "*Juliette* and the Posterity of Prosperity," *L'Esprit créateur*, 15, no. 4.

Millett, Kate. *Sexual Politics.* New York: Avon Books, 1971.

Minter, David Lee. "Aesthetic Vision and the World of *Emma,*" *Nineteenth-Century Fiction*, 21, June 1966.

Moers, Ellen. *Literary Women: The Great Writers.* New York: Doubleday, 1976.

Moler, Kenneth. *Jane Austen's Art of Allusion.* Lincoln: University of Nebraska Press, 1968.

Morgan, Susan J. "Emma Woodhouse and the Charms of Imagination," *Studies in the Novel*, 7, no. 1, Spring 1975.

Mornet, Daniel. *Rousseau: l'homme et l'oeuvre.* Paris: Hatier-Boivin, 1950.

Mudrick, Marvin. *Jane Austen: Irony as Defense and Discovery.* Princeton: Princeton University Press, 1952.

Nietzsche, Frederich. *On the Genealogy of Morals*, trans. Walter Kaufman and R. J. Hollingdale. New York: Vintage Books, 1969.

Page, Norman. *The Language of Jane Austen.* New York: Barnes & Noble, 1972.

Praz, Mario. *The Romantic Agony.* London: Oxford University Press, 1970.

Rabine, Leslie. "George Sand and the Myth of Femininity," *Women & Literature*, 4, no. 2, Fall 1976.

Rabkin, Norman. "*Clarissa:* A Study in the Nature of Convention," *Journal of English Literary History*, 23, no. 3, September 1956.

Riccoboni, Mme. *The History of the Marquis de Cressy.* 1758; London: T. Becket and P. A. de Hondt, 1765.

——. *The History of Miss Jenny Salisbury.* 1764; Dublin: A. Leathley, J. Exshaw et al., 1770.

Richardson, Samuel. *Clarissa or, The History of a Young Lady.* Oxford: Shakespeare Head Press, 1930.

——. *The History of Sir Charles Grandison.* London: Oxford University Press, 1972.

——. *Pamela.* New York: Norton, 1958.

Richetti, John J. *Popular Fiction Before Richardson: Narrative Patterns 1700–1739.* Oxford: Clarendon Press, 1969.

——. "The Portrayal of Women in Restoration and Eighteenth-Century English Literature," *"What Manner of Woman: Essays in English and American Life and Literature.* New York: New York University Press, 1977.

Robinson, Mary. *Walsingham: or the Pupil of Nature.* London, 1798.

421

BIBLIOGRAPHY

Rogers, Katharine. "The Feminism of Daniel Defoe," *Woman in the 18th Century and Other Essays,* ed. Paul Fritz and Richard Morton. Toronto: Samuel Stevens Hakkert and Co., 1976.

——. "Richardson's Empathy with Women," *The Authority of Experience: Essays in Feminist Criticism.* Amherst: University of Massachusetts Press, 1977.

Rosbottom, Ronald C. *Marivaux's Novels: Theme and Function in Early Eighteenth-Century Narrative.* Rutherford: Fairleigh Dickinson University Press, 1974.

Roth, George. *Les Pseudo-mémoires de Madame d'Epinay. Histoire de Madame de Montbrillant.* Paris: Gallimard, 1951.

Rougemont, Denis de. *Love in the Western World.* New York: Pantheon, 1956.

Rousseau, Jean-Jacques. *Confessions.* Harmondsworth: Penguin, 1975.

——. *Correspondence générale,* ed. T. Dufour. Paris: A. Colin, 1924–34.

——. *Julia; or, the New Eloisa.* Edinburgh: J. Bell, J. Dickson, and C. Elliot, 1773.

——. *Oeuvres complètes.* Paris: Bibliothèque de la Pleiade, 1969.

Rustaing de Saint-Jury, Louis. *Les Femmes Militaires, ou Relation Historique d'une Isle Nouvellement de'couverte.* Paris: Didot, 1739.

Sade, Marquis de. *Juliette,* trans. Austryn Wainwright. New York: Grove Press, 1968.

Schorer, Mark. "The Humiliation of Emma Woodhouse," *Jane Austen: A Collection of Critical Essays,* ed. Ian Watt. Englewood Cliffs: Prentice-Hall, 1963.

Scott, Sarah, and Barbara Montagu. *A Description of Millennium Hall, and the Country Adjacent.* London: J. Newberry, 1762.

Scott, Walter. Review of *Emma, Discussions of Jane Austen,* ed. William Heath. Boston: D. C. Heath, 1961.

——. *Heart of Midlothian.* New York: Holt, Rinehart, and Winston, 1969.

Séjourné, Philippe. *Aspects généraux du roman féminin en Angleterre de 1740 à 1800.* Gap: Louis-Jean, 1966.

Shannon, Edgar F. "Emma: Character and Construction," *PMLA,* 71, September 1956.

Shinagel, Michael. "*Memoirs of a Woman of Pleasure:* Pornography and the Mid-Eighteenth-Century English Novel," *Studies in Change and Revolution: Aspects of English Intellectual History 1640–1800,* ed. Paul Korshin. Menston: Scolar Press, 1972.

Showalter, Elaine. *A Literature of Their Own.* Princeton, Princeton University Press, 1977.

Shuttle, Penelope, and Peter Redgrove. *The Wise Wound.* London: Gollancz, 1978.

Slepian, B., and L. J. Morrissey. "What is Fanny Hill?" *Essays in Criticism,* 14, January 1964.

422

BIBLIOGRAPHY

Smith, Charlotte. *Emmeline.* London: Oxford University Press, 1971.

———. *The Young Philosopher.* London, 1798.

Sollers, Philippe. "Sade dans de texte," *Tel Quel,* 28, 1967.

Sontag, Susan. "Illness as Metaphor," *New York Review of Books,* January 1978.

Spacks, Patricia Meyer. *Imagining a Self: Autobiography and the Novel in Eighteenth-Century England.* Cambridge: Harvard University Press, 1976.

Staël, Mme de. *Corinne.* Paris: Garnier Frères, 1924.

———. *Correspondance générale,* ed. Beatrice Jasinski. Paris: Pauvert, 1962.

———. *Delphine.* London: G. and J. Robinson, 1803.

———. *Dix années d'exil.* Paris, 1966.

———. *Lettres choisies—1778–1817.* Paris: Klincksieck, 1970.

———. *Madame de Staël: Choix de textes thématiques et actualité.* Paris: Klincksieck, 1974.

Starobinski, Jean. *Jean-Jacques Rousseau: La Transparence et l'obstacle.* Paris: Gallimard, 1971.

———. *L'Oeil vivant.* Paris: Gallimard, 1964.

———. "Suicide et mélancolie chez Mme de Staël," *Preuves,* 190, no. 16, 1966.

Stewart, Joan Hinde. *The Novels of Mme Riccoboni.* Chapel Hill: North Carolina Studies in the Romance Languages and Literature, 1976.

Sunstein, Emily. *A Different Face: The Life of Mary Wollstonecraft.* New York: Harper and Row, 1975.

Ten Harmsel, Henrietta. *Jane Austen: A Study in Fictional Conventions.* London: Mouton, 1964.

Thomas, Donald. *The Marquis de Sade.* Boston: New York Graphic Society, 1976.

Thrale, Hester Lynch. *Thraliana: The Diary of Mrs. Hester Lynch Thrale 1776–1809,* ed. Katherine C. Balderston. Oxford: Clarendon Press, 1942.

Tissot, M. *Onanism: Or, A Treatise upon the Disorders produced by Masturbation: or, the Dangerous Effects of Secret and Excessive Venery,* trans. A. Hume. London: J. Pridden, 1766.

Tompkins, J. M. S. *The Popular Novel in England 1770–1800.* 1932; Lincoln: University of Nebraska Press, 1961.

Tortel, M. "Interventions sur la communications de Jean Biou," *Colloque d'Aix-en-Provence, 19 et 20 fevrier.* Paris: Armand Colin, 1968.

Tourné, Maurice. "Penélope et Circé, ou les mythes de la femme dans l'oeuvre de Sade," *Europe,* October 1972.

Trilling, Lionel. "Emma and the Legend of Jane Austen," *Beyond Culture: Essays in Literature and Learning.* New York: Viking Press, 1965.

———. "Mansfield Park," *Jane Austen: A Collection of Critical Essays.* Englewood Cliffs: Prentice-Hall, 1963.

Vance, Christie Mcdonald. "The Extravagant Shepherd: A Study of the Pastoral

BIBLIOGRAPHY

Vision in Rousseau's *Nouvelle Héloïse,*" *Studies in Voltaire and the Eighteenth Century,* 105, 1973.

Van Ghent, Dorothy. *The English Novel, Form and Function.* New York: Rinehart & Co., 1953.

Van Laere, François. *Une Lecture du temps dans "La Nouvelle Héloïse."* Neuchâtel: La Baconnière, 1968.

Wardle, Ralph. *Mary Wollstonecraft: A Critical Biography.* 1951; Lincoln: University of Nebraska Press, 1967.

Warner, James H. "Eighteenth Century English Reactions to *La Nouvelle Héloïse, PMLA,* September 1937.

Watt, Ian. *The Rise of the Novel: Studies in Defoe, Richardson and Fielding.* 1957; Harmondsworth: Penguin, 1972.

Wiesenfarth, Joseph. *The Errand of Form: An Assay of Jane Austen's Art.* New York: Fordham University Press, 1967.

Wilden, Anthony. Introduction to Lacan's *The Language of the Self: The Function of Language in Psychoanalysis.* New York: Dell, 1968.

Williams, Helen Maria. *Julia.* 1790; New York: Garland, 1974.

Williams, Raymond. *The Country and the City.* Frogmore: Paladin, 1975.

Willis, Lesley H. "Object Association and Minor Characters in Jane Austen's Novels," *Studies in the Novel,* 7.

Wilson, Arthur. *Diderot.* New York: Oxford University Press, 1972.

Wilt, Judith. "He Could Go No Further: A Modest Proposal about Lovelace and Clarissa," *PMLA,* January 1977.

Wolff, Cynthia Griffin. *Samuel Richardson and the Eighteenth-Century Puritan Character.* Hamden: Archon, 1972.

Wollstonecraft, Mary. *Collected Letters of Mary Wollstonecraft,* ed. Ralph Wardle. Ithaca: Cornell University Press, 1979.

——. *Maria or The Wrongs of Woman.* New York: Norton, 1975.

——. *Mary, A Fiction.* New York: Schocken Books, 1977.

——. *A Vindication of the Rights of Woman.* New York: Norton, 1975.

——. *A Wollstonecraft Anthology.* Bloomington: Indiana University Press, 1977.

Wolpe, Hans. "Psychological Ambiguity in *La Nouvelle Héloïse," University of Toronto Quarterly,* 28, no. 3, April 1959.

Woolf, Virginia. *A Room of One's Own.* Harmondsworth: Penguin, 1945.

INDEX

INDEX

Bradshaigh, Lady, 364-65
Brady, Patrick: "Structural Affiliations," 138n, 157n
Brantôme, Seigneur de, 321-23, 406
Braudy, Leo: "Fanny Hill," 185n
Brissenden, R.F.: *Virtue in Distress*, 11, 183; *"Mansfield Park,"* 263n
Brophy, Elizabeth Bergen: *Samuel Richardson*, 46n
Brothel: in *Clarissa*, 14, 35, 38, 49; in *Fanny Hill*, 74, 80, 84, 90, 100; compared with convent, 80; in male fantasy, 80; places of education, 80-81, 92-94
Brothel keepers, madams, 11, 14, 26, 35-43, 80, 92-95
Brownmiller, Susan: *Against Our Will*, 10
Burgelin, Pierre, 374n
Burney, Fanny, 314n, 317, 319, 413; *Evelina*, 263n, 312, 316; *Cecilia*, 312-14, 317, 318, 354, 407, 408; *The Wanderer*, 312, 314-18, 319, 333, 355, 358, 405, 410, 411
Burroway, Janet, "The Irony," 248n
Burrows, J.F.: "Jane Austen's *"Emma,"* 277n
Bushell, Nelson S.: "Susan Ferrier's *Marriage,"* 351n
Butler, Marilyn: *Jane Austen*, 217n, 247n

Carter, Elizabeth, 364
Catholicism, 231, 234-35; Catholic writers, 412
Chapman, R.W.: *Jane Austen*, 270n
Chapone, Hester Mulso, 359, 364; *Letters*, 359
Charles II, 323
Charpentier, John: *Rousseau*, 134n
Chateaubriand, F.R. de: *Atala*, 326-27
Chesler, Phyllis: *Women & Madness*, 408n
Chorier, Nicholas: *Satyra Sotadica*, 320n
Cinderella, 11, 108
Cixous, Hélène: "La jeune née," 406n
Class, rank, class judgments, 306, 314; in *Clarissa*, 13, 24; in *Fanny Hill*, 72, 89-90, 92-93; in *Julie*, 133, 147; in Wollstonecraft's novels, 194, 218, 219, 221, 222; in *Mansfield Park*, 246, 250,

257-58, 261, 268, 269-71, 274-75; in *Emma*, 279, 280, 282, 283, 286; in *Amelia*, 336; in *Dangerous Liaisons*, 337; in *Millenium Hall*, 343; in *Heart of Midlothian*, 347
Cleland, John, 69, 95, 322, 346, 361, 413; *Fanny Hill*, 3, 4, 170, 174, 220, 308, 329, 339, 350, 404, 405, 407, 411; analysis of, 69-100
Collyer, Mary, 329n, 331-32, 408
Communities, clubs, 151, 165, 181, 342; see Female communities
Confidante, 1, 134, 138, 305, 306, 311, 337
Constant, Benjamin, 388, 390, 392, 393
Convent: in *The Nun*, 100-31; in *Juliette*, 171; in *Delphine*, 232, 241; compared with brothel, 80; evils of, 101, 102, 128; as place of lesbianism, 102, 322, 412; as prison, 117, 241, 331, 406; as female asylum, 233, 234, 237, 355
Craik, W.A.: *Jane Austen*, 247n
Crocker, Lester: "Julie," 156n; *Nature and Culture*, 168n
Croismare, Marquis de, 366

Daiches, David, 46n, 50n
Daughters, 2, 3; in *Clarissa*, 11, 20, 26, 29, 30, 44, 52, 65; in *Fanny Hill*, 76, 81; in *The Nun*, 110-11; in *Julie*, 133, 147, 149, 159; in *Juliette*, 168; in Wollstonecraft's novels, 195-96, 211, 215, 223, 226; in *Delphine*, 239, 240; in Austen's novels, 250, 252, 262; surrogate, 92, 187, 189, 190, 255, 256, 312, 330
Death: in *Clarissa*, 14, 18-25, 50, 58-9, 63, 152, 314, 317; in *The Nun*, 116, 120, 126-27, 129; in *Julie*, 161-64, 165n; in *Juliette*, 184, 189; in Wollstonecraft's novels, 199, 200-3, 204-6, 213-14, 216, 226; in *Delphine*, 228, 230, 236n, 239, 240, 244; in *The Wanderer*, 317; in *Liaisons*, 338; and love, 135, 167, 200, 201, 205, 207, 230; as weapon, 240, 356; in biography, 380-81, 386, 387; motif of, 403, 409-10

426

INDEX

INDEX

Horney, Karen: "Neurosis," 257n
Houdetot, Countess d', 368-71, 373-74
Hysteria, 100-1, 201, 205, 209, 318, 372

Illegitimacy, 103, 108, 210, 284
Incest: in *Juliette*, 168, 187, 190, 376; in *Mansfield Park*, 246, 259n, 260, 263, 263n, 264, 274
Innocence: in *Clarissa*, 22, 24, 42; in *Fanny Hill*, 73, 77, 78, 79, 86, 89, 91; in *The Nun*, 106-7, 122-28; in *Juliette*, 186; in *Delphine*, 236; in *Mansfield Park*, 254; as seduction, 106-7, 122-28, 254
Insane asylum, *see* Madhouse
Insanity, *see* Madness

James, Robert: *Medicinal Dictionary*, 321n
Jealousy, envy: in *Clarissa*, 32-33, 37; in *Fanny Hill*, 91; in *Julie*, 149; in *Emma*, 294-95, 296; in Haywood's novels, 307; in *Military Women*, 346; in Austen's novels, 400; in biography, 372, 390-92
Johnson, Samuel: on *Amelia*, 334n
Josephs, Herbert: "Diderot's *La Religieuse*," 109

Kempf, Roger: "Sur Le Corps de Julie," 164n
Kenrick, William, 136n
King, William: *The Toast*, 320n
Kinkead-Weekes, Mark, 15n, 47n
Kirkham, Sarah, 364
Klossowski, Pierre: *Sade mon prochain*, 187n, 190n
Knight, Fanny, 398
Krafft-Ebing, Richard: *Psychopathia Sexualis*, 376n

Lacan, Jacques: *Language of the Self*, 196n
Laclos, Choderclos de: *Dangerous Liaisons*, 328, 336-40, 403-4, 409, 412; *Traité*, 339n
Lacombe, Roger G.: *Sade*, 174n
Laforgue, René: *Psychopathologie*, 374n

Laing, R.D.: *Politics of Experience*, 222n
Language: as control, 20, 340; as creator of others, 21, 38-39, 42, 47, 60, 66, 68; of female character, 29, 51, 56, 62, 153, 190, 283n, 376; imposed, 49, 50, 147; *see also* Speech, Letters, Silence
Lapdogs, 195, 254, 254n
Lascelles, Mary: *Jane Austen*, 261n
Law, 15, 24, 25, 37, 43, 52
Lawrence, James: *Empire of the Nairs*, 344n
Legacy, fortune: in *Clarissa*, 9-13, 15, 34, 38, 52, 64, 68, 313, 407-11; in *Mary, A Fiction*, 205; in *Fanny Hill*, 98; in *Cecilia*, 314
Le Gendre, Mme, 366-68
Lejeune, Philippe: *L'Autobiographie*, 362
Lely, Gilbert: *The Marquis de Sade*, 375n
Lennox, Charlotte, 319, 348, 413-14; *Euphemia*, 310-11, 312, 332, 352, 354, 406-7
Lesbianism, 81-82, 124-25, 172, 175, 177, 319-27, 341, 360; as variation of and preparation for heterosexuality, 84, 322, 339; as subversion, 84; as response to exclusive female society, 102; exaltation of, 168, 172; as political act, 172, 341; described to shock, 319, 320; satirized and exploited, 320; as physical monstrosity, 320-21; in opposition to marriage, 322, 324; (biographical) male fear of, 340, 366-68, 375
Letters: creating character, 47, 50; as elements of action, 78, 105, 144, 272, 294, 294n, 354; relationship through, 10, 50-1, 54, 56, 72-4, 78, 142, 153; as voyeuristic device, 139, 142, 144, 147; used to distance, 21, 45, 107, 200-1, 204, 298, 299; subverted, 49, 50-51, 59, 63, 144, 338; in sentimental fiction, 306, 310; in biography, 359, 361-62; in Richardson, 365-66; in Diderot, 366-67; in Sade, 377, 378n; in Staël, 392-93, 395; in Austen, 396, 400
Lévi-Strauss, C.: *Elementary Structures*, 168n
Lewinter, Roger: introduction, 102n, 107n
Lewis, C.S. "A Note," 247n
Lewis, Matthew: *The Monk*, 263n

429

INDEX

Libertine, rake: in *Clarissa*, 5, 12, 18-25, 40, 59-63, 306; in *The Nun*, 129; in *Juliette*, 181, 184, 190, 342; in *Mansfield Park*, 271; in *Liaisons*, 337

Libertinism, libertine philosophy, 21, 169, 215, 270

Litz, A. Walton: *Jane Austen*, 247n, 275n, 397n

Llangollen, Ladies of (Eleanor Butler and Sarah Ponsonby), 359, 360, 382

Locke, John, 305n

London: in *Clarissa*, 14, 49n, 59; in *Fanny Hill*, 69, 73, 79-80, 85

Love: and death, 135, 167, 200, 201, 205, 207, 230; and sexuality, 200, 203, 204; and friendship, 62, 191, 232-33, 244, 307; and religion, 233, 234; and family, 246; as goal, 193, 195, 228-29; as poison, 135; failure in, 196, 221, 250, 217n

Lucas, Charles: *Infernal Quixote*, 211n

Macaulay, Thomas Babbington; review, 315n

McDowell, Judith, 136n

Madhouse: in *The Wrongs of Woman*, 209, 210, 218, 219, 221, 406, 413; *see also* Prison, Brothel

Madness, 19; from male treatment, 19, 53; from seclusion, 102, 126-28; from sexuality, 126-28; from severed friendship, 164-66, 314; from sensibility, 212; from love, 230; from rejection, 317; motif of, 403, 408-9

Maids, servants, 332, 352-53; in *Clarissa*, 18, 23, 36, 49; in *Julie*, 142; in *Millenium Hall*, 343; wife as, 26, 326

Male antagonism to women, 22, 378

Male homosexuality, 71n, 95-98, 188

Manipulative friendship: defined, 4, 327-28, 340, 412; in *The Nun*, 114-16, 121-27; in *Julie*, 132-67; in *Juliette*, 168-90, in *Delphine*, 237-43; in *Emma*, 287; in *Marianne*, 328-32; in *Amelia*, 332-36; in *Dangerous Liaisons*, 336-40; in Ricoboni's novels, 358

Manley, Mary; *The New Atalantis*, 210n, 340-42, 345, 346

Mansell, Darrel: *The Novels of Jane Austen*, 273n, 275n, 285n, 291, 294n

Marivaux, P.C. de: *Marianne*, 2, 5, 167, 336, 337, 340, 353, 405-12, analysis of, 328-32

Marriage: as goal, 2, 69, 78, 88, 94-95, 226, 242-43, 249, 287, 289, 350; as necessity for women, 154, 341, 344; and money or property, 25, 78, 199, 314, 407; in opposition to friendship, 67-68, 140-44, 150, 151, 158, 226, 276, 281, 286, 289, 310, 322, 324, 335; fear of, 16, 207; opposed, 52-53, 207; as trap, 212, 212n, 214, 231, 237, 241, 253, 254, 344n; flawed, 261, 285, 343; parodied, 284; vicarious, 278-79, 285; utopian, 348; advice on, 350; in biography, 389, 398, 401

Masculinity in women, 320n, 355; in *Clarissa*, 32-33, 38, 46, 60, 62; in *Juliette*, 185; in *Wrongs of Woman*, 218

Masochism, 199, 206, 324

Mavor, Elizabeth: *Ladies of Llangollen*, 359n

May, Georges: *Diderot et "La Religieuse,"* 104n, 116n, 366n

Menstruation, 101, 109, 182, 404, 405

Mercken-Spaas, G., 190n, 244n

Methodists, 319, 324

Miller, Nancy: "Female Sexuality and Narrative Structure," 136n, 144n, 193n, 408n; "Juliette," 187n, 190n

Millett, Kate; *Sexual Politics*, 10

Minter, David Lee; "Aesthetic Vision," 294n

Mirrors, 30-31, 82

Misogyny, 181, 185

Modesty: as stimulant to lust, 173; denigrated, 180

Moers, Ellen: *Literary Women*, 198n

Moler, Kenneth: *Jane Austen's Art of Allusion*, 257n, 268n, 275n, 277n

Money, 407; in *Clarissa*, 14, 25, 56-57, 65; in *Fanny Hill*, 69, 78, 98; in *The Wrongs of Woman*, 224; in *Delphine*, 238-9; in *Mansfield Park*, 253, 270, 272; in *Cecilia*, 314; in *New Atalantis*, 341-42; in

430

INDEX

Marriage, 352; social friendship, 348, 350; *see also* Legacy, Property
Monthly Review, 70n
Montreuil, Anne-Prospère, 375-77, 378
Montreuil, Mme de, 375, 377-78
Montreuil, Renée-Pélagie de, 375-77, 378
More, Hannah, 268n
Morgan, Susan J.: "Emma Woodhouse," 290n, 301n
Morley, Lord: on *The Nun*, 131
Mornet, Daniel: *Rousseau*, 134n, 371n
Mothers, 2, 344n, 409, 411; in *Clarissa*, 10-13, 18, 26-31, 36, 37, 42-45; in *The Nun*, 103, 107-13, 114; in *Fanny Hill*, 76-78, 81, 92; in *Julie*, 134, 146-49, 151, 159, 165; in Wollstonecraft's novels, 193-96, 199, 205, 211, 213-15, 221, 223; in Austen's novels, 248-53, 256, 265, 272-73, 276; in *Marianne*, 329; in *Liaisons*, 337-38; *see also* Surrogate mothers
Mudrick, Marvin: *Jane Austen*, 247n, 273n, 275n, 280n, 285n, 291n

Naiveté: feminine weakness, 239; scorned, 332; as manipulation, 104-7, 114, 121-23; in *Fanny Hill*, 76
Names, naming, 18, 28-29, 44, 53, 62, 64, 76, 132
Napoleon, 154n, 391, 393, 394
Narbonne, Louis de, 388, 389
Narcissism, 406; in *Fanny Hill*, 71, 82-84, 99; in *Mary, A Fiction*, 195, 196, 198, 206, 207; in *Emma*, 299; in *Marianne*, 328, 329n, 332, 406; in *Amelia*, 332, 336, 403, 410-11; as stage of female sexuality, 82-84; as sexuality of the old, 99; in writing, 99; as fearful reaction, 196, 198, 206; as cause of lesbianism, 332
Narrator, 328; in *Fanny Hill*, 70-75, 78, 82, 88, 92, 93, 99-100; in *The Nun*, 102, 104-7, 129-30; in *Juliette*, 185; in *Marianne*, 329, 331; in *Millenium Hall*, 343
Necker, Jacques, 387, 388, 389
Necker, Suzanne, 387-89, 395

Nietzsche, Frederich: *Genealogy of Morals*, 407-8
Norris, John, 56
Nosebleed: in *Clarissa*, 22-23; in *Fanny Hill*, 85; in *The Nun*, 109; in *Julie*, 148-50; in *Lasselia*, 308; in *Female Husband*, 324-25; in *Amelia*, 334; in *New Atalantis*, 342; motif of, 404-5
Nuns: in *The Nun*, 105, 108, 115, 116, 118, 119, 366; in *Delphine*, 232, 236, 243, 244n; in *Marianne*, 329, 331

Old age, 45, 101, 242, 337
Orphans, 3, 69, 74, 79, 146, 313, 329, 353

Page, Norman: "The Language of Jane Austen," 255n, 270n
Patriarchy, 190, 358, 413; men and, 13-25; women and, 25-68, 271n, 319, 339, 341, 343, 348, 348-49, 414; patriarchal relationships, 189, 350
Phallus, 175, 179
Penis, 51, 90, 99, 175, 179, 180
Penknife, 405; in *Clarissa*, 23-25, 308; in *Lasselia*, 308; in *Amelia*, 333
Political friendship defined, 4, 346, 348; in *Clarissa*, 12, 46; in *Juliette*, 177, 190; in *Mary, A Fiction*, 199-207; in *The Wrongs of Woman*, 208-26; in *Delphine*, 226-45; in *The Wanderer*, 316-17; in *Liaisons*, 339; in *New Atalantis*, 340-42; in *Millenium Hall*, 342-44; in *Military Women*, 345-46; in *Heart of Midlothian*, 347-48; in Riccoboni's novels, 358
Pornography, 320, 327, 412
Poverty: in *Clarissa*, 37, 45; in *Fanny Hill*, 74, 76; in *Mansfield Park*, 252, 270, 271n; in *Cecilia*, 314; in *Moll Flanders*, 349; as mark of heroine, 76; as moral educator, 270-71, 270n
Praz, Mario: *The Romantic Agony*, 180n
Prison: in *Clarissa*, 17, 37; in *The Wrongs of Woman*, 221; in *Delphine*, 244; in *The Female Husband*, 325; in *Amelia*, 333; in Sade's life, 376-77
Property, 10, 19, 25, 37, 43, 52, 64; *see also* Legacy, Money

INDEX

434